# Preparing Students with Disabilities for College Success

# Preparing Students with Disabilities for College Success

## A Practical Guide to Transition Planning

edited by

**Stan F. Shaw, Ed.D.**
University of Connecticut

**Joseph W. Madaus, Ph.D.**
University of Connecticut

and

**Lyman L. Dukes, III, Ph.D.**
University of South Florida St. Petersburg

·P·A·U·L·H·
BROOKES
PUBLISHING Co.®

Baltimore • London • Sydney

**Paul H. Brookes Publishing Co.**
Post Office Box 10624
Baltimore, Maryland 21285-0624
USA

www.brookespublishing.com

Typeset by Broad Books, Baltimore, Maryland.
Manufactured in the United States of America by
Sheridan Books, Inc., Chelsea, Michigan.

The individuals described in this book are composites or real people whose situations are masked and are based on the authors' experiences. In all instances, names and identifying details have been changed to protect confidentiality.

**Library of Congress Cataloging-in-Publication Data**

Preparing students with disabilities for college success : a practical guide to transition planning / edited by Stan F. Shaw, Joseph W. Madaus, and Lyman L. Dukes, III.
     p.     cm.
   Includes bibliographical references and index.
   ISBN-13: 978-1-59857-016-8 (pbk.)
   ISBN-10: 1-59857-016-1 (pbk.)
   1. People with disabilities—Education (Higher)—United States.   2. College students with disabilities—United States.   I. Shaw, Stan F.   II. Madaus, Joseph W.   III. Dukes, Lyman L.
IV. Title.
   LC4813.P74 2010
   371.9'0474—dc22                                                                2009038321

British Library Cataloguing in Publication data are available from the British Library.

2020   2019
10    9    8    7    6    5    4

# Contents

# About the Editors and Contributors

**Manju Banerjee, Ph.D.,** is Associate Director of the Center for Students with Disabilities at the University of Connecticut. She is also a research and education consultant for Educational Testing Service in Princeton, New Jersey, and has more than 22 years of experience in the field of learning and other disabilities. She is currently Co-Principal Investigator of a $1.3 million federally funded demonstration grant project focusing on inclusive instruction by faculty in online and technology blended courses. Her interests include technology and universal design, disability documentation, and high-stakes testing.

**Loring C. Brinckerhoff, Ph.D.,** is a nationally recognized authority on learning disabilities and attention-deficit/hyperactivity disorder. He is the Director of the Office of Disability Policy at Educational Testing Service and a consultant to Harvard Medical School. He is co-author of one of the leading textbooks in the field, *Postsecondary Education and Transition for Students with Learning Disabilities* (PRO-ED, 2002). He has also written dozens of articles and book chapters for parents and professionals on high-stakes testing, disability documentation, transition from high school to college, self-advocacy skills for adolescents, and program planning for students with learning disabilities. Dr. Brinckerhoff is the past president of the Association on Higher Education And Disability (AHEAD) and recipient of its prestigious Ronald E. Blosser Dedicated Service Award. He received his doctorate in learning disabilities from the University of Wisconsin–Madison in 1984.

**Lyman L. Dukes, III, Ph.D.,** Associate Professor of Special Education at the University of South Florida St. Petersburg, joined the faculty in 2001. He is also Principal Investigator of Project 10: Transition Education Network, which is a transition-focused training and technical assistance center funded by the Florida Department of Education. Previously, he has worked as a secondary-level special education teacher as well as a rehabilitation therapist and behavioral consultant for people with significant disabilities. His current research interests include transition from school to postsecondary settings, transition assessment and the use of the summary of performance for high school students with disabilities, programmatic self-assessment for postsecondary disability services, and the use of blended instruction at the postsecondary level.

**Linda K. Elksnin, Ph.D.,** earned her doctorate in special education from the University of Virginia. Dr. Elksnin is Professor Emerita at The Citadel, which awarded her the James Self Award for Excellence in Graduate Teaching. She taught students with disabilities at the preschool, elementary, and secondary levels.

Dr. Elksnin is the co-author with Dr. Nick Elksnin of three textbooks and co-authored *Educational Assessment of Learning Problems: Testing for Teaching* (Allyn & Bacon, 1992) with Gerald Wallace and Steve Larsen. Dr. Elksnin was Co-Editor of *Assessment for Effective Intervention* and serves on the editorial boards of *Learning Disabilities: A Contemporary Journal, Learning Disability Quarterly, Journal of Learning Disabilities,* and *Exceptionality.*

Dr. Elksnin is past president of the International Council for Learning Disabilities and was a member of the Learning Disabilities Roundtable, which authored *Commentary Regarding Reauthorization of the Individuals with Disabilities Education Act.* She is a member of the International Academy for Research in Learning Disabilities.

**Nick Elksnin, Ph.D.,** has more than 25 years of experience as a school psychologist, special education consultant, and special education administrator. He earned his doctorate in educational psychology from the University of Georgia and was a postdoctoral fellow in pediatrics and psychiatry at the Medical University of South Carolina. Dr. Elksnin taught graduate courses in psychology and special education at The Citadel and the College of Charleston.

Dr. Elksnin is the co-author of the textbooks *Teaching Social-Emotional Skills at School and Home* (Love Publishing Company, 2006), *Teaching Occupational Social Skills* (PRO-ED, 1998), *Working with Students with Disabilities in Vocational-Technical Settings* (PRO-ED, 1998), *Assessment and Instruction of Social Skills: Across the Lifespan and the Curriculum* (Singular Publishing Group, 1995), and *An Introduction to Developmental Disabilities: A Neurodevelopmental Perspective* (Wadsworth Publishing, 1994). Dr. Elksnin served as Co-Editor of *Assessment for Effective Intervention* for 9 years and is on the editorial boards of *Learning Disabilities: A Contemporary Journal, Remedial and Special Education,* and *Intervention in School and Clinic.*

Dr. Elksnin has consulted with numerous school districts, private schools, Head Start, and the College Board. He is a licensed Psycho-Educational Specialist and a Nationally Certified School Psychologist. He is a frequent presenter at national conferences.

**Michael Faggella-Luby, Ph.D.,** is Assistant Professor of Special Education in the Neag School of Education at the University of Connecticut, Associate Research Scholar at the Center on Postsecondary Education and Disability, and a research scientist at the Center for Behavioral Education and Research.

Dr. Faggella-Luby's scholarly interests focus on learning disabilities, adolescent literacy, and evidence-based secondary education for all learners. He has recently taken over the postschool outcomes for students with disabilities transition survey for the Connecticut State Department of Education.

**K. Brigid Flannery, Ph.D.,** is a senior research associate/associate professor at the University of Oregon, College of Education, in Eugene. She is a research faculty member in Educational and Community Supports and also Director of the Special Education Major for the College of Education. Her current interests include research and program development to implement positive behavior support at the high school level, improving individualized education program planning at the high school level, and increasing access to and retention of students at risk or with disabilities in postsecondary education.

**John W. Graham, M.A.,** is a third-year doctoral student in educational psychology at the University of Oklahoma, Norman, at the Zarrow Center for Learning Enrichment. John is also the associate editor of the *Journal of Postsecondary Education and Disability.* Mr. Graham's area of concentration is special education with a focus in transition and self-determination.

**Carol A. Kochhar-Bryant, Ed.D.,** is Professor of Special Education at The George Washington University. She has developed and directed advanced graduate and doctoral leadership development programs in special education and conducts evaluations for public school districts, state departments of education, and federal agencies to improve educational services for learners with special needs. Trained in special education and psychology, Dr. Kochhar-Bryant has directed residential services for individuals with disabilities, directed community service coordination/case management services, and worked in in-patient psychiatric services. Her research interests focus on educating adolescents who are special learners in general and on alternative education settings, mental health concerns and system coordination, assessment of transition and independent living skills, effective transition of youth to adult life, and preparation of leadership to assist at-risk youth. She is past Governmental Relations Chair, and Past President, of the Council for Exceptional Children's Division on Career Development and Transition.

**Joseph W. Madaus, Ph.D.,** is Director of the Center on Postsecondary Education and Disability and is Associate Professor in the Department of Educational Psychology at the University of Connecticut. Prior to joining the faculty at the University of Connecticut, he was Director of the Learning Resource Center at Mitchell College in New London, Connecticut, and was Director of the University Program for College Students with Learning Disabilities at the University of Connecticut. He was a Distinguished Research Fellow in the National Institute on Disability and Rehabilitation Research Mary Switzer Fellowship program and he serves on multiple journal editorial boards. In 2007, Dr. Madaus received both the Teaching Promise and Teaching Innovation award from the University of Connecticut chapter of the American Association of University Professors. In 2008, he was named as a University Teaching Fellow, the highest teaching honor at the University of Connecticut.

**James E. Martin, Ph.D.,** holds the Zarrow Chair in Special Education at the University of Oklahoma, and is Director of the University of Oklahoma's Zarrow Center. Dr. Martin earned his doctorate in Special Education from the University of Illinois in 1983 with a focus on transition. Professor Martin has authored several books, a couple dozen chapters for edited books, numerous journal articles, and several curriculum lesson packages. Federal, state, and local funding agencies provided him with more $7,500,000 to conduct his research and writing activities. He has conducted presentations and training workshops at sites across the United States, Canada, and Europe. In 2006, the Council for Exceptional Children's Division on Career Development and Transition awarded Professor Martin the Oliver P. Kolstoe Award for his efforts to improve the quality and access to career and transition services for people with disabilities. He is also the editor for the Association on Higher Education And Disability's *Journal of Postsecondary Education and Disability.*

Dr. Martin's professional interests focus on the transition of youth with disabilities from school into further postsecondary education and the workforce and on what must be done to facilitate success in high school and postsecondary environments. In particular, he examines the application of self-determination methodology to educational and workplace settings.

**Joan M. McGuire, Ph.D.,** is Senior Research Scholar and Associate Director of the Center on Postsecondary Education and Disability and Professor Emerita of Special Education at the University of Connecticut. She is the recipient of several awards, including the University of Connecticut's AAUP Excellence Award for Teaching Mentorship, the Oliver P. Kolstoe Award from the Council for Exceptional Children's Division on Career Development and Transition, and the inaugural Communication Award from the Association on Higher Education And Disability. In addition to serving as Co-Editor of the *Journal of Postsecondary Education and Disability* and as an editorial board reviewer for several peer reviewed journals, Dr. McGuire has authored more than 85 published refereed journal articles, 2 books, and 12 book chapters. She has also authored and co-authored proposals resulting in more than $4.8 million in federal and state grants, including $3 million for demonstration projects focusing on Universal Design for Instruction (UDI). Dr. McGuire serves as a consultant to Educational Testing Service and conducts independent program and project evaluations for grant funded initiatives and disability services. Her research interests include UDI, effective strategies for inclusive college teaching, and postsecondary disability services and student outcomes.

**Juan Portley, Ph.D.,** recently completed his doctorate in special education from the University of Oklahoma. He has extensive experience working with schools in New Mexico on state and federal legislation trainings and curriculum development in transition education. He has also worked as a resource teacher for Grades 6–12, a special education coordinator, and a transition coordinator. He currently operates as an independent education consultant throughout the Southwest.

**Stan F. Shaw, Ed.D.,** is Senior Research Scholar and Associate Director at the Center on Postsecondary Education and Disability and Professor Emeritus of Special Education at the University of Connecticut. He co-authored *Postsecondary Education and Transition for Students with Learning Disabilities* (PRO-ED, 2003) and *What Every Teacher Should Know About Transition and*

*IDEA 2004* (Allyn & Bacon, 2007). He wrote the postsecondary education chapter for the international *Handbook of Special Education* (Sage Publications, 2007). He is a former editor of the *Journal of Postsecondary Education and Disability* and is currently on the editorial boards of respected professional journals, including *Career Development and Exceptional Individuals, Journal of Postsecondary Education and Disability,* and *Journal of Special Education Leadership,* among others. He is the recipient of several awards, including the Oliver P. Kolstoe Award from the Council for Exceptional Children's Division on Career Development and Transition, the University of Connecticut's AAUP Excellence Award for Teaching Mentorship, and the inaugural Communication Award from the Association on Higher Education And Disability. He has been project director for more $6 million in grants.

Dr. Shaw's current interests include transition from high school to college, implementation of the summary of performance to enhance communication between high school and postsecondary education, staff development and preparation of postsecondary disability personnel, disability policy and law, and grant writing.

**Brandi Simonsen, Ph.D.,** is an assistant professor of Special Education in the Neag School of Education and a research scientist with the Center for Behavioral Education and Research at the University of Connecticut. Dr. Simonsen teaches courses in positive behavior support, and she brings qualifications in the areas of applied behavior analysis, positive behavior support, behavior disorders, program administration and management, and research design/methodology. Dr. Simonsen's primary research interests include linking assessment to intervention and providing positive behavior support for students, especially students with or at risk for behavior disorders, in the school environment. Before joining the faculty at University of Connecticut, Dr. Simonsen was the director of a school serving students with disabilities who presented with challenging educational and behavioral needs. In addition to serving as an administrator, Dr. Simonsen has previously been certified as a teacher of elementary general education and middle-secondary special education, and she has provided consultation to public and alternative schools.

# Foreword

Progress in the education of and service supports for children, youth, and adults with disabilities has been agonizingly slow. Happily, there has been progress and we are clearly better off today than we were more than four decades ago when I entered this field. This is especially true in the area of postsecondary education and training. Still, postsecondary education and training is another of our major steep hills to climb in overcoming resistance to both internal and external attitudes and practices among professionals, as well as limited dreams and expectations of students with disabilities and their families.

*Preparing Students with Disabilities for College Success: A Practical Guide to Transition Planning* reflects not only how the field has made progress in the past but also how to make a new surge with more focus and knowledge. It is an impressive response to continuing vestiges of resistance toward fair and equitable transition planning and services to students who can, with secondary school preparation and postsecondary school supports, succeed in college and other postsecondary education and training settings.

If you are a stakeholder in the decisions related to postsecondary education or training (e.g., student, parent, secondary teacher, transition specialist, postsecondary support professional) and want *encouragement* to continue the hard transition planning, preparation, and support work that you believe in, this book is chock full of information that will encourage you. If you are a stakeholder and want *knowledge* related to strategies for planning, teaching, and supporting students in the transition process, this book will provide that knowledge. Whether you read it from cover to cover or use it as a guide to focus on specific challenges, it will be an invaluable resource for you. Although it is written primarily for professional stakeholders, I believe it could be an exceptionally helpful resource for families so that they know what is possible under the law and what is current recommended practice for professionals.

What is especially important about this book, in my opinion, is the focus on the current school population with mild to moderate disabilities that has difficulties with learning and behavior related to grade-level academic performance. The difficulties that these students have diminish expectations from school professionals, their families, and the students themselves. Hopes and dreams, especially among the students and families, go by the board as the realities of past and current performance loom large in planning for the future after high school. These experiences are similar among students and parents in which physical and sensory disabilities are involved, especially if academic performance is marginal; however, the students classified as having learning disabilities, communication disorders, emotional disorders, autism spectrum disorders, or attention deficit disorder under the category of Other Health Impaired or 504 Plans reflect two important differences. First, their disabilities are frequently invisible and thus academic failure is often attributed to being lazy, not caring, or "flaky." The lack of a visible socially recognized disability sets up entirely different social responses and attribution assumptions. Second, this population makes up an extremely large percentage of the total number of students receiving special education services or 504 plans. To be more specific, "extremely large percentage" means approximately 80% or almost 4 million students. These two differentiating factors raise the ante on the level of importance of the need for specific attention in addressing the problems inherent in these factors.

Our current educational system is not kind to the target population of *Preparing Students with Disabilities for College Success* in many ways. In most cases, instructional procedures in general education are geared for those who do not have learning or behavioral issues and the ratcheting up of academic standards of the past decade or so has left as many casualties as survivors. Those casualties are too often explained away as academic performance problems due to the students' impairments or lack of motivation rather than the instructional system. We have to do better than this and this book is a fresh guide on how to do it.

I recently received a call from a woman who immigrated to the United States from Taiwan in the 1980s. She has a daughter who has been in our educational system for her entire life. The call was to thank me for the assistance and encouragement I gave the family 10 years ago when the daughter was 8. The daughter had been receiving special education services through her school and was now enrolled in a postsecondary career training program for health care workers. I had little recall of the event in general and none of anything specific that I had said or done. In retrospect, what I said or did was not what was really important; rather, it was how they felt about themselves and the challenges after our interaction. Relating this incident is not to reflect credit on myself but to remind us all that keeping hope alive is one of the most important things that we can do for students and it does not cost families or us anything. Following up on the flicker or flame of hope is critical, though, because hope may not be enough for them to survive the educational system. The ideas in this book give professionals themselves hope and the information and resources to do their jobs professionally. The ideas come from the most knowledgeable and committed people currently in this area of transition services. Trust them. You are in good hands.

*Gary M. Clark, Ed.D.*
*Professor Emeritus*
*Department of Special Education*
*University of Kansas*

# Acknowledgments

An informal conversation with Rebecca Lazo, Senior Acquisitions Editor at Paul H. Brookes Publishing Co., resulted in the conceptualization of this book. Her efforts and good advice, combined with the excellent support of Steve Plocher and others at Paul H. Brookes Publishing Co., were essential in both the development and completion of this book. Working with our chapter authors, all of whom are longtime collaborators, made this a particularly enjoyable experience. We believe it has resulted in the fulfillment of our goal to improve the transition to college for students with disabilities.

We express our deepest gratitude to those who have contributed to our growth as we have worked in the area of transition to postsecondary education. Colleagues of particular note include Patricia Anderson, Manju Banerjee, Steve Bigaj, Loring Brinckerhoff, Michael Faggella-Luby, Sharon Field, Karen Halliday, Mark Koorland, Donna Korbel, Joan McGuire, Mark Mullins, David Parker, Sally Reis, Sue Saunders, Sally Scott, Dayle Upham, and Carrol Waite.

In addition, we respectfully acknowledge the professionals, parents, advocates, and individuals with disabilities from whom we have learned the value of believing in unlimited possibilities. Their perseverance, self-determination, and desire for change have made postsecondary education an increasing reality for students with disabilities.

Finally, we thank our families for their enduring love that allows us to take risks as we have pursued our professional goal to enhance access to productive and dignified lives for individuals with disabilities.

# Dedication to Dr. Patricia Sitlington

It's a fact. More youth with disabilities are enrolling in postsecondary education than ever before, albeit less than their peers without disabilities. Data from the National Longitudinal Transition Studies, for example, indicate that the percentage of youth that enrolled in postsecondary education in 2007 increased 16% since the 1980s. A large portion of this growth is because people believed that youth with disabilities could succeed in college and worked hard to open those pathways.

This book is dedicated to one of those people. Dr. Patricia Sitlington spent more than 30 years working to increase the success of individuals with disabilities. Pat's research, her writings, and her teachings challenged us to do better and guided us in ways that we might improve, always with the focus on increasing postsecondary education and employment opportunities of youth with disabilities. Her efforts helped to shape policies and systems and, most important, inspired individuals with the hope and promise of what can happen when people work together to improve the success of youth with disabilities.

Pat was still earnestly working toward these outcomes when she died in February 2009. Although I know she had more to contribute, I believe that she lives on each time a transition assessment is used to determine needed supports, each time another youth with disabilities successfully makes the transition to college or a job, each time that another door is opened or opened wider. . . . Eventually, through our collective efforts, there will be a time when enrollment of youth with disabilities in postsecondary education becomes comparable to that of youth without disabilities.

With love and affection for a dear friend and colleague, and a commitment to carry on,

Barbara Guy, Transition Coordinator, Iowa State Department of Education

*To my wife, partner, and best friend, Barbara Rhein,*
*who with grace, good humor, and wisdom has shared life's journey with me.*
*To my grandsons, Casey, Brady, and Derek, and their parents,*
*who are my greatest legacy and hope for the future.*
*—SFS*


*To Melissa, Patrick, Colin, and Mary:*
*You are the brightest lights in my life.*
*Thank you for sharing your love and laughter with me every day.*
*—JWM*


*To my amazing wife and best buddy, Kelli Dukes,*
*and my dear daughter, Brenna Melora Dukes.*
*You make each and every day a joy.*
*—LLD*

# 1

# Introduction

...............................................................

*Joseph W. Madaus, Stan F. Shaw, and Lyman L. Dukes, III*

Tremendous progress has been made since the late 1950s to increase access to college for students with disabilities. From early efforts that focused on veterans with physical disabilities (Atkinson, 1947; Berdie, 1955; Condon, 1962), opportunities for students with disabilities have increased significantly. By the 2003–2004 school year, more than 1 in 10 freshmen reported having a disability (National Center for Education Statistics, 2006), a figure that has more than tripled since 1978 (American Youth Policy Forum, 2002). The majority of these students are those with nonvisible mild/moderate disabilities (e.g., learning disability, speech-language, emotional disturbance, autism spectrum disorder [ASD], attention deficit-hyperactivity disorder [ADHD], other health impairments). Progress is also evident in the fact that in 2005, nearly 44% of students with disabilities enrolled in postsecondary education since leaving high school, an increase from 26% in 1990 (Cameto, 2007).

Despite these advances, however, more needs to be done. Although many students are attending college, they do so at a significantly lower rate than their peers without disabilities (Cameto, 2007). More also needs to be done to help students with disabilities remain in, and eventually graduate from, college. There are a variety of reasons that students do not complete college, including a lack of preparation in basic skills. According to the National Center for Educational Statistics (2006), 36% of all undergraduates reported taking a remedial course in 2003–2004. This coursework was most frequently in mathematics (77%), followed by writing (35%) and reading (28%). Students at community colleges were more likely to have taken a remedial course (43%) than students in 4-year institutions (28%). Students with disabilities also more often reported taking remedial courses (40%) than their peers without disabilities (35%). Because this coursework often does not count toward graduation requirements, it increases the time and costs required to complete college.

The increased need for self-determination is another significant challenge faced by students with disabilities when they attend college. An interdisciplinary team of professionals and parents support high school students with disabilities, often making decisions for the student related to coursework and accommodations. In college, the support team is gone, and the student is required to become his or her own self-advocate. The National Longitudinal Transition Study-2 (NLTS-2) reported that 87% of students in their sample received accommodations and supports in high school

1

(Cameto, 2007). Only 25% of these students, however, received accommodations in 4-year colleges, and 26% in 2-year colleges. It is interesting that 56% of the students in the NLTS-2 sample did not disclose their disability to a college because they no longer considered themselves to have a disability in college. It is not clear, however, if these students were unaware of their legal rights, or even the specific nature of their disability, that made them eligible for services in high school.

Why is college so important for students with disabilities? Data from multiple sources point to the positive effect of a college degree on the overall lifetime earnings of workers in the United States. The Commission on the Future of Higher Education (U.S. Department of Education, 2006) noted that over a lifetime, an individual with a bachelor's degree would earn an average of $2.1 million dollars, which is almost twice that of a worker with a high school education. The commission estimated that 90% of the fastest-growing jobs in the information and service economy would require postsecondary education. The College Board (2006) commented that adults with some college or an associate's degree (4.2%) and those with a bachelor's degree or higher (2.35%) are also less likely to be unemployed than those who graduated from high school (5.4%) or those who did not graduate from high school (8.8%). Research has also demonstrated that college graduates with learning disabilities have employment rates and earnings that are consistent with the American work force in general (Madaus, 2006).

This book outlines the complexities that students with disabilities face in making the transition to college, but it presents a variety of practical solutions and strategies to help students throughout the process. Through the use of vignettes, tips, and activities, each chapter translates the most up-to-date research in a user-friendly format that can be used to guide students with disabilities and their families. Each chapter focuses on early, coordinated, student-centered planning to help students develop the academic and personal skills required to successfully make the transition to college. The following sections offer an overview of each chapter.

## CHAPTER OVERVIEWS

In Chapter 2, Joan McGuire provides an overview of the legal mandates that apply to students with disabilities in both high school and college, including the key differences between the Individuals with Disabilities Education Improvement Act (IDEA) of 2004 (PL 108-446), Section 504 of the Rehabilitation Act of 1973 (PL 93-112), the Americans with Disabilities Act (ADA) of 1990 (PL 101-336), and the Americans with Disabilities Act Amendments Act (ADAAA) of 2008 (PL 110-325). With this as a foundation, McGuire explains how these legal mandates directly affect the instructional environment and increase the need for student self-determination and self-advocacy. The importance of technology-related skills and competencies is also explained, as is the range of disability supports at the postsecondary level. The chapter concludes with a discussion of long-term considerations related to the high school plan of study, as well as other postsecondary options.

Chapter 3, by Joseph Madaus, provides information related to accommodations at the college level that can be shared with students and their families. Many students with disabilities (and their families) become accustomed to receiving certain academic adjustments and services at the high school level, but are then surprised to learn that those are unavailable at the college level. To promote early planning and an increase in student self-advocacy, Madaus provides an overview of the legal foundations related to IDEA 2004 and Section 504, including how services under Section 504 may differ in high school and in college. An overview of how accommodations, both instructional and programmatic, are determined at the college level is presented. The chapter contains specific tips that secondary teachers can use to help develop student self-advocacy and preparation for making accommodation requests in college.

Self-determination is an essential skill for students with disabilities to develop and to continually refine. Chapter 4, by James Martin, Juan Portley, and John Graham, focuses on methods to assess and promote student self-determination. Martin and colleagues provide a definition of self-determination, and they describe methods that can be used with students to develop and practice these skills. Specific methods to assess student self-determination are presented, as are ways that these tools can be incorporated into the transition planning process and increase student involvement in the individualized education program (IEP) process. The chapter concludes with a discussion of how students can identify and attain their post-high school goals.

Chapter 5, by Michael Faggella-Luby, K. Brigid Flannery, and Brandi Simonsen, demonstrates how schoolwide intervention models can be used to support academic and behavioral skills that foster access to college. Noting some of the common roadblocks faced by students with disabilities in making the transition to college, Faggella-Luby and colleagues describe the role of cognitive strategy instruction and present a variety of strategies and instructional techniques that have proven successful with high school students. Schoolwide models, including response to intervention and schoolwide positive behavior supports, are also outlined, including the component tiers, the roles of various high school personnel, ways to promote student involvement, and methods to evaluate implementing these models to help students make the transition to college.

Technology is becoming increasingly ubiquitous in the lives of students, both in high school and college. The technology skills required in college are different than those required in high school and must be considered as part of careful transition planning. In Chapter 6, Manju Banerjee provides a look at trends and issues related to technology skills. She differentiates between the remedial and compensatory use of assistive technology at the secondary level and the role of technology in delivering instruction at the college level. Banerjee then outlines many of the essential technology skills and competencies that are needed in college and provides specific steps to consider in helping students prepare for these demands.

The role of the family in transition planning cannot be overstated. Chapter 7, by Carol Kochhar-Bryant, explains methods that can be used by high school personnel to foster collaborative relationships. Noting the different types of family structures that are evident today, the chapter begins with an overview of the role and the importance of the family in transition

planning and discusses specific policies and legislation that support the role
of the family. Kochhar-Bryant then explains how a disability can affect the
family system and how the role of the family will change as the student
moves through school and toward transition. The chapter presents principles
and strategies for developing effective collaboration with families, including
those parents who present challenging behaviors for both secondary and
postsecondary personnel.

It is critical that students move into postsecondary life with
documentation that will assist them in becoming eligible for services and
accommodations in college. Chapter 8, by Lyman Dukes, provides a
comprehensive look at how secondary personnel and students can work
together to gather the data that will help the student show that he or she is
both "otherwise qualified" for college and eligible for support and
accommodations. Dukes provides an overview of transition assessment,
including specific tools that can be used, and the role of the student in the
process. The chapter concludes with a discussion of the summary of
performance (SOP) requirement of IDEA 2004. Dukes presents a
comprehensive SOP for a student who will attend college and outlines how
secondary personnel can use the SOP to assist their own students.

Chapter 9, by Nick and Linda Elksnin, presents the many elements of
the college search process. The chapter begins by describing the subjective
and emotional considerations that go into the college search and presents
information to help students, families, and secondary school personnel
conduct the "systematic college search." This includes conducting an
initial search to determine a match between the student and the
institution. In addition, a more specific search is conducted to match the
needs of the student because of his or her disability and the specific
services that are offered on a given campus. The chapter also contains a
variety of tools and resources that can be used directly in the college
search process.

Following the college search, students must then navigate the array of
admissions procedures that exist at institutions throughout the country.
Chapter 10, by Manju Banerjee and Loring Brinckerhoff, examines this
process in detail. A planning time line is presented, as are specific suggestions
related to what types of documentation should be gathered both to receive
accommodations on the SAT and the ACT and to determine eligibility for
services in college. Banerjee and Brinckerhoff present a set of key questions
that students should ask related to disability services, as well as a discussion
of the pros and cons of self-disclosure when applying to college.

Chapter 11, by Stan Shaw, pulls many of the themes found in the various
chapters together. Shaw describes the transition planning process, including
time lines and the roles of key personnel, and then presents specific
suggestions related to the development of a transition IEP that includes
considering student preferences. Shaw then discusses how the concepts of
universal design can be used to incorporate transition planning into the
school's infrastructure, including career services, counseling services, and
joint programs between high schools and colleges. The chapter concludes by
presenting ways to address the needs of students with specific disabilities as
they make the transition to college.

# REFERENCES

American Youth Policy Forum and Center on Education Policy. (2002). *Twenty-five years of educating children with disabilities: The good news and the work ahead.* Washington, DC: Author.

Americans with Disabilities Act (ADA) of 1990, PL 101-336, 42 U.S.C. §§ 12101 *et seq.*

Americans with Disabilities Act Amendments Act (ADAAA) of 2008, S. 3406, PL 110-325.

Atkinson, B.H. (1947). Students in wheelchairs. *Phi Delta Kappan, 24,* 295–297.

Berdie, R.F. (1955). Counseling for physically disabled students. *Journal of Higher Education, 26,* 475–478.

Cameto, R. (2007). *4 years out: Postschool outcomes and experiences of youth with disabilities.* Presentation at the Division on Career Development and Transition Conference, Orlando, FL.

College Board. (2006). *Education pays: Second update.* Retrieved November 1, 2006, from http://www.collegeboard.com/prod_downloads/press/cost06/education_pays_06.pdf

Condon, M.E. (1962). The facilitation of the education of the physically disabled college student. *Rehabilitation Literature, 23,* 266–274.

Individuals with Disabilities Education Improvement Act (IDEA) of 2004, PL 108-446, 20 U.S.C. §§ 1400 *et seq.*

Madaus, J.W. (2006). Employment outcomes of university graduates with learning disabilities. *Learning Disabilities Quarterly, 29,* 19–31.

National Center for Education Statistics. (2006). *Profile of undergraduates in U.S. postsecondary education institutions: 2003-2004.* Retrieved November 1, 2006, from http://nces.ed.gov/pubsearch/pubsinfo.asp?pubid=2006184

Rehabilitation Act of 1973, PL 93-112, 29 U.S.C. §§ 701 *et seq.*

U.S. Department of Education. (2006). *A test of leadership: Charting the future of U.S. higher education.* Washington, DC: Author.

# Considerations for the Transition to College

*Joan M. McGuire*

# THE LEGAL LANDSCAPE

According to a report based on the National Longitudinal Transition Study-2 (Cameto, Levine, & Wagner, 2004), many students with disabilities are benefiting from the requirements under the IDEA 2004 for transition planning. The authors reported that "almost 90% of secondary school students receiving special education services have transition planning under way on their behalf, with about two-thirds having begun the process by age 14 as required by IDEA 97" (p. ES 2). This is good news considering that it has been approximately 20 years since federal policy regarding transition planning for youth with disabilities was initiated under the leadership of Will (1984), who viewed it as a bridge from school to adulthood. Cameto et al. also noted that the transition plans for students with mild disabilities (e.g., learning disabilities, other health impairments including attention-deficit/hyperactivity disorder [ADHD], hearing, or orthopedic) are the most likely to incorporate recommendations for postsecondary education accommodations. Yet, there continue to be challenges relating to the process reported by parents and secondary school personnel. Postsecondary disability service providers as well as faculty also note concerns in the transition process and preparedness of students, including documentation that is inadequate to support reasonable and appropriate accommodations, overaccommodation at the secondary level, and reluctance of students to self-advocate for their disability-related needs (Cook, Hennessey, Cook, & Rumrill, 2007).

Gaining knowledge about legislation, which differs at the secondary and postsecondary levels, is a critical starting point to understanding the elements that contribute to a successful transition to postsecondary education. Understanding the regulations for IDEA 2004, particularly those that apply to transition; Section 504 of the Rehabilitation Act of 1973 and its amendments; and the ADA 1990 and the ADAAA is essential for effective planning as college-bound students prepare for an environment that is significantly different from their high school setting.

## Transition Components of IDEA 2004

Transition components of IDEA 2004 include 1) age for beginning the transition planning process; 2) assessment, eligibility, and reevaluation; and 3) components of the individualized education program (IEP).

### Age for Initiating Planning

Unlike the requirements for transition planning under IDEA 1997 that mandated that services begin at age 14 or younger, IDEA 2004 altered the point at which planning must be initiated to age 16. The wisdom of this change has been debated (O'Leary, 2006; Shaw, 2006) because preparation for college has to begin early with a high school plan of study that equips students with the skills and knowledge necessary for the demands of postsecondary education. It is too soon to evaluate the effect of this age change on 14- and 15-year-old students, but the importance of collaborative planning involving middle school and secondary special educators, students, and parents cannot be overstated. Curriculum decisions such as course level (i.e., college preparatory, general, vocational/technical/career) and areas of study (e.g., math, science, foreign language) will affect a student's eligibility for college admission. Some researchers (Lerner, 2003; Sitlington, Clark, & Kolstoe, 2000, as cited in Hitchings, Retish, & Horvath, 2005) have pointed out that upper-level and college preparatory high school courses require students to manage complex information and heavy work loads, underscoring the need for study skills and self-awareness of their learning styles. Initiating the transition planning process at the time a student is advancing from junior high or middle school to high school makes sense because it allows more flexibility and time for preparation (Brinckerhoff, McGuire, & Shaw, 2002). Detailed steps for a cohesive transition planning approach are outlined in Chapter 11.

> Starting transition planning early helps ensure that students' curriculum choices and IEPs will address their educational needs so they can meet their postsecondary goals. Planning should also include opportunities for students to utilize and monitor the effectiveness of learning strategies and accommodations in anticipation of a postsecondary learning environment that differs significantly from that at the secondary level.

## Assessment, Eligibility, and Summary of Performance

Another major change in IDEA 2004 covers requirements for assessment to determine initial and continuing eligibility for special education, more specifically, for students with learning disabilities. Determining eligibility for services under the category of learning disability now requires states to use criteria from among three options: 1) severe discrepancy, 2) response to intervention (RTI), and 3) other alternative research-based procedures (Regulations for IDEA, 2006). An aptitude—achievement discrepancy can no longer be a required criterion for determining learning disabilities, and states must permit the use of another method, including RTI. This procedure is based on the response of a student to scientific, research-based intervention that includes progress monitoring via repeated assessments conducted at reasonable intervals during the intervention (Yell & Drasgow, 2007). It is too soon to determine the implications of these changes for the transition process, and it remains to be seen whether school districts will replace the much criticized severe discrepancy model with RTI. Zirkel and Krohn (2008) found that 1 year following the implementation of the federal regulations, approximately half of the 47 states that provided usable replies to a survey had not yet finalized their state regulations about RTI and learning disabilities. Even more challenging will be the process of evaluating and identifying older students who are not referred for initial evaluation until middle school and high school because scientific, evidence-based interventions are primarily validated for early elementary levels (Fuchs, 2003; Graner, Faggella-Luby, & Fritschmann, 2005). Shaw (2006) suggested that changes in eligibility criteria for learning disabilities will result in minimizing the dependence on psychoeducational assessments, which include standardized testing results. This would have implications for colleges and universities and their requirements for disability documentation of learning disabilities—a subject of lively discussion underscored by the lack of uniformity in approaches to assessment as well as variability in eligibility criteria across states (National Joint Committee on Learning Disabilities, 2007).

Reevaluations to document continued eligibility are another change under IDEA 2004. The IEP team must consider existing evaluation data as well as parental input, current classroom-based and district or state assessment data, and observations of teachers and related services personnel (141[a][6][c][A][i-iii]). If the team determines that no additional information is needed to verify a student's continuing eligibility, then parents must be advised of that decision. Furthermore, a reevaluation is not required if a student is no longer eligible for special education services because he or she graduates with a regular diploma, as would be the case for most college-bound students. However, the local education agency (LEA) must provide a summary of performance (SOP) with recommendations on ways to meet a student's postsecondary goals (see Chapter 8 for details about the SOP).

There are several implications of these assessment regulations. The first relates to how recently an assessment has been conducted—a component of guidelines for documenting learning disabilities and ADHD that is used by many colleges and universities as well as testing agencies such as Educational Testing Service (ETS; see http://www.ets.org for an example of such guidelines) to establish eligibility under Section 504 and the ADA. It is possible that students headed for postsecondary education will not have testing that meets the time parameters for recency, such as 3 or 5 years, because the mandate for a triennial reevaluation under IDEA 2004 now permits school districts to use professional judgment to decide whether additional data are needed for continued eligibility. Kochhar-Bryant, Shaw, and Izzo (2007) speculated that some students could exit high school without any formal testing since middle or even elementary school. At the time of mandated reevaluation, however, the LEA must notify a parent or guardian of his or her right "to request an assessment to determine whether the child continues to be a child with a disability, and to determine the child's educational needs" (IDEA 2004, § 300.305 [d][1]). The importance of disability documentation at the postsecondary level may not be clear to parents and students who sometimes assume that an IEP or Section 504 plan is sufficient to establish a need for accommodations at the postsecondary level; thus, they may not think to request updated testing. The effect of this "disconnect" between secondary and postsecondary practices could have striking implications for students because colleges and universities are not required to conduct assessments to determine eligibility, leaving the expense of any updated testing done after secondary school solely to the consumer.

A second implication centers on the SOP, which includes a summary of academic achievement and functional performance with recommendations about ways to assist the student to meet postsecondary goals. Although such a document could be useful, it is important that students understand that SOP recommendations are not binding at a college or university. Madaus and Shaw (2006) noted that "just as postsecondary institutions are not required to accept IEPs and recommendations from secondary schools, they will not be required to accept the recommendations in the SOP" (p. 278).

### IEP Components

Although early transition planning is not precluded, IDEA 2004 requires an IEP to include appropriate measurable postsecondary goals based on age-appropriate transition assessments (§ 300.320b). Students' strengths, preferences, and interests must be taken into account, reinforcing the importance of student self-advocacy, a critical skill at the postsecondary level where students must be their own spokespeople. The words of a parent of a student with learning disabilities underscore the opportunity this change in IDEA 2004 may bring. "In addition to parents backing off, the students need to learn how to become more independent. Teach your child to become a strong self-advocate and to be assertive without acting entitled or demanding" (Goldberg, 2001, p. 52).

To summarize, transition components under IDEA 2004 have been revised from IDEA 1997, and these changes in legal mandates at the secondary level can be expected to exert a ripple effect at the postsecondary level. Awareness of the different requirements between the secondary and postsecondary levels (e.g., recency of testing, evidence of substantial functional impairment, standardized test results) is imperative for professionals as they work closely with students in the transition process.

## Section 504, the ADA, and the ADAAA

Section 504 of the Rehabilitation Act of 1973 comprises civil rights legislation covering preschool, elementary, secondary, and adult education programs as well as colleges and universities that receive any type of federal financial aid. Another important civil rights law is the ADA, which extends antidiscrimination requirements to public and private colleges, testing agencies, the employment sector, and telecommunications. Understanding these laws and what they mean at the secondary and postsecondary levels will help clarify misconceptions that often underlie expectations of parents and students for services in college. In addition, there are distinct differences between these civil rights laws, which protect against discrimination on the basis of disability, and IDEA 2004, which is an entitlement law that assures a free appropriate public education (FAPE) to any student with a disability in the K–12 system with needs for special education. Reilly and Davis stated,

> Many students with disabilities and their families do not realize that making the transition from high school to college or the workplace involves leaving behind the protection under the Individuals with Disabilities Education Act (IDEA) of 1990, its 1997 amendments (PL 105-17), and its 2004 reauthorization (PL 108-446). (2005, p. 26)

## *Section 504: Subparts D and E*

Madaus and Shaw (2004) pointed out that Section 504 includes seven subparts, two of which are germane to transition planning. Subpart D extends to secondary schools, whereas Subpart E pertains to postsecondary education programs and activities. There are commonalities between elements of these two subparts, but there are also significant differences that are essential to understand in the interest of effective transition planning.

The intent of Section 504 is to assure equal access and nondiscriminatory treatment to "otherwise qualified" individuals with disabilities. Inherent in this definition are two key concepts: 1) evidence of a disability or impairment (referred to in the original statute as *handicap* but revised to reflect person-first terminology) and 2) determination of "otherwise qualified" status. Subpart A includes the following definition of *disability* that is used in Subparts D and E: any individual who (a) has a physical or mental impairment that *substantially limits* one or more major life activities, (b) has a history of such impairment, or (c) is regarded as having such impairment (§ 104.3 [j]). A major difference between Subparts D and E centers on the definition of *otherwise qualified,* which is summarized by Madaus and Shaw (2004, p. 82) from the regulations.

1. Subpart D
   A qualified person with a disability is (i) of any age during which nonhandicapped persons are provided such services, (ii) of any age during which it is mandatory under state law to provide such services to handicapped persons, or (iii) to whom a state is required to provide a free appropriate public education under section 612 of the Education of the Handicapped Act (§104.3[k][2]).

2. Subpart E
   A qualified person with a disability is one who meets the academic and technical standards requisite to admission or participation in the recipients' education program or activity (§ 104.3[k][3]).

Under Subpart D, a student may be qualified for coverage because he or she meets the age range, generally age 3–21 or until graduation, specified in IDEA 2004. At the postsecondary level, the concept of *qualified* is not dependent on age: Students must demonstrate that they have met academic requirements for admission. Transition planning must consider many factors because admissions criteria differ vastly according to a college's mission and its competitive profile. Colleges are not required to alter their technical standards, meaning that participation and level of performance in college preparatory high school courses comprise a legitimate admissions requirement of many colleges. Likewise, an admissions criterion for standardized testing such as the SAT or ACT does *not* have to be waived for students with disabilities who are encouraged to seek appropriate accommodations for the test from the testing agency. Clearly, students need to consider these admissions parameters throughout their high school years. For students whose high school curriculum has not included competitive college preparatory courses, there may be merit in initially considering options discussed later in this chapter to determine the "goodness of fit" between their postsecondary goals and institutional requirements.

Under Subpart D, each year an LEA must

(a) undertake to identify and locate every qualified handicapped person residing in the recipient's jurisdiction who is not receiving public education; and 2) take appropriate steps to notify handicapped persons and their parents or guardians of the recipient's duty under this subpart. (§ 104.32)

Under Subpart E, any preadmission inquiry regarding disability is prohibited unless the postsecondary institution is taking "remedial action to correct past discrimination" or "is taking voluntary action to overcome the effects of conditions that resulted in limited participation" (§104.42[c]). It is unlikely that a college would qualify for making a preadmission inquiry under this section of the regulations but if so, then its policies must state the purpose of such an inquiry, noting that such information is voluntary and will be treated confidentially and that refusal to answer will not result in adverse treatment of an applicant. Once a student is admitted to a college and is seeking accommodations, it becomes his or her responsibility to disclose his or her disability and provide documentation that substantiates its current effect on learning and/or another major life activity (e.g., mobility, concentration, interacting with others). As frequently noted in the literature (Brinckerhoff et al., 2002; Kochhar-Bryant et al., 2007; Madaus & Shaw, 2004; National Joint Committee on Learning Disabilities, 2007; Zirkel, 2007), colleges and universities typically require documentation beyond an IEP or Section 504 plan to determine reasonable accommodations. The courts have consistently found that colleges and universities have a right to request this in order to establish the existence of a disability *and* the current functional effect of that disability that warrants accommodation(s) (Heyward, 2004). Whereas evaluation is the responsibility of the LEA and is provided at no expense to the student or parent under Subpart D, documentation of disability is the student's responsibility and at his or her expense under Subpart E.

Under Subpart D, service decisions for an eligible student are made by a team of people knowledgeable about the student, the disability, and placement options, and these services are typically delineated in a 504 plan (Wehman, 2006). In contrast, under Subpart E, there is no mandate for special education, nor is there a range of placement options. The regulations apply to admissions and recruitment, treatment of students, academic adjustments, housing, financial aid, and nonacademic services. Academic adjustments can include changes to the length of time for completing a degree and providing auxiliary aids such as recording of texts and notetakers. Courses are with students without disabilities unless the student is participating in a fee-based special program that offers services beyond what are mandated under the law (Brinckerhoff et al., 2002).

Table 2.1 provides a summary of institutional responsibilities under the two subparts of Section 504 (Madaus & Shaw, 2004). The implications for students making the transition to postsecondary education are notable. For an effective and efficient transition to occur, awareness of differences must begin *before* a student initiates college studies. According to Miller and Newbill (cited in Wehman, 2006), "the role played by Section 504 in schools has increased dramatically in recent years" (p. 14), based in part on the growing

**Table 2.1.**   Responsibilities under subparts D and E of Section 504

| Area | Responsibilities under Section 504 subpart D (secondary level) | Responsibilities under Section 504 subpart E (postsecondary level) |
|---|---|---|
| Identification | School district | Student |
| Evaluation | School district | Student |
| Payment for evaluation | School district | Student |
| IEP or service plan | School district | Not required |
| Course selection and programming | School district | Student |
| Transition planning | School district | Student |
| Progress monitoring | School district | Student |
| Assuming educational costs | School district | Student/parent |
| Ensuring reasonable accommodations | School district | Institution (upon student eligibility) |
| Monitoring effectiveness | School district | Student |

From McGuire, J.M. (2008). *Transition materials.* Storrs: University of Connecticut, Center on Postsecondary Education and Disability; reprinted by permission.

familiarity of its relevance by advocates and parents. Wehman pointed out that "the definition of disability and eligibility requirements are much more restrictive in IDEA than they are in Section 504" (2006, p. 14–15). For some students who may not automatically be eligible for special education under IDEA 2004 (e.g., ADHD, oppositional defiant disorder [ODD]), protections and services stipulated under Section 504 will undoubtedly result in 504 plans that may or may not include assessment data.

Although this may benefit students who are not in need of special education, it may constitute a liability once the student makes the transition to college and seeks accommodations. It is unlikely that such 504 plans will meet the documentation requirements of a college or university.

> Planning ahead can also help ensure that students and their families are adequately prepared with documentation that is needed at the postsecondary level to establish the current functional impact of the disability and the rationale for reasonable accommodations.

## The ADA and ADAAA

With the intent of providing equal opportunities for people with disabilities, protections against discrimination were extended to the private sector under the ADA. This law draws much of its language from Section 504 and it uses an identical definition of a person with a disability. There are five sections or "titles" in the ADA: I) employment, II) public services, III) public accommodations, IV) telecommunications, and V) miscellaneous. Of particular relevance to college-bound students with disabilities are Titles II and III that pertain to testing, licensing, and certification. Examinations and the process for applying for them must be accessible, meaning that any modifications or auxiliary aids must be available at no cost to the test taker with a disability. Major testing agencies such as Educational Testing Service and the American College Testing program have detailed guidelines and procedures for applicants to request accommodations.

Unlike IDEA 2004, which is overseen by the Office of Special Education Programs (OSEP), the Office for Civil Rights (OCR) is the enforcement agency for both Section 504 and the ADA. Elementary and secondary schools must comply with the ADA, Section 504, and IDEA 2004 (Rothstein, 2002), whereas colleges and universities are not covered under IDEA 2004. In terms of practice, the regulations accompanying Section 504 serve as a blueprint for services at the postsecondary level.

On September 25, 2008, 18 years and 2 months after his father signed the original ADA, President George W. Bush signed into law the ADAAA, which went into effect January 1, 2009. The process leading to this historic event included advocacy efforts across multiple private, nonprofit, and individual entities because of a series of lower court and Supreme Court cases that narrowed the definition of *disability* contrary to congressional intent (http://www.law.georgetown.edu/archiveada).

The implications of the ADAAA for colleges and universities will evolve as was the case with implementing the ADA. It is reasonable to project that a broader interpretation of the construct of disability will result in an increase in the number of students seeking accommodations and equal access. Service providers at the secondary and postsecondary levels should remain abreast of changes once the regulations for the amendments are promulgated. Feldblum, Barry, and Benfer (2008) wrote a detailed analysis of the advocacy efforts that preceded the passage of the original ADA and that underscored the need for an amended version that, in their words, restores the original intent of the ADA. Their comparison of the ADA and its amended version (http://www.law.georgetown.edu/archiveada/#ADAAA) highlights these substantive changes:

- *Definition of disability.* According to the Equal Opportunity Employment Commission (http://www.eeoc.gov/ada/amendments_notice.html), the ADAAA retains the ADA's basic three-pronged definition of *disability* as an impairment that substantially limits one or more major life activities, a record of such an impairment, or being regarded as having such an impairment. It changes the way that these statutory terms should be interpreted in several ways. The amendments provide a rule of construction to counter the Supreme Court's narrow interpretation of "substantially limits a major life activity." This rule of construction states that the definition of *disability* shall be construed "in favor of broad coverage of individuals rather than the overly demanding standard applied by the courts."

- *Major life activities.* A nonexhaustive list now includes caring for oneself, performing manual tasks, seeing, hearing, eating, sleeping, walking, standing, lifting, bending, speaking, breathing, learning, reading, concentrating, thinking, communicating, and working, in addition to other bodily functions (e.g., functions of the immune system, normal cell growth, digestive, bowel, bladder, neurological, brain, respiratory, circulatory, endocrine, reproductive functions).

- *Episodic conditions.* The amendments now clarify that impairments that are episodic in nature or are in remission are considered disabilities if the impairment would substantially limit a major life activity when the condition is actively manifesting itself.

- *Mitigating measures.* The ADAAA provides that the ameliorative effects of mitigating measures should *not* be considered in determining whether an individual has an impairment that substantially limits a major life activity. An exception is made for ordinary eyeglasses or contact lenses, which may be taken into account.

- *Auxiliary aids and services.* This includes qualified interpreters or other effective methods of making aurally delivered materials available to individuals with hearing impairments; qualified readers, taped texts, or other effective methods of making visually delivered materials available to individuals with visual impairments; acquiring or modifying equipment or devices; and other similar services and actions.

The broad implications of the ADAAA are best summarized by Senator Tom Harkin, the lead sponsor of the bill in the Senate:

> This bill fulfills the promise of the ADA and greatly increases the number of people eligible for its protections. It fixes a number of glaring injustices that have come about because of the Supreme Court's misunderstanding of the original ADA and it clarifies once and for all, that anyone with a disability is eligible for the protections of the ADA. (http://harkin.senate.gov/blog/?i =f0b8bd21-242b-4058-bf5a-3dd134ad0045)

## Creating a Section 504 Plan and Planning Ahead

As secondary institutions continue to grapple with implementing IDEA 2004 and postsecondary institutions experience the effects of its changes, dialogue is critical particularly as it relates to documentation sufficient to establish a student's eligibility for reasonable accommodations in college. Too often students who have been eligible for a Section 504 plan during high school try to present this or an IEP as documentation for postsecondary accommodations. Limitations to these plans can include no background information or history, no data to indicate the nature or severity of the disability, and no discussion of the rationale for the recommended accommodations. Modifications received under 504 plans or IEPs, such as foreign language waivers, "untimed" tests, word banks for multiple choice tests, and reduced homework, raise concerns about expectations for similar alterations in college. Determining accommodations at the college level occurs as a dynamic process that takes into account the nature and severity of the disability, elements of a specific course, and what Scott described as "much more than a clerical task of implementing evaluator recommendations" (2002, p. 325).

Subpart E of the Section 504 regulations stipulate that "academic requirements that the recipient [institution] can demonstrate are essential to the program of instruction being pursued by such student or to any directly related licensing requirement will not be regarded as discriminatory" (§ 104.44[a]). This underscores a potential disconnect between secondary and postsecondary curricular choices. If a student intends to pursue a college major in international business, an exemption from foreign language at the postsecondary level is unlikely. Assuming that the student is determined "otherwise qualified" for admission, he or she may be surprised to learn that a foreign language waiver will not be granted at his or her college because foreign language proficiency is viewed as essential to an international business major. There may be options he or she would be well advised to explore *before* making a decision about his or her college of choice (e.g., availability of a study abroad program with options for demonstrating language proficiency).

The process of determining reasonable accommodations involves the student, a disability service provider, and often a faculty member teaching the course in which accommodation is requested. Courts have typically deferred to the decisions of higher education personnel, including faculty, regarding the essential components of a program or course of study (Heyward, 2004). As noted previously, colleges are not required to accept IEPs and accommodation recommendations as sufficient documentation (Madaus & Shaw, 2006), and the same can be said of Section 504 plans. Requirements for documentation may change as the legal requirements for assessment change under IDEA 2004 and as the ADAAA is implemented. More comprehensive evidence such as a detailed Section 504 plan as well as an SOP may offer alternatives to the more traditional standardized assessment battery that now characterizes the documentation requirements of many postsecondary institutions. Following is an example of a comprehensive 504 plan for Jessica.

## JESSICA'S 504 PLAN

After intense remediation in elementary school and reduced special education services during middle school and her first 2 years of high school, a determination was made to discuss Jessica's eligibility for a 504 plan for her junior year. The team met at the end of 10th grade, and Jessica was an active participant in the discussion. In addition to informal conversations about accommodations Jessica has used, the team reviewed standardized test results that verified the ongoing effect of her learning disability on her academic performance, particularly in the areas of processing speed, spelling and grammar, and organization. With input from her classroom teachers as well as the support of the special education teacher, the team decided that by using accommodations and modifications, Jessica should be able to experience success during 11th grade. There was consensus about the types of supports that Jessica would use, including extended test time, a calculator, and a computer with spellchecking. At the beginning of the next year, Jessica will talk with her teachers about the benefits of advanced organizers and her need to break down long-term assignments into segments, knowing that the special education teacher is there as a back-up resource if Jessica requires consultation. Jessica is confident that she can monitor her work, and she agreed that it is her responsibility to make contact with special education staff if she is experiencing difficulty or anxiety. The team also agreed to reconvene midway through 11th grade for an update on the effectiveness of the plan. Figure 2.1 displays Jessica's Section 504 Plan.

## A. Referral

Name: <u>Jessica Loomes</u>   Date of birth: <u>9/14/89</u>   Grade: <u>11</u>

School: <u>Victor High</u>   Date of meeting: <u>9/28/06</u>

Referred by: <u>Terry Griswold, Section 504 Coordinator</u>

Date of referral: <u>9/05/06</u>

1. Reason for referral: <u>Jessica is a junior who received special education services because of a learning disability from 4th through 10th grades. She no longer receives resource support but does use numerous accommodations for testing and in-class assignments. The purpose of this referral is to develop a 504 plan for her junior year.</u>

2. Describe interventions that have been implemented in the past to address the student's functional limitations. <u>Jessica's learning disabilities include average cognitive functioning with significant weaknesses in her speed of performance, spelling and grammar, and recall of information. She has tried audiotaped textbooks but finds them inconvenient and too time consuming to use. A detailed calendar of due dates for reading assignments along with advanced organizers for long-term assignments have been effective. Jessica has used extended time (.5), a calculator, and a word processor for the state standardized mastery tests, and she recently took the SAT with .5 extended test time and a calculator.</u>

## B. Eligibility Determination

1. Area(s) of concern: <u>Jessica needs extended time for processing materials especially when there is extensive reading and writing involved. This creates a problem for in-class activities and assignments because Jessica often has not completed the reading in time to participate in activities.</u>

2. Summary of formal performance data reviewed (note sources): Scores are reported as standard scores (mean = 100; $SD$ = 15).

   A. Cognitive abilities (data gathered from the Wechsler Adult Intelligence Scale-Third Edition [WAIS-III] administered in 10th grade)
   Verbal IQ: 106          Performance IQ: 94          Full Scale IQ: 101
   Index scores:   Verbal Comprehension Index: 111
                   Perceptual Organization Index: 95
                   Working Memory Index: 82
                   Processing Speed Index: 88

   B. Academic performance (data gathered from Woodcock Johnson III - Tests of Achievement [WJ III ACH] administered in 10th grade)
   Broad reading: 84 (letter–word, 84; fluency, 81; passage comprehension, 94)
   Broad math: 87 (calculation, 88; fluency, 81; applied problems, 90)
   Broad written language: 70 (spelling, 70; fluency, 84; writing samples, 75)

3. Summary of staff reports/comments/observations: <u>Jessica's 10th-grade teachers of English, American history, algebra 1, and earth science completed informal checklists about her in-class and homework performance. Clearly, she is a student who needs and uses accommodations. Teachers report that she is a hard worker, although she sometimes has difficulty independently initiating tasks and organizing her work.</u>

4. Summary of student/parent(s)/guardians comments: <u>Jessica wants to continue her education and plans to enroll at the community college in the paraprofessional program for becoming a teacher's aide. Her parents support her choice and are willing to work with her at home, although sometimes that can become tedious because both of them work and do not get home until dinner time.</u>

5. Other pertinent information: <u>Jessica volunteers two afternoons a week at a local child care center, and she babysits for several families in her neighborhood.</u>

6. Specify the physical or mental impairment(s): <u>Specific learning disability</u>

7. Indicate the major life activity that is affected: <u>Learning, reading, performing math calculations</u>

**Figure 2.1.** Jessica's Section 504 plan. (From McGuire, J.M. [2008]. *Transition materials.* Storrs: University of Connecticut, Center on Postsecondary Education and Disability; reprinted by permission.)

8. The term *substantially limits* means that the student is significantly restricted as to the condition, manner, or duration under which a particular major life activity is performed that the average student of approximately the same age can perform.

Using the 1–5 scale, indicate the degree of the impairment:
1 _____ negligible; 2 _____ mild; 3 _____ moderate; 4 \_\_\_X\_\_ substantial; 5 _____ extreme
If the team's determination was a 4 or more, then the student is eligible for services under Section 504, and an accommodation plan should be developed.

9. The student is qualified for the development of a 504 accommodation plan?
Yes \_\_\_X\_\_ No \_\_\_\_\_
(If no, stop here. Send the notice of Section 504 noneligibility to the parents/guardian.)

## C. 504 Accommodation Plan

Is this 504 plan an
1. Initial accommodation plan \_\_\_X\_\_\_ 2. Reevaluation _____ 3. Continuing _____
Basis for determination as a qualified individual: Long-standing history of learning disabilities and special education services dating back to the fourth grade; testing completed in 10th grade (evaluation information considered: e.g., medical records, academic evaluation)

2. The goals of this plan are
- To promote self-advocacy on the part of Jessica in anticipation of the need for her to assume such a role in college
- To provide an opportunity for Jessica to use accommodations and monitor their effectiveness

3. Services, accommodations, modifications, or assistive technology to be provided to enable the student
- To advance appropriately toward attaining her annual goals
- To be involved in and make progress in the general education curriculum
- To participate in extracurricular and other nonacademic activities
- To be educated and participate with other students with and without disabilities

Specific areas where implemented
A. Instructional strategies: advanced content classes, teacher organizers and study guides as warranted, monitor long-term assignment completion
B. Tests/quizzes/assessments: prior notice of tests/quizzes; study guides; extended time on tests and written work, with spell check and calculator where warranted
C. Behavioral: daily feedback; positive reinforcement
D. Organization: detailed class syllabus with rubrics for grading
E. Environment: preferential seating if warranted
F. Grading: consider effort invested in work
G. Materials/books/equipment: use of a computer with spellchecker; use of calculator
H. Other: _____

4. Person responsible for implementing this plan: Terry Griswold

5. Dates the plan is in effect: 10/1/06 to 6/17/07

6. The review/reassessment date for this plan is: 6/20/07

7. Team members:
Terry Griswold, 504 Coordinator
Jessica Loomes, Student
Judy Loomes, Mother
Tom Loomes, Father
Mary Addison, Special Education Coordinator
Sylvia Montgomery, Vice Principal
Jeff Ruth, Transition Coordinator
Sue Cinques, Early Childhood Teacher

I am aware of and/or have participated in the development of this plan.
Parent's signature: _____ Date: _____
Approval by 504 coordinator: _____ Date: _____

## THE LEARNING LANDSCAPE

Several characteristics that differentiate secondary and postsecondary settings take on added importance as high school students prepare for transition: curriculum choices, the instructional environment, and competence in technology skills. Each of these is addressed in the sections that follow.

## Curriculum Choices

### *Secondary*

According to IDEA 2004 regulations, transition planning must include the course of study needed to assist a student in reaching his or her transition goals (National Association of State Directors of Special Education, 2006). Yet, altering the age at which transition services must begin from 14 to 16 is puzzling because there is ample evidence that age 16 is too late in the process to specify a college preparatory or career vocational course of study (Weidenthal & Kochhar-Bryant, 2007). According to Getzel (2005), middle school offers an environment for students to explore topics and course levels in English, math, science, history, and foreign language. Because a requirement of colleges and universities for admission is satisfactory completion of specific academic units, planning a course of study as a student moves from middle school and through 4 years of high school should be discussed early by the IEP team members with input from guidance counselors and teachers as well as the student and parents.

> For college-bound students, a plan of study should include college preparatory courses as well as opportunities for career exploration, and numerous transition tools are available to guide this process (e.g., Clark, Patton, & Moulton, 2000; http://www.ncset.org/publications/default.asp).

The type of diploma a student will receive is another important conversation in a student's transition to high school. As a result of the accountability mandate under the NCLB Act to monitor graduation rates, many states are now offering multiple diploma options for students with disabilities, including honors diplomas, standard diplomas, certificates of attendance or completion, and IEP diplomas (Johnson, Thurlow, Cosio, & Bremer, 2005). As these authors noted, "it is critical to understand the impact of diploma options on the postsecondary and employment outcomes of students with disabilities" (n.p.).

Components of the standards-based education reform movement (i.e., curriculum standards and accountability for all students) that emanate in large part from the NCLB Act have other implications for curriculum choices as well. With the goal of higher educational expectations and performance for *all* students, three elements comprise what is commonly called "standards-driven reform:" 1) content standards (knowledge and skills *all* students are expected to learn); 2) assessments to determine student achievement; and 3) accountability (consequences for schools, districts, students, and, in some cases, teachers for failure to meet standards; McLaughlin & Embler, 2006). Content standards and the assessment process are particularly relevant for students preparing to go on to college. Because of the NCLB Act and its emphasis on more rigorous coursework and graduation requirements, a collaborative approach between regular and special educators is imperative in order to balance the need for high standards for *all* students and opportunities for the *individualized* transition planning process that is the hallmark of IDEA 2004. Aligning components of these two systems must occur to assure meaningful transition planning. The National Alliance for Secondary Education and Transition has developed a set of standards, benchmarks, and a toolkit that articulate quality secondary education and transition services for all youth (http://www.ncset.org/websites/naset.asp).

## CHRIS'S TRANSITION PLAN

Chris's case is an example of a collaborative planning approach that synchronizes standards-based components of NCLB and IDEA 2004 transition requirements. Chris, a student with a long-standing history of learning disabilities and ADHD, plans to continue his education at the state college that offers a 4-year degree in turfgrass science and management through its agricultural department. He has worked on self-advocacy skills in a curriculum that began in seventh grade (see Greene & Kochhar-Bryant, 2003, for numerous resources) and talks with his guidance counselor several times each year about his plans. Chris will be taking the SAT during his junior year and plans to request extra time given his slower rate of reading due to short-term memory impairments and slower processing speed. This accommodation has also been provided for Chris on the high-stakes, statewide proficiency tests required for graduation.

When he made the transition from eighth to ninth grade, Chris was not sure about a career path, but the IEP team, Chris, and his mom decided it would be in his best interest to enroll in college preparatory courses. Chris's individualized transition plan (ITP), prepared when he was in 10th grade, and his transcript reflect a collaborative planning process. With his goal of attending college, choice of curriculum as well as level of courses were important. His academic plan meets the state requirements for graduation with a standard diploma (22 credits minimum), and course selection reflects the effect of high standards on his preparation for college. Given his postsecondary goal, Chris began high school in Level B courses, the level to prepare students for colleges ranked as competitive or less competitive according to college guides. As he progressed through high school, his annual IEP meeting included input from subject area teachers about the possibility of changing to Level A courses (highly competitive). Chris and his special education teacher worked together on possible transition goals in the area of organizational skills to prepare him for the demands of college. As Chris moves on to his junior year, it will be important for him to stay abreast of requirements for documentation at the colleges he is considering to be certain he has gathered the necessary evidence to support his need for accommodations. Figure 2.2 contains Chris's ITP.

Student:   Chris Mangione

Grade:   10

Parent(s)/guardian(s):   Sylvia Mangione

Date of birth:   2/15/91

Date of meeting:   3/31/07

Student preferences/interests: Chris wants to attend Midwest State and enroll in the  turfgrass science and management program. He works during the summer as a caddy at a local golf course and helps the grounds crew maintain the fairways and putting greens. Chris has attended his planning and placement team meetings since junior high and talked about his plans with teachers and others.

Present level of performance: Chris knows that time management is hard for him. He  works part time and sometimes feels like he has too much to juggle. Long-term assignments are especially challenging for him, and he expects that it will be hard for him to keep up with all the requirements for a project he knows is required next year in his  environmental science class.

Annual goal: To develop strategies to assist Chris in completing long-term assignments in a timely manner.

1. Chris will review the components of a long-term project in environmental science that are listed in the directions provided by the teacher.

2. Chris will use a monthly calendar/planner to set a time frame for each section of the project.

3. Chris will meet with his environmental science teacher at the beginning of each week to review the tasks he is working on that week and to monitor his completion of task(s) from the previous week.

4. Chris will reflect on his work on this long-term project and ask for help if he is having difficulty completing it.

5. Chris will work with his resource teacher to develop a template for long-term planning that he can use for projects in other courses.

Chris's academic plan of study

| Grade 9 | Grade 10 | Grade 11 | Grade 12 |
|---------|----------|----------|----------|
| Algebra 1 | Geometry | Algebra 2 | Statistics |
| English 1 | English 2: American literature | English 3: British literature | English 4: World literature |
| Introduction to physical science | Biology | Environmental science/microbiology | Chemistry |
| World civilizations | U.S. history | Political perspectives | Money management/ public speaking |
| Spanish 1 | Spanish 2 | Computer literacy/ Microsoft Office 1 and 2 | Health/first aid/CPR |
| Physical education | Physical education/ keyboarding | Print making 1/ computer art | Introduction to management/starting your own business |

**Figure 2.2.**   Chris's individualized transition plan. (From McGuire, J.M. [2008]. *Transition materials*. Storrs: University of Connecticut, Center on Postsecondary Education and Disability; reprinted by permission.)

## Postsecondary

Given the broad scope of institutional missions among the more than 4,300 colleges and universities in the United States (Carnegie Foundation, 2007), taking time to identify good "matches" between a student's preferences/ interests, qualifications, and postsecondary education requirements is time well spent. Although there are no national postsecondary curriculum standards, many colleges now delineate a set of courses required of all graduates referred to as the *general education core curriculum, general institute requirements,* or *core of general studies.* The variability of specified content areas and required credit hours are highly diverse, however. For example, Meredith College specifies 51-67 semester hours of general education courses from areas including core (e.g., English, history, religion) and fields of knowledge (e.g., data analysis, abstract reasoning, and problem solving; world cultures and language; scientific literacy; arts and aesthetics; health and physical learning), whereas required courses (or demonstration of competency) at Massachusetts Institute of Technology include science; lab science; technology; and humanities, arts, and social sciences (HASS). As students explore postsecondary options, gathering details about general education requirements, including the distribution and number of credits, is an important task because choosing a college and program of study can have a widespread effect on a postsecondary plan of study.

Foreign language is one area that is particularly important for students with disabilities to consider. As noted previously, colleges are not required to substantially alter technical standards that are essential in a program of study. Although alternatives may be possible (e.g., substituting American Sign Language), it behooves the college-bound high school student to gather facts about curriculum requirements, both at the secondary and postsecondary levels, well in advance of enrolling. There are also numerous resources for secondary personnel regarding the content area of foreign language as it relates to students with disabilities (e.g., Madaus, 2003; Scott & Manglitz, 2000; Sparks & Javorsky, 2004).

In summary, both secondary and postsecondary education include curriculum requirements. There is much more latitude at the postsecondary level because a college's mission as well as a program's technical standards affect student choice. An informed student is well served to initiate and monitor curriculum choices regularly in both settings.

## Instructional Environment:
## Differences in Secondary and Postsecondary Settings

Brinckerhoff et al. (2002) included an overview of differences in secondary and postsecondary settings, including amount of instructional time, expectations for independent work, assessment of student performance, teaching styles, and structure. At the high school level, there are numerous formal and informal "checks and balances" built into the instructional and home environments that are designed to promote student success. Instructional time is more intense and structured, with teachers providing significantly more contact time and often taking attendance. Assessment of learning outcomes occurs more frequently than in college, sometimes including allowances based on student effort or degree of improvement. High school students are not required to maintain a minimum grade point average in order to remain in school, whereas colleges stipulate a minimum level of academic proficiency to assure continuing enrollment. Perhaps the single most distinguishing quality between the two settings centers on degree of structure and the ability to function independently. Studying, seeking the assistance of faculty, self-disclosing and advocating for reasonable accommodations, decision making and problem solving, and self-reliance are key ingredients for a successful college experience. For secondary students, these functions are often overseen by well-intentioned parents and special educators with a focus on success.

Elements of the transition planning process should integrate preparing students with disabilities for these differences. The importance of self-determination and its effects on student outcomes, both behavioral and learning, is well documented in the literature (Field, Sarver, & Shaw, 2003; Thoma & Wehmeyer, 2005; Wehmeyer, Gragoudas, & Shogren, 2006). Chapter 4 provides an extensive array of strategies to foster the development of this attribute in different settings.

> Plan on a collaborative process among the student, school personnel, and parents to promote student self-awareness and skills to self-advocate. Provide multiple opportunities for students to practice, evaluate, and revise strategies that empower them to be in charge of their learning and the learning process.

## Technology Skills

The U.S. Department of Labor (2008–2009; http://www.bls.gov/oco/ocos066.htm) reported that the description of the changing landscape of postsecondary settings with respect to technology constitutes a call for vigilance in preparing college-bound students. According to the report in the *Occupational Outlook Handbook,* "Most college and university faculty extensively use computer technology, including the Internet; e-mail; CD-ROMs; and programs, such as statistical packages. They may use computers in the classroom as teaching aids and may post course content, class notes, class schedules, and other information on the Internet" (n.p.). On a positive note, there is widespread interest in the importance of technology competencies for high school graduates, with national educational technology standards already developed and revised by the International Society for Technology in Education (http://www.iste.org/). According to Swanson (2006), 47 states now have technology standards for students, yet only four actually test students on these standards (Arizona, New York, North Carolina, Utah).

Despite developing technology standards and emphasizing the importance of these skills for a digital age and global economy, a report by the National Council on Disability stated that "the rapid acquisition of educational technology has not sufficiently addressed the needs of students with disabilities. Access for students with disabilities is just beginning to be identified as an important factor when purchasing educational technology" (2000, p. 25). In a study comparing students with and without disabilities, the rates of computer and Internet use are both about 10 percentage points lower for those with disabilities (DeBell & Chapman, 2006). Another survey indicated that most 4-year college freshmen are computer literate (Sax, Astin, Korn, & Mahoney, 2000), with almost four out of five freshmen reporting using a personal computer frequently during the year prior to entering college. The percentage of freshmen with higher family incomes that used computers frequently, however, was larger than for freshmen with lower family incomes (Sax et al., 2000), raising concerns for students with disabilities from lower socioeconomic settings.

The widespread use of educational technologies at the postsecondary level has implications for the preparation of college-bound high school students. The requirements for transition planning under IDEA 2004 specify identifying assistive technology devices and/or services needed to assist the student in attaining transition goals. This may or may not encompass instruction in educational or learning technologies, broadly defined as "any application of technology, particularly computer and information technology, which contributes to the learning process" (Finnis, 2004, n.p.). Research on the technology competencies of students with disabilities is disturbing. A survey of college students with learning disabilities and ADHD and students without disabilities found that both groups reported high threshold levels of comfort and fluency with learning technologies (Parker & Banerjee, 2007). Notable differences in specific skills were found, however. Students with disabilities indicated a lower level of comfort with e-mail and multitasking on a computer (e.g., online literature searches including reading online) than did their peers without disabilities. Given students' need for technology skills that are taught and practiced *before* their postsecondary studies, transition planning that addresses these skills should begin as early as possible to avoid the need to learn skills simultaneously with taking college classes. See Chapter 6 for in-depth coverage of this topic.

## STUDENT SUPPORT SERVICES: LADDERS TO LEARNING OR SCAFFOLDS FOR ACCESS?

Proactively planning for transition to college should address several key factors that relate to how smoothly and effectively the process occurs. Madaus and Shaw (2004) noted that "Section 504 is outcome neutral and focuses on access" (p. 82). Identical results (e.g., successful degree completion) are *not* ensured under this law, suggesting that students who are preparing for a new environment and expectations are well advised to understand:

- Differences in services, rights, and responsibilities of students, parents, and secondary and postsecondary institutions under IDEA 2004 and Section 504

- Differences in self-advocacy and self-determination

### Services in High School and College

As discussed previously, under IDEA 2004, all students with disabilities must have available to them a FAPE that emphasizes special education and related services (e.g., counseling services, speech-language services) designed to meet their unique needs and prepare them for further education, employment, and independent living. Education must be delivered to the maximum extent possible in settings that include children without disabilities, and school districts bear the responsibility of evaluating children to determine their eligibility for services, which are delineated in an IEP. If a student with a disability is not progressing according to the provisions of his or her IEP, then the district must reconvene to determine adjustments necessary to assure an appropriate education. Modifications and accommodations (e.g., extended test time, use of recorded texts) must be available as necessary for a student to participate in the general education curriculum, including nonacademic and extracurricular activities. Districts are responsible for developing a transition plan for eligible students no later than age 16. Subpart D of Section 504 also requires school districts to provide eligible students with a FAPE, although there is no federal funding that accompanies this civil rights law (Shaw & Rhein, 2008). Key responsibilities of secondary schools for eligible students with disabilities are *individualized* support services, *free* education, annual evaluation of progress, and rights of parents.

The mandate under Subpart E of Section 504 for colleges and universities is significantly different to ensure equal access. The statute states, "No otherwise qualified individual with a disability shall, solely by reason of his or her disability, be excluded from participation in, be denied the benefits of, or be subjected to discrimination under any program or activity receiving Federal financial assistance" (29 U.S.C. § 794). Subpart E covers all aspects of student life, including admissions, recruitment, academic programs and adjustments (often referred to as *accommodations*), treatment of students, and nonacademic services (34 C.F.R. § 104.42-104.44, 104.47). Rothstein (2002) noted treatment of students can include access to housing, student health services, financial aid, athletic or cultural facilities, and campus transportation systems.

Unlike the legal requirement for services in high school, there is no mandate for colleges and universities to provide special education, *individualized* support services, or *free* education. Section 504 and the ADA assure equal access to qualified students, not entitlement. The notion of "qualified" is dynamic because a student who does not meet the academic standards of a college or university is subject to dismissal, and the courts have consistently upheld this standard (Heyward, 2004; Rothstein, 2002). Colleges are not required to identify students with disabilities. In fact, it is a student's responsibility to self-identify and provide disability documentation that verifies his or her eligibility *and* the need for reasonable accommodations. Colleges are not required to assure protections retroactively. In the case of a student who chooses not to disclose his or her disability, and then experiences failure in a course because of not receiving accommodations, there is no obligation to alter or excise a failing grade from a transcript.

Discussion regarding services a student can expect at the college level needs to take place during the transition planning process because there is no legally prescribed model for postsecondary disability services. Table 2.2 provides an overview of disability support services that may be available, illustrating the importance of identifying the kinds of supports a student expects to need when embarking on college studies. Madaus noted

> Section 504 requires that the institution designate an institutional contact person, or "a responsible employee" (104.7[a]), who ensures that qualified students with disabilities receive individually appropriate accommodations (e.g., extended test time, separate exam locations) and auxiliary aids (e.g.,

**Table 2.2.**  Continuum of postsecondary support services

| Decentralized services | Loosely coordinated services | Centrally coordinated services | Data-based services |
|---|---|---|---|
| Disability contact person may have multiple responsibilities | Disability contact person | Full-time disability coordinator<br><br>Services located in Office for Students with Disabilities or other on-campus sites (e.g., learning or academic skills center) | Full-time program director; assistant director and/or additional staff<br><br>Services located in Office for Students with Disabilities |
| Basic services as mandated under Section 504 | Generic 504 support services and accommodations | Full range of accommodations | Full range of accommodations |
| Few formal policies | Procedures in place for gaining access to services | Policies and procedures in place | Comprehensive policies and procedures |
|  | Peer tutors available for all students | Emphasis on student self-advocacy | Emphasis on student self-advocacy |
|  | Students referred to other on-campus services (e.g., counseling and/or career services, residential life) | Assistive technology may be available<br><br>Specially trained disability specialists may be available | Assistive technology available<br><br>Individualized support plan available |

From McGuire, J.M., & Shaw, S.F. (2005). *Resource guide of support services for students with learning disabilities in Connecticut colleges and universities* (p. 6). Storrs: University of Connecticut, Center on Postsecondary Education and Disability; adapted by permission.

access to assistive technology). This person is not required to have training in special education or disabilities and may have other responsibilities on the campus. Institutions may not charge additional fees to students for providing such accommodations. (2005, p. 33)

Some colleges and universities are now extending their services to incorporate content tutoring and instruction in study skills, organizational and time management skills, and special learning strategies instruction (Harding, Blaine, Whelley, & Chang, n.d.). It behooves college-bound high school students to systematically explore the type of postsecondary setting and the degree of disability support services anticipated in order to make an informed decision about choice of schools to which to apply.

Although decisions about reasonable accommodations are made on a case-by-case basis, Scott noted

More controversial accommodations include the use of a *word bank* (a list of terms including distraction terms approved by the instructor that may be used during a test) for students with specific word-retrieval deficits; a *formula sheet* (a list of relevant formulas approved by the instructor to be used during a test) for students with memory deficits or extensive number and letter reversals; an *interpreter* (someone to clarify questions not related to test content) for students with reading comprehension deficits; and *alternate test formats* (such as an oral exam rather than a written exam) for students with a particular combination of learning disability deficits that limit the effectiveness of others forms of accommodations. (2002, p. 309)

## TYLER: PREPARING FOR CHANGE

A conversation between the parent of Tyler, a college-bound student with ADHD and emotional disabilities, and his guidance counselor, who is helping Tyler gather information to support his accommodation needs in college, illustrates some of the disconnects between secondary and postsecondary settings. Tyler receives resource support from a special education teacher as well as modifications and accommodations in testing. His mother plays an active role advocating for him with his guidance counselor and classroom teachers. Box 2.1 displays the text of a telephone conversation between Tyler's mother and his guidance counselor. It is not clear how the list of accommodations she outlines has been determined, nor is it clear whether Tyler is using any accommodations and whether they are effective in assuring him an equal opportunity to demonstrate his learning. Several of her comments suggest that Tyler may be ill-prepared for making the transition to college. First, she initiates the conversation with the guidance counselor about how she perceives Tyler's needs. In a college setting, Tyler must assume responsibility for self-disclosing to the disability office. Although some parents continue to assume an active role with college disability personnel (D. Korbel, personal communication, August 25, 2008), the research is unequivocal regarding the relationship between a student's self-determination, self-advocacy, and outcomes (Levinson & Ohler, 1998; Skinner & Lindstrom, 2003). Tyler's mother indicates the accommodations Tyler must have "in order to do well in college." Accommodations from high school do not automatically transfer into a college setting. Furthermore, the context and technical requirements of a course for which accommodations are requested come into play. College faculty are not required to modify grading requirements, although many are willing to engage in a dynamic process of discussing a student's specific situation. The overall intent of antidiscriminatory protections for college students is assuring equal access, not guaranteed success. Tyler will be expected to meet the academic regulations of the college he attends with or without the provision of reasonable accommodations.

Scott accurately pointed out that caution is needed with such accommodations because of concerns about compromising an essential aspect of the test. When considering the example of Tyler, the history of accommodations he used on tests as well as their efficacy would be important as would recent documentation and collaboration about the appropriateness of an accommodation with the faculty teaching the course. Chapter 3 provides a detailed analysis of the accommodation process.

Finally, use of the proverbial "we" throughout Tyler's mom's conversation raises concerns about Tyler's ability to advocate on his own behalf once he graduates and progresses into an environment where the expectations are vastly different. His engagement in his own learning will play a major role in the successes or challenges he will experience as a college student.

**Box 2.1.** Transcript of a telephone conversation

The following is a transcript of the telephone call between Tyler's mother (Mrs. Williams) and his guidance counselor (Jeff Scott).

Mrs. W: Hi, Mr. Scott. Thanks so much for returning my call. I think Tyler told you that we've been talking with several of the colleges he is interested in to find out what we need to do to get Tyler the help he'll need in order to do well in college. I know that a PPT meeting is scheduled in the spring, but I'd like to stay on top of this. Here are some of the things that Tyler must have when he leaves Miller High for college:

- Untimed tests

- No multiple choice tests

- Modified homework

- Study guides from teachers before tests

Mr. Scott: Sure thing, Mrs. Williams. Actually, this is the first time I've heard about some of these accommodations because Tyler hasn't mentioned them. I know that he's responsible for speaking with his teachers when he needs extra time or has questions about assignments. I'll definitely check with him to talk more about how these accommodations are working for him.

Mrs. Williams: Well, I do know that Tyler felt he could have done better on the test he just had with Mr. Jamison, his U.S. history teacher. Tyler really likes Mr. Jamison, but he did say he studied a lot for the test the night before, and he thinks he would have done much better if Mr. Jamison tested him orally. That way he could have asked questions if he didn't understand what Mr. Jamison was looking for. In fact, I have a call into Mr. Jamison to talk about this.

Mr. Scott: What I'd like to do, Mrs. Williams, is to meet with Tyler and then to talk with his teachers. I'll also touch base with Mrs. Elliott, his resource teacher, to find out more about what Tyler is doing with her and what accommodations he uses. I've made a note to get back to you as soon as I've had these conversations.

Mrs. Williams: Okay, thanks, but I don't want to waste too much time on this as we really have to get things together to make a packet that we can discuss when we go for college interviews.

From McGuire, J.M. (2008). *Transition materials.* Storrs: University of Connecticut, Center on Postsecondary Education and Disability; reprinted by permission.

## CHOICES ABOUND

Although making the transition to traditional 2- and 4-year settings has been emphasized, other options exist for students who may not have a clear sense of their direction toward postsecondary educational goals. Getzel (2005) listed considerations to explore when choosing among postsecondary educational institutions: a student's career goals; level and type of support services; academic preparedness; and size, location, and accessibility. Each of these factors should be continuously examined as a student progresses from middle school and through high school.

As a result, in part of the Carl D. Perkins Vocational and Applied Technology Education Act Amendments of 1990 (PL 101-392) and 1998 (PL 105-332), there has been a shift in the concept of *vocational education* to *career-vocational* or *career technical education* (Greene & Kochhar-Bryant, 2003). Innovative collaborations exist between high schools and community colleges offering 2 + 2 programs in which high school students have the opportunity to earn college credit at the same time as earning standard high school credit. These tech prep courses and programs offer students the possibility of a 4-year career pathway consisting of the last 2 years of high school plus 2 years of a community college associate's degree program. According to the U.S. Office of Vocational and Adult Education (n.d.), roughly 47% of the nation's high schools (or 7,400 high schools) offer one or more tech prep programs. Nearly every community and technical college in the nation participates in a tech prep consortium, as do many 4-year colleges and universities. This option alters the notion that vocational education is strictly for students who do not plan to attend college and opens doors to more advanced skills through an associate's degree or a certificate in a specific career field. It is an option that should be considered based on students' strengths and preferences.

Community college settings enroll the majority of students with disabilities (Berkner & Choy, 2008) and are an excellent resource to consider in the transition planning process. They provide options including a terminal degree, certificates, and academic preparation for transfer to 4-year colleges. Typically, a high school degree or equivalent (GED certificate) comprises the sole requisite for enrollment, although admissions standards are set by each state. Matriculation (in the literature and college catalogues, these are typically referred to as articulation agreements) agreements between community colleges and 4-year colleges are designed to provide a smooth transition for students from community college graduates into 4-year colleges. Typically, "they either guarantee that the associate's degree will satisfy all freshman and sophomore general education requirements at the four-year university or specify a list of courses that will be treated as equivalent" (http://www.finaid.org/otheraid/partnerships.phtml). Working together, a student, parents, and guidance counselor should initiate a discussion about these options with the awareness that periodic and planned review of goals is important regardless of whether the high school embraces the spirit of commencing transition planning at age 14.

> In addition to initiating discussion of postsecondary education options, it is helpful to review a student's interests, strengths, and activities as sources of guidance for long-term education and career goals.

Many states are now offering online opportunities for high school students. The National Education Association (n.d.) noted that the number of students participating in online courses is large and growing dramatically and projected that by 2006, a majority of high school students will have had an online course before graduating. The association pointed out issues such as the unique social, educational, and emotional needs of high school students that must addressed. Yet, for some students with special learning needs or students for whom regular classrooms are not effective, this option may offer an alternative to the components of a traditional college preparatory high school plan.

For students who are academically motivated, some high schools have designed early college experience programs in collaboration with a regional college or university. While still in high school, students take university courses taught at their high school by instructors who are certified as adjunct professors and earn college credit. Another option is advanced placement courses offered on the campus of a regional university. These courses are typically offered based on available space and/or the signed consent of college instructors. Finally, with the vastly expanding number of college courses now offered through distance education, choices of when and where to enroll have multiplied exponentially and may present more options for some high school students.

## SUMMARY

The operative concept in considering preparation for making the transition to college is *informed and sustained* planning. Some have noted that many transition decisions need to be made by 10th grade (Hallahan & Kauffman, 2000), and options may narrow if the process begins at that stage. This chapter has noted critical areas that must be addressed to assure that college-bound students with disabilities have the requisite skills for a smooth and effective transition. These include

- Identifying the laws (i.e., IDEA 2004, Subparts D and E of Section 504, the ADAAA) that apply to secondary and postsecondary settings

- Knowing the transition-related components of IDEA 2004

- Knowing the rights and responsibilities of students, parents, and high schools under the IDEA 2004 and Section 504, Subpart D, and colleges and universities under Subpart E

- Identifying differences between high school and college including curriculum choices, instructional environments, and the importance of technology skills

- Knowing about college-level disability services and how they differ from services at the secondary level

- Understanding options in the transition planning process that relate to preparing for postsecondary education

- Recognizing the role that self-determination and self-advocacy play in transition

# REFERENCES

Americans with Disabilities Act (ADA) of 1990, PL 101-336, 42 U.S.C. §§ 12101 *et seq.*

Americans with Disabilities Act Amendments Act (ADAAA) of 2008, PL 110-325, 42 U.S.C. §§ 12101 *et seq.*

Berkner, L., & Choy, S. (2008). *Descriptive summary of 2003-2004 beginning post-secondary students: Three years later* (NCES 2008-174). Washington, DC: U.S. Department of Education, National Center for Education Statistics, Institute of Education Sciences.

Brinckerhoff, L.C., McGuire, J.M., & Shaw, S.F. (2002). *Postsecondary education and transition for students with learning disabilities.* Austin, TX: PRO-ED.

Cameto, R., Levine, P., & Wagner, M. (2004). *Transition planning for students with disabilities: A special topic report of findings from the National Longitudinal Transition Study-2.* Retrieved August 13, 2008, from http://eric.ed.gov/ERICDocs/data/ ericdocs2sql/content_storage_01 /0000019b/80/29/e5/9c.pdf

Carl D. Perkins Vocational and Applied Technology Education Act Amendments of 1990, PL 101-392, 20 U.S.C. §§ 2301 *et seq.*

Carl D. Perkins Vocational and Applied Technology Education Act Amendments of 1998, PL 105-332, 20 U.S.C. §§ 2301 *et seq.*

Carnegie Foundation. (2007). *The Carnegie classification of institutions of higher education: Basic classification tables.* Retrieved August 22, 2008, from http://www.carnegiefoundation.org/classifications/index.asp?key=805

Clark, G.M., Patton, J.R., & Moulton, R. (2000). *Informal assessments in transition planning.* Austin, TX: PRO-ED.

Cook, L., Hennessey, M.L., Cook, B.G., & Rumrill, P.D. (2007). The views of university faculty members and service providers regarding the increased enrollment of students with learning disabilities. *Learning Disabilities: A Multidisciplinary Journal, 14,* 205–215.

DeBell, M., & Chapman, C. (2006). *Computer and internet use by students in 2003* (NCES 2006–065). Washington, DC: U.S. Department of Education, National Center for Education Statistics.

Feldblum, C.R., Barry, K., & Benfer, E.A. (2008). *The ADA Amendments Act of 2008.* Retrieved November 3, 2008, from http://www.law.georgetown.edu/archiveada/ documents/ADAarticlefinalforwebsite_001.pdf

Field, S., Sarver, M., & Shaw, S. (2003). Self-determination: A key to success in postsecondary education for students with learning disabilities. *Remedial and Special Education, 24,* 339–349.

FinAid. (n.d.). *College partnerships and articulation agreements.* Retrieved August 7, 2008, from http://www.finaid.org/otheraid/partnerships.phtml

Finnis, J. (2004). *Myths and facts of learning technology.* Retrieved March 6, 2006, from http://www.techlearning.com/story/showArticle.jhtml?articleID=22101447

Fuchs, D. (2003, Spring). On responsiveness-to-intervention as a valid method of LD identification: Some things we need to know. *Perspectives, 29,* 28–31.

Getzel, E.E. (2005). Preparing for college. In E.E. Getzel & P. Wehman (Eds.), *Going to college: Expanding opportunities for people with disabilities* (pp. 69–87). Baltimore: Paul H. Brookes Publishing Co.

Goldberg, L.S. (2001). What is a parent to do? The parent's roles in college planning for children with learning disabilities. In T.A. Citro (Ed.), *Transition skills for post secondary success: Reflections for students with learning disabilities* (pp. 51–58). Weston: Learning Disabilities Association of Massachusetts.

Graner, P.S., Faggella-Luby, M.N., & Fritschmann, N.S. (2005). An overview of responsiveness to intervention: What practitioners ought to know. *Topics in Language Disorders, 25,* 93–105.

Greene, G., & Kochhar-Bryant, C.A. (2003). *Pathways to successful transition for youth with disabilities.* Upper Saddle River, NJ: Merrill Prentice Hall.

Hallahan, D.P., & Kauffman, J.M. (2000). *Introduction to special education* (8th ed.). Boston: Allyn & Bacon.

Harding, T., Blaine, D.D., Whelley, T., & Chang, C. (n.d.). *A comparison of the provision of educational supports to students with disabilities in AHEAD versus non-AHEAD affiliated institutions.* Retrieved August 26, 2008, from http://www.rrtc.hawaii.edu/products/

Heyward, S. (2004). *Disability and higher education: Guidance for Section 504 and ADA compliance.* Horsham, PA: LRP.

Hitchings, W.E., Retish, P., & Horvath, M. (2005). Academic preparation of adolescents with disabilities for postsecondary education. *Career Development for Exceptional Individuals, 28,* 26–35.

Individuals with Disabilities Education Act Amendments (IDEA) of 1997, PL 105-17, 20 U.S.C. §§ 1400 *et seq.*

Individuals with Disabilities Education Act (IDEA) of 1990, PL 101-476, 20 U.S.C. §§ 1400 *et seq.*

Individuals with Disabilities Education Improvement Act (IDEA) of 2004, PL 108-446, 20 U.S.C. §§ 1400 *et seq.*

Johnson, D.D., Thurlow, M., Cosio, A., & Bremer, C.D. (2005, February). *Diploma options for students with disabilities.* Retrieved August 7, 2008, from http://www.ncset.org/publications/viewdesc.asp?id=1928

Kochhar-Bryant, C.A., Shaw, S., & Izzo, M. (2007). *What every teacher should know about transition and IDEA 2004.* Boston: Allyn & Bacon.

Lerner, J. (2003). *Learning disabilities: Theories, diagnosis, and teaching strategies.* Boston: Houghton Mifflin.

Levinson, E.M., & Ohler, D.L. (1998). Transition from high school to college for students with learning disabilities: Needs, assessment, and services. *High School Journal, 82,* 62–69.

Madaus, J.W. (2003). What high school students with learning disabilities need to know about college foreign language requirements. *Teaching Exceptional Children, 36*(2), 62–66.

Madaus, J.W. (2005). Navigating the college transition maze: A guide for students with learning disabilities. *Teaching Exceptional Children, 37,* 32–37.

Madaus, J.W., & Shaw, S.F. (2004). Section 504: Differences in the regulations for secondary and postsecondary education. *Intervention in School and Clinic, 40,* 81–87.

Madaus, J.W., & Shaw, S.F. (2006). The impact of the IDEA 2004 on transition to college for students with learning disabilities. *Learning Disabilities Research and Practice, 21,* 273–281.

McGuire, J.M. (2008). *Transition materials.* Storrs: University of Connecticut, Center on Postsecondary Education and Disability.

McGuire, J.M., & Shaw, S.F. (2005). *Resource guide of support services for students with learning disabilities in Connecticut colleges and universities.* Storrs: University of Connecticut, Center on Postsecondary Education and Disability.

McLaughlin, M.J., & Embler, S. (2006). High-stakes accountability and students with disabilities: The good, the bad, and the impossible. In P. Wehman (Ed.), *Life beyond the classroom: Transition strategies for young people with disabilities* (4th ed., pp. 183–200). Baltimore: Paul H. Brookes Publishing Co.

National Alliance for Secondary Education and Transition. (2005). *National standards and quality indicators: Transition toolkit for systems improvement.* Retrieved January 16, 2007, from http://www.nasetalliance.org/

National Association of State Directors of Special Education. (2006). *The Individuals with Disabilities Education Act: Comparison of IDEA regulations (8/3/2006) to IDEA regulations (3/12/1999).* Alexandria, VA: Author.

National Council on Disability. (2000). *Transition and postsecondary outcomes for youth with disabilities: Closing the gap to postsecondary education and employment.* Retrieved April 20, 2008, from http://www.ncd.gov/newsroom/publications/2000/transition_11-01-00.htm

National Education Association. (n.d.). *Guide to online high school courses.* Retrieved August 25, 2008, from http://www.nea.org/technology/onlinecourseguide.html

National Joint Committee on Learning Disabilities. (2007). The documentation disconnect for students with learning disabilities: Improving access to post-secondary disability services. *Learning Disability Quarterly, 30,* 265–274.

No Child Left Behind Act of 2001, PL 107-110, 115 Stat. 1425, 20 U.S.C. §§ 6301 *et seq.*

O'Leary, E. (2006). New and improved transition services: Individuals with Disabilities Education Improvement Act of 2004. *LDA Newsbriefs, 41*(1), 1, 4–5.

Parker, D.R., & Banerjee, M. (2007). Leveling the digital playing field: Assessing the learning technology needs of college-bound students with LD and/or ADHD. *Assessment for Effective Intervention, 33*(1), 5–14.

Regulations for the Individuals with Disabilities Education Act (2006), 34 C.F.R. § 300.1 *et seq.*

Rehabilitation Act Amendments of 1992, PL 102-569, 29 U.S.C. §§ 701 *et seq.*

Rehabilitation Act of 1973, PL 93-112, 29 U.S.C. §§ 701 *et seq.*

Reilly, V.J., & Davis, T. (2005). Understanding the regulatory environment. In E.E. Getzel & P. Wehman (Eds.), *Going to college: Expanding opportunities for people with disabilities* (pp. 25–48). Baltimore: Paul H. Brookes Publishing Co.

Rothstein, L.F. (2002). Judicial intent and legal precedents. In L.C. Brinckerhoff, J.M. McGuire, & S.F. Shaw (Eds.), *Postsecondary education and transition for students with learning disabilities* (pp. 71–106). Austin, TX: PRO-ED.

Sax, L.J., Astin, A.W., Korn, W.S., & Mahoney, K.M. (2000). *The American freshman: National norms for Fall 2000.* Los Angeles: University of California, Higher Education Research Institute, Graduate School of Education and Information Studies.

Scott, S.S. (2002). The dynamic process of providing accommodations. In L.C. Brinckerhoff, J.M. McGuire, & S.F. Shaw (Eds.), *Postsecondary education and transition for students with learning disabilities* (pp. 295–332). Austin, TX: PRO-ED.

Scott, S.S., & Manglitz, E. (2000). Foreign language learning: A process for broadening access for students with learning disabilities. *Journal of Postsecondary Education and Disability, 14,* 23–37.

Shaw, S.F. (2006). Legal and policy perspectives on transition assessment and documentation. *Career Development for Exceptional Individuals, 29,* 108–113.

Shaw, S.F., & Rhein, B.A. (2008). *Section 504 referral, eligibility and accommodation form.* Storrs: University of Connecticut, Center on Postsecondary Education and Disability.

Skinner, S.G., & Lindstrom, B.D. (2003). Bridging the gap between high school and college: Strategies for the successful transition of students with disabilities. *Preventing School Failure, 47,* 132–137.

Sparks, R.L., & Javorsky, J. (2004). College students classified with ADHD and the foreign language requirement. *Journal of Learning Disabilities, 37,* 169–178.

Swanson, C.B. (2006). *Tracking U.S. trends.* Retrieved August 25, 2008, from http://www.edweek.org/ew/articles/2006/05/04/35trends.h25.html

Thoma, C.A., & Wehmeyer, M.L. (2005). Self-determination and the transition to postsecondary education. In E.E. Getzel & P. Wehman (Eds.), *Going to college: Expanding opportunities for people with disabilities* (pp. 49–68). Baltimore: Paul H. Brookes Publishing Co.

U.S. Department of Labor, Bureau of Labor Statistics. (2008–2009). *Occupational outlook handbook.* Retrieved August 26, 2008, from http://www.bls.gov/oco/ocos066.htm

U.S. Office of Vocational and Adult Education. (n.d.). *Tech prep education.* Retrieved August 22, 2008, from http://www.ed.gov/about/offices/list/ovae/pi/cte/tpreptopic2.html

Wechsler, D. (1991). *Wechsler Adult Intelligence Scale-Third Edition [WAIS-III].* San Antonio, TX: Harcourt Assessment.

Wehman, P. (2006). Transition: The bridge from youth to adulthood. In P. Wehman (Ed.), *Life beyond the classroom: Transition strategies for young people with disabilities* (4th ed., pp. 3–39). Baltimore: Paul H. Brookes Publishing Co.

Wehmeyer, M.L., Gragoudas, S., & Shogren, K. (2006). Self-determination, student involvement, and leadership development. In P. Wehman (Ed.), *Life beyond the classroom: Transition strategies for young people with disabilities* (4th ed., pp. 41–69). Baltimore: Paul H. Brookes Publishing Co.

Weidenthal, C., & Kochhar-Bryant, C. (2007). An investigation of transition practices for middle school youth. *Career Development for Exceptional Individuals, 30,* 147–157.

Will, M.C. (1984). *OSERS programming for the transition of youth with disabilities: Bridges from school to working life.* Washington, DC: U.S. Department of Education, Office of Special Education and Rehabilitative Services.

Woodcock, R.W., McGrew, K.S., & Mather, N. (2000). *Woodcock-Johnson III Tests of Achievement.* Itasca, IL: Riverside.

Yell, M.L., & Drasgow, E. (2007). Assessment for eligibility under IDEIA and the 2006 regulations. *Assessment for Effective Intervention, 32,* 202–213.

Zirkel, P.A. (2007). What does the law say? *Teaching Exceptional Children, 40*(1), 74–76.

Zirkel, P.A., & Krohn, N. (2008). RTI after IDEA: A survey of state laws. *Teaching Exceptional Children, 40,* 71–73.

# Let's Be Reasonable

## Accommodations at the College Level

*Joseph W. Madaus*

### WHAT YOU'LL LEARN IN THIS CHAPTER:

✔ How requirements for modifications differ between the Individuals with Disabilities Education Improvement Act (IDEA) of 2004 (PL 108-446) and Section 504 of the Rehabilitation Act of 1973 (PL 93-112), Subpart E

✔ How Section 504 requirements for modifications differ between Subpart D and Subpart E

✔ The impact of Section 504, Subpart E on determining reasonable accommodations

✔ The impact of court cases in determining reasonable accommodations at the postsecondary level

✔ Other key factors involved in determining reasonable accommodations at the postsecondary level

✔ The difference between instructional/course accommodations and program accommodations

✔ Practices at the secondary level to help students learn to self-advocate for reasonable accommodations

✔ Methods to help gather key documentation at the secondary level to assist students in requesting future accommodations

## MARIE

Marie is a freshman majoring in physical therapy. She goes to the learning disability support office 2 days before her second examination in organic chemistry. She tells the director that she attempted the first examination without accommodations and did not perform as well as she wanted, so she would like extended time for the second examination. She also tells the director that she received extended time on examinations throughout high school. She provides the director with a Section 504 plan that verifies that she used extended test time, but it does not provide any evidence of a disability. The director calls her high school guidance counselor, who states that Marie was tested for a learning disability but did not meet the criteria for eligibility. Instead, she was put on a Section 504 plan because she "needed a little extra time on examinations." Marie's request for extended time on examinations in college is denied. She and her family are confused and angry.

## STEVEN

Steven is junior who is entering the nutritional sciences program. His learning disability documentation shows substantial limitations in written language and spelling. He was not penalized for spelling mistakes throughout high school and at a previous college that he attended. He comes to the disability support office upset because he met with a faculty member and his new advisor in the nutritional sciences program and was told he could not receive a similar accommodation within the program.

## STEPHANIE

Stephanie is a freshman who self-disclosed her attention-deficit/ hyperactivity disorder (ADHD) to the disability services office. She requested extended test time and a separate location for her psychology 101 examinations. These requests were approved, and Stephanie was provided with a letter for her psychology professor that verified she was registered with the disability services office and that outlined her specific accommodation needs. She was told to give the letter to the professor and discuss her disability and examination needs with him. On the day of the first examination, Stephanie arrives at the disability services office to take the examination. She is told that the examination is not in the disability services office, nor were arrangements made with the professor. What went wrong?

In each case, the student presented what he or she believed to be clear evidence of need for accommodation or modification within his or her college courses. In each case, the student did not receive the accommodations expected. As you read this chapter, think about some of the reasons for the decisions that were made by the college. How do they differ from the decision-making process at the secondary level? What can secondary personnel learn from these cases to help their students as they make the transition to postsecondary education?

## CHAPTER OVERVIEW

As Chapter 2 demonstrated, there are significant legal differences between the secondary and college environments in relation to the scope of required services for students with disabilities. One of the most significant differences that students encounter during transition relates to requesting and receiving accommodations at the college level. At the secondary level, it is the role of the special education team to determine the types of accommodations and modifications needed by the student (Salend, 2008). Decisions might be made and accommodations put into place with little to no input, reflection, or effort on the part of the student. As a result, the student may become a passive recipient of services, accustomed to prearranged accommodations without having to reflect on the need for or true benefit of the accommodations.

In contrast, the student must be an active participant in the accommodation process at the college level. As this chapter highlights, a college student is responsible for self-disclosure of the disability to the proper campus contact person and at the proper time. The student is responsible for providing necessary supporting evidence of the disability and of the need for requested accommodations. The student may be responsible for determining and carrying out the logistics (e.g., time, place, transporting the examination) of the accommodations. The student must be involved in evaluating the effectiveness of any received accommodations. In summary, the student must be ready to take an active and, indeed, proactive role throughout the accommodation process. How can secondary personnel help the student prepare for these changes?

This chapter provides an overview of the accommodation decision-making process at the college level. Some foundational differences in legislation between the secondary and postsecondary levels related to accommodations are discussed. The accommodation process at the college level is examined, including the central role of the student. Throughout the chapter, suggestions are offered related to how to help students at the high school level become actively involved in the accommodation process to be ready for their role at the college level.

## IMPACT OF LEGISLATION

In order to provide a free appropriate public education (FAPE) to *all* students, including those with disabilities, secondary schools work under the auspices of IDEA 2004 and Section 504 of the Rehabilitation Act of 1973. Although these two laws have different purposes (see Chapter 2 for a detailed explanation), they serve as the means by which students with disabilities receive access to a FAPE.

At the postsecondary level, the nature of protections and services changes. The coverage of IDEA 2004 does not apply once the student graduates from secondary school or reaches the maximum age at which the local education agency (LEA) is required to provide services. Instead, qualified students with disabilities may be eligible for civil rights protection under the Americans with Disabilities Act Amendments Act (ADAAA) of 2008 (PL 110-325) and under Section 504. The nature and scope of these civil rights protections are very different than the entitlement mandates of IDEA 2004.

The fact that Section 504 applies to both secondary and postsecondary schools can create additional confusion, as some students and families may expect equivalent services in both academic settings. Different sections of the law apply to each environment, however, which can result in significant differences in relation to providing accommodations and services at each level. Understanding the fundamentals of these laws in relation to providing accommodations and modifications at both the secondary and postsecondary levels is an important starting point.

## IDEA 2004 and Accommodations

According to IDEA, each LEA is responsible for providing a FAPE that "emphasizes special education and related services" (§ 300.1 [a][1]) for eligible students with disabilities.

In order to provide these services, the local district is responsible for identifying and evaluating students with potential disabilities and for periodically reevaluating students with known disabilities. If a child is found eligible for special education, then the LEA is responsible for developing an individualized education program (IEP). The IEP must contain "a statement of the program modifications or supports that will enable the child to advance toward annual learning goals (§ 300.320 [B][4]). The IEP must also include a "statement of any individual appropriate accommodations that are necessary" to measure the student's performance on state and districtwide assessments (§ 300.320 [B][6][i]).

### Definition of Accommodation

Thurlow defined *accommodations* as "changes in materials or procedures that provide access to instruction and assessments for students with disabilities" (2002, p. 1) and enable the student to show his or her knowledge and ability, rather than the effect of the disability. The term *accommodation* is often used interchangeably with the term *modification,* and, in fact, IDEA uses the terms in a comparable manner in regard to state and district assessments (Thurlow, 2002). Using the term *modification* can result in confusion, however. As Salend pointed out, valid testing accommodations are "designed to provide students with access to tests *without altering the tests*" (2008, p. 16, emphasis added). Specific methods, procedures, and equipment may be changed to allow participation, but these modifications should not change the fundamental nature of the test's content, construct, or results (Salend, 2008). In order to be most effective, the accommodation or modification must be individualized to include consideration of the student, the curriculum, and the classroom (Hogan, 2005; Williams, 2001). Specific accommodations should not be automatically considered or provided to students with specific disabilities (Salend, 2008), nor does the fact that a student has a disability mean that the student necessarily requires accommodations (College Board, 2008).

## Accommodation Use at the Secondary Level

Accommodations and modifications are commonly used because of the increasing numbers of students with disabilities now gaining access to the general education curriculum and participating in state and districtwide assessments (Wagner, Newman, Cameto, Levine, & Marder, 2003). According to data from the National Longitudinal Transition Study-2 (NLTS-2), 87% of students with disabilities received accommodations and supports in high school (Newman, 2008). Specific accommodations included both instructional and assessment accommodations and modifications. Nearly two thirds of students with disabilities in general education classes received some modification to their program, with 52% receiving "some modifications" and 11% receiving "substantial modifications." Approximately three quarters of all students with disabilities received extended time for examinations, whereas two thirds received additional time to complete assignments. An additional one third of students received modified grading standards (Wagner et al., 2003).

## Long-Term Considerations for Students

Many accommodations and modifications are indeed appropriate and provide immediate benefit in that they allow the student to show his or her true knowledge, rather than the impact of the disability. Because of the typical lack of student involvement in the special education process at the secondary level (from determining accommodations to self-advocating for specific needs to evaluating the usefulness of accommodations), however, students may be surrounded by a well-intentioned, but ultimately problematic, "bubble of support" that results in a lack of control (Noonan Squire, 2008, p. 126). The process used for setting up accommodations and modifications for a student may impede the development of long-term goals or the skills and behaviors necessary for success in postsecondary environments for the following reasons (Agran & Hughes, 2008; Getzel & Thoma, 2008; Hadley, 2007; LaFrance Holzer, 2006; Madaus, 2006; Madaus, Gerber, & Price, 2008; Newman, 2008; Noonan Squire, 2008; Salend, 2008; Stodden & Jones, 2002):

- Students with disabilities tend to be minor players in developing their IEP and in setting goals based on their preferences and interests.

- The special education team may determine necessary accommodations without requiring the student to consider how the accommodations align with his or her specific disability.

- Accommodations may be put into place without the need for student self-advocacy or self-reflection regarding their effectiveness.

- Some accommodations may be embarrassing or isolating to students.

- Students may become dependent on the accommodations and services and expect them to continue into the college setting, where they may not be available or may be delivered in a different manner than that to which a student is accustomed.

- Students may use accommodations as a means to deal with anxiety and stress rather than learning methods to internally handle these issues.

- Students with disabilities can enter college without an understanding of their disability and how to articulate their needs in the new environment.

- Many college students and adults who received secondary special education services do not consider themselves to be people with disabilities in their adult lives and do not self-disclose or request accommodations. Self-determination skills that teach young adults to understand the nature and impact of their disability and their legal rights and responsibilities are critical. This will allow for a more informed decision related to self-disclosure. However, research points to limited instruction in this area at the secondary level (see Chapter 4 for more information about self-determination).

## Section 504, Subpart D

As noted in Chapter 2, secondary schools are mandated to provide services to students with disabilities under Section 504 of the Rehabilitation Act of 1973. Although both IDEA 2004 and Section 504 provide services and protections to students with disabilities, Section 504 is a civil rights law that is designed to prevent discrimination against individuals on the basis of a disability. Unlike IDEA 2004, Section 504 is a general education law (Zirkel & Kincaid, 1993). The importance and use of Section 504 to provide services to students with disabilities has increased since the late 1980s as a result of increased Office for Civil Rights (OCR) attention, the work of advocacy groups, and the growth of the numbers of students with hidden disabilities (Blazer, 1999; Council of Administrators of Special Education, 1999; Madaus & Shaw, 2008b; Smith, 2002). Literature related to Section 504 implementation at the secondary level indicates some important trends related to transition for students with disabilities (Madaus & Shaw, 2008b; "Misidentification," 2004; "Over-Providing," 2004). Among these findings are the following.

- There has been increased usage of Section 504 since the late 1990s to provide services to students with disabilities.

- Services are sometimes provided to students who do not have a diagnosed disability but who struggle in an academic area.

- Section 504 is sometimes used as a "consolation prize" for students who are ineligible for IDEA services.

- Section 504 is sometimes used as a means to provide services to students without the stigma of a special education label.

Although Section 504 also applies to colleges and universities, different subparts of the regulations apply. The services provided under Section 504 at the secondary level may not carry over to the postsecondary level, and students who receive services without a diagnosed disability may not be eligible for services at the postsecondary level.

## Section 504, Subpart E

Once a student with a disability exits the secondary school, the special education services offered by IDEA 2004 end. Likewise, the services offered under Section 504, Subpart D, also end. Qualified students with disabilities may be eligible for services under Section 504, Subpart E, however. As noted previously, and as explained in Chapter 2, Section 504 is a civil rights law that prohibits discrimination against qualified students with disabilities by focusing on accessibility to both physical and instructional environments. In order to provide access, the regulations require postsecondary institutions to consider academic adjustments and, if necessary, modifications. In this regard, the regulations state

> A recipient [educational institution] to which this subpart applies shall make such modifications to its academic requirements as are necessary to ensure that such requirements do not discriminate or have the effect of discriminating, on the basis of handicap, against a qualified handicapped applicant or student. Academic requirements that the recipient can demonstrate are essential to the instruction being pursued by such student or to any directly related licensing requirement will not be regarded as discriminatory within the meaning of this section. Modifications may include changes in the length of time permitted for the completion of degree requirements, substitution of specific courses required for the completion of degree requirements, and adaptation of the manner in which specific courses are conducted. (§ 104.44 [a])

These Section 504 regulations also provide specific consideration of adjustments for accommodations and evaluation. The regulations note

> In its course examinations or other procedures for evaluating students' academic achievement, a recipient [educational institution] to which this subpart applies shall provide such methods for evaluating the achievement of students who have a handicap that impairs sensory, manual, or speaking skills as will best ensure that the results of the evaluation represent the student's achievement in the course, rather than reflecting the student's impaired sensory, manual, or speaking skills (except where such skills are the factors that the test purports to measure). (§ 104.44 [C])

## Definition and Types of Accommodations

The modifications outlined in the language of Section 504 all relate to ensuring that a student with a disability has "an equal opportunity to participate in, and benefit from, the programs or activities of the college or university" (HEATH Resource Center, 2006, p. 55). These modifications are typically referred to as *academic adjustments*. OCR noted that "academic adjustments may include auxiliary aids and modifications to academic requirements as are necessary to ensure equal educational opportunity" (U.S. Department of Education, 2007a). In other words, the terms *accommodation, academic adjustments, modifications,* and *auxiliary aids* refer to making alterations to instruction, assessment, program requirements, or physical space to allow equal access for students with disabilities. Or, as Souma, Rickerson, and Burgstahler noted, accommodations can be defined as "the removal of a barrier to participation and learning" (2002, p. 4).

Souma et al. stated that the emphasis of accommodations is on providing equal access to the "content and activities of a course" (2002, p. 4) rather than an outcome. Likewise, the HEATH Resource Center advised "academic adjustments ensure access, not necessarily success" (2006, p. 55).

## Considerations in Determining Accommodations

Although the regulations of Section 504 and the ADA and the publications of OCR seem clear in regard to the responsibilities of postsecondary institutions to provide specific academic adjustments for students with disabilities, colleges have the ability to make individualized decisions related to student accommodation requests. This decision making requires a careful balance between student needs and institutional standards.

The regulations, which provide a list of possible academic adjustments, include accommodations such as course substitutions, alternate examination formats, and extended time. Colleges do not need to provide modifications that fundamentally alter requirements of a program, however (Brinckerhoff, McGuire, & Shaw, 2002; HEATH Resource Center, 2006). OCR clearly advised students in making the transition:

> Your postsecondary school is not required to lower or effect substantial modifications to essential requirements. For example, although your school may be required to provide extended testing time, it is not required to change the substantive content of the test. In addition, your postsecondary school does not have to make modifications that would fundamentally alter the nature of a service, program or activity or would result in undue financial or administrative burdens. (U.S. Department of Education, 2007a)

These considerations will be discussed throughout the rest of this chapter.

## What Accommodations Are Available and Which Are Used?

Data from multiple studies indicate that testing accommodations are the most commonly provided and received accommodations in college (Harding, Blaine, Whelley, & Chang, 2001; Lewis & Farris, 1999). Data from the NLTS-2 likewise indicated that students with disabilities most commonly reported receiving examination accommodations, including extended test time (65%) or some other type of examination accommodations (12%; Newman, 2008). Twenty-five percent of the students reported receiving note-taking assistance, whereas 14% received accommodations related to "technology/books on tape/braille."

## What Does This Mean for Students in Transition?

Although both IDEA 2004 and Section 504, Subpart D refer to the responsibility of a local district to provide a FAPE for students with disabilities, neither the regulations of Section 504, Subpart E nor the ADA require this of postsecondary institutions. Much of the responsibility that had been carried by the local district and the IEP team shifts to the student. To preview a discussion that will follow in this chapter, college students with disabilities

- Must be "otherwise qualified" for admission to an institution, regardless of the disability
- Must be "otherwise qualified" for admission into a program or major within the institution, regardless of the disability
- May receive reasonable accommodations and auxiliary aids, provided that they do not fundamentally alter the technical requirements of a course or major or the skills required for professional licensing

These requirements are in keeping with the intent of Section 504 and the ADA, namely to ensure access to qualified students with disabilities (see Chapter 2 for more specific information related to the concept of "otherwise qualified"). As the next section discusses, however, accommodation decisions in college must strike a balance between the rights, needs, and responsibilities of the student and the rights and responsibilities of the college.

## ACCOMMODATIONS AT THE COLLEGE LEVEL: A BRAVE NEW WORLD

Although colleges and universities are required to consider and, if appropriate, provide reasonable accommodations for students with disabilities, the role and responsibilities of the student become more pronounced in college. These include learning about and following the process set forth by the college for self-disclosure, submitting necessary documentation, and requesting and receiving accommodations. As the following section discusses, the student is also responsible for the timely request of accommodations and for monitoring the effectiveness of received accommodations. Each step is addressed in this section.

### Self-Disclosure

Whereas local school districts were responsible for identifying students with potential disabilities, colleges and universities are under no similar obligation. At the college level, it is the responsibility, and choice, of the student to seek out necessary support services and to self-disclose to the appropriate person or office on campus. Although many colleges have a dedicated office for disability services, some do not. Colleges must only determine a contact person to whom students with disabilities can self-disclose and submit the required documentation to provide evidence of the disability and receive accommodations. The contact person may be part of a different campus office (e.g., academic advisor, counseling services). This information should be available on the college web site or in the print catalog. But if in doubt, students should consult with the admissions office or the dean of students office. Students must be aware that finding this information is their responsibility; not knowing who the contact person is does not constitute a reasonable excuse for not requesting accommodations in a timely fashion.

Colleges are not required to have disability specialists but must designate a person to be the disability contact person for the campus. If a disability office or support service cannot be found on a college's web site or in the print catalog, then check with the dean of students office, the admissions department, or the affirmative action office.

As noted, self-disclosure is an individualized choice—students are not required to do so. Indeed, according to the NLTS-2, only 36% of students with disabilities who received special education services in high school disclosed disabilities to a postsecondary institution (Newman, 2008). The majority of students (56%) did not disclose because they do not consider themselves to have a disability, whereas 8% consider themselves to have a disability, but chose not to self-disclose. Without disclosure, however, students may not be eligible to receive reasonable accommodations.

## Documentation

The documentation requirement of colleges and universities is one of the most confusing parts of the transition process. At the high school level, the special education team was responsible for conducting, compiling, and maintaining evaluation data related to a student's disability. Colleges are under no similar obligation, and, in fact, OCR, which enforces compliance with Section 504 and the ADA, clearly noted that colleges are not responsible to conduct or pay for an evaluation to document a disability and need for academic adjustments.

In an extremely useful publication for students making the transition to college titled *Students with Disabilities Preparing for Postsecondary Education: Know Your Rights and Responsibilities,* OCR advised students that colleges "will probably require you to provide documentation that shows you have a current disability and need an academic adjustment" (U.S. Department of Education, 2007a). OCR also clearly noted that it is the responsibility of the student or family to assume the costs of any necessary evaluations (U.S. Department of Education, 2007b).

## Documentation Requirements May Vary

Colleges may require students to submit documentation to verify the nature of the disability and the need for accommodations. There is no standard set of documentation requirements, however. Although some professional organizations have promulgated guidelines (e.g., the Association on Higher Education And Disability [AHEAD], Educational Testing Services [ETS], the College Board), adherence by colleges is not required. Data from a national examination of components of learning disability documentation guidelines at postsecondary institutions demonstrated the variation in requirements. Madaus and Banerjee (2008) surveyed postsecondary disability service providers from a range of institutional types regarding the components of documentation required and the relative importance placed on these components. The results indeed indicated disparities. For example, it was reported that five different standards of documentation requirements were being followed by respondents (e.g., AHEAD Guidelines, AHEAD Best Practices, ETS Guidelines). Forty-three percent of the respondents reported that documentation could be no more than 3 years old, whereas 24% would accept documentation that was up to 5 years old. An additional 33% would consider the age of a student's documentation on a case-by-case basis and thus had no set recency requirement. There was also great variation in relation to whether the college requires a discrepancy in identifying a learning disability. Forty-nine percent of the respondents indicated that their school requires a severe discrepancy between aptitude and achievement, whereas 51% do not. There was additional variation related to the size of the discrepancy in the schools that require such evidence. Understandably, these differences can create significant confusion for students and professionals working in transition.

One additional finding that directly affects transition planning was that disability service providers place great emphasis on formal measures of ability and achievement when making eligibility decisions related to students with learning disabilities. This may be contrary to the trend in the K–12 arena to focus more on informal, formative data, but it is an important trend for secondary personnel to bear in mind when selecting individually appropriate transition assessments.

In addition, the IDEA 2004 regulations note that secondary schools are not responsible for providing documentation to determine a student's eligibility for services after high school, nor are they responsible for conducting evaluations on students who are exiting special education due to graduation. When combined with the move toward informal, curriculum-based data, schools may be inclined to not conduct reevaluations with standardized data. IDEA 2004, however, also requires the IEP team to develop "appropriate measurable postsecondary goals based upon age-appropriate transition assessments related to training, education, employment, and, where appropriate, independent living skills" (§ 300.320 [b][1]) for students age 16 and older. For students who have college as a goal, best practices in transition planning would suggest that the IEP team carefully consider the requirements that the student will need to satisfy to receive accommodations and be successful in those environments. The IEP team and the student should research documentation requirements and these should be incorporated into the transition assessment process. To enhance the possibility of a successful transition, this may involve using standardized measures that are administered later in the student's high school career (Madaus & Shaw, 2006, 2007).

## What Does This Mean for Students Making the Transition?

Understanding the documentation requirements of colleges can be a daunting process. Box 3.1 contains suggestions to involve students in this process. Following are some key points to remember ("Admissions for

---

**Box 3.1.** Involving students in the documentation process

The documentation requirements of colleges can be confusing to seasoned professionals, let alone to students and families. There are steps, however, that students can take to participate in the process and, in so doing, perhaps increase their own understanding of their disability.

Most colleges post their documentation requirements to their disability service web site or make the requirements available in print format. As part of the transition process, students could

- Research the documentation requirements of their institution of choice (or of several colleges as part of a practice exercise). In some cases, this will be as simple as typing *disability documentation* into the college's web site search function. In other cases, more research may be needed. High school teachers could help the student navigate the web site to find the appropriate information. If the information is not available on the Internet, then high school teachers and students could research the contact information for disability services, student affairs, or admissions and move to the next step.

- Print the documentation guidelines or contact the disability services office and request a hard copy be mailed.

- Review the documentation requirements with a high school special education teacher, transition coordinator, or case manager. The professional could help the student understand (if even in broad terms) what each component of the documentation is asking for.

- Work with that person to ensure that all required components are available in the student's file.

- Work with the case manager to understand what the documentation says about the student and how it describes the nature of the student's strengths and needs.

- Contact the college disability service provider with any questions as this process continues. The case manager or transition teacher could help the student prepare a list of questions to cover during the telephone call or e-mail exchange.

- Make copies of required documentation, including one copy for the college and one copy to keep for personal records.

---

Students with Disabilities," 2008; Brinckerhoff et al., 2002; Madaus, Bigaj, Chafouleas, & Simonsen, 2006; Madaus & Shaw, 2006; U.S. Department of Education, 2007b).

- An IEP or a high school Section 504 plan may be useful in recording and documenting services received in high school, but it may be insufficient for determining eligibility for services in college.

- Although college disability service providers may look at informal data or observations from high schools, they tend to require formal assessment data in making eligibility decisions.

- The nature of a student's disability can change over time. Even if a student has a clear record of receiving special education services for several years, this may not be sufficient to support an accommodation request in the new college environment.

- The existence of a disability does not equate to eligibility or need for accommodations.

- It is up to the student to provide evidence of a current and substantial limitation to a major life function. It is in the student's best interest to have a comprehensive evaluation conducted as late as possible in the student's high school career.

- Updated evaluations that align with college documentation requirements could occur as part of the individually appropriate transition assessment requirement of IDEA 2004.

## REVIEW 1: MARIE

Marie submitted a Section 504 plan and a copy of a psychoeducational evaluation. None of the documents provided evidence of a documented learning disability. The telephone call to her case manager revealed that the school determined Marie did not have a learning disability, but that she would benefit from extended test time. Therefore, one of the primary reasons that Marie's request was denied was that she did not present evidence of a current disability that substantially limited her learning.

## Timing Is Everything

The timing of a student's self-disclosure and accommodation request is also an important consideration. Although some colleges request this information at the time of admission (see Chapter 2), such disclosure cannot be used against the student in the admission decision (U.S. Department of Education, 2007a). It is also important to note that disclosure in the admissions process may not suffice as documentation to substantiate accommodation requests after enrollment. Students who self-disclose during admission should verify their status with the disability services office.

Give careful consideration to whether you wish to send documentation to the admissions department. Unless this is specified by the disability services office or is part of the admissions process, the documentation should be sent directly to the disability services office. This will help to ensure that the materials are kept confidential and are viewed by people with knowledge about the content.

Students may self-disclose at the start of their college career or at any point thereafter. Without disclosure, however, colleges need not provide accommodations. If a student chooses to not self-disclose and performs poorly in a class, then the student's grade may remain as part of the academic record because accommodations or services cannot be provided retroactively (Madaus, 2005).

Students must also make timely requests for accommodations within a semester. Many colleges require accommodation requests be made at the outset of the semester in order to allow time to review the request and if the request is approved, time to determine the logistics of implementing the accommodation. Requests made shortly before an examination or other course event may not be honored. OCR offered the following valuable advice to students.

> Although you may request an academic adjustment from your postsecondary school at any time, you should request it as early as possible. Some academic adjustments may take more time to provide than others. You should follow your school's procedures to ensure that your school has enough time to review your request and provide an appropriate academic adjustment. (U.S. Department of Education, 2007a)

As OCR noted, some accommodations take more time to be put into place. For example, whereas a request for extended test time might be processed and put into place within a few days, requests for a notetaker or electronic books might take several weeks.

## REVIEW 2: MARIE

As Review 1 described, Marie's request for extended time was denied because she did not submit evidence of a current disability. A second issue, however, with Marie's request related to her timing. She requested the accommodation 2 days before the examination. This did not allow enough time for her information to be gathered and reviewed or for her professor to be notified.

## How Does the Student Actually Request Accommodations?

The process for requesting specific accommodations can vary from college to college. Although colleges are increasingly using web-based systems for requesting accommodations, many will still require the student to make (and keep) an appointment with the appropriate person or office on campus. This is likely to be true especially for initial requests. Because needs can change (as can course schedules) over time, students may be required to request accommodations each semester, even if they are requesting the same one(s).

It is also important to understand that the process for requesting some types of accommodations may differ. For example, requests for testing accommodations or housing accommodations may go through the disability services office at the outset of the semester. Requests for program accommodations (discussed later in this chapter) may require the student to follow a slightly different procedure and to submit different materials.

Regardless of the specific accommodation requested, multiple court cases and OCR investigations have consistently noted that the student is responsible for following established procedures for requesting accommodations and for providing documentary evidence to support the request (Charmatz, 2006; "Legal Roundup," 2008).

## Accommodations Are Not One Size Fits All

Each college is allowed to consider a variety of factors in determining accommodations. A foundational consideration is if the student has provided compelling evidence of a current and substantial limitation to a major life function, such as learning. This is often determined through evaluating the student's documentation. Although the importance of documentation was discussed previously, it is imperative to note that certain documentation might be considered sufficient for some, but not all, accommodation requests. For example, submitted documentation might provide evidence of a disability and support for a request for extended test time. The same evidence, however, might not be sufficient for a more complex accommodation, such as changing a test format or a course substitution. In such cases, the student might be required to provide additional necessary documentation above and beyond that which was already submitted. Because students with similar disabilities might not benefit from identical services (U.S. Department of Education, 1998), decisions must be made student by student.

Requirements of a specific course are a second consideration for accommodations. Remember that the language of Section 504 states that colleges must provide academic adjustments in "its course examinations or other procedures for evaluating students' academic achievement" (§104.44 [c]). The regulations also state

> Academic requirements that the recipient can demonstrate are essential to the instruction being pursued by such student or to any directly related licensing requirement will not be regarded as discriminatory. (§104.44 [a])

Therefore, if a student is enrolled in a particular course that requires evidence of mastery of a skill or concept that can be considered essential to that course, then he or she may not be eligible for particular accommodations. For example, a student with a clear impairment in written language might not be penalized for spelling mistakes (or might be provided with access to an adaptive technology) on a history or political science essay examination. The same student, however, might not receive that accommodation in a course in which spelling is determined to be essential, such as pharmacy or nutritional sciences courses.

The requirements and teaching methods used in a particular course will also help determine if a particular accommodation is necessary. For example, a student might need extended time on course examinations but enroll in a course in which examinations are not timed or grading occurs through alternate means, such as a mastery model. A student may need note-taking assistance for some courses, but not for courses in which the notes are posted online or provided in class. Or, a student might need a reader for examinations that feature heavy literacy demands, but not for courses in mathematics or sciences that have lighter reading demands. For these reasons, it can be useful for a student to attend the first class and to learn about the course requirements prior to finalizing accommodation requests.

> Students might want to attend the first class before requesting specific accommodations. The student can then receive the course syllabi and learn about the requirements of the course. This will allow for a more informed decision about accommodation needs. Students (especially freshmen), however, should self-disclose and submit necessary documentation before this time.

A third consideration for accommodations relates to technical requirements for a student's major, program of study, or intended career. Although a college must consider requested accommodations, if a particular skill, course, or plan of study is considered essential for entry into a particular career or for professional licensing, then accommodations or modifications need not be provided. This was one of the findings in the case of *Guckenberger v. Boston University* (1997). The court wrote that "a university can refuse to modify academic degree requirements—even course requirements that students with learning disabilities cannot satisfy—as long it undertakes a diligent assessment of the available options." The court continued, noting that

> Although BU ultimately has the right to decline to modify its degree requirements—and that decision will be given great deference—it must do so after reasoned deliberations as to whether modifications would change the essential academic standards of its liberal arts curriculum. (National Association of College and University Attorneys, 1997)

## REVIEW 3: STEVEN

Despite the clear evidence of a learning disability that affects Steven's spelling, it was determined that correct spelling would be an essential component of the nutritional science program, particularly his clinic placement. In that setting, Steven would be responsible for writing case notes that outlined the dietary considerations of hospital patients. It was determined that spelling would not be considered essential for his coursework and that adaptive technology could assist him during his field placements.

As Chapter 2 noted, an international business major may be required to complete courses in foreign language, regardless of the impact of a disability or a past history of receiving a course waiver while in high school.

In addition to these factors, students and families should be aware that colleges do not need to grant all requested accommodations (Hawke, 2004), nor provide the "best" or "optimal" accommodations. Colleges must consider the recommendations provided in a student's documentation and the specific requests of the student, but they are allowed to provide different accommodations if they are reasonable and effective (Hawke, 2004). In this regard, OCR clearly noted

> Colleges are not required to provide the most sophisticated auxiliary aids available; however, the aids provided must effectively meet the needs of a student with a disability. An institution has flexibility in choosing the specific aid or service it provides to the student, as long as the aid or service selected is effective. These aids should be selected after consultation with the student who will use them. (U.S. Department of Education, 1998)

## What Does This Mean for Students Making the Transition?

It is essential that students understand the following:

- Requesting accommodations must be done on a case-by-case and course-by-course fashion.

- An accommodation needed for one (or even multiple) course might not be needed or reasonable in all courses.

- An accommodation approved for one course or at one time in a program of study might not be approved for another course or at another time in a program of study.

- An accommodation might be appropriate for a student in one major but not for a student in another.

- Documentation that was sufficient for determining eligibility for some accommodations might not be sufficient for other accommodation requests.

Although students may rely on accommodations to help deal with test anxiety (Hadley, 2007), test anxiety is not considered to be a disability under Section 504 and the ADA (Hawke, 2004). In the case of *McGuiness v. University of New Mexico School of Medicine* (1998), both a district court and appeals court found that a disorder that was limited to particular subjects did not constitute a disability. Although some colleges may provide accommodations or services in such cases, students may need to develop individualized compensatory approaches and not rely on testing accommodations.

- Although college guides that describe disability services list available accommodations, these should be considered only as potential accommodations.

- Colleges can make reasoned deliberations about what constitutes an essential requirement or technical standard. Students with disabilities may be required to fulfill these requirements or standards.

## Where the Rubber Meets the Road

Just as the specific process for requesting accommodations can vary from college to college, so too can the specific process for putting accommodation requests into place. Students must carefully research, understand, and follow the specific process at a particular college. Without following the process, the student may not receive the accommodation requested.

For example, at some colleges, the student is provided with a letter from the disability services office that outlines particular accommodations for each professor. It is the student's responsibility to provide the letter to the professor and, often, to self-advocate in relation to the accommodation. This may involve explaining the nature of the disability to the professor, as well as explaining the need for accommodation. Although many professors will have experience receiving such letters and working with students with disabilities, some may not. The student may need to explain more about the accommodation needed and the process in such cases.

> The HEATH Resource Center (2006, p. 52) outlined several important skills that students need to communicate with faculty regarding accommodation requests: 1) expressing thoughts and feelings honestly and directly, 2) making eye contact that is firm but not glaring, 3) speaking appropriately in an audible voice, 4) using a speech pattern that is clear, 5) using "I" language and not "you" language, 6) making appointments to further discuss issues and concerns, 7) knowing about their disability and how it is likely to affect their educational experience, and 8) being aware of nonverbal presentation using body cues and postures.

In some cases, the student and the professor will work out the specific logistics of the accommodation (e.g., time, place). In other cases, the student may be referred back to the disability services office to determine the logistics. Again, the student must be an active participant in the process. He or she must ensure that he or she knows what process will be followed, where the examination will be held, and what materials (if any) can be brought into the examination. Not knowing these components of the accommodation process may result in the student not receiving a requested (or even an approved) accommodation.

Students must also understand that providing accommodations can take some logistical work, particularly in large courses. Professors should be provided with sufficient lead-time to work out the specifics of the accommodation (e.g., Where will the test be held? How will it be transported and returned? How will it be secured?). As a courtesy, students might check in with the professor one or two classes before the examination to ensure that accommodations are in place.

---

### REVIEW 4: STEPHANIE

Stephanie was provided with a letter from the disability services office. The university procedure was that she should give this to her professor and discuss the arrangement for accommodations with him. Stephanie told the disability services office that she did not give the letter to the professor because she felt awkward doing so, and could never find the "right time." Then a few classes passed and she forgot. She assumed that the examination would be given at the disability services office because she took high school examinations in the resource room. Because she never self-disclosed to the professor, however, he did not know that she needed an accommodation. Because he teaches a large section of the course, he makes arrangements for a separate room, proctored by a graduate assistant. Stephanie was directed back to the regular classroom and was able to take the examination with a late start. She worked out the details for accommodations on subsequent examinations with her professor.

---

## Monitoring the Effectiveness of Accommodations

Based on the previous factors, disability service providers must make decisions about the general appropriateness of an accommodation. The regulations of both Section 504 and the ADA refer to the fact that the college must provide effective accommodations and auxiliary aids and that colleges may not provide a student with an accommodation or service that is less effective than an accommodation or service provided to others. Decisions regarding what accommodation(s) would be most appropriate should be made in consultation with the student. The college is also entitled to "analyze the appropriateness of an aid or service in its specific context" (U.S. Department of Educaiton, 1998) and to make a decision accordingly.

The student plays an important role in this process. If the student receives an accommodation that was not useful or not needed, or if there were specific components of the accommodation that were not helpful, then it is up to the student to report this to the disability service provider. Together (and sometimes with input from the faculty member), alternatives can be worked out. But this cannot happen without input from the student. If students find an accommodation is not working, OCR advised the following:

> Let the school know as soon as you become aware that the results are not what you expected. It may be too late to correct the problem if you wait until the course or activity is completed. You and your school should work together to resolve the problem. (U.S. Department of Education, 2007a)

# BEYOND THE CLASSROOM: OTHER CONSIDERATIONS

In most cases, accommodations or academic adjustments are related to specific course examinations or evaluation procedures. In some cases, however, adjustments to specific program requirements may be necessary. Although decisions related to course accommodations might be made in conjunction with a course professor, decisions related to these program requests are often made in conjunction with campus academic administrators. Like course accommodations, these decisions are made on a case-by-case basis and will require the student to follow particular procedures.

## Reduced Course Load

Taking a reduced course load is a common program accommodation for students with disabilities. For some students, this is an appropriate and reasonable accommodation. For others, taking fewer courses can mean too much free time, and less structure, in their day. Other implications to consider are the impact of carrying less than a full-time credit load on athletic eligibility, financial aid, health insurance, student housing, and eligibility for dean's list status. In addition, a reduced course load will result in a longer degree completion period.

## Course Substitutions

Course substitution is another significant program accommodation. Section 504 specifically addresses this topic, noting that colleges must consider "substitution of specific courses required for the completion of degree requirements" (§ 104.44 [a]). As with instructional accommodations, however, several factors must be considered. First, if the course (e.g., foreign language, math) is considered to be an essential component of a program of study, then a college may require that students complete the requirement, regardless of the impact of the disability. Section 504 also states, "academic requirements that the recipient can demonstrate are essential to the instruction being pursued by such student or to any directly related licensing requirement will not be regarded as discriminatory within the meaning of this section" (§ 104.44 [a]).

Making this factor more confusing is that at some colleges, varying majors require varying amounts of specific coursework. For example, a liberal arts major may be required to take four semesters of foreign language, whereas an engineering student might only be required to take two semesters (Madaus, 2003).

Furthermore, some colleges may require additional documentary evidence related to the impact of the disability on learning a language or in fulfilling math requirements. This may go beyond what is contained in documentation provided to determine eligibility for services and may involve letters from past teachers and tutors and evidence of past attempts to learn the material.

Researching essential requirements of potential majors and, if necessary, the course substitution process, as part of the college search process is an important step. Knowing that a college or a major within a college will require and will not substitute coursework in areas that were waived in high school should be a critical part of the decision-making process. Madaus (2003) presented more information and suggestions related to course substitutions.

## Personal Attendants

Although personal attendants, individualized services, or devices might be part of a high school student's IEP, Section 504 and the ADA both specifically note that colleges are not required to provide such services. Section 504 regulations state, "recipients need not provide attendants, individually prescribed devices, readers for personal use or study, or other devices or services of a personal nature" (§ 104.44 [d][2]). This may appear confusing because some services, such as a reader, might be provided as a reasonable accommodation for examinations. OCR noted, however, that "readers may be provided for classroom use but institutions are not required to provide readers for personal use or for help during individual study time" (U.S. Department of Education, 1998). Other personal services noted by OCR (U.S. Department of Education, 2007b) include providing eyeglasses or personal tutoring (unless this is provided to other students).

## What Does This Mean for Students Making the Transition?

- Students should research not only the admissions requirements for a college, but also the degree requirements. Getting into college is important, but getting out with a degree is the main objective.

- If a particular content area (e.g., math, foreign language) is a graduation requirement and is of concern, then students should contact the disability services office and find out if the college has a course substitution process.

- If the requirement is essential for a particular major, then the student should be prepared to attempt the requirement or select a different major or, in some cases, a different college.

- Students and high school teachers should gather sufficient supporting documentation that outlines the difficulty in a particular content area and any specific supports, tutoring, or decisions made regarding high school waivers or lower-level courses.

## LONG-TERM PERSPECTIVE ON ACCOMMODATIONS

Although accommodations and modifications are sometimes very appropriate and necessary to enable a student to show his or her true knowledge rather than the impact of the disability, it is important for high school IEP teams to take a long-term perspective when making decisions related to accommodations. The NLTS-2 reported that only 36% of students self-disclosed a disability to their college, and roughly one quarter received accommodations. In the NLTS-2 sample, 56% of the cohort did not self-disclose because they did not consider themselves to be people with disabilities.

**Box 3.2.**   Teaching students about accommodations

In order to help students self-advocate for accommodations at the college level, allow them to begin the process in high school. Consider the following steps.

- Work with the student to go through the requirements of each course, including instructional demands (e.g., notetaking, course readings) and assessment requirements (e.g., examinations, papers).

- Brainstorm areas in which the student does well and areas that present challenges.

- Determine if there are strategies that can be used to tap into student strengths and to overcome student weaknesses. Can these strategies be developed and replace the need for accommodations (even over time)?

- Discuss what accommodations or modifications were used in the past. Ask the student to reflect on the effectiveness of these accommodations.
  In what specific situations were they helpful?
  In what way(s) were they helpful?
  In what situations were they burdensome?
  In what way(s) were they burdensome?
  In what situations did they not make a difference or were not used?

- Brainstorm possible accommodations for a course with the student. At first you may need to explain specifically what the accommodation would entail and how it might help to compensate for the disability. As the student becomes able to do so, shift this role to him or her and ask him or her to explain this to you.

- If an accommodation is going to be requested, allow the student to request the accommodation from his or her teachers. To do this, help the student practice how and when to request the accommodation(s). Provide and practice with a script.

- Select one or two teachers who might be understanding, and begin with those teachers. Ask the student to reflect on how the request went. What should be repeated, and what should be done differently?

- Involve the student in setting up the accommodations. This may involve developing a routing sheet with logistical details (e.g., time, place, accommodation) that must be discussed and signed by all teachers and the student.

- After the accommodation was provided, ask the student to reflect on its effectiveness. Loop back to discussions about the student's disability, and how the accommodation helped (or did not make a difference).

*(continued)*

(continued)

Like many strategies, this approach will take effort. The student must be actively involved in the decision-making and evaluation process. Over time, he or she may internalize this thought process and become more self-determined. As the research on adults with disabilities shows, this is a critical lifetime skill.

A study of 500 graduates with learning disabilities from three universities nationwide (all of whom self-disclosed at the college level) found that 73% of the respondents believed their learning disabilities affected their work performance to some extent (Madaus, 2008). Only 55% self-disclosed to their employer, however, and of those, only 12% actually requested accommodations. The primary reason for nondisclosure was that there was no reason or need to, but fear of stigmatization, job loss, or damaging relationships was also reported. Instead of receiving accommodations, the graduates used a range of strategies that reflected a degree of self-determination. These included setting goals and priorities (60%), time management (50%), arriving early to work (48%), and staying late at work (47%).

The research clearly demonstrates that accommodation use becomes less common as young adults move through college and into the workplace. In order to help students adjust to this decreased reliance on accommodations, students should be taught strategies and skills to compensate for their disability. This involves careful reflection on accommodation need and use. Developing skills and self-understanding may be a more important long-term gain than reliance on accommodations (Madaus et al., 2008).

## Helping Students Get Ready

As this chapter has stressed, college students with disabilities must be ready to immediately be active participants in the accommodation process. They must be aware of the college procedures for self-disclosure, requesting accommodation, and putting accommodations into place. High school is a great stage on which to learn and rehearse these skills. Students should be early and active participants in the accommodation decision-making process. This involves understanding the "what" (What specific accommodations are needed? What specific accommodations are useful? What do I need to do to request and arrange these accommodations?), "why" (Why do I need these accommodations?), and "how" (How does this accommodation relate to my disability?) of accommodations. Box 3.2 contains some specific suggestions that can be implemented with students early in their high school career. Box 3.3 contains a list of helpful resources that can be shared with students and their families as they begin the college exploration process.

**Box 3.3.** Useful resources

- The National Collaborative on Workforce and Disability for Youth created an extremely useful workbook for students with disabilities titled *The 411 on Disability Disclosure*. The workbook contains sections on self-determination, rights and responsibilities, and accommodations. It also contains scripts to help students during the disclosure process in college, employment, and social situations. The workbook can be downloaded from http://www.ncwd-youth.info/411-on-disability-disclosure.

- The Wisconsin Department of Public Instruction offers *Opening Doors to Postsecondary Education and Training*. Included are topics related to the differences between high school and college, planning tips for college, considerations for the IEP process, and preparation at the high school level for college. The guide is available at http://dpi.wi.gov/sped/pdf/tranopndrs.pdf.

- The *Guidance and Career Counselors' Toolkit: Advising High School Students with Disabilities on Postsecondary Options* is available from the HEATH Resource Center. The toolkit provides sections on counseling students during the transition process, services and strategies, college and career options, and procedural concerns. The toolkit can be downloaded at http://www.heath.gwu.edu/images/stories/Toolkit.pdf.

- The Office for Civil Rights has a guide for students called *Students with Disabilities Preparing for Postsecondary Education: Know Your Rights and Responsibilities*. It is available at http://www.ed.gov/about/offices/list/ocr/transition.html.

- Madaus (2003) presented information related to foreign language course substitutions for students with LD. The article provides specific suggestions for students to prepare for a possible substitution request. The article can be downloaded from the Council for Exceptional Children's Division for Learning Disabilities web site at http://www.dldcec.org/pdf/foreign_language.pdf.

## SUMMARY

Colleges are required to provide students with disabilities with reasonable academic adjustments in order to ensure access to instruction and programs. Because colleges operate under different legal mandates than high schools in regard to providing services to students with disabilities, the nature, type, and process for requesting and receiving accommodations can vary significantly. Making students and their families aware of these differences early in high school is an important part of effective transition planning, as is allowing students to be active participants in the accommodation decision-making process. As the research on adult outcomes shows, this active involvement and development of self-advocacy and self-determination can have significant long-term effects.

## REFERENCES

Admissions for students with disabilities. (2008). *Disability Compliance for Higher Education, 13*(12), 16.

Agran, M., & Hughes, C. (2008). Asking student input: Students' opinions regarding their individualized education program involvement. *Career Development for Exceptional Individuals, 31*(2), 69–76.

Americans with Disabilities Act Amendments Act (ADAAA) of 2008, PL 110-325.

Blazer, B. (1999). Developing 504 classroom accommodation plans: A collaborative, systematic parent-student-teacher approach. *Teaching Exceptional Children, 32,* 28–33.

Brinckerhoff, L.C., McGuire, J.M., & Shaw, S.F. (Eds.). (2002). *Postsecondary education and transition for students with learning disabilities* (2nd ed.). Austin, TX: PRO-ED.

Charmatz, M.P. (2006). *Students must follow procedures to receive accommodations.* Retrieved August 8, 2008, from http://www.dche.com

College Board. (2008). *Eligibility and review.* Retrieved August 28, 2008, from http://professionals.collegeboard.com/testing/ssd/application/eligibility-review

Council of Administrators of Special Education. (1999). *Section 504 and the ADA: Promoting student access* (2nd ed.). Fort Valley, GA: Author.

Getzel, E.E., & Thoma, C.A. (2008). Experiences of college students with disabilities and the importance of self-determination in higher education settings. *Career Development for Exceptional Individuals, 31*(2), 77–84.

Guckenberger v. Boston University, 974 F. Supp. 106 (D. Mass. 1997).

Hadley, W.M. (2007). The necessity of academic accommodations for first-year college students with learning disabilities. *Journal of College Admission.* Retrieved September 12, 2008, from http://findarticles.com/p/ articles/mi_qa3955/is_200704/ai_n19198046

Harding, T., Blaine, D.D., Whelley, T., & Chang, C. (2001). *A comparison of the provision for educational supports to students with disabilities in AHEAD versus non-AHEAD affiliated institutions.* Honolulu: University of Hawaii.

Hawke, C.S. (2004). Accommodating students with disabilities. *New Directions For Community Colleges, 125,* 17–27.

HEATH Resource Center. (2006). *Guidance and career counselors' toolkit: Advising high school students with disabilities on postsecondary options.* Washington, DC: George Washington University.

Hogan, T. (2005). Modifications for students with learning disabilities in inclusive settings. *Kappa Delta Pi Record, 41*(3) 118–123.

Individuals with Disabilities Education Improvement Act (IDEA) of 2004, PL 108-446, 20 U.S.C. §§ 1400 *et seq.*

LaFrance Holzer, M. (2006). *The test-taking strategy intervention for college students with learning disabilities.* Unpublished doctoral dissertation, University of Connecticut, Storrs.

Legal roundup. (2008). *Disability Compliance for Higher Education, 13*(12), 12.

Lewis, L., & Farris, E. (1999). *Students with disabilities in postsecondary education: A profile of preparation, participation, and outcomes.* Washington, DC: National Center for Education Statistics.

Madaus, J.W. (2003). What high school students with learning disabilities need to know about college foreign language requirements. *Teaching Exceptional Children, 36*(2), 62–67.

Madaus, J.W. (2005). Helping students with learning disabilities navigate the college transition maze. *Teaching Exceptional Children, 37*, 32–37.

Madaus, J.W. (2006). Employment outcomes of university graduates with learning disabilities. *Learning Disabilities Quarterly, 29*, 19–31.

Madaus, J.W. (2008). Employment self-disclosure rates and rationales of university graduates with learning disabilities. *Journal of Learning Disabilities, 41*, 291–299.

Madaus, J.W., & Banerjee, M. (2008). *An examination of service provider perceptions of learning disability documentation components.* Storrs, CT: Center on Postsecondary Education and Disability.

Madaus, J.W., Bigaj, S., Chafouleas, S., & Simonsen, B. (2006). What key information can be included in a comprehensive summary of performance? *Career Development for Exceptional Individuals, 29*(2), 90–99.

Madaus, J.W., Gerber, P.J., & Price, L.A. (2008). Adults with learning disabilities in the workforce: Lessons for secondary transition programs. *Learning Disabilities Research and Practice, 23*(3), 148–153.

Madaus, J.W., & Shaw, S.F. (2006). The impact of the IDEA 2004 on transition to college for students with learning disabilities. *Learning Disabilities Research and Practice, 21*(4), 273–281.

Madaus, J.W., & Shaw, S.F. (2007). Transition assessment: Introduction to the special issue. *Assessment for Effective Intervention, 32*, 130–132.

Madaus, J.W., & Shaw, S.F. (2008a). Preparing school personnel to implement Section 504. *Intervention in School and Clinic, 43*(4), 226–230.

Madaus, J.W., & Shaw, S.F. (2008b). The role of school professionals in implementing Section 504 for students with disabilities. *Educational Policy, 22*(3), 363–378.

McGuiness v. University of New Mexico School of Medicine, 170, F.3d 974 (10th Cir. 1998).

Misidentification under 504 and IDEA can be avoided. (2004, October). *Section 504 compliance handbook,* 5–7.

National Association of College and University Attorneys. (1997). *Guckenberger v. Boston U.* Retrieved July 21, 2009, from http://www.nacua.org/documents/ Guckenberger_v _BostonU.txt

Newman, L. (2008). *National picture of the postsecondary experiences of students who had received special education services in high school. Findings from the National Longitudinal Transition Study-2.* Presentation at the AHEAD Annual Conference, Reno, NV.

Noonan Squire, P. (2008). A young adult's personal reflection and review of research on self-determination. *Career Development for Exceptional Individuals, 31*(2), 126–128.

"Over-providing" under Section 504 may create personal liability. (2004, December). *Special Education Law Update, 1*, 10–12.

Rehabilitation Act of 1973, PL 93-112, 29 U.S.C. §§ 701 et seq.

Salend, S.J. (2008). Determining appropriate testing accommodations: Complying with NCLB and IDEA. *Teaching Exceptional Children, 40*, 14–23.

Smith, T.E.C. (2002). Section 504: What teachers need to know. *Intervention in School and Clinic, 37*, 259–266.

Souma, A., Rickerson, N., & Burgstahler, S. (2002). *Academic accommodations for students with psychiatric disabilities.* Seattle: University of Washington.

Stodden, R.A., & Jones, M.A. (2002). *Supporting youth with disabilities to access and succeed in postsecondary education: Implications for educators in secondary school.* Retrieved September 12, 2008, from http://www.ncset.org/publications/ viewdesc.asp?id=706

Thurlow, M. (2002). *Accommodations for students with disabilities in high school.* Minneapolis, MN: National Center on Secondary Education and Transition.

U.S. Department of Education. (1998). *Auxiliary aids and services for postsecondary students with disabilities.* Washington, DC: U.S. Government Printing Office.

U.S. Department of Education. (2007a). *Students with disabilities preparing for postsecondary education: Know your rights and responsibilities*. Washington, DC: U.S. Government Printing Office.

U.S. Department of Education. (2007b). *Transition of students with disabilities to postsecondary education: A guide for high school educators*. Washington, DC: U.S. Government Printing Office.

Wagner, M., Newman, L., Cameto, R., Levine, P., & Marder, C. (2003). *Going to school: Instructional contexts, programs, and participation of secondary school students with disabilities*. Menlo Park: CA: SRI International.

Williams, J. (2001). *Adaptations and accommodations for students with disabilities: Resources you can use*. Washington, DC: National Information Center for Children and Youth with Disabilities.

Zirkel, P., & Kincaid, J. (1993). *Section 504, the ADA, and the schools*. Horsham, PA: LRP.

# 4

# Teaching Students with Disabilities Self-Determination Skills to Equalize Access and Increase Opportunities for Postsecondary Educational Success

*James E. Martin, Juan Portley, and John W. Graham*

## WHAT YOU'LL LEARN IN THIS CHAPTER:

✔ Why self-determination is important from a historical and practical perspective

✔ How to provide opportunities for students to develop and practice self-determination skills

✔ What self-determination tools are available to meet the needs of your students and how to use these tools in your transition education program

✔ How to facilitate student-directed individualized education program (IEP) transition planning meetings and how this approach benefits students

✔ What questions students need to answer to develop a comprehensive plan to attain their goals

Postsecondary educational programs must provide students with disabilities opportunities to gain access to programs and support services (Scott, 2002). To utilize available opportunities, students with disabilities need to request access to programs and then use supports to attain their educational goals. Students with disabilities need to learn and use self-determination skills to gain access to programs and supports to achieve at a level equal to their peers without disabilities (Anctil, Ishikawa, & Scott, 2008; Shaw & Dukes, 2006). This chapter examines strategies that educators may use to teach their students self-determination skills as a means to increase the likelihood of postsecondary educational success.

First, self-determination and its importance for educational success is explained. Second, the chapter describes self-determination assessment tools educators may use to identify students' self-determination skills and those they need to learn. Third, how student leadership of the high school IEP process provides important opportunities to teach self-determination skills is addressed. Fourth, opportunities to help students develop goal attainment skills is discussed. Fifth, infusing self-determination methodology into the classroom, family, and workplace is described as another means to increase students' self-determination skills. The chapter closes with a series of questions that students need to answer in order to take self-determined action.

## SELF-DETERMINATION BACKGROUND

### Definitions

Field, Martin, Miller, Ward, and Wehmeyer (1998) defined *self-determination* as a set of skills, knowledge, and beliefs that facilitate an individual's engagement in goal-directed, self-regulated behavior. Self-determined individuals take control of their lives and assume the roles of successful adults (Mithaug, Mithaug, Agran, Martin, & Wehmeyer, 2003). Martin and Marshall (1995) believed that self-determined students establish goals based on an awareness of their needs and interests. Next, they develop plans, implement their plans, evaluate progress, and make needed adjustments to attain their goals. Wehmeyer (1994) considered goal attainment skills as the most important self-determination component. Goal attainment is a two-step process in which one first selects goals that match interests and skills and then uses those plans to guide action to achieve the identified goals (Martin et al., 2003). School instructional activities should be viewed as learning opportunities that educators use to increase the likelihood of self-determined actions (Mithaug, 1996). Self-determination becomes "evident" when students persistently act to attain educational goals (Mithaug, 2005, p. 163).

### Importance of Adjustment

Mithaug, Martin, and Agran (1987) suggested that a major obstacle to successful transition occurs when students fail to adapt to dynamic working, community, and educational environments. Research suggests that when students use strategies to regulate their choices and actions to obtain what they want, they will maximize their adjustment to the learning environment (Wehmeyer et al., 2007). When students are more self-determined they become more likely to adjust their behaviors to attain desired goals (Mithaug et al., 2003).

The self-determined learning theory (Mithaug et al., 2003) proposes that learning is equated with adjustment. That is, students learn when their attempts to attain goals are ineffective and they must make adjustments. Students learn by adjusting their strategies, support system, and other aspects of their plans. The likelihood of attaining desired goals increases when students align their choices, actions, evaluations, and adjustments with their self-identified needs and interests (Martin et al., 2003).

## Link Between Self-Determination and Academic and Vocational Success

A growing body of research indicates a strong connection between student self-determination skills, academic performance, and post–high school outcomes (Konrad, Fowler, Walker, Test, & Wood, 2007; Martin et al., 2003). A 20-year longitudinal study of individuals with learning disabilities found that self-determination attributes predicted post–high school success (Goldberg, Higgins, Raskind, & Herman, 2003; Raskind, Goldberg, Higgins, & Herman, 1999). For example, Goldberg et al. (2003) determined that students who identified post–high school goals during early adolescence had better post–high school outcomes. Liebert, Lutsky, and Gottlieb (1990) reported that college students with physical or learning disabilities and with higher self-determination scores obtained better grades than students with lower self-determination levels. Parker (2004) found self-determination skills resulted in improved academic outcomes for college students with attention-deficit/hyperactivity disorder (ADHD).

Wehmeyer and Schwartz (1998) measured the self-determination of students with learning disabilities and intellectual disabilities prior to exiting high school. After completing school, students with superior levels of self-determination had higher employment rates. Wehmeyer and Palmer (2003) replicated the aforementioned study and found the same result. Martin, Mithaug, Oliphint, Husch, and Frazier (2002) compared the employment outcomes of workers with disabilities who completed a systematic self-determination assessment and job placement process with those who did not complete the assessment. Those who completed the self-determination assessment kept their jobs significantly longer than those who did not.

## Equalizing Success for Groups Who Have Had Historically Marginalized School Outcomes

Students with disabilities from minority ethnic, racial, and cultural backgrounds should learn self-determination skills to increase the likelihood of post–high school success (Leake & Boone, 2007; Trainor, Lindstrom, Simon-Burroughs, Martin, & McCray-Sorrells, 2008; Zhang & Benz, 2006). Goff, Martin, and Thomas (2007) found that setting post–high school transition education and employment goals enabled African American students at risk for school failure to overcome peer pressure to not succeed in school. In a Division on Career Development and Transition (DCDT) position paper on improving post–high school outcomes for diverse youth, Trainor et al. (2008) suggested that educators increase student opportunities to develop self-determination skills as a means to improve the chances of post–high school success.

- Self-determined students choose goals that match their interests and skills.

- Self-detemined students develop a plan to attain their goals, evaluate their performance, and make needed adjustments.

- Students with disabilities who learn self-determination skills improve their likelihood of academic and post–high school success.

- Assessing self-determination behaviors provides an opportunity for students, educators, and family members to identify student strengths, needs, and opportunities to learn and practice self-determination skills.

The next section provides an overview of self-determination assessment tools and describes how the tools can be used to support transition education.

## ASSESSING SELF-DETERMINATION

Assessing students' self-determination skills and opportunities for students to learn these skills precedes instruction (Martin & Sale, in press). Self-determination assessment provides a baseline level of students' skills and details that they need to learn. It is critical that educators examine available self-determination assessment tools to find one that meets the needs of their students. For example, readers may download the AIR Self-Determination Scale (Wolman, Campeau, DuBois, Mithaug, & Stolarski, 1994), The Arc Self-Determination Scale (Wehmeyer & Kelchner, 1995), and the Self-Determination Assessment Battery (Hoffman, Field, & Sawilowsky, 2004) free of charge from the University of Oklahoma's Zarrow Center web site (http://education.ou.edu /zarrow). Secondary personnel are encouraged to download and examine each one while reading the following assessment descriptions.

### AIR Self-Determination Scale

The authors of the AIR Self-Determination Scale (Wolman et al., 1994) believe that self-determined individuals set goals, make plans, and follow through with action to attain identified goals. The degree of self-determination depends on students' knowledge and skills, as well as the opportunity to learn and practice those skills at school and home. The AIR Scale includes educator, parent, and student versions. The educator and parent versions require teachers and family members to use their knowledge of the student to complete the tool. A graphic profile displays performance on each section in a bar chart format and depicts an overall score.

### The Arc Self-Determination Scale

Wehmeyer described *self-determination* as "acting as the primary causal agent in one's life and making choices and decision regarding one's quality of life free from undue external influence" (1992, p. 302). Students should complete The Arc assessment independently if they have the necessary reading skills. In the "autonomy" section, a Likert-type scale is employed as a means of answering specific questions. The "self-regulation" section asks students to write the middle of a story when given the beginning and end. The "psychological empowerment" subscale provides two-item forced choice questions, and the "self-realization" section provides forced choice (i.e., agree-disagree) items. Educators use tables in the manual to convert raw scores into percentile ranks and then complete the student's profile.

## Self-Determination Assessment Battery

This battery uses Field and Hoffman's (1994) self-determination conceptualization that includes the following sections: 1) know yourself, 2) value yourself, 3) plan, 4) act, and 5) experience outcomes and learn. Parents, educators, and students all provide evaluation input into measuring the student's degree of self-determination. This battery includes a 38-item observational checklist, a knowledge scale, student scale, teacher perception scale, and parent perception scale. Educators use the manual to score each assessment.

## Using Self-Determination Assessment Results

Students and their IEP teams may use the results of self-determination assessments in developing transition plans that facilitate entry into and success in postsecondary education. First, the results of self-determination assessment should be placed in the present level of academic and functional performance sections of the IEP to aid in identifying self-determination strengths and limits. Second, the identified self-determination limits provide a pool of potential behaviors that can be converted into annual transition goals to assist students in attaining post–high school education, employment, and independent living goals. Third, using self-determination assessment annually allows students and the IEP team to see self-determination skill growth across time. Fourth, using the AIR Self-Determination Scale or another self-determination assessment tool annually will enable students and their IEP teams to see growth at school and home in the opportunities students have to learn and practice self-determination skills. Postsecondary educational staff should be encouraged to examine student self-determination profiles to determine possible support needs.

---

- Several free self-determination assessments are available that provide educators the means to identify self-determination strengths and needs.

- Secondary special educators need to use self-determination assessments as part of their annual transition assessment process to identify annual transition goals to enable students to attain their post–high school goals.

- Educators need to teach students to become actively involved in their IEP transition planning process as a means to increase students' self-determination skills.

## STUDENT LEADERSHIP OF THE IEP MEETING PROCESS

The Individuals with Disabilities Education Improvement Act (IDEA) of 2004 (PL 108-446) requires that students attend their IEP transition planning meetings (Johnson, 2005). The IEP meeting and subsequent goal attainment process provides students and families excellent opportunities to identify and practice the self-determination skills necessary for success in secondary and postsecondary educational settings (Rusch, Hughes, Agran, Martin, & Johnson, 2009). Increased student participation in the educational planning process enables students to increase their self-determination skills (Martin, Van Dycke, Christensen, et al., 2006) and enables IEP team members to become more involved in setting goals, making decisions, and solving problems (Wehmeyer, Palmer, Agran, Mithaug, & Martin, 2000). Unfortunately, students seldom become involved in educational planning discussions when they attend educator-directed IEP meetings. The next section outlines some of the common reasons and presents strategies to increase student involvement.

### Lack of Student Involvement

The mandate for students to attend their transition IEP meeting implies that students become involved in IEP meeting discussions. But without systematic IEP meeting instruction, students do not understand the purpose of the meeting, do not understand their role, do not understand discussions, and feel that adult IEP team members do not listen to them when they talk (Lehmann, Bassett, & Sands, 1999; Lovitt, Cushing, & Stump, 1994; Morningstar, Turnbull, & Turnbull, 1995; Powers, Turner, Matuszewski, Wilson, & Loesch, 1999).

Over three consecutive years, Martin, Marshall, and Sale (2004) examined the perceptions of secondary IEP team members who participated in educator-directed IEP meetings. In most cases, students did not know the reasons for the meeting, did not know what to do, did not understand what was said, and talked significantly less compared with all other participants. General education teachers and students felt less comfortable sharing thoughts and understood the process significantly less than other IEP team members. Special education teachers talked the most, and special educators and parents talked more about student interests than did the students.

To verify these findings, Martin, Van Dycke, Christensen, et al. (2006) observed secondary teacher-directed IEP transition meetings. The results indicated that special education teachers talked 51% of the time, family members 15%, general educators and administrators 9%, support staff 6%, and students 3%. The authors concluded, "It seems naïve to presume that students attending their transition IEP meetings will learn how to actively participate and lead this process through serendipity—yet this is precisely what current practice tends to expect." Students with disabilities can learn the skills to become actively involved in their IEP meetings, however, if they are taught what to do and given opportunities to become involved (Test et al., 2004).

### Teaching Students to Become Leaders of IEP Meetings

Students need to be taught what to do at their IEP meetings and how to attain their IEP goals. Martin, Marshall, Maxson, and Jerman (1999) developed the

**Table 4.1.**   Self-Directed Individualized Education Program (IEP) steps

 1.  Student begins meeting by stating the purpose.
 2.  Student introduces everyone.
 3.  Student reviews past goals and performance.
 4.  Student asks for others' feedback on performance.
 5.  Student states school and transition goals.
 6.  Student asks questions if confused.
 7.  Student deals with differences in opinion.
 8.  Student states support needs.
 9.  Student summarizes goals.
10.  Student closes meeting by thanking everyone.
11.  Student works on attaining IEP goals all year.

Reprinted with permission from Sopris West Educational Services. *The Self-Directed IEP,* by James E. Martin, Laura Huber Marshall, Laurie Maxson, Patty Jerman © 1999.

Self-Directed IEP to teach students how to participate in and lead their own IEP meetings (see Table 4.1). Students learn to set goals, develop a plan, self-evaluate past performance, and use self-advocacy skills—*all of which increase students' level of self-determination.* Several research studies examined the effectiveness of the Self-Directed IEP and the results of these studies have established the Self-Directed IEP as an effective instructional practice (Horner et al., 2005; Odom et al., 2005).

Snyder and Shapiro (1997) found that the Self-Directed IEP substantially increased the IEP participation of students with behavior problems. Sweeny (1997) compared students who received instruction with the Self-Directed IEP with those who had teacher-directed IEP meetings. She found that students in the Self-Directed IEP group attended significantly more IEP meetings, had significantly higher levels of involvement in their IEP meetings, and knew significantly more goals following the meeting. Snyder (2000) found that students with learning disabilities showed a substantial increase in talking and making meaningful contributions at their IEP meetings when they used the Self-Directed IEP steps at their IEP meetings, and students and teachers found it to be a useful instructional tool. Snyder (2002) used the Self-Directed IEP to teach students with intellectual disability and behavior problems to actively participate in their IEP meetings. These studies demonstrated that the Self-Directed IEP teaches students with different disabilities the skills to actively participate in the IEP planning process.

The Self-Directed IEP has been used to teach secondary-age students with intellectual disability, and these students have learned to lead their meetings; state the meeting purpose; introduce everyone; review past goals and performance; express transition interests, skills, and goals; and close the meeting (Allen, Smith, Test, Flowers, & Wood, 2001). Martin, Van Dycke, Christensen, et al. (2006) compared the results of students randomly assigned to teacher-directed IEP meetings with Self-Directed IEP instructional groups. They found that students in the Self-Directed IEP instructional group started and led significantly more IEP meetings, talked a significantly increased percent of the time during the meetings, engaged in significantly more IEP meeting leadership steps, reported significantly higher positive perceptions of their IEP meetings, and received significantly increased Self-Determination scores. Van Dycke (2005) found that the written IEP documents of students who received Self-Directed IEP instruction contained more comprehensive vision statements and more employment and independent living outcome statements than students who had teacher-directed IEP meetings.

## Teaching Educators to Provide IEP Leadership Opportunities

Student IEP meeting leadership depends on opportunities to become an active IEP team member and understand one's role during the meeting. The self-directed IEP instructional program can teach students needed skills; however, the opportunity to participate must be available. Students who had visual impairments received instruction with the Self-Directed IEP lesson materials in which an audio and visual PowerPoint presentation was included that explained the role of each team member (Wu, Martin, & Isbell, 2009). When the training was provided, students talked more, special educators talked less, and students engaged in more IEP leadership steps. Educators may download the IEP team instruction PowerPoint file at the University of Oklahoma's Zarrow Center web site (http://education.ou.edu/zarrow/). Click on the self-determination educational materials section to find the team leadership PowerPoint file.

- Educators can use the Self-Directed IEP instructional program to teach students the skills to become active participants at their IEP meetings and then use the IEP team instruction PowerPoint at each IEP meeting to teach the team what each member needs to do to increase the opportunities for student participation.

- As students become advocates during IEP meetings, their self-determination levels increase.

- Research suggests that students with increased self-determination skills will be better prepared for postsecondary education.

- At student-directed IEP meetings, students participate in the determination of annual academic and transition goals.

- Identifying goals based on an understanding of students' interests, skills, and limits represents the first and easiest step of the goal attainment process.

## GOAL ATTAINMENT

High school students' goal attainment skills may predict the enrollment of students with disabilities in postsecondary educational programs (Halpern, Yovanoff, Doren, & Benz, 1995). Johnson, Sharpe, and Stodden (2001) believed that students with disabilities need to learn goal attainment and other self-determination skills while in high school to increase their likelihood of postsecondary educational success. The U.S. Department of Education's Office of Special Education Programs' (2001) *Expert Strategy Panel Report* on students with disabilities' access to and participation in the general education curriculum indicated that capacity-building materials are needed to teach students goal attainment and other self-determination skills. Research suggests, however, that most youth with disabilities lack goal attainment skills (Mithaug et al., 2003). Fuchs et al. (1997) found that having a goal does not increase the academic performance of students with disabilities. To improve performance, students must systematically be taught goal attainment skills (Fuchs et al., 1997). Unfortunately, most teachers do not teach goal attainment skills due to a lack of time, materials, understanding of how to teach the concept, and simple means to infuse goal attainment into the curriculum (Wehmeyer et al., 2000).

Self-determination definitions used by special educators consider the process of attaining self-chosen goals as the most important self-determination component. Ward (1988) considered self-determination as the attitude and ability that leads individuals to define goals and to take the initiative in achieving those goals. Martin, Marshall, and Maxson (1993) believed that self-determined individuals know what they want and how to get it. From an awareness of personal needs, self-determined individuals set goals and then doggedly pursue those goals. This involves asserting their presence, making their needs known, evaluating progress toward meeting their goals, adjusting their performance as needed, and creating unique approaches to solve problems. Field and Hoffman (1994) said that self-determination is a person's ability to define and achieve goals from a base of knowing and valuing oneself.

A goal serves three important functions (Bandura, 1986). First, it defines the immediate performance an individual hopes to produce. Second, it highlights which aspects of the performance to observe or monitor during self-regulation. Finally, the proximal goal and associated standards serve as the criteria for self-evaluation of the performance. This evaluative aspect of self-regulation is a critical source of continuing motivation for goal-directed activity due to its relationship to self-reaction and self-perceptions of competence.

## Students Need to Learn to Attain Their Own Academic and Transition Goals

After students with disabilities participate in student-directed IEP meetings, they need to work on attaining their annual academic and transition goals. The Take Action instructional program (Marshall et al., 1999) teaches students a simple and effective means to achieve academic and transition goals.

## Take Action Instructional Program

Take Action consists of seven lessons that educators use to systematically teach students goal attainment skills. First, students learn how to break long-term goals into short-term goals. Second, students learn to develop a plan to attain an identified goal. They are taught that a good plan contains six parts:

**Table 4.2.**   Take Action questions for each plan part

1.  Standard: What will I be satisfied with?
2.  Motivation: Why do I want to do this?
3.  Strategy: How will I do this?
4.  Schedule: When will I do this?
5.  Support: What help will I need?
6.  Feedback: How will I get feedback on what I did?

standard, motivation, strategy, schedule, support, and feedback. To complete each part, students answer a question as detailed in Table 4.2. Third, students learn to identify the support needed to attain a goal and how to obtain feedback on their performance. Fourth, students learn to write a plan to attain a goal. Students learn to critique plans and predict if plans will work. Fifth, students learn to develop a plan to attain a goal. Sixth, students learn to evaluate plans and actions, then they learn how to make adjustments in the plan if the goal was not attained. Seventh, students use the Take Action process to attain their goals. The Take Action manual includes a set of modified lessons for students who would benefit from a less complex goal attainment plan. Instead of using seven lessons to teach the Take Action process, the modified version has three lessons. Students complete the process in one day compared with a week for the more complex Take Action process.

## Impact of Take Action Lessons

Two research studies have examined the effectiveness of the Take Action lessons. German, Martin, Marshall, and Sale (2000) used Take Action to teach high school students with cognitive disabilities goal attainment skills. Prior to using the plan, students attained few of their daily goals. After learning the Take Action process, they achieved 80%–100% of their goals and the results were maintained for several weeks. Martin, Marshall, and El-Kazimi (2009) used Take Action with students in middle school. Instruction using Take Action produced statistically significant increases in goal attainment skills and self-determination skills for all participating students. The mean percentages for students with IEPs showed higher growth than those in general education or those who had been identified as gifted and talented.

## Summary and Implications

Goal attainment represents the most important self-determination skill, and students with disabilities need to learn this skill to increase their likelihood of high school and postsecondary education success. Educators may use the Take Action instructional program in resource settings or general education classes to teach this critical skill set. It is critical that the Take Action process be applied and practiced time and again in order for students to attain postsecondary education academic and personal goals.

- Students need to use the Take Action process weekly.

- Students need to use the Take Action process to attain all of their IEP goals.

## SANDY ESTABLISHES A PLAN
## USING THE TAKE ACTION QUESTIONS

Sandy, a high school junior, sets a long-term goal of leading her IEP meeting for her senior year. Her short-term goal involves knowing her strengths, preferences, and interests and increasing her self-determination skills. To develop a plan, she answers six planning questions regarding what she would be satisfied with, why she wants to accomplish the goal, the strategy she hopes to use, the schedule she sets to achieve the goal, the support she might need, and how to obtain feedback on her progress.

*Standard:* What will I be satisfied with?
Knowing enough about myself that I can actively participate in my next IEP meeting and discuss my transition plans.

*Motivation:* Why do I want to do this?
I want to obtain more information about myself so that I can make better decisions and participate in transition planning discussions.

*Strategy:* What methods should I use?
I will complete a vocational interest inventory, an adaptive behavior assessment, and a self-determination assessment. I will use the results to determine my IEP and transition goals and develop further action steps to achieve those goals. My teacher will teach me skills to participate in my IEP meetings.

*Schedule:* When will I do this?
I will begin by asking my teachers to help me search for viable assessments and begin completing them during the next month so I can share the results at my upcoming IEP meeting. I will start meeting weekly with my teacher so she can teach me IEP leadership skills.

*Support:* What help do I need?
I will need to request help from my teachers and parents to find and complete the right assessments. My teacher and parents will need to also complete the adaptive behavior and self-determination assessment so I can learn more about myself. I also need my teacher to show me how to become more involved in my next IEP meeting.

*Feedback:* How will I get information on my performance?
I will see the results of the assessment. My teacher and I will both complete a checklist depicting how well I did on participating in my IEP meeting.

## DOUG ESTABLISHES A PLAN
## USING THE TAKE ACTION QUESTIONS

Doug, a high school junior, sets a long-term goal of participating in an upcoming extracurricular activity for his junior year. His short-term goal involves exploring the variety of extracurricular activities offered by his school to decide his interests in the choices. The planning steps in Doug's decision include satisfying his desire to participate in extracurricular activities, motivating him to accomplish the goal, choosing the strategy he hopes to use, setting the schedule to achieve the goal, deciding on the support he might need, and gaining feedback on his progress.

*Standard:* What will I be satisfied with?
I want to know the extracurricular activities available in my high school that I can become involved in.

*Motivation:* Why do I want to do this?
I want to become more involved in school activities that interest me so that I can make more friends and feel a part of the high school.

*Strategy:* What methods should I use?
I will visit the theater class, football practice, and cross country practice during the first week of school. I will then talk with my homeroom teacher to decide the activities I enjoyed the most in order to develop further action steps to achieve my goal.

*Schedule:* When will I do this?
Tomorrow I will find out when the theater class meets, and I will ask the coach when I can visit him about the football and cross country teams and then participate in a couple of practices.

*Support:* What help do I need?
I need help from my parents to pick me up from school once practice ends. I will also have to find out what equipment is needed for the team sports and how I can get the proper equipment. I will ask my mom to help develop questions I can ask the theater students, teachers, and coaches to help me decide what I really want to do.

*Feedback:* How will I get information on my performance?
I will evaluate my performance by asking the theater teacher and the coaches how I did during my visits.

## QUESTIONS TO GUIDE SELF-DETERMINED ACTION
## AND INFUSE SELF-DETERMINATION INTO THE CLASSROOM

The self-determined learning model of instruction (Mithaug, Wehmeyer, Agran, Martin, & Palmer, 1998) organizes self-determination skills in a sequence of questions that enable students to self-direct their learning. In this model, students answer 12 questions to take self-determined action (Wehmeyer et al., 2000). First, students must choose a goal to accomplish. Goals must have one major criterion—they must be achievable for the student. The goal must have meaning for the student, should come from the student, and a pathway to that goal must be planned by the student with the assistance of the IEP teacher, the family, and all other stakeholders that participate in the student's instructional environment.

Questions 1–4 assist students in developing a goal; questions 5–8 enable students to build a plan; questions 9–12 help students reflect about what has been learned. The questions from the self-determined model of instruction are similar to the Take Action process, but differ in scope and purpose. The questions are as follows.

1. What do I want to learn?
2. What do I know about it now?
3. What must change for me to learn what I do not know?
4. What can I do to make this happen?
5. What can I do to learn what I do not know?
6. What could keep me from taking action?
7. What can I do to remove these barriers?
8. When will I take action?
9. What actions have I taken?
10. What barriers have been removed?
11. What has changed about what I do not know?
12. Do I know what I want to know?

The preceding case studies about Sandy and Doug demonstrate how self-determination instruction can be infused into everyday instructional settings. Infusing self-determination instruction into special education and general education classrooms by using the Take Action process provides a means for students to begin to self-direct their own learning. Questions from the Take Action plan and from the self-determination model of instruction provide ready-to-use prompts for students to take self-determined action.

## SUMMARY

Students who are self-determined set goals based on an understanding of their interests, skills, and limits. They will then develop a plan to attain their goals, evaluate their progress, and make adjustments to their plan. Students who do this have a greater likelihood for high school and postsecondary education success.

Numerous opportunities exist in secondary schools to teach students self-determination skills and to enable them to begin to direct their own educational activities. Good self-determination instruction begins with assessment. The assessment process enables educators to understand the scope of self-determination skills and it will identify which skills students currently possess and which they need to learn. The IEP and transition planning process provides an excellent opportunity for students to learn to become more self-determined. For students to take advantage of this opportunity, educators need to teach them the skills that will allow them to actively participate and lead their IEP meetings.

Goal attainment represents the most important self-determination skill. After students express their goals at the IEP meeting, it logically follows that students then need to learn to attain their IEP academic and transition goals. It is essential to provide opportunities for students to develop weekly plans to attain their goals and to evaluate and adjust their plans at the end of each week.

Infusing self-determination instruction and concepts into secondary schools provides opportunities for all students, with and without disabilities, to better develop self-determination skills. The research clearly demonstrates the positive impact that self-determination skills have on academic and post–high school outcomes. Secondary teachers are encouraged to assess students' level of self-determination, teach them to actively participate and lead their IEP and transition planning meetings, teach them goal attainment skills, provide them with opportunities to attain their IEP academic and transition goals, and infuse self-determination concepts into core and exploratory classes.

## REFERENCES

Allen, S.K., Smith, A.C., Test, D.W., Flowers, C., & Wood, W.M. (2001). The effects of Self-Directed IEP on student participation in IEP meetings. *Career Development for Exceptional Individuals, 24,* 107–120.

Anctil, T.M., Ishikawa, M.E., & Scott, A.T. (2008). Academic identity development through self-determination: Successful college students with learning disabilities. *Career Development for Exceptional Individuals, 31,* 164–174.

Bandura, A. (1986). *Social foundations of thought and action: A social cognitive theory.* Upper Saddle River, NJ: Prentice Hall.

Field, S., & Hoffman, A. (1994). Development of a model for self-determination. *Career Development for Exceptional Individuals, 17*(2), 159–169.

Field, S., Martin, J.E., Miller, R., Ward, M.J., & Wehmeyer, M.L. (1998). Self-determination for persons with disabilities: A position statement of the Division on Career Development and Transition. *Career Development for Exceptional Individuals, 21,* 113–128.

Fuchs, L., Fuchs, D., Karns, K., Hamlett, C., Katzaroff, M., & Dutka, S. (1997). Effects of task-focused goals on low-achieving students with and without learning disabilities. *American Educational Research Journal, 34,* 513–543.

German, S.L., Martin, J.E., Marshall, L., & Sale, R.P. (2000). Promoting self-determination: Using Take Action to teach goal attainment. *Career Development for Exceptional Individuals, 23,* 27–38.

Goff, C., Martin, J.E., & Thomas, M. (2007). The burden of acting white: Implications for transition. *Career Development for Exceptional Children, 30, 134–146.*

Goldberg, R.J., Higgins, E.L., Raskind, M.H., & Herman, K.L. (2003). Predictors of success in individuals with learning disabilities: A qualitative analysis of a 20-year longitudinal study. *Learning Disabilities Research and Practice, 18*(4), 222–236.

Halpern, A., Yovanoff, P., Doren, B., & Benz, M. (1995). Predicting participation in post secondary education for school leavers with disabilities. *Exceptional Children, 62*(2), 151–165.

Hoffman, A., Field, S., & Sawilowsky, S. (2004). *Self-Determination Assessment Battery user's guide* (3rd ed.). Detroit, MI: Center for Self-Determination and Transition, College of Education, Wayne State University.

Horner, R.H., Carr, E.G., Halle, J., McGee, G., Odom, S., & Wolery, M. (2005). The use of single subject research to identify evidence-based practice in special education. *Exceptional Children, 71,* 165–179.

Individuals with Disabilities Education Improvement Act (IDEA) of 2004, PL 108-446, 20 U.S.C. §§ 1400 *et seq.*

Johnson, D.R. (2005). Key provisions on transition: A comparison of IDEA 1997 and IDEA 2004. *Career Development for Exceptional Individuals, 28,* 60–63.

Johnson, D., Sharpe, M., & Stodden, R. (2001). The transition to postsecondary education for students with disabilities. *Impact 13*(1), 2–5.

Konrad, M., Fowler, C.H., Walker, A.R., Test, D.W., & Wood, W.M. (2007). Self-determination interventions on the academic skills of students with learning disabilities. *Learning Disability Quarterly, 30*(2), 89–113.

Leake, D.W., & Boone, R. (2007). Multicultural perspectives on self-determination from youth, parent, and teacher focus groups. *Career Development for Exceptional Individuals, 30*(2), 104–115.

Lehmann, J.P., Bassett, D.S., & Sands, D.J. (1999). Students' participation in transition-related actions: A qualitative study. *Remedial and Special Education, 20,* 160–169.

Liebert, D., Lutsky, L., & Gottlieb, A. (1990). Postsecondary experiences of young adults with severe physical disabilities. *Exceptional Children, 57,* 56–63.

Lovitt, T.C., Cushing, S.S., & Stump, C.S. (1994). High school students rate their IEPs: Low opinions and lack of ownership. *Intervention in School and Clinic, 30,* 34–37.

Marshall, L.H., Martin, J.E., Maxson, L., Hughes, W., Miller, T., McGill, T., & Jerman, P. (1999). *Take Action: Making goals happen.* Longmont, CO: Sopris West.

Martin, J.E., & Marshall, L.H. (1995). ChoiceMaker: A comprehensive self-determination transition program. *Intervention in School and Clinic, 30,* 147–156.

Martin, J.E., Marshall, L.H., & El-Kazimi, N. (2009). *Increasing goal attainment skills for students enrolled in middle school English classes.* Manuscript submitted for publication.

Martin, J.E., Marshall, L.H., & Maxson, L.L. (1993). Transition policy: Infusing self-determination and self-advocacy into transition programs. *Career Development for Exceptional Individuals, 16,* 53–61.

Martin, J.E., Marshall, L.H., Maxson, L.M., & Jerman, P.L. (1999). *The Self-Directed IEP.* Longmont, CO: Sopris West.

Martin, J.E., Marshall, L.H., & Sale, R.P. (2004). A 3-year study of middle, junior high, and high school IEP meetings. *Exceptional Children, 70,* 285–297.

Martin, J., Mithaug, D., Cox, P., Peterson, L., Van Dycke, J., & Cash, M. (2003). Increasing self-determination: Teaching students to plan, work, evaluate, and adjust. *Exceptional Children, 69,* 431–446.

Martin, J.E., Mithaug, D.E., Oliphint, J.H., Husch, J.V., & Frazier, E.S. (2002). *Self-directed employment: A handbook for transition teachers and employment specialists.* Baltimore: Paul H. Brookes Publishing Co.

Martin, J.E., & Sale, R.P. (in press). Self-determination instruction. In P. Wehman & J. Kregel (Eds.), *Community-based instruction* (3rd ed.). Austin, TX: PRO-ED.

Martin, J.E., Van Dycke, J.L., Christensen, W.R., Greene, B.A., Gardner, J.E., & Lovett, D.L. (2006). Increasing student participation in IEP meetings: Establishing the self-directed IEP as an evidenced-based practice. *Exceptional Children, 72*(3), 299–316.

Martin, J.E., Van Dycke, J.L., Greene, B.A., Gardner, J.E., Christensen, W.R., Woods, L.L., & Lovett, D.L. (2006). Direct observation of teacher-directed secondary IEP meetings: Establishing the need for student IEP meeting instruction. *Exceptional Children, 72*(2), 187–200.

Mithaug, D.E. (1996) *Equal opportunity theory.* Thousand Oaks, CA: Sage Publications.

Mithaug, D.E., (2005). On persistent pursuits of self-interest. *Research and Practice for Persons with Severe Disabilities, 30,* 163–167.

Mithaug, D.E., Martin, J.E., & Agran, M. (1987). Adaptability instruction: The goal of transitional programming. *Exceptional Children, 53,* 500–505.

Mithaug, D.E., Mithaug, D., Agran, M., Martin, J., & Wehmeyer, M. (2003). *Self-determined learning theory: Predictions, prescriptions, and practice.* Mahwah, NJ: Lawrence Erlbaum Associates.

Mithaug, D.E., Mithaug, D., Agran, M., Martin, J.E., & Wehmeyer, M. (2007). *Self-instruction pedagogy: How to teach self-determined learning.* Springfield, IL: Charles Thomas.

Mithaug, D.E., Wehmeyer, M.L., Agran, M., Martin, J.E., & Palmer, S. (1998). Self-determined learning model of instruction: Engaging students to solve their learning problems. In M. Wehmeyer & D.J. Sands (Eds.), *Making it happen: Student involvement in educational planning, decision-making, and instruction* (pp. 299–328). Baltimore: Paul H. Brookes Publishing Co.

Morningstar, M.E., Turnbull, A.P., & Turnbull, H.R., III. (1995). What do students with disabilities tell us about the importance of family involvement in the transition from school to adult life? *Exceptional Children, 62,* 249–260.

Odom, S.L., Brantlinger, E., Gersten, R., Horner, R.H., Thompson, B., & Harris, K.R. (2005). Research in special education: Scientific methods and evidence-based practices. *Exceptional Children, 71,* 137–148.

Office of Special Education Programs. (2001). *Students with disabilities' secondary education, transition, and employment* (Expert Strategy Panel Report). Washington, DC: Author.

Parker, D.R. (2004). *Voices of self-determined college students with ADHD: Undergraduates' perceptions of factors that influence their academic success.* Unpublished doctoral dissertation, University of Connecticut, Storrs.

Powers, L.E., Turner, A., Matuszewski, J., Wilson, R., & Loesch, C. (1999). A qualitative analysis of student involvement in transition planning. *Journal for Vocational Special Needs Education, 21,* 18–26.

Raskind, M.H., Goldberg, R.J., Higgins, E.L., & Herman, K.L. (1999). Patterns of change and predictors of success in individuals with learning disabilities: Results from a twenty-year longitudinal study. *Learning Disabilities Research and Practice, 14,* 35–49.

Rusch, F.R., Hughes, C., Agran, M., Martin, J.E., & Johnson, J.R. (2009). Toward self-directed learning, post–high school placement, and coordinated support: Constructing new transition bridges to adult life. *Career Development for Exceptional Individuals, 32,* 53–59.

Sale, R.P., & Martin, J.E. (2004). Self-determination instruction. In P. Wehman & J. Kregel (Eds.), *Community-based instruction* (2nd ed., pp. 67–94). Austin, TX: PRO-ED.

Scott, S.S. (2002). The dynamic process of providing accommodations. In L.C. Brinckerhoff, J.M. McGuire, & S.F. Shaw (Eds.), *Postsecondary education and transition for students with learning disabilities* (pp. 295–332). Austin, TX: PRO-ED.

Shaw, S.F., & Dukes, L.L. (2006). Postsecondary disability program standards and performance indicators: Minimum essentials for the office for students with disabilities. *Journal of Postsecondary Education and Disability, 19,* 14–24.

Snyder, E.P. (2000). *Examining the effects of teaching ninth grade students receiving special education learning supports services to conduct their own IEP meetings.* Unpublished doctoral dissertation, Lehigh University, Bethlehem, PA.

Snyder, E.P. (2002). Teaching students with combined behavioral disorders and mental retardation to lead their own IEP meetings. *Behavioral Disorders, 27,* 340–357.

Snyder, E.P., & Shapiro, E. (1997). Teaching students with emotional disorders the skills to participate in the development of their own IEPs. *Behavioral Disorders, 22,* 246–259.

Sweeny, M. (1997). *The effects of self-determination training on student involvement in the IEP process.* Unpublished doctoral dissertation, Florida State University, Tallahassee.

Test, D.W., Mason, C., Hughes, C., Konrad, M., Neale, M., & Wood, W.M. (2004). Student involvement in individualized education program meetings. *Exceptional Children, 70,* 391–412.

Trainor, A.A., Lindstrom, L., Simon-Burroughs, M., Martin, J.E., & McCray-Sorrells, A.M. (2008). From marginalized to maximized opportunities for diverse youth with disabilities: A position paper of the Division on Career Development and Transition. *Career Development for Exceptional Children, 31,* 56–64.

Van Dycke, J.L. (2005). *Determining the impact of the self-directed IEP instruction on secondary IEP documents.* Unpublished doctoral dissertation, University of Oklahoma, Norman.

Ward, M.J. (1988). The many facets of self-determination. *National Information Center for Children and Youth with Handicaps, Transition Summary, 5,* 2–3.

Wehmeyer, M.L. (1992). Self-determination and the education of students with mental retardation. *Education and Training in Mental Retardation, 27,* 302–314.

Wehmeyer, M. (1994). Perceptions of self-determination and psychological empowerment of adolescents with mental retardation. *Education and Training in Mental Retardation and Developmental Disabilities, 29,* 9–12.

Wehmeyer, M. (1995). *The Arc's Self-Determination Scale: Procedural guidelines.* Retrieved December 23, 2008, from http://education.ou.edu/zarrow/?p=38&z=39

Wehmeyer, M.L., Agran, M., Hughes, C., Martin, J.E., Mithaug, D.E., & Palmer, S.B. (2007). *Promoting self-determination in students with developmental disabilities.* New York: Guilford Press.

Wehmeyer, M., & Kelchner, K. (1995). *The Arc Self-Determination Scale.* Retrieved December 23, 2008, from http://education.ou.edu/zarrow/?p=38&z=3

Wehmeyer, M.L. & Palmer, S.B. (2003). Adult outcomes for students with cognitive disabilities three-years after high school: The impact of self-determination. *Education and Training in Developmental Disabilities, 38,* 131–144.

Wehmeyer, M.L., Palmer, S.B., Agran, M., Mithaug, D.E., & Martin, J.E. (2000). Promoting causal agency: The self-determined learning model of instruction. *Exceptional Children, 66,* 439–453.

Wehmeyer, M.L., & Schwartz, M. (1998). The relationship between self-determination and quality of life for adults with mental retardation. *Education and Training in Mental Retardation and Developmental Disabilities, 33,* 3–12.

Wolman, J.M., Campeau, P.I., DuBois, P.A., Mithaug, D.E., & Stolarski, V.S. (1994). *AIR Self-Determination Scale and user guide.* Retrieved December 23, 2008, from http://education.ou.edu/zarrow/?p=38&z=3

Wu, P.F., Martin, J.E., & Isbell, S. (2009). *Using brief IEP team instruction plus the self-direct IEP to increase students with visual impairments participation in secondary transition IEP meetings.* Manuscript submitted for publication.

Zhang, D., & Benz, M.R. (2006). Enhancing self-determination of culturally diverse students with disabilities: Current status and future directions. *Focus on Exceptional Children, 38*(9), 1–12.

# Using a Schoolwide Model to Foster Successful Transition to College

## Providing Comprehensive Academic and Behavioral Supports to All Learners

*Michael Faggella-Luby, K. Brigid Flannery, and Brandi Simonsen*

---

### WHAT YOU'LL LEARN IN THIS CHAPTER:

✔ How comprehensive academic and behavioral supports foster a successful transition to college

✔ How secondary curriculum demands and individual learner characteristics can prevent successful high school completion and potential transition to college

✔ What is involved in implementing a schoolwide model for academic and behavioral supports

✔ What specific academic and behavioral supports at the secondary level enhance the transition to college

✔ What the roles and responsibilities are for secondary personnel implementing a schoolwide model

# UNDERSTANDING THE CHALLENGES OF COLLEGE PREPARATION

The demands of the secondary school curriculum are often significantly challenging to individuals with disabilities and can prevent successful high school completion and potential transition to postsecondary education. Successful transition to college requires early and adequate preparation in academic and social skills to meet and overcome roadblocks to postsecondary education.

## Successful Transition to College

Preparation must begin early for students with disabilities to successfully transition through the secondary school gateway to postsecondary education and, ultimately, the world of work. All students deserve the academic and behavioral preparation that will enable them to have equal opportunity and full participation in college and society through independent living and economic self-sufficiency. Such comprehensive postsecondary outcomes require implementing an equally comprehensive schoolwide model of service delivery. Even with more students with disabilities attending postsecondary institutions than at any point since the late 1980s, as a group, these students still lag behind their general education peers in matriculating to 4-year colleges or universities, community colleges, and vocational schools (Wagner, Newman, Cameto, & Levine, 2005). In part, this may be due to a persistent gap between the demands of the secondary curriculum and the characteristics of students with disabilities. In short, students with disabilities must first successfully achieve adequate secondary school outcomes as preparation for achieving postsecondary transition outcomes. Fortunately, schoolwide models are under development to improve academic and behavioral outcomes for secondary students (see Box 5.1).

This chapter presents a three-tier schoolwide model for secondary schools that employs logic from Response to Intervention (RTI) and Schoolwide Positive Behavior Supports (SWPBS). Examples of evidence-based instruction in the academic (e.g., cognitive strategy instruction) and behavioral (e.g., SWPBS) domains are presented to illustrate the kinds of practices that educators, administrators, families, students, and other stakeholders can generalize to their own unique context. Implementing a schoolwide model may increase the quality of secondary school service delivery by ensuring that all students are adequately prepared for high school graduation and their subsequent transition to the postsecondary world.

## Roadblocks to Postsecondary Education

During the middle and high school years, students simultaneously face new structural, developmental, behavioral, and academic challenges that can exhaust their abilities, leaving them overwhelmed and falling behind. In particular, the secondary school academic emphasis on discipline-specific knowledge is perhaps its most defining characteristic and places a significant demand on students. Students face further roadblocks to postsecondary education when the demands of the secondary curriculum do not match individual learner characteristics.

Though the characteristics of learners with disabilities are varied, some general trends have emerged that help to illustrate potential areas of challenge as students attempt to meet the demands of the secondary curriculum

**Box 5.1.** Case 1: Structure, discipline put sky-high goals in reach

As a middle school student, Andrew Franz could not seem to complete simple chores in a timely manner. Taking out the trash, changing the cat litter, finishing assignments on time—none of it seemed to matter.

Then his mother introduced him to Luanne Todd, a certified Strategic Instruction Model professional developer.

"I do not know how she found her, but it was just what I needed," says Andrew.

He and Luanne worked together on the Assignment Completion Strategy and using the Quality Quest Planner. It was a journey that was not without its ups and downs. But through perseverance, their efforts began to pay off.

"One morning, according to his mother, Andy had an 'epiphany' about knowing what day it was and taking out the garbage without her reminder," says Luanne. "She was thrilled!"

Using the strategy gave Andrew structure and discipline that have become intrinsic parts of his life. Even now, as a student at the University of Alabama pursuing a degree in criminal justice, he uses a modified form of the strategy to keep on top of assignments and commitments.

"The Assignment Completion Strategy has by far affected my scholastic career more than anything else I have learned," he says. "It not only helped correct my path but also gave me the foundation to keep going and succeed on the highest levels."

When Andrew graduates from college, he will be commissioned as an officer in the U.S. Air Force. His academic success has made him a top candidate for a highly competitive position of pilot or navigator within the Air Force.

"I would just like to say that although the Assignment Completion Strategy is great, Luanne was the one that did all the hard work setting it up and teaching me for hours when I could not understand it," Andrew says. "She not only deserves recognition but also a medal! It is safe to say she was the single person who put me on the path I am today, and I owe her a ton."

Andrew's story is one of success because a dedicated teacher helped him to learn and apply a self-regulated strategy that has played an important role in his successful transition to postsecondary life, but

- What about other students who might improve their ability to transition into the postsecondary world of college with this kind of instruction?

- Is there a way for schools to offer this kind of instruction to all students?

- What if the student has behavioral needs?

- What would a schoolwide service delivery system look like to meet the needs of all learners?

From The University of Kansas Center for Research on Learning. (2009). *30 × 30: Thirty stories of success, hope and innovation.* Lawrence: Author; reprinted by permission.

described previously. For example, nationally, more than a quarter of all eighth-grade students cannot read material essential for daily living, and more than two thirds of secondary students (general and special education) score below the proficient level on the National Assessment of Educational Progress (NAEP; Perie, Grigg, & Donahue, 2005). More specifically, early epidemiological research on the characteristics of students with learning disabilities and other students at risk found that these students' basic academic skills often plateau prior to reaching the secondary level. In addition, these students have difficulty behaviorally when interacting with peers and adults, fail to set and attain goals, and are challenged by problem-solving tasks and generalizing learning to new contexts (see Deshler & Schumaker, 2006).

Students who lack appropriate academic or behavioral strategies are unable to master the critical content necessary for adequate progress throughout school. As each school year passes, students miss more and more of the knowledge they will be expected to apply later in school and life. Failure to master critical content has an immediate effect on school performance, causing a significant roadblock to postsecondary education.

## Overcoming Roadblocks to Postsecondary Education

Adequate preparation in academic and social skills is necessary for successful transition to postsecondary education (and life) and requires careful planning and comprehensive allocation of schoolwide resources. Each year schools are asked to meet new district, state, and federal initiatives (e.g., No Child Left Behind [NCLB] Act of 2001 [PL 107-110]; Individuals with Disabilities Education Improvement Act [IDEA] of 2004 [PL 108-446]) that require schools to "do more with less." Legislative pressures compel schools to move beyond disjointed and narrow programs or interventions that function as Band-Aids to larger systemic problems.

Fortunately, two emerging research findings indicate that schools and, more important, classroom teachers, can affect the preparation of students for college by focusing change in classroom-level teaching practices. First, the most robust form of school reform occurs when instructional changes are made at the classroom level, immediately improving course performance and increasing graduation rates (Rowan, Correnti, & Miller, 2002). Second, the most robust change at the classroom level involves ensuring instruction is direct and explicit (e.g., Faggella-Luby & Deshler, 2008; Swanson, 1999). Explicit instruction makes the process and content of learning transparent across academically diverse groups of students.

Schools need to use a broad approach in order to be more efficient and comprehensive in implementing these initiatives and creating a safe learning environment. Schools can use a comprehensive, schoolwide system to support the development of a climate that increases retention of students whose behavior (academic and/or social) interferes with their learning, achievement, and postsecondary education preparation.

## TOWARD A SCHOOLWIDE COMPREHENSIVE SERVICE DELIVERY MODEL

This section places a schoolwide model within the current context of education in the United States, describing the model in terms of a continuum of academic and behavioral supports to meet the needs of all learners. The section concludes with a discussion of the roles of various educators in implementing a schoolwide model.

## A Schoolwide Model within the Current Secondary Context

As mentioned previously, NCLB and IDEA 2004 are catalysts for rethinking how schools conduct typical educational practice. Specifically, these laws necessitate the development of schoolwide models in two important ways. First, schools are now held accountable under NCLB for the outcomes of *all* students through annual yearly progress (AYP) reports. So-called high-stakes assessments hold schools responsible by drawing attention to the outcomes of not only typically achieving students (reported previously as a mean score across the school), but also the outcomes of traditionally marginalized subgroups (e.g., English language learners, students from low socioeconomic backgrounds, ethnic minorities, students with disabilities). This may be the first time many schools have measured the progress of these subgroups. When the progress of any one of these subgroups is discovered to be inadequate, schools must refine their implementation of educational practices to enhance their learning outcomes. Such self-examination, using student outcomes as a metric, provides evidence of system efficacy, teacher effectiveness, and student response to instruction.

In addition, a second and related element of the legislative mandates is that for the first time, up to 15% of federal special education dollars (under IDEA 2004) have been made available for schools to spend on evidence-based early intervention and prevention services. Flexible use of special education dollars allows schools to leverage previously unavailable resources to design schoolwide models that 1) promote the completion of college prep coursework by reconceptualizing the service delivery model and 2) potentially minimize the likelihood of students who are at risk academically and behaviorally requiring special education (Simonsen et al., in press).

Within the current context, it is not uncommon for schools to attempt implementation of evidence-based practices. In fact, the problem is most likely that schools are attempting implementation of many different, and often competing, practices that tax limited school resources. Competing practices pull schools in many different directions, confusing practitioners (and ultimately students) about real priorities and often obscuring results of robust interventions. In response to this challenge, however, complementary three-tiered schoolwide prevention models for academic and social behavioral supports have surfaced: RTI and SWPBS. Emerging research supports RTI and SWPBS as efficient and effective ways to organize school resources and deliver instruction to all students in both academic (e.g., Kovaleski, Gickling, Morrow, & Swank, 1999; Marston, Muyskens, Lau, & Canter, 2003; Vaughn, Linan-Thompson, & Hickman, 2003) and social (Horner et al., 2009; Netzel & Eber, 2003) domains.

At a practical level, schools are facing the challenge of establishing a climate in which students feel safe and secure while at the same time increasing all students' abilities to meet appropriately challenging academic standards. Schools are the place for students to learn academic content, "how to learn" (e.g., time management, critical thinking, task planning), and social skills necessary to live in a community together (e.g., interpersonal skills, self-advocacy, problem solving). A schoolwide model, described in detail next, provides the essential framework for implementing a continuum of academic and behavioral supports that are appropriate for every student as part of preparation for postsecondary environments.

## Critical Components of a Schoolwide Model

A unified, three-tier schoolwide model for academic and behavioral support has been proposed by Sugai (2001; see Figure 5.1). The model has received national attention and been adopted by the National Association of State Directors of Special Education (NASDSE; 2006) as a "picture" of RTI. In brief, the model is composed of three tiers of increasingly intense instructional intervention based on regular assessments of student rate and level of performance. The model functions on the premise that evidence-based practices, employed effectively and efficiently with fidelity, will result in improved student outcomes, including successful transition to college. The critical elements of the three tiers and additional key features of a schoolwide model are illustrated in Figure 5.1 and described next. In addition, Tables 5.1 and 5.2 illustrate specific programs, practices, and interventions related to each tier.

### Universal or Primary Prevention (Tier 1)

In Tier 1, prevention focus is placed on the outcomes, data, practices, and systems throughout the whole school. In other words, interventions are

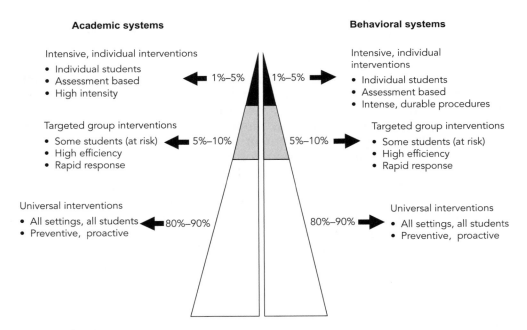

**Figure 5.1.**   A schoolwide model. (From Cole, C., & Sugai, G. [2008, January 17]. *SWPBS: Establishing district & community capacity [beyond classroom management]*. Retrieved September 9, 2009, from http://www.pbis.org/common/pbisresources/presentations/district_1_18_08.ppt; reprinted by permission.)

**Table 5.1.** Examples of systems and practices in each of the three tiers of schoolwide positive behavior support

---

*Universal Level (Tier 1):* Prevent the development of problem behaviors by focusing on all students and staff across all settings (e.g., schoolwide, classroom, nonclassroom/noninstructional settings).

- A schoolwide leadership team develops the action plan and monitors progress on implementing schoolwide systems and practices
- Expectations, rules, and procedures for discipline are clarified and taught to staff and students
- Systems are developed to acknowledge students for demonstrating the expectations and encourage continued performance of these in their day-to-day work.
- A data system is implemented that tracks student behavior (academic and social) and allows for efficient review of data for decision making.
- Sound instructional practices and relevant curriculum are implemented.
- Structures or systems that support relationships between students and staff are developed.

*Targeted Group Level (Tier 2):* Provide services, in addition to the universal services, to groups of individuals who require more support.

- Monitor and supervise the implementation of practices (Hawken & Horner, 2003; Leedy, Bates, & Safran, 2004; Sinclair, Christenson, Evelo, & Hurley, 1998).
- Teach organizational and study skills (Swain-Bradway & Horner, in press).
- Teach social skills (Bremer & Smith 2004; Lane et al., 2003; Moote, Smyth, & Wodarski, 1999).
- Provide personal support (e.g., girls group, grief group, anger management group).
- Provide academic support.

*Individualized Level (Tier 3):* Develop individualized behavioral support plans for students who are resistant to the primary and secondary prevention efforts and need to receive more intensive supports.

- Conduct functional behavioral assessment (O'Neill et al., 1997).
- Provide wraparound services (Eber, Sugai, Smith, & Scott, 2002; Epstein et al., 2005).
- Conduct futures planning (Cheney, Malloy, & Hager, 1998).
- Provide work experiences and other activities that relate to individually constructed post–high school outcomes and that build linkages to natural and paid supports (Cheney et al., 1998; Malloy & Cormier, 2004).

---

implemented in all environments (classroom and nonclassroom) for all students by all staff to increase desired academic and behavioral outcomes. For example, a core reading comprehension program across all middle school language arts classrooms would be considered a primary prevention practice for establishing and teaching clear expectations of behavior in this school.

## Targeted Group or Secondary Prevention (Tier 2)

In Tier 2, prevention focus is placed on individual or small groups of students who do not respond to primary prevention practices and thus require additional support. So called, non- or limited-responders are considered "at risk" and may require additional instruction in either learning or behavioral practices to benefit more fully from universal practices. In Tier 2, outcomes, data, practices, and systems are employed to determine the necessary evidence-based instructional practices to improve the rate and level of students' responses. For example, cognitive strategy instruction (described next) may be employed with small groups of students using explicit pedagogy to provide students with independent access to content area knowledge and critical thinking. Behaviorally, the "Latino Talking Circle" that focuses on a culturally relevant support system for Latino girls to develop strategies to succeed in school might be employed.

**Table 5.2.** Examples of evidence-based practices in each of the three tiers related to literacy supports at the secondary level

---

*Universal Level (Tier 1)*

Accelerated Reader: Computer-based learning system; students read books and answer comprehension questions (http://www.renlearn.com/ar)

Concept-Oriented Reading Instruction (CORI): Curriculum stressing engagement, reading comprehension, and conceptual learning with science content (http://www.cori.umd.edu)

Questioning the Author: Helps engage and motivate students by working with teachers to ask open-ended discussion questions (Beck, McKeown, Hamilton, & Kucan, 1997)

Strategic Instruction Model (SIM): Two-prong approach focusing on learning strategy and content-enhancement instruction (http://www.ku-crl.org/sim)

Success for All: Comprehensive, schoolwide model for students at risk, including 60-minute literacy classes (http://www.successforall.net)

Transactional strategies instruction: Flexible form of comprehension strategy instruction blending well with other programs (e.g., Project CRISS: *CR*eating *I*ndependence through *S*tudent-owned *S*trategies; http://www.projectcriss.com)

*Targeted Group Level (Tier 2)*

Peer-Assisted Learning Strategies (PALS): Peer tutoring program using dyads to work together on reading skills (http://kc.vanderbilt.edu/pals)

Reciprocal Teaching: Improving strategic reading for comprehension through strategies with increasing opportunities for collaborative practice (Palincsar & Brown, 1984)

*Individualized Level (Tier 3)*

Benchmark Word Detectives: Teaches decoding by analogy through spelling patterns using key words (http://www.benchmarkschool.org/word_id_intro.html)

Corrective Reading 2008 (Science Research Associates [SRA]): Direct instruction decoding and comprehension program (http://www.sraonline.com/?isbn=0076181804)

Lindamood-Bell: Three component sensory-cognitive instructional program for addressing student language processing needs: Lindamood Phoneme Sequencing (LiPS), Seeing Stars (SS), and Visualizing and Verbalizing (V/V) (http://www.lindamoodbell.com)

---

Each intervention has more than 10 peer-reviewed research articles related to its effectiveness in improving literacy outcomes in secondary environments. Not all studies involved students with disabilities. See Deshler, Palincsar, Biancarosa, and Nair (2007) for more information.

Several of the universal level interventions have components that make them appropriate for Tier 2 and Tier 3 levels in which instruction can be individualized and delivered with intensity.

## Individualized or Tertiary Prevention (Tier 3)

In Tier 3, prevention focus is placed on individual students who have not responded to either primary- or secondary-level interventions. Consequently, outcomes, data, practices, and systems are individualized and student specific. For example, an individualized academic intervention may focus on explicit instruction of skills necessary for decoding multisyllabic words, and an individualized behavioral intervention would focus on function-based support strategies.

Simonsen and colleagues (in press) suggest schools need to establish systems that facilitate data-based decision making because data help determine when a student is 1) responding to and benefiting from the current tier of intervention or 2) not responding to the current instruction and requires additional supports in a subsequent tier. Within this model, schools create structures for regularly collecting and using student data from each tier for instructional and programmatic decision making. To support this effort, a standing school-based team is formed to regularly review data; web-based or electronic data management programs are used for efficient input and generation of visual progress reports (e.g., graphs); and all staff are trained to prioritize, ask questions of, and review data to inform instructional decisions (see Simonsen & Sugai, 2007). By creating efficient and effective systems around assessment, schools make implementing the three tiers feasible. Moreover, the systems help to clearly illustrate teacher effectiveness on student progress, making this schoolwide model more than just another education initiative practitioners are forced to try or assessments students must take. Instead, data become a lever of change and a mark of progress, giving evidence to support practitioner and administrative decision making in a unified effort to improve student outcomes.

One way for building level teams to begin is by conducting a self-assessment around each critical component of the schoolwide model. For example, schools might examine what assessments they currently use to gather student data related to placement. Are these measures used for screening, progress monitoring, or evaluation? Are the measures norm referenced? How are data shared with administrators, practitioners, or other stakeholders? How are data used to inform decision making? Once these questions are answered, schools can decide to either eliminate superfluous assessments, integrate assessments with others to provide a more complete picture of student characteristics, modify the assessment, or sustain use if it provides critical student data.

## Practitioner Roles within a Schoolwide Model at the Secondary Level

Successfully implementing a schoolwide RTI model is occurring in elementary and middle schools throughout the nation. The application of this model in high schools, however, is in its early stages. This chapter encourages secondary personnel in general, and transition personnel in particular, to develop a schoolwide model in their schools to foster productive postsecondary outcomes for all students, including those with disabilities. Realization of an effective schoolwide model requires that schools maximize capacity by leveraging human resources. Practitioners, including special educators, general educators, and school support personnel from a variety of disciplines, as well as administrators in each of these areas, play pivotal and complementary roles within the model. It is only through the collective efforts of all school personnel (in partnership with the broader school stakeholder community) that a schoolwide model can be effectively and efficiently implemented in the high school setting.

### Special Educators

The role of the special educator is of primary importance. Within a schoolwide model, special educators continue an active role as case managers for students with disabilities. In addition, because students with disabilities are served throughout the tiers of a schoolwide model, special educators are optimally situated to play an expanding role as "interventionists." As interventionists, special educators 1) collect and interpret data; 2) deliver instruction to students who are academically and behaviorally diverse; 3) collaborate with general educators, support personnel, and administrators; and 4) ensure evidence-based instructional methods are implemented with fidelity (Simonsen et al., in press). Although many educators may complete these activities, special educators' training in instruction, assessment, behavior management, curriculum modification, and accommodation provide them with the specific expertise to excel within an interventionist role (for more, see Simonsen et al., in press).

### General Educators

General educators are essential to successfully implementing a schoolwide model because they are the primary deliverers of Tier 1 content instruction. They create universal access by determining and mapping critical course content, making instructional decisions about enhancements to support learning of challenging content, teaching in a manner that is overt and precise, determining regular evaluations to measure student learning, and using assessments to determine if content has been mastered or needs to be retaught. General educators also collaborate with related services personnel, especially interventionists, around planning for academic diversity, progress monitoring, and instructional decision making, with the goal of helping all students succeed in the general education curriculum.

### Other Personnel

Without question, high school personnel from a variety of other disciplines (e.g., counselors, school psychologists, speech-language pathologists [SLPs]) play critical roles within a schoolwide model. These professionals help ensure sufficient capacity across all three tiers by performing training, consulting, and collaborating in partnership with interventionists. Roles may include supporting general educators in Tier 1 classrooms, implementing push-in or pull-out programs in Tier 2, and providing intensive and explicit individualized instruction in Tier 3.

### Administrators

Finally, a schoolwide model requires considerable administrative support. Administrators 1) establish, support, and play an active role in schoolwide data-based decision-making teams; 2) communicate regularly with faculty, students, and stakeholders; 3) take responsibility for leading implementation of a schoolwide effort; and 4) build capacity by developing practitioner and stakeholder leadership skills.

In summary, schools will need to draw on the diversity of professional expertise found in their staff for a schoolwide model to function effectively and efficiently. In the next sections, evidence-based academic and social behavioral interventions that should be included within a schoolwide model at the secondary level are described.

# ACADEMIC INTERVENTIONS

Students with disabilities often require academic interventions to meet the grade-level demands of secondary curriculum. Cognitive strategy instruction is an evidence-based academic intervention that fits within the multitiered system to support individual and group learning needs in secondary schools.

## Cognitive Strategy Instruction

Cognitive strategy instruction is one of the best researched and most powerful interventions that can be implemented as part of a schoolwide model to improve academic preparation for college coursework. Deshler and Schumaker (2006) defined these *learning strategies* as an individual's approach to a task, including how one thinks and acts when planning, executing, and evaluating performance on a task and its outcomes.

Learning strategies are different from basic or study skills, which usually consist of a simple procedure or set of steps applied in a unique situation (e.g., steps to solve a long division problem, procedure for outlining an essay). Instead, learning strategies have four critical features. First, an "approach" requires holistic thinking that begins with initial recognition of a problem, continues with strategy execution to bring about task completion, and finally concludes with evaluation of the efficiency and effectiveness of the actual approach used. A strategy must help a learner complete a task successfully *and* in a timely and suitable manner. Second, strategies focus on how a student thinks and how a student acts—neither is sufficient alone for successful application of a strategy. Third, a strategy focuses on a continuum of performance including what happens before, during, and after a task. Fourth, strategy use is reinforced (and considered successful) when students observe their own performance and improved results as a result of effort and application of the strategy to solve a learning problem (Deshler & Schumaker, 2006). All students have their own approaches to tasks, but these approaches are not always successful. For example, there are many ways to fail an examination, just as there are many ways to prepare for an examination. Cognitive strategy instruction improves student learning by providing both a procedure to follow *and* a metacognitive problem-solving process that allows for student success and generalization of the approach to new contexts. Consequently, strategies move beyond a skills approach (e.g., if all you have is a hammer to solve a problem, you only look for nails to hit) into a broader ability to strategically analyze and complete tasks (e.g., having a full toolkit and knowing what to use in different situations). In upcoming sections, data will be highlighted indicating that students with disabilities who learn to be strategic learners can achieve similar success as students without disabilities (Deshler & Schumaker, 2006). The ability to do so increases the likelihood of academic success once in college.

## Research on Cognitive Strategy Instruction in Secondary Schools

Considerable research has been conducted on strategy instruction (e.g. Swanson, 1999; Swanson, Hoskyn, & Lee, 1999). Early research demonstrated that successful students were able to generate and use strategies independently, whereas some students, especially those with disabilities, lacked this ability to the detriment of academic performance (Deshler & Schumaker, 2006). Consequently, several teams began programs of research to discover if instruction in the components of strategies used by successful students would improve academic outcomes for students who struggle (Pressley & Hilden, 2006). Results of this work indicated that both students at risk for failure and students with disabilities can be taught through overt and explicit instruction to independently use strategies (Faggella-Luby & Deshler, 2008).

Strategies have been found to improve academic preparation for adolescents with learning disabilities and emotional/behavioral disabilities in the areas of reading (e.g., Faggella-Luby & Deshler, 2008; Mastropieri, Scruggs, & Graetz, 2003), mnemonics for remembering (e.g., Wolgemuth, Cobb, & Alwell, 2008), written expression (e.g., Graham & Harris, 2003), problem solving in math (e.g., Fuchs et al., 2003), peer collaboration across content areas (e.g., Baker, Gersten, Dimino, & Griffiths, 2004; Mastropieri, Scruggs, Spencer, & Fontana, 2003), and test taking (Hughes, Deshler, Ruhl, & Schumaker, 1993). In addition, strategy instruction for students with disabilities at the postsecondary level has also been found to improve academic performance in the areas of mnemonics (Patwa, 2003) and decreasing test anxiety (LaFrance-Holzer, 2007).

Individually, these studies tell us about conditions and methods that were successful for improving student outcomes and successful preparation for completing college prep coursework. Collectively, these studies generate a solid foundation from which teachers can draw guidelines for instructional practice. It is essential to identify the most robust instructional elements, given the limited time for secondary practitioners to affect student performance before graduation. Swanson and colleagues have conducted the most complete analyses of elements relative to improving instruction for students with learning disabilities through a quantitative comparison of explicit instruction, study methods, and outcomes (e.g., Swanson, 1999; Swanson et al., 1999). Using meta-analytic methodology, they identified six core instructional components related to the greatest student improvements: 1) daily reviews, 2) teacher statement of lesson objectives for instruction, 3) teacher presentation of new material, 4) teacher-guided student practice, 5) independent student practice, and 6) formative evaluation of student progress (Swanson, 1999).

---

Note that each of the six core components related to student improvement identified by Swanson et al. (1999) are not exclusive to strategy instruction. How might each of these six components appear in daily lesson plans? How might you construct a lesson plan that draws upon this list of instructional practices to meet learning objectives?

---

## Cognitive Strategy Instruction Pedagogy in Secondary Schools

One way of operationalizing Swanson's core instructional components, or pedagogy, can be found in the eight stages of instruction (see Table 5.3)

**Table 5.3.**   What are the Strategic Instruction Model stages of instruction?

*Acquisition*

Stage 1: Pretest and make commitments. Students are pretested with grade-level materials to determine baseline performance and to assess the appropriateness of a strategy for instruction. Both the teacher and student then commit to engage in the learning process.

Stage 2: Describe. Teachers describe the overt and covert components of a strategy, including self-regulation activities, as well as a rationale for how students can apply the strategy through real-world examples.

Stage 3: Model. Modeling is the heart of strategy instruction and is composed of four components: 1) teacher-led advance organizer in which strategy components are reviewed and redefined as the teacher helps students to connect the strategy directly to their own learning; 2) teacher successfully presents strategy actions and thinking by vocalizing the process through a think-aloud; 3) student enlistment to mediate learning as teachers check student understanding while guiding successful use of the strategy, reteaching as necessary; and 4) a postorganizer is used to review critical elements of the strategy, reinforce personal applications, and clearly communicate teacher expectations.

Stage 4: Verbal practice. Self-regulation formally begins as students review strategy purpose (for future application) and steps so that they may be applied with automaticity (allowing for additional cognitive resources to focus on the content being learned rather than on individual steps).

Stage 5: Controlled practice and feedback. Student responsibility for strategy use grows via multiple opportunities, individual to each learner, for strategy practice with ability-level materials (enabling students to focus on learning the strategy prior to engaging in more challenging grade-level materials). It is essential that teachers provide regular corrective feedback during this stage.

Stage 6: Advanced practice and feedback. Once students have mastered strategy components on ability-level materials, they begin practicing on more challenging material as they transition toward grade-level materials. As before, it is essential that teachers provide regular corrective feedback, analyzing individual student performance and instructing as necessary.

Stage 7: Posttest and make commitments. In the final acquisition stage, posttests confirm student mastery of strategy components (a cause for celebration), and the teacher works with students to formally begin the process of learning how, when, and why to apply the strategy in new situations (i.e., generalization).

*Generalization*

Stage 8: Generalization. Students are explicitly taught to generalize their use of the strategy in new settings or with new tasks with the teacher 1) orienting students to the idea of using the strategy in new settings; 2) prompting student activation, purposefully using the strategy in a novel setting while monitoring performance and continuing feedback; 3) guiding student adaptation of how the strategy might be altered to fit new setting demands; and 4) periodically checking student maintenance of strategy mastery.

*Source:* Deshler and Schumaker (2006).

included within the Strategic Instruction Model (SIM) Learning Strategy Curriculum developed at The University of Kansas Center for Research on Learning. During 30 years of research, Drs. Deshler, Schumaker, and colleagues have conducted methodologically rigorous and educationally significant (i.e., student outcomes resulting in passing grades) research related to adolescents with learning disabilities (Deshler & Schumaker, 2006). The Learning Strategy Curriculum includes three strands corresponding to acquisition, storage, and expression strategies (see http://www.ku-crl.org for more information). Each strategy is explicitly taught using eight instructional stages, including seven stages during strategy acquisition and a four-phased generalization stage to prepare students to use the strategy to meet alternative setting demands (Kline, Schumaker, & Deshler, 1991). Strategies have been used to help students complete high school coursework and successfully transition to college (see Box 5.2 for Zech and Paula's story).

**Box 5.2.** Case 2: Hockey player wins face-off against reading struggles

Paula Hamp, reading specialist and Strategic Instruction Model professional developer, of Sioux City, Iowa, has seen many successes over the years. One that stands out as especially inspiring involves a young man who came to her for tutoring while playing for a local U.S. hockey league team.

Zech was a very bright young man who was severely dyslexic and still needed to complete two high school credits to graduate.

Once I started working with him, I realized that Zech could not read. He had the skills to sound out letters and letter combinations, but no skills to put it all together. Even though he needed his American government and economics credits, he first needed additional reading skills.

I spent time teaching him the Word Identification and Self-Questioning strategies. During the course of his hockey season, I was able to teach him to use the strategies independently, and he was able to complete his coursework.

Days before he went home, his parents came into town from the East Coast and took me out to eat. Near the end of the dinner, his father touched my arm and said, "Paula, I really can't thank you enough."

There was a long pause at which time he began to cry. He collected himself and continued. "I remember just last year my son struggled to read *The Little Yellow Duck,* and last week he called me and said 'Dad, listen to this!' and he read aloud from his American government book. He read words such as *judicial, legislative,* and *executive."*

The whole time tears streamed down his face. "We then discussed current political issues that related to what he had just read. I never thought I'd see this day. Thank you."

I had to confess, "It's not me. It's Zech learning the Kansas strategies and applying them!"

Two years later, Paula received an e-mail from Zech. He was playing hockey for the University of Massachusetts, where he was earning a 2.98 grade point average. And, he told her, he was still using the strategies! Since that time, Zech graduated from the university as a First Team All-Academic and has gone on to play professional hockey.

From The University of Kansas Center for Research on Learning. (2009). *30 × 30: Thirty stories of success, hope and innovation.* Lawrence: Author; reprinted by permission.

## Instruction Relative to Group Size

Research has shown that the best outcomes in learning strategy instruction result when instruction occurs in small groups of no more than six students (Deshler & Schumaker, 2006). The reality of secondary school instruction, however, is that not all instruction can occur within small-group settings. Consequently, additional pedagogical sequences are required for large (20–30 students) and moderate (10–15 students) groups.

### Large-Sized Groups

In a parallel line of research, Deshler, Schumaker, and colleagues have investigated the effects of content enhancement routines to assist teacher planning and instruction in large-group content area courses (e.g., Lenz, Deshler, & Kissam, 2004). This research has validated a three-phase instructional methodology (cue, do, review) for large-group instruction that is adapted here specifically for strategy instruction. First, teachers *cue* students to the strategy by announcing and explaining strategy steps, purpose, and areas of potential generalization. Second, teachers *do* the instruction by guiding students through using the strategy in a collaborative manner, highlighting the strategy's critical elements as much as possible. Finally, teachers conclude with a *review* of strategy steps, purpose, and areas of generalization. A key limitation of this type of instruction is the abbreviated nature, which results in fewer students learning to use the strategy independently. Regular assessment can identify students who do not respond to this methodology and require additional instruction.

### Moderate-Sized Groups

To address the limitations of the cue-do-review methodology, an emerging pedagogy for strategy instruction with moderate-sized groups is under development (e.g., Faggella-Luby, Schumaker, & Deshler, 2007). The four-phase methodology (I do it, We do it, Y'all do it, You do it), referred to as embedded strategy instruction, was developed to aid teachers desiring a way to routinely weave strategies within and across classes. First, during the *I do it* phase, students learn by watching as the teacher introduces and describes the steps and purpose of the strategy prior to carrying out a think-aloud model of the entire strategy highlighted by verbal problem solving. Second, during the *We do it* phase, students learn by sharing as they coconstruct and use the strategy in partnership with the teacher. During this phase, students perform each strategy step, explain how they are thinking about the steps, and practice with examples that allow teachers to evaluate understanding and reinstruct if necessary. Third, during the *Y'all do it* phase, students learn together in cooperative learning dyads, providing opportunities to explain thinking to each other, while the teacher circulates to different groups, evaluating understanding and providing corrective feedback. Finally, during the *You do it* phase, students learn by independently practicing the strategy, recording progress over time. Teachers use independent practice to circulate and provide brief, specific, and constructive feedback, reinstructing, as needed, for those students who continue to struggle. Although this pedagogy is not as explicit as the eight stages presented previously, both the teacher *and* the student play a role in instruction, resulting in higher likelihood of independent strategy use.

The pedagogies suggested for large and moderate groups require additional explanation for successful implementation. Clearly, as group size increases, intensity of instruction will inevitably decrease as the context demands that teachers provide fewer opportunities to respond, limited amounts of guided practice, and often less individualized practice. If approximately 80% of students (corresponding to a schoolwide model) are responding well to large-group instruction (i.e., mastering the critical content and components of the strategy), then the chosen method of instruction can be considered appropriate. If fewer than 80% of students are responding, however, teachers must be willing to become more explicit in their instruction. That is, instruction will more closely align with the eight stages of acquisition and generalization from the Learning Strategy Curriculum. This trend holds equally true for teachers working with moderate-sized groups (about 15% of the total student population).

> Note that the difference between instructional conditions is not just about the decrease in group size (e.g., fewer students taught at one time). Rather, as group size decreases, teachers are able to increase use of explicit pedagogical elements such as providing opportunities for guided or independent practice and additional teacher-led corrective feedback.

## Supporting Individual Learners to Meet Curriculum Demands

Strategy instruction does not occur in a set "place." Rather, strategies might be considered along a continuum of building blocks for content literacy with relative intensity of instruction matching learner needs for adequate responsiveness to instruction. The key difference will be variations in intensity of instruction based on contextual factors such as group size, amount of independent practice, or opportunities to respond.

The Building Blocks for Content Literacy are a set of five sequential and hierarchical levels, with each prior level forming the foundation for those above. *Content literacy* refers to the fluent use of listening, speaking, reading, and writing skills and strategies required for learning in each of the academic disciplines (Lenz & Ehren, 1999). For learning to occur, students must master the components of each level. First, and most foundational, is mastery of the language underpinnings that support curriculum content and learning strategy use. Without language, literally nothing can be communicated nor consequently learned. Second, mastery is required of entry-level literacy skills. For students in secondary schools, this might mean mastery of the alphabetic principle, basic decoding of multisyllabic words, or additional fluency practice. Third, mastery of specific cognitive strategies are selected and implemented independently by the user to solve a variety of learning challenges. For example, a student might be studying for an examination on the basic trigonometric functions and remembers to use the mnemonic SOH-CAH-TOA (e.g., *Sine* = *O*pposite leg divided by the *H*ypotenuse; *Cosine* = *A*djacent leg divided by the *Hypotenuse*; *Tangent* = *Opposite* leg divided by the *Adjacent* leg) as part of a first-letter mnemonic strategy. As illustrated previously, strategies are an approach to a task that makes use of appropriate skills based on self-regulated decision making. Level four is mastery of subject matter knowledge, including facts and concepts that are unique to each discipline (e.g., math, science, history, literature). Acquisition of subject matter requires an array of strategies that can be flexibly and automatically employed by the learner to understand the unique language of the content. Finally, the fifth level is mastery of higher-order thinking, including problem solving and generalization from the facts and concepts of one discipline to another (or into real-life situations). Without mastery of subject matter knowledge, higher-order thinking has nothing to draw from (see Deshler et al., 2001).

In summary, understanding that there are prerequisite skills and language necessary to learn strategies, along with realizing that strategies are themselves essential building blocks in the acquisition of and higher-order thinking of subject matter, is of great importance to strategy instruction. In short, strategies are not an end in and of themselves, but a critical link in developing independent learning. Finally, it is critical to note that strategy instruction provides an opportunity to explore a variety of subject matters. Whether a student is working on an adaptive or functional curriculum, controlled and advanced practice require texts (e.g. textbooks, authentic historical texts, job applications) to increase domain knowledge. Moreover, in the interest of creating self-determined individuals with disabilities who can enjoy the outcomes supported by IDEA 2004 (e.g., equal opportunity, full participation in society, and economic self-sufficiency), documents from beyond the school walls, such as college and job applications, health insurance paperwork, driver education manuals, and Internet literacy, can provide a wealth of relevant content to blend into strategy practice.

## Cognitive Strategy Instruction in a Multitiered System

Appropriate implementation of strategy instruction requires teachers to think carefully about four factors:

1.  What are the demands of my content area with which students seem to struggle?

2.  Which strategy will be most effective at helping my students meet these demands?

3.  What is the most appropriate pedagogy, given the context of my classroom (e.g., group size, student abilities, instructional resources)?

4.  How am I going to measure student response to instruction?

Finally, it is important to consider how the stages of acquisition and generalization complement the critical elements of a schoolwide model. First, pretest screening provides essential information about individual learner strengths and areas of challenge, clearly indicating whether strategy instruction is warranted. In addition, screening provides baseline data to measure future student responsiveness to instruction during progress monitoring and posttesting. Second, verbal, controlled, and advanced practice requires teachers to perform regular progress monitoring to assess student rate and level of growth as affected by the instructional sequence. Consequently, instructional intensity, including number of practice trials, group size, and instructional time, can be shifted to maximize learner outcomes. Third, the stages of instruction provide a framework for teachers to self-assess their own levels of implementation (treatment integrity). If teachers adopt only some components of the stages of instruction and do not see sufficient student response, then they may be inclined to implement with higher levels of fidelity before additional measures are taken. Finally, engaging in the steps helps teachers to successfully mediate student learning by transferring strategy responsibility and understanding to the student. Moreover, engaging in strategy instruction may promote teacher fluency with evidence-based practices and encourage dialogue across departments and programs to successfully support implementation and generalization for students to postsecondary environments.

## SOCIAL/BEHAVIORAL INTERVENTIONS

Just as students with disabilities often require academic interventions, some students may also benefit from social/behavioral interventions to support development of social competence that is appropriate for secondary schools. Positive behavior support (PBS) is an evidence-based social/behavioral intervention providing a system of climate and supports for learning.

### Climate and Supports for Learning

As discussed, today's schools have increased accountability for students' academic success. Academic achievement and social competence do not exist in isolation; they are related (Maguin & Loeber, 1995; Morrison, Anthony, Storino, & Dillon, 2001; Nelson, Benner, Lane, & Smith, 2004; Roeser & Eccles, 2000). The practices high schools often use to address problem behaviors (e.g., detention, suspension) remove students from the learning environment, directly affecting potential for academic growth (Colvin, Kameenui, & Sugai, 1993; Farmer, 1996; Mayer, 1995).

In addition, secondary students often remove themselves from instructional environments. In an analysis of high school office discipline referral (ODR) data from 2006–2007 in a schoolwide information system (SWIS) database (May et al., 2003), researchers found that "tardy" and "skip from class or school" were two of the top three reasons students were referred to the office (Flannery, McGrath Kato, Fenning, & Bohanon, 2007). Students who are excluded and who have deficits in both academic performance and social competence are at an even greater risk of dropout than students with problems in only one of these areas (McKinney, 1989). This is a major barrier for students with disabilities in completing high school and gaining access to college.

As discussed, secondary schools have a number of evidenced-based practices to guide academic instruction. Though the curriculum for social competence (e.g., classroom rules, expected social norms) and the responsibility to teach social skills is traditionally less explicit than academic skills, it is present in what Jackson (1968) coined the "hidden curriculum" in the school. For example, all schools and classrooms have established expectations for behavior. There are schoolwide expectations about how students should interact with each other (e.g., language, public display of affection, fighting) and how to behave in class, at assemblies, at athletic events, and in the hall. Unfortunately, students are often given only global information and a high school handbook as a means of teaching these expectations. Many students do not understand these expectations until they see others receive consequences for violating the expectations (Flannery, Dickey, Nakayama, Calderhead, & Sugai, 2003). Students with disabilities need explicit feedback and, often, individualized interventions to help them adjust to the demands of the school setting. This supports the need for more explicit instruction related to appropriate expectations. In addition, these needs continue in postsecondary educational settings with variations across environments (e.g., residence halls, classrooms, activity centers) and professors.

> The team might want to examine its handbook and training on expectations for alignment with postsecondary education and work expectations. Making these connections more obvious helps the students see the relevance as well as prepares them for the future. Where there are differences in expectations, students may require additional transition planning to prepare for future environments of postsecondary education (i.e., additional freedom, intermittent contact with professors, and flexible schedules).

Many states, as part of adopting statewide academic content standards, have begun to establish an explicit curriculum in some of these social competence and work force skill areas. States now require documenting things such as "essential skills" (Oregon) or "standards of the heart" (Wisconsin) in order for a student to receive a high school diploma. These skill standards were developed based on the skills necessary for success as a caring, contributing, productive, and responsible citizen and employee. These standards include problem solving, collaborative decision making and teamwork, and healthy and positive relationships among students and between students and adults. Developing more explicit standards in nonacademic areas can be used to assist schools in developing a more explicit curriculum linked to increasing students' social competence.

## Schoolwide Positive Behavior Support

Comprehensive schoolwide efforts may relate to an improvement in perceived positive interactions between secondary students and the school personnel who serve them (Glover, 2005). SWPBS is a systemic approach for improving the social competence and academic achievement of all students. SWPBS is not a specific model, but an approach that uses effective practices, interventions, and systems-change strategies. SWPBS creates a consistent, predictable, and positive environment for all students, which is critical to the high school survival of many students with disabilities who have social skills deficits. The SWPBS model is based on a three-tiered approach to prevention (Lewis & Sugai, 1999; Sugai et al., 2000; Walker et al., 1996), which was described previously.

The systematic implementation of SWPBS is built on the following components: 1) operationally defined and valued outcomes for all students, 2) systems supports, 3) data-based decision making, and 4) research-based practices for both prevention and intervention (see Figure 5.2).

### Operationally Defined and Valued Outcomes

Students making the transition to and being successful in postsecondary education will be required to have solid academic knowledge as well as behaviors needed to work in a group learning environment. Outcomes include the behavior or academic targets that provide the focus of implementation. At the high school level, some outcomes may be measured through data such as graduation rate, credit accrual, suspensions/expulsion rates, attendance rates, and passing state assessments. School team members identify desired outcomes (e.g., graduating, reducing office discipline referrals), link these outcomes to data that are routinely collected, and then review these data regularly to facilitate ongoing decision making to determine the effects of interventions on their desired outcomes.

### System Supports

Supports are needed at the classroom, school, and district levels to implement SWPBS as a successful, effective, and sustainable program. These systems include

**Figure 5.2.** Schoolwide positive behavior support (SWPBS) systemic implementation. (From OSEP Center on Positive Behavioral Interventions and Supports. [2009]. *What is school-wide positive behavioral interventions & supports?* Retrieved August 12, 2009, from http://www.pbis.org/common/cms/documents/WhatIsPBIS/ WhatIsSWPBS.pdf; reprinted by permission.)

development of a leadership team, with support from administrators; communication with staff and faculty; and the provision of training, policy, and organizational supports. The leadership team should be representative of the school faculty and staff (e.g., teachers, security, counselors). In high school, this often results in a fairly large team, with representatives from each of the departments or divisions, and often operates through subcommittees. This team regularly reviews existing data, develops an action plan for implementation, and communicates through department and faculty meetings.

Implementing a new system also requires communicating clearly, training, and coaching. The reason schoolwide models have been slow to develop in high schools relates to the difficulty in creating a school structure that effectively addresses challenging behaviors and fosters success for all students. Professionals concerned with transition to postsecondary education should be involved in developing this systemic effort and should also support the provision of ongoing training and team building so that these evidence-based practices can be implemented.

### Data-Based Decision Making

Collecting and using data to aid in decision making is a major feature of the team process within SWPBS. Data are essential for defining the behavioral outcomes as well as monitoring the ongoing effect of the intervention practices on behavior. This includes developing data management systems that provide staff efficient access to data in order to inform decisions at every level and to measure the implementation efforts. In a problem-solving model, it is critical that responses are based on reviewing data on a regular and frequent basis for identifying problems early and documenting success. Data may indicate that a disproportionate number of referrals are coming from the hallways between classes or that the students with the highest rate of ODRs are also those students who are failing classes during the time of referral. This data-driven approach encourages a focus on solving problems rather than the traditional focus on "problem students" or the inabilities of students with specific disabilities (e.g., ADHD, traumatic brain injury, autism spectrum disorder [ASD]) to function "normally."

The type of data being used for decision making depends on what is being monitored or considered. At the universal and targeted level, schools are examining data such as ODRs, number of classes passed, credits accrued, state assessment scores, and attendance. Problems identified at this level of data collection can be addressed by implementing universally designed strategies that are effective for students with and without disabilities. In addition, schools regularly look at this aggregated data by some subgroups such as grade, disability, or cultural groups. For example, a school recently found that although their suspension and expulsion rate overall was acceptable, disaggregated data for students from minority ethnic groups had a much higher rate of suspension and expulsion. This school implemented several interventions, including developing student cultural leadership groups, to engage students in school life and educate staff regarding their different cultures. As another example, if data indicate that students with Asperger syndrome are being disciplined at a high rate during lunch, then a small group or individualized intervention to address student problems or practice appropriate lunch behaviors might be required.

> Schools should consider how different types of data interact for individuals or groups of students. Perhaps they should consider that there is a decrease in office discipline referrals and suspensions (good) but then add in the fact that expulsion and drop-out rates are up. Or maybe they should consider that students who are failing three or more courses are also those who are frequently late for or absent from those same classes.

Data also are used to 1) describe, choose, and evaluate goals/outcomes and 2) guide which practices should be selected and/or adapted to achieve goals/outcomes. One school collected ODR data, and after reviewing the data, the team was concerned about the number of students who were tardy to class. The team did not find specific classes or times of day that were a problem, so they checked their universal system, rather than targeting the large group of students with many class tardies. The team surveyed teachers regarding the implementation of the tardy policy (e.g., the 5-minute rule, the consequences), and they surveyed students related to the function of the behavior—why were they late. Both of these pieces of information gave the school a number of areas to improve before they put an elaborate system in place to deal with tardies (e.g., teacher consistency of policy implementation, students struggling academically so they avoid going to class, teachers themselves not being on time for class).

### Evidence-Based Practices for Both Prevention and Intervention

Focusing on prevention and using evidence-based practices are two key foundational components of the SWPBS. Focusing on prevention is evident at all three levels of the system. For example, at the universal level, schools implement strategies to prevent problem behaviors and provide a positive host environment for the entire school community. This is done by establishing and teaching schoolwide behavioral expectations, establishing an acknowledgment system, and ensuring staff are using effective instructional practices and relevant curriculum. School leaders increasingly expect investment in practices and procedures that are supported by rigorous research evidence. An example of an evidence-based practice is the Check and Connect program (Sinclair, Christenson, Evelo, & Hurley, 1998). The Check is for the close monitoring of students and their school performance. The Connect focuses on the connection between staff and student as well as partnerships between the school, family, and community service providers. Each student has an individual (e.g., a teacher, support staff, administrator) who reviews the student's performance (e.g., attendance, office referrals, grades) and quickly intervenes if necessary. This individual also serves as an advocate and provides feedback and encouragement to the student, emphasizing the importance of remaining in school.

A number of resources have been developed to assist schools in selecting evidence-based practices. A task force established by the Council for Exceptional Children (CEC) identified research methodologies that met evidence-based criteria. These findings as well as guidelines for identifying evidence-based practices are available at the CEC research web site (http://www.cecdr.org). The U.S. Department of Education (2003) has sponsored a web site that describes evidence-based practices (http://www.whatworks.ed.gov). Finally, members of the Office of Special Education Programs Center on Positive Behavioral Interventions and Supports (2007) described evidence-based practices and the literature that provides the evidence behind SWPBS in a brief report available on the web site http://www.pbis.org.

## Research on Schoolwide Positive Behavior Support in High Schools

SWPBS began in elementary and middle schools; however, there is emerging evidence regarding the use of SWPBS in high schools (Bohanon et al., 2006; Bohanon, Flannery, Malloy, & Fenning, 2009; Bohanon-Edmonson, Flannery, Eber, & Sugai, 2005; Moroz, Fenning, & Bohanon, 2006; Warren et al., 2003).

Bohanon and colleagues (2006) demonstrated the effectiveness of universal (Tier 1) SWPBS interventions in an urban high school with a racially and ethnically diverse population. An external team from a university collaborated with the school staff to gather relevant data and implement the basic components of SWPBS (e.g., defining and teaching schoolwide expectations, rewarding appropriate behavior, using data for decision making). During implementation, there was a 20% reduction in ODRs as well as a decrease in the proportion of students receiving support at the secondary and tertiary level.

Moroz et al. (2006) implemented a classwide intervention within the context of universal schoolwide procedures to address student tardiness. Two classrooms in an urban high school that had a high rate of tardiness participated. The students were directly taught the expected behaviors necessary to prevent tardies and provided acknowledgment of on-time behavior. These two classrooms experienced significant reductions in student tardies when compared with nonparticipating classrooms. Being to class on time and having basic academic support skills (e.g., using a planner, monitoring assignments, setting goals) are critical elements for success in postsecondary education, so supports of this nature at the secondary level can have a direct effect on students' future success.

Swain-Bradway and Horner (in press) described an example of an intervention at the secondary level. The school initially implemented a behavior education program (BEP; Crone, Horner, & Hawken, 2003). After an initial period of success, the students rapidly returned to their former social behavior patterns within the classroom setting. Informal interviews with the students indicated that they valued the positive adult interactions provided by BEP implementation, but their continued academic failure was negatively affecting classroom behavior. As a result, an academic support class was added to provide academic enabling skills (e.g., using a planner, monitoring assignments, setting goals). Following its implementation, students experienced positive outcomes such as reductions in ODRs, improvement in behavior, organization, and rate and quality of assignment completion. This pilot study provides an example of the interplay between academic and social competence and highlights the need for high schools to develop preventative interventions that address and monitor such.

## APPLYING LESSONS LEARNED FOR SUCCESSFUL IMPLEMENTATION OF A SCHOOLWIDE MODEL FOR ACADEMIC AND BEHAVIOR SUPPORTS

As high schools implement schoolwide models to support students' academic and social behavior, researchers are beginning to document features of effective high school implementation.

### Attention to Infrastructure and Capacity

Because high schools group departments by content area, faculty and staff are typically more accustomed to working within departmental models, rather than thinking in the context of school models. For teachers, the departmental model drives their understanding and perceptions of the school system (Murphy et al., 2001). Pedagogical beliefs and practices differ systematically from one teaching field to another. For example, mathematics and foreign language faculty approach teaching from a sequential and cumulative fashion, whereas English and social studies faculty emphasize comprehension of general principles and fundamental processes.

When implementing a schoolwide model, departmental structures should be recognized and utilized as the mechanism for sharing information, supporting teachers, and implementing change. School teams must have clear lines of communication with the departments and a representative voice on the schoolwide team. Some high schools have found it more productive to share general information in all-school meetings and follow up in departments to discuss, digest, and provide feedback regarding issues and solutions. There may also be benefits to differentiating implementation of a specific strategy by department. For example, science teachers may have specific behavior rules associated with lab activities and a specific academic strategy (e.g., writing lab reports). Because of the differences between departments, it is critical to obtain consensus on the desired behaviors or instructional outcomes and then to work with departments to ensure all staff and students are clear about expectations.

The role of administration is also critical. The participation and leadership of the administrators will affect the success of any initiative. In high schools, a school administrator is often assigned to be a member of a schoolwide team, but this administrator is only one of the administrators in the high school. If an initiative is to be successfully implemented schoolwide, then the implementation team and the assigned administrator will need to work closely with the larger administrative team to develop procedures and strategies to keep the group updated on the implementation plan.

### Involvement of Students

As schools develop strategies and contexts that will promote student academic and social success, they need to consider both the features of the school environment and the characteristics of the students. The participation and "buy-in" of students is critical at the high school level. The National School Resource Network (1980) indicated that participation by those most affected by rules was important to achieve buy-in. High school students are looking for active participation in choices and decision making, want autonomy, and want to identify with and be included in peer groups. Students want to be engaged in school by having a voice in policy decisions, school organization, discipline, academic areas, and activities (Joselowsky, 2007).

Schools need to look for ways to gain input from students (including those groups of students who usually remain unheard) with respect to the school climate and suggestions for change (Joselowsky, 2007). Schools have included students as members of their schoolwide leadership team, but more often, students comprise a coexisting team that either meets regularly or as specific topics and issues arise. Some successful schools have a mechanism to obtain ongoing feedback from students through surveys, feedback boxes, teams of students representing student peer groups, and so forth. Moreover, such participation in this process by students with disabilities provides occasion to practice self-determination and leadership skills (Wehmeyer, Gragoudas, & Shogren, 2006).

> When building capacity for a schoolwide model, it is important to consider stakeholder involvement. One important constituency is students with disabilities. In fact, student development of self-determination and self-advocacy can be accelerated for students with disabilities involved in youth leadership opportunities. Moreover, such students could provide a valuable perspective within a multitiered model.

## Development of Relevant Expectations and Alignment with Policies

One of the underpinnings of a schoolwide model is developing positively stated and taught student expectations and rules that are consistently communicated and implemented. This clarity provides a foundation for a common culture and predictability for students and staff. This inclusive approach provides supports for students with disabilities to develop appropriate skills and behaviors to succeed in secondary and postsecondary environments. As a corollary, it does not allow for "accepting" inappropriate behaviors that might be typical for students with ASDs or Tourette syndrome that would not be adaptive to postsecondary education settings. Each school identifies the academic and behavioral expectations that are endorsed and emphasized by students, families, and educators that are then taught and consistently communicated and implemented schoolwide. Whenever possible, these should also align with and support achievement of any state standards that students and staff are expected to meet.

For example, with SWPBS, schools develop three to five positive expectations that are typically stated in one- to two-word phrases. Some high schools have adopted the same expectation language as their feeder middle and elementary schools, which is often something such as, *Be Respectful, Be Responsible, Be Safe.* In other high schools, the expectations are often constructed around a word such as *PRIDE* (Perseverance, Respect, Integrity, Diversity, Excellence), align with their school mascot (e.g., Lancer PRIDE, the Dragon Way, Viking Code), or align with their school initials (WHS—*Worth, Honor, Success).* In defining their expectations and rules, high schools focus not only on social behaviors, such as "use appropriate voice," but also on behaviors related to academic engagement, such as getting to class on time, bringing appropriate materials, turning in homework, and actively engaging in the learning process. These are the same skills that will be needed by students in order to be successful in less structured postsecondary educational settings.

When developing expectations and rules, school staff and students need to use language that aligns with the particular high school environment and its cultural expectations. Though the definitions may remain the same, the rules or how the expectations are implemented may vary from location to location within the school or from school to school. How a student is to behave in a classroom is different than in the hallway, cafeteria, or assembly. The important thing is the clarity of the expectations and rules so that students and staff feel that the responses are provided in a fair manner. School staff will need to have discussions, sometimes lengthy, to arrive at agreed-on schoolwide rules. Schools have agreed about some rules at a schoolwide level and then each department develops the rules for these schoolwide expectations that are appropriate for their respective teaching environments. For example, one school has PRIDE as their acronym for expectations, in which *P* represents participation. The health/physical education (PE) department describes this expectation as "get involved in activities, discussion, and wear PE uniform"; the language arts department describes it as "volunteer to read and be prepared to participate with the correct books, pencil, and planner"; and the English as a second language program describes it as "come to school every day and join a club." Because the students are moving across multiple environments as well as multiple teachers they also need to learn the skills to identify nuances in how expectations change. Transition teachers can adapt this approach to clarify for students that these skills are needed in postsecondary environments. For example, when describing Respect, teachers can discuss how in class discussions in college, a number of diverse views will be shared and students may not agree with them. That is okay, but students need to be respectful by listening and responding in a nonthreatening manner. Another school has a *P* in its acronym, but it stands for Personally Responsible. When discussing this expectation, teachers can talk about how students will need to be responsible for their work and request the tutoring or assistance they need. Special education teachers can also share that students show personal responsibility in college when they self-advocate and request the necessary accommodations. Students will need to identify variations in expectations from different people and settings when they graduate from high school and enter a new career or a postsecondary education setting. With the increased focus on post–high school success, some high schools also are beginning to frame these expectations and rules as they would relate to employment or postsecondary education. In other words, they use their schoolwide expectations as a tool to teach about expectations in post–high school environments. This is intended to improve both student buy-in and generalization of rules to the postsecondary environments.

## Data Collection for Decision Making

Data analysis for decision making on a schoolwide basis is somewhat new for high schools. Administrators and staff need to establish schoolwide outcomes, measures to monitor student progress, and acceptable standards for successfully achieving outcomes. Currently, schools have access to academic data at the end of a quarter (grades) or year (state academic assessments) and to social data (e.g., ODRs for major behaviors and attendance data) on an ongoing basis. Though these might be good measures, there is much discussion in the high schools about data that is important at the classroom level. By collecting ongoing progress monitoring data, teachers are able to make decisions about instructional conditions on a weekly basis, avoiding waiting for quarterly grades to determine if students are learning adequately. Because of the strong correlation between academic performance and social competence, it is important that schools examine multiple types of data when identifying issues of concern and determining interventions. For example, schools may analyze attendance records, on-task behavior, classes passed, and progress monitoring data. Given the varied settings involved in college, it might also be helpful for transition personnel to collect data related to social behaviors in after-school activities, sports, and on the school bus.

## SUMMARY

In summary, optimal preparation for transition to postsecondary education requires comprehensive implementation of academic and behavioral supports via a schoolwide model. There are two important reasons for using such a model of service delivery. First, transition to college begins with successfully completing high school, a task that is proving insurmountable for almost one third of all secondary school students, especially students with disabilities (Allensworth & Easton, 2007). This may be due in part to a mismatch between the demands of the secondary curriculum and common academic and behavioral characteristics of students with disabilities. Second, current rates of college enrollment (still lower than desired) and college graduation (considerably lower than desired) for students with disabilities demonstrate the need for further preparation in self-regulatory academic and social-behavioral strategies to facilitate meaningful learning. Secondary schools can teach students important social-behavioral skills that are critical to success in the postsecondary environment.

Implementing a schoolwide model improves postsecondary outcomes for students with disabilities in secondary schools. Such a model involves universal screening, research-based pedagogical practices, regular progress monitoring, and assessing rates of teacher fidelity of implementation. Equally important is how schools draw upon existing professional resources, including teachers, support personnel, and administration, throughout the school.

Two research-based interventions to consider are strategy instruction and SWPBS. Strategy instruction is well researched and focused on teaching students how to learn, encouraging future independent problem solving.

Research indicates that struggling adolescent learners, including those with identified disabilities, learn most efficiently when teachers use overt and explicit pedagogies such as those contained in the eight stages of the Learning Strategy Curriculum (e.g., Deshler & Schumaker, 2006; Swanson, 1999). Strategies are an essential element along a continuum of building blocks for content literacy at both the secondary and postsecondary level.

SWPBS has been implemented nationally in a number of high schools and is increasing each year. The active involvement of students in developing and implementing SWPBS is beginning to occur as well. The foundational principles remain constant across grade levels, but it is even more critical that a strong infrastructure and communication system is in place at the high school level.

The work in secondary schools is not yet complete, however. Although educational challenges around early literacy and SWPBS at the elementary school level have received considerable focus since the 1980s, similar work with adolescents is just beginning. Continued research is needed on schoolwide models (and others) to validate the dual application of RTI and SWPBS logic. In addition, the research community has a responsibility to validate and disseminate evidence-based practices and pedagogies for adolescent learners as well as standardized screening and progress monitoring assessments. Teacher preparation programs and ongoing school professional development must seek to infuse the principles of the schoolwide model as a critical part of their training. Finally, and perhaps most important, stakeholders in the community (e.g., students with disabilities, parents, relatives, educators) must be vigilant in these efforts, holding researchers and policy makers accountable for fiscal and programmatic decisions.

After decades without proactive systematic efforts to improve postsecondary outcomes for students with disabilities, it is time to implement a better model. Embracing the schoolwide model will have a dual effect on schools. First, infusing research-based practices such as strategy instruction and SWPBS will increase student performance in the classroom. Second, increased student performance will decrease the number of dropouts and increase graduation rates. By avoiding the current model that waits for students to fail before intervening with unsystematic and disconnected programs, a schoolwide model uses preventative means to change the landscape of the American classroom from one of frustration and failure for students with disabilities to one of opportunity and successful transition to college.

## REFERENCES

Allensworth, E., & Easton, J.Q. (2007). *What matters for staying on-track and graduating in Chicago Public High Schools: A close look at course grades, failures and attendance in the freshman year.* Chicago: Consortium on Chicago School Research.

Baker, S., Gersten, R., Dimino, J., & Griffiths, R. (2004, January). The sustained use of research-based instructional practice: A case study of peer-assisted learning strategies in mathematics. *Remedial and Special Education, 25*(1), 5–24.

Beck, I.L., McKeown, M.G., Hamilton, R.L., & Kucan, L. (1997). *Questioning the author: An approach for enhancing student engagement with text.* Newark, DE: International Reading Association.

Bohanon, H., Fenning, P., Carney, K., Minnis-Kim, M., Anderson-Harris, S., Moroz, K., et al. (2006). School-wide applications of positive behavior support in an urban high school: A case study. *Journal of Positive Behavior Interventions, 8*(3), 131–145.

Bohanon, H., Flannery, H., Malloy, J., & Fenning, P. (2009). *Utilizing positive behavior supports in high school settings to increase school completion rates. Exceptionality, 17,* 1–30.

Bohanon-Edmonson, H., Flannery, B., Eber, L., & Sugai, G. (Eds.). (2005). *Positive behavior support in high schools.* Retrieved July 30, 2007, from www.pbis.org/highschool.htm

Bremer, C.D., & Smith, J. (2004). Teaching social skills. *Information brief: Addressing trends and developments in secondary education, 3*(5).

Cheney, D., Malloy, J., & Hager, D. (1998). Finishing high school in many different ways: Project RENEW in Manchester, New Hampshire. *Effective School Practices, 17*(2), 45–54.

Cole, C., & Sugai, G. (2008, January 17). *SWPBS: Establishing district & community capacity (beyond classroom management).* Retrieved September 9, 2009, from http://www.pbis.org/common/pbisresources/presentations/district_1_18_08.ppt

Colvin, G., Kameenui, E.J., & Sugai, G. (1993). School-wide and classroom management: Reconceptualizing the integration and management of students with behavior problems in general education. *Education and Treatment of Children, 16*(4), 361–381.

Crone, D.A., Horner, R.H., & Hawken, L.S. (2003). *Responding to problem behavior in schools: The behavior education program.* New York: Guilford Press.

Deshler, D., Palincsar, A., Biancarosa, G., & Nair, M. (2007). *Informed choices for struggling adolescent readers: A research-based guide to instructional programs and practices.* Newark, DE: International Reading Association.

Deshler, D.D., & Schumaker, J.B. (2006). *Teaching adolescents with disabilities: Accessing the general education curriculum.* Thousand Oaks, CA: Corwin Press.

Deshler, D., Schumaker, J., Lenz, B., Bulgren, J., Hock, M., Knight, J., et al. (2001, May). Ensuring content-area learning by secondary students with learning disabilities. *Learning Disabilities Research and Practice, 16*(2), 96–108.

Eber, L., Sugai, G., Smith, C., & Scott, T.M. (2002). Wraparound and positive behavioral interventions and supports in the schools. *Journal of Emotional and Behavioral Disorders, 10*(3), 171–180.

Epstein, M., Nordness, P.D., Gallagher, K., Nelson, R., Lewis, L., & Schrepf, S. (2005). School as the entry point: Assessing adherence to the basic tenets of the wraparound approach. *Behavioral Disorders, 30*(2), 85–93.

Faggella-Luby, M., & Deshler, D. (2008). Reading comprehension in adolescents with LD: What we know. What we need to learn. *Learning Disabilities Research and Practice, 23*(2), 70–78.

Faggella-Luby, M.N., Schumaker, J.S., & Deshler, D.D. (2007). Embedded learning strategy instruction: Story-structure pedagogy in heterogeneous secondary literature classes. *Learning Disability Quarterly, 30*(2), 131–147.

Farmer, C.D. (1996). Proactive alternatives to school suspension: Reclaiming children and youth. *Journal of Emotional and Behavioral Problems, 5*(1), 47–51.

Flannery, K.B., Dickey, C., Nakayama, N., Calderhead, W., & Sugai, G. (2003). *Transition from 8th grade to 9th grade: Focus groups with 9th graders.* Unpublished manuscript, University of Oregon.

Flannery, K.B., McGrath Kato, M., Fenning, P., & Bohanon, H. (2007). *Office discipline referral patterns in high schools implementing school-wide positive behavior support (SWPBS): Preliminary findings.* Unpublished manuscript, University of Oregon.

Fuchs, L., Fuchs, D., Prentice, K., Burch, M., Hamlett, C., Owen, R., et al. (2003, June). Explicitly teaching for transfer: Effects on third-grade students' mathematical problem solving. *Journal of Educational Psychology, 95*(2), 293–304.

Glover, D. (2005). *The impact of a school-wide positive behavior support plan on high school students' perceptions of school climate and peer relationships.* Unpublished dissertation, Loyola University, Chicago.

Graham, S., & Harris, K. (2003). Students with learning disabilities and the process of writing: A meta-analysis of SRSD studies. In H.L. Swanson, K. Harris, &

S. Graham (Eds.), *Handbook of learning disabilities* (pp. 323–344). New York: Guilford Press.

Hawken, L.S., & Horner, R.H. (2003). Evaluation of a targeted intervention within a school wide system of behavior support. *Journal of Behavioral Education, 12,* 225–240.

Horner, R.H., Sugai, G., Smolkowski, K., Eber, L., Todd, A., Nakasato, J., & Esperanza, J., (2009). A randomized wait-list controlled effectiveness trial assessing school-wide positive behavior support in elementary schools. *Journal of Positive Behavior Interventions, 11*(3) 133–144.

Hughes, C., Deshler, D., Ruhl, K., & Schumaker, J. (1993, July). Test-taking strategy instruction for adolescents with emotional and behavioral disorders. *Journal of Emotional and Behavioral Disorders, 1*(3), 189–198.

Individuals with Disabilities Education Improvement Act (IDEA) of 2004, PL 108-446, 20 U.S.C. §§ 1400 *et seq.*

Jackson, P.W. (1968). *Life in classrooms.* Austin, TX: Holt, Rinehart & Winston.

Joselowsky, F. (2007) *Youth engagement, high school reform, and improved learning outcomes: Building systemic approaches for youth engagement.* Retrieved June 10, 2008, from bul.sagepub.com/cgi/content/abstract/91/3/257

Kline, F., Schumaker, J., & Deshler, D. (1991, June). Development and validation of feedback routines for instructing students with learning disabilities. *Learning Disability Quarterly, 14*(3), 191–207.

Kovaleski, J., Gickling, E., Morrow, H., & Swank, P. (1999, May). High versus low implementation of instructional support teams: A case for maintaining program fidelity. *Remedial and Special Education, 20*(3), 170–183.

LaFrance-Holzer, M. (2007). *The Test-Taking Strategy as an intervention for college students with learning disabilities.* Unpublished dissertation, University of Connecticut, Storrs.

Lane, L.K., Wehby, J., Menzies, H.M., Doukas, G.L., Munton, S.M., & Gregg, R.M. (2003). Social skills instruction for students at risk for antisocial behavior: The effects of small-group instruction. *Behavioral Disorders, 28*(3), 229–48.

Leedy, A., Bates, P., & Safran, S.P. (2004). Bridging the research-to-practice gap: Improving hallway behavior using positive behavior supports. *Behavioral Disorders, 29*(2), 131–138.

Lenz, B.K., Deshler, D.D., & Kissam, B. (2004). *Teaching content to all: Evidenced practices for middle and high school settings.* Boston: Allyn & Bacon.

Lenz, B.K., & Ehren, B. (1999). Strategic content literacy initiative: Focusing on reading in secondary schools. *Stratenotes, 8*(1), 1–6.

Lewis, T.J., & Sugai, G. (1999). Effective behavior support: A systems approach to proactive school-wide management. *Focus on Exceptional Children, 31*(6), 1–24.

Maguin, E., & Loeber, R. (1995). Academic performance and delinquency. In M. Tonry (Ed.), *Crime and justice: An annual review of research* (Vol. 20, pp. 145–264). Chicago: University of Chicago Press.

Malloy, M., & Cormier, G. (2004). Project RENEW: Building the community's capacity to support youths' transition from school to adult life. In D. Cheney (Ed.), *Transition of secondary students with emotional or behavioral disorders: Current approaches for positive outcomes* (pp. 180–200). Arlington, VA: Council for Children with Behavioral Disorders.

Marston, D., Muyskens, P., Lau, M., & Canter, A. (2003). Problem-solving model for decision making with high-incidence disabilities: The Minneapolis experience. *Learning Disabilities Research and Practice, 18*(3), 187–200.

Mastropieri, M., Scruggs, T., & Graetz, J. (2003). Reading comprehension instruction for secondary students: Challenges for struggling students and teachers. *Learning Disability Quarterly, 26*(2), 103–116.

Mastropieri, M., Scruggs, T., Spencer, V., & Fontana, J. (2003, February). Promoting success in high school world history: Peer tutoring versus guided notes. *Learning Disabilities Research and Practice, 18*(1), 52–65.

May, S., Ard, W., III., Todd, A.W., Horner, R.H., Glasgow, A., Sugai, G., et al. (2003). *School-wide information system*. Available online at University of Oregon, Educational and Community Supports web site: http://www.swis.org

Mayer, G.R. (1995). Preventing antisocial behavior in the schools. *Journal of Applied Behavior Analysis, 28,* 467–478.

McKinney, J.D. (1989). Longitudinal research on the behavioral characteristics of children with learning disabilities. *Journal of Learning Disabilities, 22,* 141–150.

Moote, G., Smyth, N.J., & Wodarski, J.S. (1999). Social skills training with youth in school settings: A review. *Research on Social Work Practice, 9,* 427–465.

Moroz, K., Fenning, P., & Bohanon, H. (2006). *The effects of guided practice, publicly posted feedback, and acknowledgement on classroom tardies in an urban high school implementing school-wide positive behavioral interventions and supports.* Unpublished dissertation, Loyola University, Chicago.

Morrison, G.M., Anthony, S., Storino, M., & Dillon, C. (2001). An examination of the disciplinary histories and the individual and educational characteristics of students who participate in an inschool suspension program. *Education and Treatment of Children, 24,* 276–293.

Murphy, J., Beck, L., Crawford, M., Hodges, A., & McGaughy, C. (2001). *The productive high school: Creating personalized academic communities.* Thousand Oaks, CA: Corwin Press.

National Association of State Directors of Special Education. (2006). *Response to intervention: Policy considerations and implementation.* Alexandria, VA: Author.

National School Resource Network. (1980). *Resource handbook on discipline codes.* Cambridge, MA: Oelgeschlager, Gun & Hahn.

Nelson, J.R., Benner, G.J., Lane, K.L., & Smith, B.W. (2004). Academic achievement of K-12 students with emotional and behavioral disorders. *Exceptional Children, 71,* 59–73.

Netzel, D., & Eber, L. (2003, March). Shifting from reactive to proactive discipline in an urban school district: A change of focus through PBIS implementation. *Journal of Positive Behavior Interventions, 5*(2), 71–79.

No Child Left Behind Act of 2001, PL 107-110, 115 Stat. 1425, 20 U.S.C. §§ 6301 *et seq.*

O'Neill, R.E., Horner, R.H., Albin, R.W., Sprague, J.R., Storey, K., & Newton J.S. (1997). *Functional assessment for problem behavior: A practical handbook* (2nd ed.). Pacific Grove, CA: Brooks/Cole.

OSEP Center on Positive Behavioral Interventions and Supports. (2007). *Is school-wide positive behavior support an evidence-based practice? A research summary.* Retrieved August 22, 2008, from http://www.pbis.org

OSEP Center on Positive Behavioral Interventions and Supports. (2009). *What is school-wide positive behavioral interventions & supports?* Retrieved August 12, 2009, from http://www.pbis.org/common/cms/documents/WhatIsPBIS/WhatIsSWPBS.pdf

Palincsar, A.S., & Brown, A.L. (1984). Reciprocal teaching of comprehension-fostering and monitoring activities. *Cognition and Instruction, 1,* 117–175.

Patwa, S. (2003). *The effect of a strategic instruction intervention on the mastery of information by postsecondary students with learning disabilities.* Unpublished doctoral dissertation, University of Connecticut, Storrs.

Perie, M., Grigg, W., & Donahue, P.W. (2005). *The nation's report card.* Washington, DC: National Center for Education Statistics.

Pressley, M., & Hilden, K. (2006). Cognitive strategies: Production deficiencies and successful strategy instruction everywhere. In D. Kuhn & R. Siegler (Eds.), *Handbook of child psychology: Cognition, perception, and language* (6th ed., Vol. 2, pp. 511–556). New York: Wiley.

Roeser, R.W., & Eccles, J.S. (2000). Schooling and mental health. In A.J. Sameroff, M. Lewis, & S.M. Miller (Eds.), *Handbook of developmental psychopathology* (2nd ed., pp. 135–156). New York: Kluwer Academic/Plenum.

Rowan, B.R., Correnti, R., & Miller, R.J. (2002). What large-scale, survey research tells us about teacher effects on student achievement: Insights from the prospects study of elementary schools. *Teachers College Record, 104*(8), 1525–1567.

Simonsen, B., Shaw, S., Faggella-Luby, M., Sugai, G., Coyne, M., Rhein, B., Madaus, J., & Alfano, M. (in press). A school-wide model for service delivery: Redefining special educators as interventionists. *Remedial and Special Education.*

Simonsen, B., & Sugai, G. (2007). Using school-wide data systems to make decisions efficiently and effectively. *School Psychology Forum, 1,* 46–58.

Sinclair, M.F., Christenson, S.L., Evelo, D.L., & Hurley, C.M. (1998). Dropout prevention for high risk youth with disabilities: Efficacy of a sustained school engagement procedure. *Exceptional Children, 65,* 7–21.

Sugai, G. (2001, June 23). *School climate and discipline: School-wide positive behavior support.* Paper presented at the National Summit on Shared Implementation of IDEA, Washington, DC.

Sugai, G., Horner, R.H., Dunlap, G., Hieneman, M., Lewis, T.J., Nelson, C.M., et al. (2000). Applying positive behavior support and functional behavioral assessment in schools. *Journal of Positive Behavior Interventions, 2*(3), 131–143.

Swain-Bradway, J., & Horner, R.H. (in press) High school implementation of the behavior education plan. In D. Crone, R. Horner, & L. Hawkin (Eds.), *Responding to problem behavior in schools: The behavior education program.* New York: Springer.

Swanson, H.L. (1999). Reading research for students with LD: A meta-analysis of intervention outcomes. *Journal of Learning Disabilities, 32*(6), 504–532.

Swanson, H.L., Hoskyn, M., & Lee, C. (1999). *Interventions for students with learning disabilities.* New York: Guilford Press.

The University of Kansas Center for Research on Learning. (2009). *30 x 30: Thirty stories of success, hope and innovation.* Lawrence: Author.

U.S. Department of Education. (2003). *What works clearinghouse.* Available at http://www.whatworks.ed.gov

Vaughn, S., Linan-Thompson, S., & Hickman, P. (2003, June). Response to instruction as a means of identifying students with reading/learning disabilities. *Exceptional Children, 69*(4), 391–409.

Wagner, M., Newman, L., Cameto, R., & Levine, P. (2005, June 1). *Changes over time in the early postschool outcomes of youth with disabilities.* A report of findings from the National Longitudinal Transition Study (NLTS) and the National Longitudinal Transition Study-2 (NLTS-2).

Walker, H.M., Horner, R.H., Sugai, G., Bullis, M., Sprague, J.R., Bricker, D., et al. (1996). Integrated approaches to preventing antisocial behavior patterns among school-age children and youth. *Journal of Emotional and Behavioral Disorders, 4*(4), 194–209.

Warren, J.S., Edmonson, H.M., Griggs, P., Lassen, S.R., McCart, A., Turnbull, A., & Sailor, W. (2003, Spring). Urban applications of school-wide positive behavior support: Critical issues and lessons learned. *Journal of Positive Behavior Interventions, 5,* 80–91.

Wehmeyer, M.L., Gragoudas, S., & Shogren, K. (2006). Self-determination, student involvement, and leadership development. In P. Wehman (Ed.), *Life beyond the classroom: Transition strategies for young people with disabilities* (4th ed., pp. 41–69). Baltimore: Paul H. Brookes Publishing Co.

Wolgemuth, J., Cobb, R., & Alwell, M. (2008, February). The effects of mnemonic interventions on academic outcomes for youth with disabilities: A systematic review. *Learning Disabilities Research and Practice, 23*(1), 1–10.

# Technology Trends and Transition for Students with Disabilities

*Manju Banerjee*

## WHAT YOU'LL LEARN IN THIS CHAPTER:

- ✔ How assistive technology supports students with disabilities

- ✔ What are remedial and compensatory functions of assistive technology

- ✔ Differences in use of assistive technologies in high school and college

- ✔ How instructional technology is used in postsecondary education

- ✔ What technology skills and competencies are needed for college

- ✔ What steps to take for instructional technology preparedness in college

- ✔ What other technology factors affect equal access in postsecondary education

## MARY'S STORY

Mary was diagnosed with a reading disorder in third grade. She has been using audio books from Recording for the Blind & Dyslexic (RFB&D) ever since she can remember. Now, in high school, she downloads her textbooks from the RFB&D web site onto her iPod and listens to her books during the bus ride to school. Mary wants to go to college after she graduates. She and her transition coordinator believe that Mary has the necessary experience with assistive technologies for college success. Mary and students like her may be surprised to learn that many colleges now have laptop requirements for entering freshmen and technology competency standards for graduation. Assistive technologies used in grade school may not be enough for the technology-mediated postsecondary environment.

> Often referred to as the Net Generation or Millennials, today's students have grown up in a rich digital environment where technology is both transparent and ubiquitous. Technology has always been part of their lives, from the Internet to laptops, iPods, games, instant messaging (IM), cell phones, and pagers. They take technology for granted—they expect it to be integral to their lives and to serve them, including in education. (Campbell, Oblinger, et al., 2007)

## CHAPTER OVERVIEW

There is no dearth of testimony regarding the tremendous rate at which technology is influencing instructional pedagogy, knowledge acquisition, and interaction and communication in higher education. This chapter focuses on the traditional and contemporary role of technology in education and its significance for students with disabilities making the transition from high school to postsecondary education. Included are discussion of the expanding role of technology in higher education and implications for technology competency for college courses, legal mandates regarding assistive technology in school and college, issues of technology ownership, and availability of assistive technologies in postsecondary education. Both the promise and potential pitfalls of technology for students with disabilities making the transition to college are addressed.

Until recently, basic computer word processing skills were the only technological competencies required of college students for a general baccalaureate degree. Students equipped with knowledge of word processing and the rudiments of electronic messaging could declare themselves technologically literate. This view has undergone a radical transformation in recent years. College students today are by far the largest group of Internet users in the general population (Allen & Seaman, 2007). According to the U.S. Department of Labor report on trends and challenges for work in the 21st century, "We are living in a new economy—powered by technology, fueled by information, and driven by knowledge" (1999). The impact of technology in education is being felt both at the secondary and postsecondary levels. In

1994, the percentage of classrooms in the United States with at least one computer with Internet access was 3%; in 2002, the percentage was at 92% (North Central Regional Educational Laboratory, 2003). In 2005–2006, the average number of computers to students in classrooms across the country was 1:4 (U.S. Census Bureau, 2006). This is an unprecedented adoption rate for any technology by schools in the United States, even surpassing textbooks (Leu, Kinzer, Coiro, & Cammack, 2004).

## INFUSION OF TECHNOLOGY IN HIGHER EDUCATION

Technology is redefining traditional perceptions and approaches in higher education as it is mandated by law, recognized by educators as a significant element of contemporary education, and validated by its prolific use by students. Awareness of the ways in which technology has transformed and is continuing to reshape postsecondary education is an important component of a successful college experience for all students (Parker & Banerjee, 2007), but it is of particular significance to students with disabilities making the transition to college. Technology is no longer an access tool, but instead it has redefined the threshold of skills required for successfully completing postsecondary education. For the current generation of college students, with or without disabilities, being fluent in technology is not a novelty, but rather an essential element of college survival (Brinckerhoff & Banerjee, 2006). High school students making the transition to college need to be prepared to enter an educational arena in which technology is regularly used to engage, communicate, and assess student learning.

### Technology Trends and Disabilities

Technology in education is an ongoing phenomenon that picked up momentum in the early 1980s with the advent of the personal computer and the introduction of the Internet into the public domain. For students with disabilities, personal computers were the "great equalizer" that afforded flexibility in learning and expression while extending an individual's potential for academic success (Day & Edwards, 1996). Students whose essays and writing scores on high-stakes tests were constrained by weak spelling skills could use a computer with a built-in spell checker, hence eliminating spelling as a hindrance to the writing process (Thompson, Thurlow, Quenemoen, & Lehr, 2002). Word processing and computational capabilities inherent within computers allowed students to circumvent a host of academic challenges including poor grapho-motor skills, limited numeration proficiencies, weak decoding, and poor abilities to visualize abstract concepts.

Special education teachers and disability service providers turned to the capabilities of the computer to further their students' basic literacy skills, introduce learning strategies augmented with technology, and compensate for functional limitations within the individual with technology tools (McNaughton, Hughes, & O'fiesh,1997). For students with disabilities, computers afforded flexibility in learning and expression, and provided an array of supports that had the potential to increase the individual's learning capabilities (Day & Edwards, 1996). Assistive technologies became the solution for students with disabilities, both in grade school and in college.

**Box 6.1.**   Examples of assistive technologies often used by students with learning disabilities

- Word processing with automatic spell check, grammar check, thesaurus, and dictionary, autosummarizing tools
- Word prediction and outlining features
- Built-in calculators within commonly used programs
- Audiobooks
- Personal FM systems (i.e., systems that use a microphone and headset for students with auditory impairments)
- Optical character recognition systems with speech synthesis and text-to-speech software (i.e., voice output systems that read back text displayed on a computer screen)
- Speech recognition systems (i.e., systems that allow the user to operate the computer by speaking to it)
- Data managers (technologies that store personal information for students with organization and memory impairments)
- Closed-circuit television (CCTV)
- Large-print books
- Electronic notebooks

### Assistive Technology

Assistive technologies help bridge the gap between a student's current level of academic functioning and the expected level of proficiency in a given educational context (Anderson-Inman, Knox-Quinn, & Szymanski, 1999). Assistive technologies were first introduced as a component of rehabilitation services in the late 1950s (Mull & Sitlington, 2003). According to the Technology-Related Assistance for Individuals with Disabilities Act (Tech Act) of 1988 (PL 100-407), "assistive technology is any item, piece of equipment, or product system whether acquired commercially off the shelf, modified or customized, that is used to increase, maintain, or improve functional capabilities of individuals with disabilities" (§ 140 25). See Box 6.1 for examples of assistive technologies often used by students with learning disabilities. Assistive technology solutions for students with disabilities can broadly be classified into two categories (Silver-Pacuilla, Ruedel, & Mistrett, 2004). The first provides remedial support of specific skills through repetition, drill/practice, and real-time feedback, and the second provides compensatory support for functional limitations due to the disability. Each of these assistive technology solutions are discussed further in the following sections.

*Assistive Technology as Remedial Support*   The expectation that students will acquire basic literacy skills in reading, writing, and math by the time they graduate from high school is often erroneous. According to a report by the National Center on Education Statistics (NCES, 2004), 42% of community college freshmen and 20% of freshmen in 4-year institutions enroll in at least one remedial course. These percentages represent one third of all college freshman. Assistive technologies support remedial coursework by:

- Creating multiple opportunities for drill and practice

- Functioning as an extension of instruction

- Providing corrective feedback in real time (i.e., instantly)

- Allowing students to work independently at their own pace and own time

- Supporting user-controlled and self-determined choices by the student within the learning process

There are many technologies that offer remedial support. Consider the following illustrations. The Geometer's Sketchpad (http://www.keypress.com/x5521.xml) is an educational technology tool that can be used to remediate basic skills in numeration, operations, algebraic thinking, geometry, and measurement at the high school level. Dynamic visualization of core mathematical concepts in Geometer's Sketchpad can be used by instructors and students to supplement remedial instruction in algebra and geometry. Another example is the Criterion online writing evaluation. The Criterion is a web-based application produced by the Educational Testing Service (ETS) that provides K–12 teachers, as well as writing instructors at community colleges and other institutions of higher education, with remedial and diagnostic feedback on students' essays. Students draft and submit essays and receive immediate feedback in the form of a holistic score and diagnostic annotations within each essay that guide writing instruction (see http://criterion.ets.org). Other examples include software that creates a test bank of items for drill and practice.

It is important to note, however, that assistive technology for remediation of basic skills for students with disabilities at the postsecondary level is not as common as in high school. The use of assistive technology by college faculty to instruct students in skill remediation is not regular practice. College faculty are content experts and typically not concerned with software and/or technological devices that focus on basic skill remediation. The onus, therefore, is on students to identify assistive and other technologies that can help them practice basic skills in reading, writing, and math. If properly used, the Internet can be a great resource for remediation. In preparation for college, high school students may wish to learn skills for Internet literacy and web navigation to identify *credible* sites that can provide them with another explanation on a given topic (e.g., quadratic equations, causes of the Civil War). Web sites can provide information that is scaffolded with multimedia or is at a lower readability level than the textbook and therefore can facilitate learning. Opportunities for problem solving and practice can be greatly expanded through the Internet (Leu et al., 2007). Of course, students need to be aware of the caveat that comes with any Internet search—many sites and links on the Internet are unstable, often personal opinions, or simply inaccurate. Internet literacy is of paramount importance for post–high school

**Box 6.2.**   Examples of Internet skills

Skills required for learning in open environments such as the Internet are different from skills required for learning in closed environments such as a textbook.
   Internet literacy includes ability to

- Identify a clearly defined question or search query, which starts the reading or search process

- Navigate links and locate information to read

- Critically evaluate the information identified

- Synthesize the information (through the choices made about sites to visit and links to follow)

- Communicate the information in writing or oral format

*Source:* Leu et al. (2007).

transition, and students should start developing awareness and fluency with Internet literacy skills in middle and high school. (See Box 6.2.)

*Assistive Technology as Compensatory Support*   Compensatory support for individual academic challenges due to a disability is the second way assistive technology can be used at the postsecondary level. A student with visual impairment or decoding deficits who uses text-to-speech software is applying assistive technology in its compensatory capacity to circumvent difficulties in reading print. When students are confronted with words and phrases they cannot read, they typically either skip the word or ask for assistance. Computers equipped with speech capabilities can provide students with instant and repeated audio feedback at the word, sentence, and paragraph level.

Assistive technologies that serve a compensatory function are often identified as technology-based *accommodations*. Their primary function is to augment the student's strengths while compensating or circumventing the deficits. Accommodations at the postsecondary level are individualized changes or alterations to the planning, delivery, and assessment of instruction and learning that are designed to ensure equal opportunity for access by students with disabilities. A human reader is an accommodation often used by students with a reading disorder or visual impairment. The assistive technology counterpart to a human reader is audio books and/or a variety of stand-alone and packaged text-to-speech software and hardware. In a similar vein, accommodations such as a notetaker or scribe can be supplanted by audio recorders such as Audacity (http://www.audacity.sourceforge.net) and other note-taking technologies such as the Pulse smartpen (http://www.livescribe.com). In their compensatory role, assistive technologies serve to:

- Circumvent a specific functional limitation
- Allow students to keep pace with their peers in basic skills areas

- Create opportunities for equal access and participation

- Provide a range of accommodation that any eligible student with a disability is legally entitled to receive

## Differences in Assistive Technology Use in High School and College

It is important for students making the transition from high school to college to recognize that different parameters influence the availability, use, and adoption of assistive technologies between these two educational settings. If assistive technology is documented as part of a student's individualized education program (IEP), then schools are obligated to invest in acquiring and training the individual to use the technology. For example, if books in audio format are listed in a student's IEP, then the school must procure either membership with audio book lending libraries such as RFB&D or provide an alternative text-to-speech option. Use and adoption of assistive technology in high school is guided by instructional, remedial, and compensatory objectives as mandated by the Individuals with Disabilities Education Improvement Act (IDEA) of 2004 (PL 108-446).

At the postsecondary level, use and availability of assistive technology is dependent on eligibility for equal access and the college's obligation to provide "reasonable" accommodations, according to the Americans with Disabilities Act (ADA) of 1990 (PL 101-336) and the Americans with Disabilities Act Amendments Act (ADAAA) of 2008 (PL 110-325). A college may determine that books in alternate format are not a reasonable accommodation for a particular individual. As a result, students who develop familiarity with a particular assistive technology in high school, such as an assistive technology suite of tools (e.g., WYNN literacy software), may be disappointed to learn that the same is not automatically assured in a college setting. In other words, past familiarity with a particular assistive technology and/or past usage does not guarantee the same in college. Students have to demonstrate eligibility for a particular assistive technology through a review process based on disability documentation, history of use of assistive technology, intake interview, and institutional considerations of "reasonableness" and "undue burden." The role of assistive technology in college is not necessarily for skill improvement, content mastery, or academic success, although enhanced academic performance may result from using such technologies. The role of assistive technology in higher education is to serve as an accommodation for functional limitations due to the disability. For example, use of text-to-speech software as an accommodation for weak decoding skills will not necessarily improve reading fluency on its own, but will allow the student to keep pace with peers, given the volume of reading in college.

### Assistive Technology and IDEA 2004

Prior to 1988, there were several laws that addressed the benefits of assistive technology for individuals with disabilities, but none mandated its use. Since then, laws specifically addressing the assistive technology needs of people with disabilities have been passed. The Tech Act provided federal funds and required states and territories to develop programs related to the training and delivery systems for assistive technology devices and services for all individuals including children. The Tech Act was amended in 1998 as the Assistive Technology Act of 1998 (PL 105-394), further validating the importance of assistive technology in the lives of individuals with disabilities. The Tech Act amendment extended funding to 50 states and 6 territories to develop permanent, comprehensive, statewide programs of technology-related assistance.

Although the Tech Act of 1998 was the first to define assistive technology devices and services for individuals with disabilities, it was the Individuals with Disabilities Education Act (IDEA) of 1990 (PL 101-476) that first outlined the school's responsibility to provide assistive technology to students with disabilities. IDEA 1990 made it clear that school districts as public agencies were obligated to provide both assistive technology devices and services if it was "required" for the student to receive a free appropriate public education (FAPE). It therefore fell to the IEP team to determine what, if any, assistive technology was necessary.

Under IDEA 1990, assistive technology can be part of 1) special education (i.e., specifically designed instruction to meet individual needs), 2) related services (i.e., services that the student needs to benefit from special education), and/or 3) supplemental aids and services (i.e., aids and services provided in regular education classes or other education-related settings to enable students with disabilities to be educated with their peers without disabilities). Determination of assistive technology needs must be made on a case-by-case basis. For example, use of a school-purchased assistive technology device in a student's home may be permitted if the IEP team determines that the student needs access to this device in order to receive a FAPE. Ownership of the assistive technology, however, remains with the school, but may be transferred to the student, if necessary. The school cannot charge the student for normal wear and tear of the device.

IDEA 1990 makes a distinction between assistive technology devices and assistive technology services. Assistive technology devices are any items, pieces of equipment, or product systems, whether acquired commercially or off the shelf, modified, or customized, that can be used to increase, maintain, or improve the functional capabilities of a student with a disability. Assistive technology services are any services that directly assist a student with a disability in selecting, acquiring, and/or using an assistive technology device. Assistive technology services may include the following.

- Providing evaluation services to determine the assistive technology needs of a student, including functional evaluation in the student's customary environment

- Purchasing, leasing, or otherwise procuring the assistive technology devices

- Selecting, designing, fitting, customizing, adapting, applying, maintaining, repairing, or replacing assistive technology devices

- Coordinating and using other therapies, interventions, or services with assistive technology devices such as those associated with education and rehabilitation plans and programs

- Training and providing technical assistance to the student and/or the family (if appropriate)

- Training and providing technical assistance to educators, rehabilitation personnel, employers, and others associated with the student

Students must be assessed in order for them to receive assistive technologies under IDEA 1990. The IEP team must evaluate the student's functional capabilities and determine whether these capabilities can be increased, maintained, or improved through use of an assistive technology device or assistive technology services.

The Individuals with Disabilities Education Act Amendments (IDEA) of 1997 (PL 105-17) noted that assistive technology must be "considered" on all IEPs. The intent of the amendment was to encourage IEP personnel to develop expertise and knowledge about assistive technologies for students with disabilities.

### Assistive Technology and ADA 1990

Policies and protocol regarding the provision and use of assistive technology in postsecondary institutions are informed by ADA 1990. The onus is on the student to establish both need and eligibility for the technology. Students must present evidence of their need, which is then reviewed by postsecondary disability services personnel, and a determination is made regarding eligibility for appropriate assistive technology. Often, students must use the assistive technology at predetermined locations on campus, such as the media center or the computer lab in the disability services office, if the technology is a specialized piece of hardware or software that requires a user license. Some institutions offer short-term loans for equipment, but, in many instances, the student must purchase his or her own device or software if he or she has a preference for a particular technology not offered by the institution. The repertoire of assistive technologies is vast and constantly changing as new versions of products are introduced and innovative options are discovered. Postsecondary institutions typically do not evaluate students to identify an "assistive technology match." Students are responsible for articulating and advocating for their technology needs.

## Implications of Assistive Technologies for the Transition to College

Students making the transition to college need to be aware of the changes in legal mandate as well as use, availability, and ownership of assistive technologies in college. Students need awareness of and familiarity with specific assistive technologies that complement and reinforce their own approach to learning. By the time they are ready to start postsecondary education, students should be familiar with a core set of assistive technologies that they know how to access and use. Owning assistive technologies is one avenue to consider. Colleges and universities have varied policies regarding student ownership of assistive technologies. Some colleges provide short-term loans of hardware and equipment, but most require students to come to a technology lab to use specific assistive technologies. Other institutions provide assistive technology training as a fee-for-use service. High school students should meet with their transition counselors to discuss their legal rights regarding assistive technologies and options for ownership that may or may not be available in the college of their choice.

Special education teachers and other transition personnel should familiarize students with assistive technologies that are commonly used as accommodations and may be readily accessible in postsecondary settings. Three key considerations for transition coordinators preparing students for college include 1) developing student awareness of assistive technologies that facilitate "access" to reading, writing, organizing, and test taking; 2) training students on strategies for using assistive technologies for college-level coursework; and 3) promoting student independence and fluency with individualized assistive technologies.

Secondary personnel should prepare students (and their families) for the types of assistive technology accommodations that are both commonly available and not so readily available in postsecondary institutions. Students may expect to see assistive technologies such as membership to audio book lending libraries, a simple four-function calculator, a laptop computer or portable word processor for written examinations, and PowerPoint notes from the professor in lieu of a notetaker. Other assistive technologies often available in college include closed-circuit television (CCTV) and FM systems that focus the instructor's voice toward the listener. More personalized assistive technology options such as computer-aided real time (CART) transcription services, hand-held personal digital assistants (PDAs), and smartphones and smartpens are typically not provided to students by colleges and universities.

Awareness of assistive technologies that can be expected and those that may not be expected in college is an important aspect of transition planning. An appropriate starting point is exposure to instructional environments, activities, and assignments that simulate college-level demands. For example, secondary service personnel may engage high school students in identifying assistive technologies for active listening and notetaking in large lecture situations, discussion groups, and/or labs. Other practice tasks should include technologies that facilitate formal writing, reading, compiling information from multiple textbooks and online resources, organizing references, and preparing for oral presentations.

After students and transition personnel have identified individualized assistive technologies, the next step is developing independent strategic use of these technologies to achieve a specific goal. For example, audio books by themselves may not improve a student's reading comprehension. Students need to learn ways to use audio books with an active listening strategy (Banerjee, 2003). Similarly, technologies that allow students to record a lecture may not be effective unless students are also familiar with strategies for integrating class notes with other sources of information in that class. In the case where class notes are recorded as an audio file, students need to know ways to integrate and gain access to visual and auditory sources of information for enhancing their comprehension. (See Box 6.3.)

Finally, individualized assistive technologies and strategies must be practiced frequently so that students can develop independence and fluency with these technologies in context. One workshop or a single demonstration is typically not enough. It is recommended that secondary transition

---

**Box 6.3.** Active listening strategies for audiobooks

The following is an example of an active listening strategy for students with learning disabilities to apply when listening to audiobooks. Some students follow all four steps in chronology while others may skip one or two of the steps identified based on their preference for engagement with the listening process.

### STEP 1. PRELISTENING

The student is directed to view the cues and prompts that are traditionally intrinsic to a textbook but are not available when the book is converted into an audio file. These cues include paragraph demarcations, subtitles, bold print, print size variations, color, and the beginning and end of each section. During prelistening, the student takes mental or written notes about text versus graphics, pictures, and other visual information contained within the section. For example, the student may note that the text contains several flow charts which he or she may find helpful to see rather than listen to.

### STEP 2. GIST LISTENING

The student starts the audio file and listens to a section of the recording. Pace, volume, and length of listening section are controlled by the student. For example, the student may wish to listen to several pages or sections all at once or may wish to listen to only a few sentences at a time. The object of gist listening is to get the "gestalt" of the information without getting overwhelmed or losing the thread of the audio discussion. Students often prefer to listen to an entire fiction novel or short story during gist listening without pausing the recording. Other students prefer to stop at frequent intervals to self-monitor their comprehension and understanding of the audio information.

### STEP 3. STRATEGIC LISTENING

During strategic listening, the student pauses the audio play at self-paced intervals to either talk aloud or take notes on the information that he or she just heard. Notes may include information from other sources that are dropped into a note-taking format.

### STEP 4. REVIEW LISTENING

At the review listening stage, the student relistens to selected sections of the audio book to reinforce his or her understanding of the content.

---

counselors work in concert and collaboration with content teachers to facilitate the use of assistive technologies in the general education curriculum. For example, English teachers may be persuaded to be receptive to students submitting an essay outline using Inspiration software (http://www.inspiration.com). (See Box 6.4.)

## Box 6.4.   Technology-enhanced learning strategies

Inspiration is organizational software that allows students to sort and develop ideas for writing and presenting information in a visual and text-based outline format. Built-in templates within the software scaffold students as they work on a variety of topics, ranging from chronological sequencing of a time line to comparing and contrasting opposing views on a topic.

Teachers can model and demonstrate use of the Inspiration software in class and then have students use features within Inspiration to create mind maps and organizational flow charts and to brainstorm ideas for an assignment.

The following features of Inspiration highlight the uses of this technology as a learning tool.

1.  Make visual displays (diagrams, flow charts, concept maps) of your readings and notes.

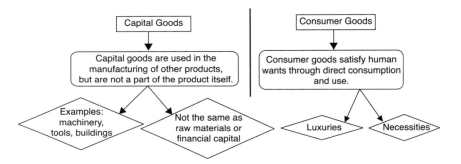

2.  Instantly switch back and forth between diagrams and outlines.

    A.  Capital goods
        1.  Capital goods are used in the manufacturing of other products, but are not a part of the product itself.
            a.  Examples:  machinery, tools, buildings
            b.  Not the same as raw materials or financial capital

3.  Use preexisting templates to organize your readings and notes.

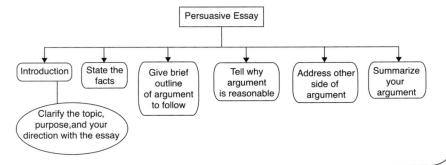

*(continued)*

(continued)

4.  Use signs, diagrams, and clip art to make your visual displays easier to follow.

Diagrams created in Inspiration® by Inspiration Software®, Inc. Clip art © 2009 Inspiration Software®, Inc. Used with permission.

## Instructional Technologies

Technologies used by faculty for instruction and communication in college serve a different purpose from technologies commonly identified as assistive or access technologies. Instructional technologies are used to plan, deliver, and assess learning through technology-mediated approaches. The Educational Testing Service defines information and communication technologies (ICT) literacy as "using digital technology, communication tools, and/or networks to access, manage, integrate, evaluate, and create information in order to function in a knowledge society" (2007, p. 11).

Institutions of higher education have been steadily increasing their adoption of instructional technologies. Early instructional technologies such as the mainframe-based learning systems were unwieldy and cumbersome. Later innovations made instructional technologies user friendly, cost effective, and highly efficient as a mode of communication and delivery. Then, the widespread use of the Internet revolutionized the way information could be stored, accessed, presented, and taught (Klotz, 1997). The Internet has now become a repository of instructional material, a medium of delivery, and a forum for communication among faculty, students, and administrators in higher education. For the purposes of this chapter, *instructional technology* is broadly defined to include hardware (e.g., computers, handheld devices, smartphones), software, and the Internet, as well as web-based systems of communication and instructional delivery tools (e.g., WebCT, Blackboard).

Instructional technologies engage students with disabilities in ways that have yet to be explored. Both assistive technologies and instructional technologies mediate the way students learn and interact in educational settings. The difference is that the focus of assistive technology is on compensation and remediation of *individual* limitations, whereas educational technologies are generic and involve learning in general. The following section underscores the increasing importance of instructional technologies for all college students, including students with disabilities.

### Instructional Technology Trends in Postsecondary Education

Understanding technology trends and the ways in which college students are adopting and using technologies is a necessary starting point for exploring the implications of instructional technologies for students with disabilities. In 2005, 52.8% of undergraduate students reported owning a laptop computer; the number was up to 75.8% in 2007 (EDUCAUSE Center for Applied Research, 2007). Frequency of Internet use is highest among teenagers and adolescents (ages 12–17), with 51% reporting that they use the Internet daily (Lenhart, 2007). By 2005, more than half (57%) of adolescents who were Internet users had also reported being media creators, having their own web page or blog and /or having posted their own creations, stories, photographs, or videos online (Pew Internet and American Life Project, 2005).

A distinguishing characteristic of the current generation of college students is use of real-time technologies that allow them to interact synchronously via text messaging and communicate in new and unique ways (Pew Research Center, 2007). According to the Pew Internet and American Life Project college survey (2005), 26% of college students use instant messaging to communicate, compared with 12% of other Internet users. Nearly three quarters (73%) of college students surveyed said that they use the Internet more than the library, whereas only 9% say they use the library more than the Internet for information searching. Students report using e-mail to set up appointments with professors (62%), discuss grades (58%), and get clarification on assignments (75%).

Networking is the fastest growing application of technology in higher education. College students are the most active users of social networking sites such as Facebook, MySpace, myYearbook, and Friendster; and of those who use social networks, 48% log onto the site several times a day (Lenhart, 2007). The opportunity to network has transformed the way colleges and universities conduct traditional campus-based practices. Information about college admissions, programs, support services, housing, and extracurricular activities are no longer confined to the pages of a college brochure or guide. More campus transactions are conducted through the high-speed interconnectivity of file servers, multiuser systems, and the Internet, as opposed to in-person contacts. High school students entering postsecondary institutions need to develop familiarity with communication in virtual environments and "netiquette" for such communication.

Online and technology-blended courses have been increasing exponentially since the mid-1990s. According to the NCES (2004) report, in 1995, 33% of all institutions of higher education offered some form of distance education courses to their students. This number jumped to 44% in 1997, an 11% jump in just 2 years. In 2000–2001, 56% of postsecondary institutions offered distance learning courses to their students. By Fall 2005, nearly 3.2 million students were enrolled in online courses (Allen & Seaman, 2007). Many courses today are technology-blended courses, which means technology is part of the instruction. Technology-blended courses are not asynchronous, such as online courses, but are often conducted with live access to the Internet and include use of course management software such as WebCT/Vista or Blackboard. Typically, blended courses combine face-to-face time with online learning.

As the conceptual framework of higher education changes, competencies and skills that define literacy for college students are also evolving (North Central Regional Educational Laboratory, 2003; Pew Research Center, 2007). College students today are more adept at using technology than any generation before them. As skills and competencies for instructional technologies become commonplace for all college students, high school students with disabilities must prepare for a technology-mediated environment that goes beyond access technologies.

### Implication of Instructional Technologies for Students with Disabilities

College students use technologies in ways that blur the line between academic and nonacademic uses, while demonstrating skills and competencies for instructional technologies. Yet, many students with disabilities, particularly learning disabilities and/or attention-deficit/hyperactivity disorder (ADHD), report a reduced level of comfort with instructional technologies (Parker & Banerjee, 2007). Parker and Banerjee noted that "despite their increasing participation in higher education, postsecondary students with these high incidence disabilities can encounter new barriers to educational access if they are not able to develop self-regulated, strategic approaches to using learning technologies" (p. 6). Readiness for college must therefore include use and familiarity with traditional assistive technologies, as well as mainstream instructional technologies.

Teachers and high school students can benefit from understanding three key elements of postsecondary instructional technologies. These elements can broadly be categorized as 1) accessibility of web-based instructional technologies, 2) learning strategies for mainstream technologies, and 3) technology competency requirements for admission and graduation from college. Each of these elements and their implications for transition are discussed in the following sections.

*Accessibility of Web-Based Instructional Technologies* Despite considerable progress, many instructional technologies continue to be inaccessible to students with disabilities. According to Hitchcock and Stahl (2003), most of the new technologies introduced since the mid-1980s have been inaccessible to individuals with disabilities. Finding accessible solutions to instructional technologies at the postsecondary level is complex because of the need for synchronization among multiple players. True access requires coordination among five key players and the student. These key players are designers of browsers (e.g., Internet Explorer, Netscape, America Online), vendors of assistive technologies (e.g., JAWS), web designers (e.g., alt tags, captioning), creators of markup language editors (e.g., Dreamweaver), and vendors of instructional software (e.g., WebCT, Blackboard). Accessibility is compromised if any one of these participants fails to recognize the needs of students with disabilities or the interdependency among them in creating an accessible environment. If the capability of one product is constrained by the limits of another, then full accessibility cannot be achieved.

Using the web and web-based information is commonplace in postsecondary research and inquiry. Yet, accessibility on the web is inconsistent. Students who are blind need audible outputs (e.g., screen readers that read web content using synthesized speech) or tactile outputs (e.g., a refreshable braille device to access web-based information). Students with reading disorders may also need audible output options such as text-to-speech software, whereas students with low vision may need screen magnification software that allows them to zoom into portions of the visual screen. Individuals who are deaf or hard of hearing and therefore unable to gain access to audio content need videos that are captioned or audios with transcription. Clearly, access to information delivered via the web has varied implications for students with different disabilities. High school personnel, and particularly transition coordinators, need to be able to query targeted postsecondary institutions regarding these and other accessibility features of the instructional technology system within the institution. Questions for postsecondary disability service providers should include queries about technology and software ownership, short-term loan of equipment for access, purchase of personalized devices, preference technologies, availability of technology training, tech maintenance services, course-authoring tools such as WebCT used by the college, procedures for online registration and accessibility, and technology competency requirements. (See Box 6.5.)

Unfortunately, many of the federal and statutory regulations addressing access for students with disabilities were passed before the Internet era (Edmonds, 2004). In 1998, Congress amended Section 508 of the Vocational Rehabilitation Act of 1973 (PL 93-112) to require all electronic and information technologies used by federal departments and agencies to be accessible to individuals with disabilities. In 1999, the U.S. Department of Education clarified that this mandate covers all state entities, including public colleges and universities. Edmonds noted, however, that although Section 508 addresses procurement of software, hardware, and other information technologies, it does not specifically apply to courseware and course management systems (e.g., WebCT, Blackboard) used by institutions for tech-blended and online courses. There are no specific regulations regarding accessibility of information technology in ADA 1990. Consequently, there are few legal guidelines that institutions of higher education must observe to ensure that their online and blended courses are accessible to individuals with disabilities from the start. Access is provided through accommodations as a retrofitted arrangement. Colleges and universities *may choose* to adopt laws similar to Section 508 to show compliance with accessibility requirements of ADA 1990. Some of these laws apply only to state agencies, whereas others include state universities and colleges within their purview. DO-IT (Disabilities, Opportunities, Internetworking, and Technology) organization directs the National Center on Accessible Distance Learning (NCADL), which is a center funded by the U.S. Department of Education that offers guidance and resources on making online and distance learning courses accessible. See the National Assistive Technology Technical Assistance Partnership (NATTAP; http://resnaprojects.org/nattap/RESNA.html) for more information on state accessibility regulations and resources.

High school students must therefore be prepared to identify and request accommodations for features of online and tech-blended courses that may pose barriers to gaining access to the course. Many commonly used course-authoring tools (e.g., WebCT, Blackboard) can be confusing to students with cognitive disabilities, such as learning disabilities. These students may have difficulty following real-time synchronous discussions and/or communication via e-mail

**Box 6.5.** Postsecondary disability service provider queries regarding assistive and instructional technologies

High school students preparing for transition to college should consider asking the following questions regarding assistive and instructional technologies to disability student services (DSS) office personnel:

- Does the DSS office offer demonstration and training on assistive technologies? What are the qualifications of staff who provide such trainings?

- Does the DSS office have trained technology specialists on staff?

- Does the DSS office have an assistive technology lab?

- Does the DSS office offer strategy instruction with technology? In other words, are there ways to enrich evidence-based learning practices with assistive and other instructional technologies?

- What are the assistive technologies on site that may be available for students with disabilities?

- Are assistive technologies available only in the DSS office, or can they be obtained at other locations as well, such as in the library, student center, writing lab, and so forth?

- Does the office provide short-term loans of equipment and software to students? What are the conditions of such loans?

- Is there training for students on instructional technologies such as WebCT and Blackboard on campus?

- Does the college or DSS office offer students summer trainings on assistive and instructional technologies?

- Does the college make recommendations regarding computer and software purchase? Is there a discount available for purchasing software through the college/university bookstore or other recommended source?

- Does the DSS office have information to guide students in their purchase of software that often serves as an accommodation, such as text-to-speech software, note-taking software, portable devices, and so forth?

- What is the DSS office's protocol for helping students problem-solve regarding technology issues and concerns?

or through an on-screen dialogue box. Deficits in speed of information processing can be heightened when students have to participate in live/real-time online discussions. It is therefore important for students with specific disabilities to be aware of the challenges of accessing the web and web-based courses at postsecondary institutions. Transition coordinators can promote

---

**Box 6.6.**  Example of an individualized education program
annual goal and short-term objective for building
technology skills

| | |
|---|---|
| *Annual Goal:* | Mary will demonstrate grade-appropriate planning and organizational skills on a computer for all of her writing assignments in English class. |
| *Short-Term Objective:* | Mary will be able to use Inspiration software to create outlines for at least two writing assignments every week in English class for a semester; she will receive feedback on the Inspiration-created outlines for the writing exercise that attests to mastery in creating draft outlines (i.e., a grade of *B* or higher). |

---

online communication skills by incorporating such skill development as annual
or short-term objectives in students' IEPs. (See Box 6.6.)

*Strategies for Instructional Technologies*  Strategies for using
instructional technologies is another area in which students with
disabilities must be cognizant. Students must be familiar with skills and
strategies specific to the digital medium to identify and gain access to
information in technology-based environments. One such skill is
navigation. Navigation within a textbook is linear and sequential, but
multimedia technologies can present navigational options that are more
exploratory in nature and often hierarchical. Functional limitations in
visual processing, visual sequencing, and cognitive flexibility can create
challenges in navigation in open learning environments such as the
Internet. Without prior experience in nonlinear navigation, students with
perceptual disabilities run the risk of getting lost in Internet cyberspace
(Leu et al., 2004).

Contemporary studies in literacy (Cope & Kalantzis, 2000; Lankshear
& Knobel, 2003; Lewis & Fabos, 2005) suggest that reading is a function of
the technology within which it is hosted. According to Leu et al. (2004),
there is no doubt that the Internet and other ICT are shaping new
perspectives on literacy. As reading in non–print-based media becomes
commonplace at the postsecondary level, the need to understand
strategies for reading on the Internet and alternative media becomes
critical for students with disabilities.

Students with cognitive disabilities may lack the proficiencies for
instructional technologies because of functional limitations due to the
disability. Many of the instructional communication technologies are visual
and involve written exchanges (e.g., e-mail). Fluency in visual processing
across multiple screens and the ability to retain positional memory during

scrolling is a necessary skill in such a learning environment. High school students making the transition to college need to be aware of these learning demands and develop strategies for addressing challenges inherent within some instructional technologies. For example, students may address loss of positional memory in moving from one screen to another by viewing information in split-screen format on their computer monitor. Software that allows the user to use two computer screens at once is another option. Scrolling can be reduced by decreasing font size. Students should work with their transition coordinator and/or a technology specialist as part of their transition planning to identify solutions for effective participation within instructional technologies.

Research-based evidence on learning strategies for technology-mediated environments is limited but emerging. Suggestions for developing strategies for students with disabilities planning to make the transition to college include awareness, use, and fluency with strategies for:

- Reading on the Internet

- Generating search words and phrases for online searches

- Conducting research using remote access e-databases

- Organizing desktop or hard drive using file management software

- Postings on course management systems such as Blackboard or WebCT

- Using e-tools within common word processing programs

- Participating in real-time online threaded discussions

- Deciphering refereed information from personal opinions

- Writing a research paper using electronic resources

- Using text, visuals, audio, and animation for class presentations

Students with disabilities need to be aware of instructional technologies used by college faculty, as well as have the opportunity to develop skills and fluency with technology strategies while in high school. Opportunities for fluency and practice are enhanced when teachers incorporate instructional technologies into the planning, delivery, and assessment of student learning in their coursework.

*Postsecondary Requirements for Technology Competency* Many colleges and universities have technology competency requirements that students must fulfill prior to graduation. These competencies range from simple skills such as being able to submit an e-mail with an attachment to creating a word processing document with clip art and scanned images, multimedia presentations, web pages, working with databases, conducting online literature searches, and working with statistical software. Some institutions of higher education use iSkills (http://www.ets.org/iskills), a standardized technology competency assessment test developed by the Educational Testing Service to assess critical thinking in a digital environment.

No doubt, students with disabilities need to be prepared for mainstream technologies as part of their transition planning for college. See the technology preparation for transition worksheet and checklist by Brinckerhoff and Banerjee (2006) for information on technology readiness for college.

## SUMMARY

For students with disabilities, the importance of preparing to use technology in college is undeniable. As students seek admission into postsecondary institutions in large numbers, they need to be aware of the ways technology has changed the postsecondary landscape and the profile of the average college student. Until now, the primary emphasis of transition planning and technology has been on technologies for access and accommodations. Students, teachers, IEP teams, and high school transition coordinators must now add readiness for postsecondary instructional technologies to students' transition portfolios. Awareness and development of skills and strategies for tech-blended and online learning is imperative if students with disabilities are to become successful college graduates.

## REFERENCES

Allen, I.E., & Seaman, J. (2007). *Online nation: Five years of growth in online learning.* Retrieved October 12, 2008, from http://www.sloanconsortium.org/publications /survey/pdf/online_nation.pdf

Americans with Disabilities Act (ADA) of 1990, PL 101-336, 42 U.S.C. §§ 12101 *et seq.*

Americans with Disabilities Act Amendments Act (ADAAA) of 2008, PL 110-325.

Anderson-Inman, L., Knox-Quinn, C., & Szymanski, M. (1999). Computer supported studying: Stories of successful transition to postsecondary education. *Career Development for Exceptional Individuals, 22*(2), 185–212.

Assistive Technology Act Amendments of 2004, PL 108-364, 29 U.S.C. §§ 3001 *et seq.*

Assistive Technology Act of 1998, PL 105-394, 29 U.S.C. §§ 3001 *et seq.*

Banerjee, M. (2003, July). *A strategies toolbox for students with learning disabilities: Reading with audio textbooks.* Presentation at the Association on Higher Education and Disability (AHEAD), Dallas, TX.

Brinckerhoff, L., & Banerjee, M. (2006). *Tech preparation: New challenges and opportunities for college-bound teens with LD and/or ADHD.* Retrieved September 4, 2006, from http://www.schwablearning.org/pdfs/expert_loring.pdf?date=8-21-06&status=new

Campbell, J.P., Oblinger, D.G., et al. (2007). *Ten top teaching and learning issues-2007.* Retrieved October 12, 2008, from http://connect.educause.edu/Library/EDUCAUSE+ Quarterly/TopTenTeachingandLearning/44831

Campus Computing Project. (2002). *Use of technology in college instruction expands.* Retrieved March 13, 2008, from http://www.adec.edu/user/2001/campus_ computing.html

Cope, B., & Kalantzis, M. (2000). Multiliteracies: The beginning of an idea. In B. Cope & M. Kalantzis (Eds.), *Multiliteracies: Literacy learning and the design of social futures* (pp. 3–8). London: Routledge.

Day, S.L., & Edwards, B.J. (1996). Assistive technology for postsecondary students with learning disabilities. *Journal of Learning Disabilities, 29*(5), 486–492. Retrieved February 7, 2007, from http://www.ldonline.org/ld_indepth/technology/post secondary_tech.html

Edmonds, C. (2004). Providing access to students with disabilities in online distance education: Legal and technical concerns for higher education. *American Journal of Distance Education, 18*(1), 51–62.

Educational Testing Service. (2007). *Digital transformation: A framework for ICT literacy.* Retrieved October 5, 2008, from http://www.ets.org/Media/Tests/Information_and_ Communication_Technology_Literacy/ictreport.pdf

EDUCAUSE Center for Applied Research. (2007). *The ECAR study of undergraduate students and information technologies-2007*. Retrieved October 12, 2008, from http://connect.educause.edu/Library/ECAR/TheECARStudyofUndergradua/45075?time=1189954853

Hitchcock, C., & Stahl, S. (2003). *Assistive technology, universal design, universal design for learning: Improved opportunities*. Retrieved November 9, 2008, from http://jset.unlv.edu/18.4/issuemenu.html

Individuals with Disabilities Education Act Amendments (IDEA) of 1997, PL 105-17, 20 U.S.C. §§ 1400 *et seq.*

Individuals with Disabilities Education Act (IDEA) of 1990, PL 101-476, 20 U.S.C. §§ 1400 *et seq.*

Individuals with Disabilities Education Improvement Act (IDEA) of 2004, PL 108-446, 20 U.S.C. §§ 1400 *et seq.*

Klotz, G. (1997). *Mathematics and the world wide web*. Retrieved May 6, 2008, from http://forum.swarthmore.edu/articles/epadel

Lankshear, C., & Knobel, M. (2003). *New literacies: Changing knowledge and classroom learning*. Buckingham, UK: Open University Press.

Lenhart, A. (2007). *A timeline for teens and technology*. Retrieved April 11, 2008, from http://www.pewinternet.org

Leu, D.J., Kinzer, C.K., Coiro, J.L., & Cammack, D.W. (2004). Towards a theory of new literacies emerging from the Internet and other information and communication technologies. In R.B. Ruddell & N. Unrau (Eds.), *Theoretical models and processes of reading* (5th ed., pp. 1570–1613). Newark, DE: International Reading Association.

Leu, D.J., Zawilinkski, L., Castek, J., Banerjee, M., Housand, B., Liu, Y., & O'Neil, M. (2007). What is new about the new literacies of online reading comprehension. In L. Rush, J. Eakle, & A. Berger, (Eds.), *Secondary school literacy: What research reveals for classroom practices* (pp. 37–68). Chicago: NCTE/NCRLL.

Lewis, C., & Fabos, B. (2005). Instant messaging, literacies, & social identities. *Reading Research Quarterly, 40*(4), 470–501.

McNaughton, D., Hughes, C., & O'fiesh, N. (1997). Proofreading for students with learning disabilities: Integrating computer and strategy use. *Learning Disabilities Research and Practice, 12*(1), 16–28.

Mull, C.A., & Sitlington, P.L. (2003). The role of technology in the transition to postsecondary education of students with learning disabilities. *Journal of Special Education, 37*(1), 26–32.

National Center on Education Statistics. (2004). *The condition of education—2004*. Retrieved October 21, 2008, from http://nces.ed.gov/pubs2004

North Central Regional Educational Laboratory. (2003). *21st century skills: Literacy in the digital age*. Retrieved October, 2, 2007, from http://www.ncrel.org/engauge/skills/skills.htm

Parker, D.R., & Banerjee, M. (2007). Leveling the digital playing field: Assessing the learning technology needs of college-bound students with LD and/or ADHD. *Assessment for Effective Intervention, 33*(1), 5–14.

Pew Internet and American Life Project. (2005). *Teens and technology*. Retrieved March 20, 2008, from http://www.pewinternet.org/pdfs/PIP_Teens_Tech_July2005web.pdf

Pew Research Center. (2007). *How young people view their lives, futures, and politics: A portrait of "generation next."* Retrieved September 20, 2008, from http://people-press.org/reports/pdf/300.pdf

Seidel, A.B. (2008, November). *Integrating digital text into the life of a person with dyslexia*. Paper presented at the International Dyslexia Association, Seattle.

Silver-Pacuilla, H., Ruedel, K., & Mistrett, S. (2004). *A review of technology-based approaches for reading instruction: Tools for researchers and vendors*. Retrieved October 9, 2008, from http://www.nationaltechcenter.org/matrix/docs/AReviewTechnology-BasedApproaches_final.pdf

Technology-Related Assistance for Individuals with Disabilities Act of 1988, PL 100-407, 29 U.S.C. §§ 2201 *et seq.*

Thompson, S.J., Thurlow, M.L., Quenemoen, R.F., & Lehr, C.A. (2002). *Access to computer-based testing for students with disabilities* (Synthesis Report 45). Retrieved December 8, 2008, from http://cehd.umn.edu/NCEO/OnlinePubs/Synthesis45.html

U.S. Census Bureau. (2006). *Facts for features: Back to school 2006–2007.* Retrieved November 8, 2008, from http://www.census.gov/Press-Release/www/releases/archives/facts_for_features_special_editions/007108.html

U.S. Department of Labor. (1999). *Future works: Trends and challenges for work in the 21st century.* Washington, DC: Author.

Vocational Rehabilitation Act of 1973, PL 93-112, 29 U.S.C., 701 *et seq.*

# 7

# How Secondary Personnel Can Work with Families to Foster Effective Transition Planning

*Carol A. Kochhar-Bryant*

## WHAT YOU'LL LEARN IN THIS CHAPTER:

- ✔ The role of families in fostering effective transition planning
- ✔ How policies support the participation of families in education and transition
- ✔ How family systems are affected by a disability
- ✔ How the family's role changes along the developmental path to transition
- ✔ Principles and strategies for effective school–family collaboration
- ✔ How to work with parents who present challenging behaviors in secondary and postsecondary settings
- ✔ Multicultural implications for school–family collaboration for transition

**CONVERSATION WITH A
PARENT OF A SECONDARY STUDENT**
I believe that my son's teachers and school counselor have worked harder
with my child because I have reached out and stayed involved. Some
parents say you have to be your child's case coordinator to get the
services they need, and they are right. You have to stay involved, reach
out, and be a good communicator. My son has many needs, and I have
had to work across many agencies—the schools, mental health services,
substance abuse, and the courts. Good communication is my
responsibility too and it gets results. For me, life has rewarded action and
a positive attitude. Carrying into the school or college the baggage of
anger, resentment, and a jaded spirit won't help communication and
won't support my son's dreams for his future (personal communication,
September 14, 2008).

## CHAPTER OVERVIEW

Over the past century, parents and families have been powerful advocates for
inclusive secondary education and access to transition services for their
children with special learning needs. Educational research has provided
ample evidence that the participation of families is the most crucial factor in
a child's ability to benefit from education and make successful transitions to
postsecondary environments. Secondary personnel recognize that children
do not exist in isolation; rather, they develop as part of a web of relationships
among the family, school, and community. The strength of these
relationships determines the effectiveness of the collaborative process in
secondary education and transition to postsecondary settings.

Children do not come with instruction manuals but neither do
school–family relationships. It is essential that secondary personnel
appreciate that parents are finding their way as their children develop and
that they too must adjust their relationships with their children during that
passage. This chapter examines 1) the crucial role of parents and families in
the transition process; 2) change in the family's role along the developmental
path to transition; 3) parents who present challenging behaviors; and 4)
principles and strategies for secondary personnel to facilitate effective family
participation.

## MANY KINDS OF FAMILIES

There are many kinds of family units with which secondary professionals will
develop relationships, and, therefore, *family* is defined in the broadest terms,
including the following:

- Traditional families with a father, a mother, and children
- Blended families from a previous divorce

- Single-parent families

- Extended families (grandparents, aunts and uncles, cousins)

- Families with a grandparent or godparent in a parental role

- Families with an older adult sibling in a parental role

- Same-sex parent families

- Families of adopted and foster children, including surrogate parents appointed by the courts

This definition includes blood relatives as well as caregivers who may or may not be legal guardians.

Regardless of the form of the family, a common characteristic is that each represents a unit that acts responsibly to protect, care for, and nurture children and youth until they graduate and gain independence. Families demonstrate a wide spectrum of abilities and dispositions when they collaborate with secondary personnel. Some may communicate appreciation as they reach out to teachers, counselors, and administrators, and others may be suspicious, mistrustful, or simply inexperienced with the expectations of the school system. Some may communicate lack of confidence in the professionals or may be frustrated with the performance of their son or daughter during the high school years and on standardized tests. They may harbor fears that their child may not qualify for admission to college. Socioeconomic and cultural differences among families and school personnel are also a source of barriers to parent participation in their children's educational programs (Price, 2005).

Families vary in makeup, stability, socioeconomic levels, education, and expectations for their children. Communities also vary in size, history, geography, and socioeconomic levels. Within these communities are entities that care for and have contact with families and students. As Epstein (2001) advised, "educators need to know the context in which students live, work and play" (p. 5). They need to work in partnership with the other important people in students' lives. The whole child must be considered and all the aspects that affect the child within home, school, and community.

Awareness and sensitivity to the pressures, values, and perspectives family members bring are the starting point for productive parent participation. Sometimes parents may attend a school conference or meeting because they wish to discuss family challenges before focusing on their teenager's education and transition goals. Sensitivity of educators and an openness to listen and learn about families' perspectives and life circumstances, beliefs, and needs are the foundation for parent partnerships. The vignette in Box 7.1 shows how both parents and teachers walked a tightrope when it came to preparing Andrew for transition to postsecondary life. Consider the vignette as you discuss the following.

- What biases or fears can you identify in the parents about the school and teachers?

- What factors threatened Andrew's high school completion?

**Box 7.1.**    Walking the tightrope to transition

Andrew's mother and father, Michelle and Richard, have felt that since Andrew started attending a general education class in their small rural high school, they have not had the same level of connection with his school program as they had in middle school. The last few IEP meetings have included discussions around transition but they get the sense that the special education teachers really do not think Andrew will be able to achieve a regular diploma so that he can attend community college. Although Andrew is maintaining Cs and Ds, he has great difficulty with standardized tests. At the last meeting, Andrew's father felt that he had to "get in a few faces" in order to get the accommodations they thought Andrew needed. His mother tried to smooth things over. She did not want the school perceiving them as hostile or overly demanding parents. She has been warned by her friend from the autism support group, who also had a son at the high school a few years ago, that if they asked for too much, then they would be labeled with a "reputation for trouble." Everyone seems to be anxious about improving the school's test scores, and more families are becoming concerned.

Attending transition meetings at school is difficult for Richard. He dropped out of school when his mother died in order to help his father with the family plumbing business. He was not upset about that because he did not like school. He always believed that the teachers were only interested in students who were going to college—the ones from the "good side of town." So school left him with bad memories. He prefers to let his wife go to the transition meetings alone, and he will only go with her when she is really worried about a specific meeting. He does not want his children to have the same experiences, so he is pushing for them to continue their education beyond high school. According to Michelle and Richard, the only person at the school who seems to understand is Mr. Harris, the transition coordinator, whose job is to make sure that "this thing called transition" happens for Andrew. He dropped by their house last summer before the school year began to talk with them about Andrew's plans and goals for the future. According to Richard, that is where "this crazy idea about going to the community college came from." But as long as Mr. Harris thought Andrew could do college-level work, and if Andrew wanted to try it, then Richard would support him. The personal home visit by Mr. Harris really convinced Richard that this could be a possibility for his son.

Andrew and his mother met with Mr. Harris and the resource room teacher. The teachers had attended a workshop and learned new strategies to help students with special needs to take the high school exit examination. They offered to meet with Andrew and Michelle to work though some of their concerns and help them better understand the testing process. The teachers explained the different types of testing

*(continued)*

(continued)

accommodations, such as having Andrew take the test in a quiet place to reduce distraction. They discovered that some of the possible accommodations had not been made available to Andrew when he took and failed the practice I-STEP+ (high school exit examination). This process really helped Andrew and his family relieve some of the pressure they were feeling. The family could focus on the next phase of Andrew's life—a job for the summer and a search for the right college with services to accommodate Andrew.

- How did teachers engage the parents in helping Andrew prepare for the exit examination?

- What is Andrew's postsecondary goal, and how supportive are his parents of the goal?

In this example, Andrew's parents negotiated carefully and persistently for accommodations in testing for their son. It is a story of competing needs between parents and professionals as well as parents' sometimes misguided misperceptions about teachers and schools that can impede constructive communication and collaboration.

## RESEARCH AND LEGISLATION UNDERSCORE THE VALUE OF FAMILY PARTICIPATION

More than 30 years of research in the United States provides ample evidence that parent involvement in education improves the performance of students, including those with disabilities (Kreider, Caspe, Kennedy, & Weiss, 2007; Zarrett & Eccles, 2006). When families are directly engaged with their children's education, students show increased test scores, higher academic achievement, and improved attitudes toward learning and have better social behavior, higher self-esteem, fewer placements in special education, higher school attendance rates, and lower drop-out rates (Abrams & Gibbs, 2002; Newman, 2004; Pena, 2000; Raimondo & Henderson, 2001; Wandry & Pleet, 2002). Parents who are actively involved in school also experience better relationships with their children's teachers (Christenson & Sheridan, 2001).

The National Longitudinal Transition Study-2 (2005), sponsored by the U.S. Office of Special Education, provides the first national picture of family involvement and its effect on student achievement. The study involved a survey of 9,230 parents and guardians of students with disabilities to examine the involvement of families in their children's (age 13–16) education. Several findings are relevant for transition planning for youth with disabilities.

- Youth whose families are more involved in their schools are not as far behind grade level in reading, tend to receive better grades, and have higher rates of involvement in organized groups and with individual friendships than youth with less family involvement in school (Newman, 2004).

- In the domain of independence, youth whose families are more involved in their schooling are more likely than youth from less-involved families to experience greater success in gaining access to college.

- Family expectations for the future help shape the achievements of youth with disabilities, particularly with regard to academic achievement (Newman, 2004).

- During the middle and high school years, parents' participation in school or community-sponsored college outreach programs also supports adolescent learning and development by influencing students' postgraduation plans.

The fourth point is particularly true for low-income, minority, and immigrant youth. For example, when parents attend meetings at the school that provide basic information about college-entrance processes, SAT preparation, financial aid, and course placements, they begin to imagine their children as college students, feel more comfortable in the school setting, build support groups with other parents, and are more likely to assist their children in navigating the school and college application system (Jacobs & Bleeker, 2004). Youth whose parents possess these qualities are more likely to graduate high school and attend college (Dearing, McCartney, Weiss, Kreider, & Simpkins, 2004; Kreider et al., 2007).

## Laws Strengthen the Role of Families in Education Transition Planning

Several education laws have strengthened the role of families in the education and transition planning for their children. Box 7.2 summarizes laws that have expanded the role of family participation in education and transition.

## Roles and Responsibilities of Parents and Postsecondary Personnel in Transition Planning

The primary role of parents during transition planning is to encourage and support students to plan for and achieve their educational goals and develop their self-determination skills. Although the Individuals with Disabilities Education Improvement Act (IDEA) of 2004 (PL 108-446) requires that transition services begin at age 16, parents should feel comfortable asking for transition planning to begin earlier if they believe it is needed. In order for an individualized education program (IEP) to meet a student's transition needs, both parents and school personnel must collaborate in the transition assessment process. *Transition assessment* is defined as a planned, continuous process of obtaining, organizing, and using information to assist individuals with disabilities of all ages and their families in making all critical transitions in students' lives both successful and satisfying (Clark, 2007). Although secondary personnel perform assessments through instruments and observations, parents participate by sharing their daily knowledge of their child about his or her goals, dreams, and strengths. Answering the following questions may help guide parents,

---

**Box 7.2.** Laws that support the participation of families in education and transition

The Individuals with Disabilities Education Improvement Act (IDEA) of 2004 (PL 108-446), No Child Left Behind Act of 2001 (PL 107-110), and the Higher Education Opportunity Act of 2008 (PL 110-315) strengthened the role of parents in their children's individualized education programs and transition plans in the following ways.

- IDEA 2004 authorizes related services that directly support parents of students with disabilities, including counseling and parent training (20 USC 1401 22, 26).

- IDEA 2004 encourages parents to become more involved in their children's education and work in other ways as partners with educators and policy makers (Abrams & Gibbs, 2002; Christie, 2005; Henderson & Mapp, 2002).

- NCLB mandates that every Title I school have a written parent involvement policy that includes parents in its development (Education Commission of the States, 2004).

- The Higher Education Opportunity Act of 2008 establishes a national center to provide technical assistance and information on best and promising practices to students with disabilities and their families, including information that assists students with disabilities in planning for college.

---

secondary personnel, and students in preparing and participating in effective IEP meetings related to transition planning.

- *What does the young person want to do with his or her life?* What are his or her dreams, aspirations, or goals? The youth's answers should be incorporated into all aspects of transition planning. If a young person is nonverbal or has difficulty communicating, help parents use their knowledge of their child to strengthen self-determination skills (see Chapter 4). Be sure that transition planning and services reflect students' preferences and choices.

- *What are the young person's needs, abilities, and skills?* Assist parents to understand the degree of independence their child needs and identify the tasks with which their child needs assistance. Many parents could benefit from understanding how to gauge such decisions.

- *What are the outcomes that the youth and parents want?* Encourage parents and their children to bring ideas and suggestions about postsecondary goals to the transition planning meeting. For example, they might suggest suitable colleges of technical education programs, summer college preparation seminars, or a desire for campus-based employment or residence.

- *If a student intends to enroll in college, is he or she taking the courses needed to meet college entrance requirements?* Provide information to students and parents about making appropriate course selections and provide information about diploma options and their implications for access to 2- and 4-year colleges.

- *Who will attend the transition IEP conference?* Help parents to encourage their son or daughter to attend the conference and together prepare parents and youth for the meeting. If the youth does not attend, then parents may represent their desires and wishes. Assist parents and their teenage children to become familiar with the roles and functions of team members and how to identify the community agencies that should be present (e.g., vocational rehabilitation). Parents need to know that they can request that a specific community agency representative be invited to the IEP meeting if the youth is receiving services from that agency. Becoming familiar with adult service systems or agencies early on can be helpful in making future decisions. Have available a copy of the daily school schedule each quarter or semester and information about available classes so they can participate in selecting classes (Pacer Center, 2007).

- *How do young people develop self-advocacy skills?* Provide parents with information about the meaning and importance of self-advocacy skills for their son or daughter in the postsecondary setting. In the meeting, direct questions to the student, even when it is the parents who may provide answers. It is important to encourage young people to have and state (by any means available to them) their own opinions. It is important for students to understand their disability and to ask for the accommodations they may need.

- *What kinds of accommodations will students need when they go on to postsecondary education?* Before parents and youth can determine the accommodations that will be needed after high school, they need information about what is available, about their child's functional skills, and the results of relevant assessments.

- *Who will be responsible for what part of the transition plan in the IEP?* Help parents and youth understand who is responsible for each transition goal and include specific time lines in the IEP.

It is essential that secondary personnel not assume that parents instinctively know their role in transition planning, and be prepared to provide information, instruction, encouragement, and support. Secondary school personnel and administrators, through their own involvement, must show students how to look beyond high school toward postsecondary education. This is accomplished by initiating, designing, and evaluating effective transition plans and coordinating services. Table 7.1 summarizes the roles and responsibilities of parents and secondary personnel. Students with disabilities can succeed in making the transition from secondary to postsecondary education settings if the student, parents, and professional personnel work together to design and implement effective transition plans.

**Table 7.1.**   Roles and responsibilities of parents and secondary personnel in transition planning

| Parents' role | Secondary personnel role |
|---|---|
| To contribute to successful transition planning, parents should<br><br>  Be involved in transition planning and ensure that the student is also included<br><br>  Help the student develop realistic goals<br><br>  Encourage the student to develop future educational plans and to explore realistic postsecondary options<br><br>  Help the student select high school courses that meet postsecondary requirements<br><br>  Collaborate with secondary and postsecondary staff to make decisions regarding programs, services, and resources<br><br>  Help the student collect and maintain an ongoing personal file that includes school and medical records, IEP, résumé, and samples of academic work<br><br>  Communicate confidence in the student's ability to be successful in a postsecondary setting<br><br>  Encourage the student to develop maximum independence in the learning, study, and living skills critical to success in postsecondary settings | To contribute to successful transition planning, secondary school personnel should<br><br>  Form a transition team consisting of a coordinator, the student, the parent(s), administrators, teachers, and related services personnel<br><br>  Include the student and parents in the entire transition planning process<br><br>  Demonstrate sensitivity to the culture and values of the student and family<br><br>  Develop an appropriate packet of materials to document the student's secondary school program and to facilitate service delivery in the postsecondary setting<br><br>  Provide administrative support, resources, and time to foster collaboration among team members<br><br>  Inform the student about statutes, rules, and regulations that ensure his or her rights<br><br>  Provide appropriate course selection, counseling, and academic support services<br><br>  Ensure that the student learns effective studying, time-management, test-preparation, and test-taking strategies<br><br>  Help the student use a range of academic accommodations and technological aids, such as electronic date books, videodisc technology, texts on CD, grammar and spell checkers, and word processing programs<br><br>  Help the student to evaluate his or her dependence on external supports and adjust the level of assistance when appropriate<br><br>  Help the student develop appropriate social skills and interpersonal communication abilities<br><br>  Help the student develop self-advocacy skills, including a realistic understanding of the learning disability and how to use this information for self-understanding and communication with others<br><br>  Foster independence through increased responsibility and opportunity for self-management<br><br>  Encourage the student to develop extracurricular interests and to participate in community activities<br><br>  Inform the student and parent(s) about admission requirements and demands of diverse postsecondary settings<br><br>  Inform the student and parent(s) about services that postsecondary settings provide, such as disabilities services, academic services, and computer-based writing services<br><br>  Ensure the timely development of documentation and materials in keeping with application time lines<br><br>  Help the student and parent(s) select and apply to postsecondary institutions that will offer both the competitive curriculum and the necessary level of disability support services<br><br>  Develop ongoing communication with postsecondary personnel |

From National Joint Committee on Learning Disabilities. (1994). *Secondary to postsecondary education transition planning for students with learning disabilities* (pp. 2–5). Retrieved September 4, 2009, from http://www.ldonline.org/article/Secondary_to_Postsecondary_Education_Transition_Planning_for_Students_with_Learning_Disabilities; adapted by permission.

# THE FAMILY'S CHANGING ROLE
# ALONG THE DEVELOPMENTAL PATH

It is important that secondary personnel appreciate that school–family relationships are not intuitive for parents and that they are navigating their way along the developmental path, along with their children. They are concerned with their children's progress, often anxious about standardized tests and graduation, and feel responsible for their long-term postsecondary outcomes. Sometimes these feelings become very intense and parents may behave in ways that seem inappropriate or excessive to educators. The first step for creating positive relationships with parents, however, is to gain—and communicate—an appreciation for the depth of their sense of responsibility for their sons and daughters with disabilities.

Creating a stable identity and becoming complete and productive adults is the major task facing adolescents (Carnegie Council on Adolescent Development, 1995). Over time, adolescents develop a sense of themselves that transcends the many changes in their experiences and roles. They find their role in society through active searching, which leads to discoveries about themselves. The changes experienced during puberty bring new awareness of self and others' reactions to them. For example, sometimes adults perceive adolescents to be adults because they physically appear to be adults; however, they are not. They do, however, need room to explore themselves and their world, and they need opportunities to grow into adult roles. Developmental tasks represent our culture's definition of "normal" or typical development at different points in the life span. The Carnegie Council on Adolescent Development (1995) synthesized research to identify eight developmental tasks that enable adolescents to create an identity and prepare for adult roles. Table 7.2 builds on the council's developmental tasks for adolescents and describes changes in parents' roles that are needed along the developmental path to adulthood.

## Parents and Service Coordination

Obtaining and coordinating services for their children with disabilities is an important way in which many families' roles change. Because most schools do not provide direct help to parents to coordinate services needed outside the school, parents frequently serve as their children's "case managers" or "service coordinators" during the school years and particularly as they approach transition to the postsecondary world. Box 7.3 provides the perspective of one parent on service coordination.

For example, parents may be working among multiple agencies—vocational rehabilitation, psychological services, speech-language services, tutorial services—to provide appropriate support services for their child who is preparing to make the transition to college. For many students in transition to postsecondary education, coordinating activities that often fall to parents may include assisting their child to 1) identify and visit colleges that are a good match for the student's interests and needs; 2) understand and determine the kinds of evaluations that may be needed by the college in order to request accommodations in the classroom; 3) complete college application forms; 4) communicate by e-mail and telephone with campus advisors;

**Table 7.2.** Change in the family's role along the developmental path to transition

| Adolescent development tasks | How parents' roles must change |
|---|---|
| *Achieving new and more mature relations with others in their age group.* Adolescents learn to interact with others in more adult ways. Physical maturity plays an important role in peer relationships and peer groups. | Monitoring by parents can be a useful boundary-setting tool because it allows parents to place limits on the adolescent's outside activities. As adolescents proceed through secondary years, they gain independence when parents allow greater freedom to their teenagers to spend time on their own with peers and make personal decisions. |
| *Achieving a masculine or feminine social role.* Adolescents develop their own definition of what it means to be male or female. Adolescents need changes to test and develop their masculine and feminine social roles. | As teenagers develop, they need to be encouraged to think about sex role stereotypes, both in terms of their social role and career role. They need to know that adults will support their decisions to prepare for career roles that may be nontraditional for males or females. |
| *Accepting one's physical self.* The beginning of puberty and the rate of body changes for adolescents varies tremendously. How closely their bodies match the well-defined stereotypes of the "perfect" body for young women and young men will affect their ability to adjust to these changes. | Adolescents who do not match the stereotype may need extra support from adults to improve their feelings of comfort, acceptance, and self-worth regarding their physique. They may need support to make realistic decisions about career goals. |
| *Achieving emotional independence from parents and other adults.* Children internalize their parents' values and attitudes. Adolescents, however, must achieve emotional independence by defining their own values and attitudes moving toward self-reliance. | This change is smoother if the adolescent and parents can agree on some level of independence that increases over time (e.g., setting curfews, expectations about homework and grades). |
| *Preparing for an economic career.* In society, an adolescent reaches adult status when he or she is able to financially support him- or herself. This task has become more difficult than in the past because the job market demands increased education and skills. | Adult guidance and support is needed to help the teenager reach this developmental task, typically by late adolescence or early adulthood. Guidance and support also is needed after the adolescent completes his or her education and gains some entry-level work experience. Parents can facilitate this process by encouraging and permitting work during summers and career-related service activities that support postsecondary goals. |
| *Preparing for marriage and family life.* Sexual maturation is the basis for this developmental task. Achieving this developmental task is difficult because adolescents often confuse sexual feelings with genuine intimacy. Indeed, this developmental task is usually not achieved until late adolescence or early adulthood. | Parents can share values and attitudes about the importance of marriage, preparation to become a parent, and the seriousness of the responsibility of caring for a child. These messages can be conveyed through discussing family experiences, modeling behavior, watching films, reading books and magazines, and counseling. |
| *Acquiring a set of values and an ethical system as a guide to behavior—developing an ideology.* As adolescents learn to develop abstract thinking, they are able to develop their own set of values and beliefs. They typically internalize their parents' values and attitudes, but also must achieve emotional independence by defining their own values and attitudes moving toward self-reliance. | Parents must learn to shift from directing, teaching, and demanding standards of behavior and attitudes to employing practices that build on the base of internalized values. In other words, they promote the independent decision making of their teenager by guiding by example and allowing and supporting individual decisions about dress, behavior, and postsecondary goals. |
| *Desiring and achieving socially responsible behavior.* Children define themselves and their world within the family. Adolescents define themselves and their world from their new social roles. Status within the community, beyond that of family, is an important achievement for older adolescents and young adults. | Adolescents and young adults become members of the larger community through employment (financial independence) and emotional independence from parents. Parents should actively teach work behaviors in the home and encourage community activities, volunteering, and service. |

*Sources:* Carnegie Council on Adolescent Development (1995), Havinghurst (1972), and Perkins (1997).

**Box 7.3.**    Parent perspective on involvement with the school

Since my daughter needed services from several agencies when she was in high school, I became a "case manager" for her. I knew I needed to do this so that we would be prepared for when she graduated. I had a huge file with all of the paperwork from multiple agencies—mental health, speech and language, health services, and others. It was so much to keep track of and coordinate, but I had to stay organized. Because I was organized and informed, I could advocate for my daughter with her teachers and was much better prepared to participate in the transition planning process for her. In fact, her counselor looked to me for a better understanding of the services she would need in the postsecondary setting.
—Conversation with the parent of a high school student

5) contact and coordinate appointments with support service agencies and accompany their child on visits; 6) assist with reapplication for accommodations on an annual basis; and 7) select appropriate college courses that meet the requirements of the terminal degree. Although most students can manage these tasks with relative independence, many will require initial or ongoing support from a parent or mentor as they enter and progress through the college curriculum.

Educators and policy makers have recognized the need to strengthen parent participation in the secondary school as well as increase schools' support of families (Kreider et al., 2007; Morningstar & Wehmeyer, 2008). It is important that schools be explicit in their communication with parents about role expectations. Furthermore, postsecondary institutions are also creating parent advisory councils to improve relationships with families who remain an ongoing support to their sons and daughters throughout the 2 or 4 years of study.

## PRINCIPLES AND STRATEGIES
## FOR EFFECTIVE SCHOOL–PARENT COLLABORATION

Research has demonstrated that one reason for the continuing poor outcomes of school-to-postsecondary transition planning is the absence of family-focused approaches at the secondary level that promote the students' and families' determination of transition goals and services (Ames & Dickerson, 2004; Education Commission of the States, 2004; Turnbull, Turnbull, Erwin, & Soodak, 2006). Furthermore, there is consensus in the research literature that effective parent participation in transition planning is built on several assumptions: 1) the primary educational environment is in the family; 2) parent participation is a major factor in improving the quality of education and transition services and a child's long-term postsecondary success; 3) the benefits of parent participation extend from preschool through high school; and 4) children who are minorities and are from low-income families have the most to gain when schools involve parents (Ames & Dickerson, 2004; Lightfoot, 2001; National Center for Family Literacy, 2004; Newman, 2004; Raimondo & Henderson, 2001; Zhang, Wehmeyer, & Chen, 2005).

It is important to understand the difference between strategies that call for more *parent involvement* and strategies that are *family-centered* or aimed at promoting family empowerment and decision making. Models of transition planning and coordination are taking a family-centered approach in which the transition coordinator incorporates assessments of family needs into the IEP for students through to the age of majority. The coordination functions are guided by family support principles, which emphasize family strengths, and principles of family empowerment, including students as lead decision makers with their parents in planning for their educational progress and later for postsecondary life. Family-centered strategies are based on the following principles.

- Informed choice among graduation and transition service options is ensured for the individual and his or her family.

- Transition services are coordinated around the postsecondary goals of the student and family, not around the needs of the school or program.

- The ability of ordinary citizens to help students plan for transition and participate in community life is recognized.

- Parents are children's first teachers and have a lifelong influence on their values, attitudes, and aspirations.

- Most parents, regardless of economic status, educational level, and/or cultural background care deeply about their children's education and postsecondary success and can provide substantial support if given specific opportunities and knowledge.

- Schools must take the lead in eliminating, or at least reducing, traditional barriers to parent participation in transition planning (Ames & Dickerson, 2004; Christie, 2005; Education Commission of the States, 2004; Novick, 2001; Turnbull et al., 2006).

As mentioned previously, a family-support philosophy emphasizes an empowerment model that builds on family strengths and develops home–school relationships that are based on mutual respect and responsibility. The important themes for the participation of parents and family members in the service coordination process are summarized in Table 7.3.

Secondary teachers recognize that their efforts to improve students' learning and performance are integrally related to the family circumstances and home life. The following comment by a secondary educator indicates the importance of school–family communication.

**Table 7.3.**   Themes for families participating in service coordination and transition

| Theme | Description of positive practices |
| --- | --- |
| Parents/families as active partners | Parents and families are partners with professionals in the service delivery process and must be viewed as collaborators, not service recipients. The collaborative view fosters a perception that parents and families are active and not passive in the service delivery process and should enjoy equal status with professionals in the team decision-making process. |
| Parents/families as team members | Parents and families are involved in assessing their child's transition needs and participate with members of the interdisciplinary team in developing individualized service plans and transition plans. Parents are invited and participate in each annual IEP meeting for their children who need special services. They participate in any decision about placement change or change in level of services. Parents can be valuable participants in service planning and evaluating, developing policy, and planning for training of service coordinators (Hausslein, Kaufmann, & Hurth, 1992). |
| Parents/families as transition coordinators | Parents are encouraged to be closely involved and supportive of their adolescent children in the process of preparing for and making the transition between services, such as between secondary school and postsecondary settings and employment. They partner with transition coordinators to provide parent-training seminars or to speak in classes about transition and preparation for employment and self-advocacy. |
| Parents/families as decision makers | Parents/families are lead decision makers regarding the assessments and the services to be provided, in cooperation and consultation with professionals. |
| Parent/family training for advocacy | Parent training and resources are provided to help family members and guardians better advocate and coordinate services for their children or wards. Families are educated and empowered to acquire and to assist in creating transition services and supports and are informed about available community and outreach services. |

## COMMENTS OF A SECONDARY EDUCATOR

Although it takes time and effort to actively involve many of the parents of my students in regular home–school communication, I have found that setting up a system at the beginning of the year and being consistent is well worth the effort, both in terms of the students' success in school and my effectiveness as a teacher. We can never underestimate the value of the information and influence of a teenager's parents and siblings. We cannot afford to leave them out of the process, for long after our involvement with a teenager is over, they remain. They are the constants and the greatest advocates in a teenager's life. Better communication with parents means feeling more connected with the child (personal communication, August 5, 2008).

Weaknesses in parent–professional collaboration typically stem from a lack of understanding among secondary personnel about the meaning of parent partnership in the context of secondary education and transition planning. Such partnerships mean that parents play a central role in promoting a culture of cooperation that is key to enabling young people to achieve transition success. As the teacher commented previously, professionals come in and out of students' lives, but parents remain forever. Comprehensive transition planning addresses multiple developmental domains, including education, employment, personal responsibility, relationships, home and family, leisure pursuits, community involvement, and physical and emotional health. Parents have been and will remain important influences and supports related to these domains long after high school graduation.

## Principles and Strategies for Facilitating Effective Collaboration

Although there is ample evidence of the positive effects of family involvement, many schools inadvertently discourage family involvement. Educators in many public schools are concerned with the immediate needs of children and youth, often with little awareness of family life circumstances or the engagement of parents. Some educators speculate that such a narrow focus may contribute to lower levels of family involvement (National Coalition for Parent Involvement in Education, 2001; North Central Regional Educational Laboratory, 2001; Pleet, 2000). Large classes also impede family participation because teachers have minimal time to spend with individual students and meet with family members outside class, and there are few incentives to do so. Many factors influence the relationship of parents and professionals in their children's schools, including the effect of the disability on the family, the type and severity of the disability and its effect on the school, and the effect of culture on attitudes about disabilities. The following strategies can facilitate successful parent involvement.

1. *Create a welcoming school environment.* The school climate is the educational and social atmosphere of a school. A welcoming school climate treats parents with respect and encourages a wide range of participation. As a result, parents feel accepted, respected, and needed, and they are more likely to become involved in the school (Blank, 2001; North Central Regional Educational Laboratory, 2001). Administrator support for parent participation is essential for facilitating family involvement because teachers often need encouragement and incentives to extend themselves to family members. A welcoming school climate can be created in several ways.

   - Embrace a philosophy of partnership and be willing to share power with families. Make sure that parents and school staff understand that the responsibility for children's educational development is a collaborative enterprise (Mapp, 2004).

   - Establish flexible policies that encourage parent participation at a variety of levels.

   - Permit parents to visit the school during open houses, parent–teacher conferences, art and music events, and athletic and academic programs.

   - Provide opportunities for parents to voice their comments and concerns.

   - If the parents are not fluent in English, then arrange to have a resource person—either a teacher or another parent—communicate with the parents in their first language.

   - Create a parent center at the school, staffed by a parent liaison, where parents can congregate, plan school activities, work on classroom projects, and learn about the educational process, transition planning, and disabilities.

- Provide parent education and support programs (e.g., parenting classes, seminars for parents on helping children learn at home, skills improvement classes), publicize parent involvement efforts, and personally thank and honor parents who have volunteered their efforts.

- Provide ongoing professional development in family participation for all school staff, which should address developing skills to work with parents and families, reducing barriers to parent involvement, communicating with families who are culturally and linguistically diverse, and improving two-way communication between school and home (North Central Regional Educational Laboratory, 2001).

The goal of improving access and progress of students with disabilities in general education depends on teachers' competence in working closely with parents.

2. *Provide well-trained and available staff.* Many school administrators report that levels of parent involvement are linked to adequate numbers of well-trained staff. Effective secondary education and transition support depends on well-prepared teachers and administrators who understand the value of direct participation of parents and have the skills to facilitate such engagement. Many school personnel, however, lack these skills (Henderson & Mapp, 2002; U.S. Government Accountability Office, 2003).

3. *Overcome communitywide barriers.* Administrators and teachers consistently reported socioeconomic barriers to parent participation, including poverty, lack of transportation, families with multiple jobs and single-parent households, and negative school experiences in their past (Ames & Dickerson, 2004; McDonough, 2007). Many students live with extended family members rather than their parents. In many schools, only a few of the students live with both parents, and overall, 20% of children do not have parents who actively provide care for them (Kreider et al., 2007; Nord & West, 2001). School personnel can overcome these persistent barriers by raising awareness of the barriers and creating a systematic plan to provide opportunities for developing positive relationships with teachers and administrators. Examples of such actions include the following.

- Preparation for transition planning meetings for families and students.

- Parent-to-parent meetings and support network for students continuing their education.

- Workshops for parents of youth with disabilities on topics related to transition and postsecondary education, including shifts in legal requirements, responsibilities of postsecondary agencies, and how parents can foster adult independence skills.

- Distribution of printed materials to parents of children receiving special education services to orient them to postsecondary life, opportunities, expectations, and preparation.

- Guidebooks for parents on how to facilitate discussion about future goals and life in postsecondary education (e.g., choosing a major and selecting courses in college, building relationships on campus, working with faculty, staying safe and healthy, developing money management skills, locating services on campus, asking for help).

- Student-led panels to discuss their views about what is most helpful for them.

4. *Building parents' confidence in the eligibility determination and IEP process.* Parents report that they are generally not comfortable enough with the IEP process to request changes in their children's goals (Henderson & Mapp, 2002). Families that expressed reservations about their level of involvement in the process were disproportionately from African American, Hispanic, and Asian/Pacific Islander families and from low-income households (Christie, 2005; Epstein, 2001; Henderson & Mapp, 2002). Many districts are taking steps to ensure that parents are not presented with the IEP for the first time at the IEP meeting and then are expected to sign it. Many are using ombudsmen who assist families with the process and with dispute resolution (Henderson, 2008).

5. *Overcoming attitudinal barriers.* In a large national Study of State and Local Implementation and Impact of IDEA (SLIIDEA; 2003), parents reported that some school personnel create attitudinal barriers, including prejudicial feelings toward students in special education and their parents and ambivalence about parent involvement in advisory councils (U.S. Government Accountability Office, 2003). Administrators have sought to overcome these barriers by welcoming organized groups of parents or parent advisory councils and helping these groups find common ground with the overall improvement goals of the school.

6. *Increasing the availability of multilingual resources.* In many school districts that experience an influx of non–English-speaking families, teachers and administrators are making efforts to provide a range of printed materials and interpreters who could intervene on behalf of non–English-speaking parents (Ames & Dickerson, 2004; Bernhard, Freire, Pacini-Ketchabaw, & Villanueva, 1998; Brilliant & Duke, 2001; Christie, 2005; Henderson & Mapp, 2002; SLIIDEA, 2003). In addition, parent support groups or parent mentors who share the language can be helpful in engaging parents.

7. *Making time.* Many teachers are disappointed with the poor turnout of parents at conferences and question the usefulness of such conferences (Black, 2005). Secondary personnel can benefit from support from school administrators to gain greater clarity about their role in working with parents of students with disabilities and to find sufficient time in their schedule to spend with parents (Abrams & Gibbs, 2002; Ames & Dickerson, 2004; Ammon et al., 2000).

## "HELICOPTER" PARENTS IN THE POSTSECONDARY SETTING

The popular terms *helicopter parent* (Cline & Fay, 2006), *tether parent,* or *millenial generation* parent (Shapira, 2008) are pejorative terms for a person

---

**Box 7.4.**   My helicopter parent

My mom has always been my greatest advocate; I know that. I pushed back a lot when I was in the high school alternative education center and was embarrassed when she would come to school to meet my counselor and teachers. It was okay that she drove me to community college several days a week because I was afraid to drive and really didn't want to own a car. But then she insisted on meeting all my teachers and wanted to talk to them about my difficulties with stress and pressure from having multiple projects and asked them to help me to organize the work. It was as though she wanted me to have special consideration. I know she meant well and she really wanted to see me go on to a 4-year college, but I didn't want any special treatment. I just wanted to be like everyone else and succeed on my own. If I got a C, then so be it. I would have to learn how to do better the next time. I have to find a way to explain to her that I need her to step away and give me some space. I will make it on my own.
—Conversation with a community college student

---

who pays extremely close attention to his or her child or children, particularly at secondary and postsecondary educational institutions. Such parents have been placed into several nuanced categories.

- The *agent* is pushy and will accompany his or her young adults to career fairs, query test results, and intervene with administrative decisions.

- The *white knight* appears on short notice to "save the day" or intervene in problems in high school or college.

- The *black hawk* crosses the line from close attention to unethical behavior such as writing college term papers, preparing admissions essays, and negotiating employment salaries.

In general, helicopter parents rush in at the slightest crisis to prevent any harm or failure from falling on their children at the expense of letting them learn from their own mistakes. Box 7.4 provides an illustration of the helicopter parent from the student's perspective.

A Harvard Graduate School of Education report indicated that about one sixth of American teachers leave the profession every year (Berg, Donaldson, & Johnson, 2005). According to research by the Center for the Study of Teaching and Policy (Elfers, Knapp, Zahir, & Plecki, 2005), the stress of dealing with difficult parents is one of the top reasons teachers choose to depart (Tingley, 2006). Among new teachers, communication with parents is the most frequently cited challenge and the area in which they feel least prepared (MetLife Survey of the American Teacher, 2005).

## Why Do Helicopter Parents Exist?

There are numerous reasons why parents are being labeled as *helicopters,* and there is also some controversy regarding these labels. Some of these reasons are practical and others are a result of social and cultural changes. First, since the 1990s, there has been a concerted effort on the part of schools to engage more parents in their children's K–12 education. Parents began to spend more time in schools and classrooms. At the same time, teachers were equipped with telephones and computers in their classrooms, and parents were able to call, e-mail, and text message teachers frequently. Current educational laws, as well as the Family Educational Rights and Privacy Act (FERPA) of 1974 (PL 93-380), have also recognized the importance of family in the educational process. There have been clear messages to parents to get involved. Some families tend to become less involved as their children progress through middle and high school, but others have become even more active. Parents are seldom assisted in the process of fading back in the high school years and in the transition to college and, in fact, often receive mixed messages. The question is at what point does a parent go from "helpful" to "helicopter?"

Many parents have a need to protect their children, particularly those with disabilities, from a tougher and more competitive culture. There is a lot of competition to get into college and into freshman classes, and parents are intervening to gain any advantage they can. Again, as a result of ubiquitous technology, college students are tethered to their parents through cell phones, e-mail, and instant messaging. Parents' position is that they are consumers paying increasingly higher tuition, fees, and housing and that they need to protect their investment. They argue that the playing field has become much more competitive. If parents do not get involved, then their children will not have any advantage, which is particularly important if the child has a disability. Employers, however, say they want graduates who are self-reliant (Redmond, 2008). College administrators are struggling with a growing phenomenon and seeking strategies that both support parents and respect their concerns while trying to teach the importance of student independence. The dean of students at Georgia Tech described how when parents drop their children off for the fall semester, he commends the parents for their successful efforts but also lets them know that they now need to let go so their children can independently problem-solve, make decisions, and learn to cope (Fortin, 2008).

A report on *60 Minutes* (CBS, 2008) discussed how the children of baby boomers, born between 1982 and 1995 are overmanaged and very pressured and treated by their parents as pieces of Baccarat crystal or something that is fragile and could be easily shattered (Levine, 2006). Levine believed that children are being coddled and protected to a degree that threatens their ability to strike out on their own and form healthy relationships and work skills. They are not permitted to search on their own and find solutions to problems in their lives. In the past, parents would drop their children at the college steps and move out of the way. Today, parents call the administrative offices to intervene in things such as mediating roommate disputes, questioning a professor's grading system, or complaining about housing accommodations. Some researchers have offered a different view, asserting that labeling parents helicopter parents criticizes and disrespects the role they have in raising their children and that the stereotype has been harmful (Cole, 2007).

## Strategies for Working with Helicopter Parents: Understanding Partnership

Perceived hyper-involvement of parents often reflects the natural anxieties and concerns that parents have for their children once they leave the home and enter postsecondary education. It reveals a sense of deep responsibility they have for their children's success and long-term transition outcomes. Effective secondary personnel work with parents from a position of understanding the depth of that responsibility. The following principles for secondary education personnel will increase the chances for quality collaboration with parents.

- Begin with the premise that parents have the right and responsibility to be involved in their child's education and, particularly, in transition planning. Many parents deemed to be difficult are actually those who have experienced unresponsive teachers or administrators when they have brought concerns forward. This includes teachers and administrators who view parents as needing to be managed rather than as people with whom to partner.

- Recognize that working successfully with parents is a legitimate focus for staff development (Tingley, 2006).

- Principals and administrators set the tone in the building, so it is important that parents perceive the school as welcoming and inviting.

- Help parents view the secondary and transition process as a pathway to independence, along which they will need to relinquish their assumption of control over their child's future and adopt a role of mentor or guide. Appreciate that this is a most difficult psychological process for many parents and one for which they have not been prepared.

- Provide parents with information about transition rights, responsibilities, philosophy of self-determination, and factors that contribute to a successful transition. Include information about how parents can continue to guide their child in planning for graduation while strengthening their child's ability and confidence to make decisions.

- Make sure the school has a clear, written process for addressing parental objections about transition planning processes.

Administrators can support teachers not only by intervening in a timely manner when parents present behavior for which they are unprepared, but also by helping teachers develop collaboration strategies themselves. Teachers need to feel confident they can count on their administrator for support and guidance when the *involved* parent becomes the *impossible* parent. Secondary teachers can help overinvolved parents gain perspective by using the following strategies.

- Allow parents to express issues and concerns in a parent-teacher conference after school.

- Try to identify the underlying concerns of the parents.

- Make sure student assignments have detailed instructions and clear deadlines.

- Have the parent speak with the principal or assistant principal about the quality of the education that their child is receiving.

- Invite the parent to participate in planning educational experiences or field trips. Direct involvement may be helpful and a win-win for all.

- Send home weekly feedback and/or grade sheets on the child's performance and progress.

Secondary teachers and counselors can consider the following principles for guiding parents who might be considered overinvolved with their children. These could be integrated into parent training or parent handbooks.

- Encourage students to discuss their concerns about their future, but let them develop their own solutions. Problem solving is an important path to self-determination that should begin in the early grades, but particularly strengthened in the secondary years.

- Be available to answer questions about homework, but avoid giving the answers or doing the work for the child, even if the assignment seems too difficult.

- Understand that the parent's role is to create the conditions or environment in which their child can succeed in the secondary education class and during the transition to postsecondary education, engaging their child to the fullest extent possible.

- Respect teachers' schedules by making appointments and using e-mail. A child's teacher is usually happy to meet, but he or she also needs time to teach and prepare for class.

- Hold children accountable and let them experience the consequences of their actions. Especially by middle school, it is important to make a child responsible for studying, bringing homework home, and turning in assignments.

- The parents' role is to prepare their child to be a responsible and capable adult, so parents should decrease their involvement over time and let their child live his or her own life (Haller & Moorman, 2008).

## MULTICULTURAL IMPLICATIONS FOR SCHOOL–FAMILY COLLABORATION

There are various needs and issues that need to be addressed regarding school-family collaboration in multicultural contexts. These are discussed next.

### What Are the Unique Needs of Families Who Are Culturally and Linguistically Diverse?

The needs of students who are culturally and linguistically diverse are largely unmet in today's schools, as reflected by two important statistics. First, a disproportionate percentage of Hispanic, African American, and Native American students drop out or do not obtain a high school diploma (Garcia,

2005; National Center for Education Statistics, 2002; U.S. Department of Education, 2003). Second, and equally as important, is the disproportionate percentage of Latino, African American, and Native American students placed in special education classes (Cummins, 2001; Northwest Evaluation Association, 2005; Obiakor & Wilder, 2003). Although special education may meet the needs of students with disabilities, it can be inappropriate for students without disabilities. Research has demonstrated that improperly placing students who are culturally and linguistically diverse in special education can negatively affect their educational outcomes and potential career possibilities (Artiles, 2003; Cummins, 2001; Kochhar-Bryant & Greene, 2008; Obiakor & Wilder, 2003; Salend, Garrick-Duhaney, & Montgomery, 2002). These conditions and the growth in diversity of the student population are driving many changes in curriculum and instruction, student assessment, school organizational structure, administration, personnel preparation, and transition services. Students who are culturally and linguistically diverse demand a different lens on the educational environment and the needs of the students, particularly if they also have disabilities.

Children for whom English is not their primary language have numerous challenges to learning that require special responses on the part of teachers and administrators so that all students are given every opportunity to succeed in school and to make successful transitions to the postsecondary world. These challenges include 1) language differences that require teachers to understand how students learn to speak and read English when their primary language is different; 2) how student's immersion in the mainstream language affects academic progress and student assessment; 3) how student and family cultures affect students' learning and progress and curriculum and instruction; 4) how students who are culturally and linguistically diverse are evaluated and referred to special education so as to avoid over- or underrepresentation; 5) implications of culture and language for gaining access to community services; 6) attitudes and practices that negatively affect student groups that are culturally and linguistically diverse; and 7) implications of culture for high school transition planning and employment preparation.

These challenges demand that educators appreciate the complex interaction of language, culture, and professional knowledge and attitudes in the education and transition of students who are culturally and linguistically diverse. According to many observers, the implications of this new reality are not being fully considered by those advocating or undertaking school reform and improvement (Mcleod, 2005; Zehler, Fleischman, Hopstock, Pendzick, & Stephenson, 2003). The Council for Exceptional Children (2001) developed specific content standards for teachers and administrators that address diversity and the role of families in the educational process. Secondary personnel, counselors, and administrators must be familiar with the special needs of students with and without disabilities who are culturally and linguistically diverse.

## Barriers to Transition to
## Postsecondary Education for Students and
## Families Who Are Culturally and Linguistically Diverse

Significant barriers exist to making a successful transition for youth with disabilities and their families who are culturally and linguistically diverse during the secondary years. These are grouped below into three categories: 1) characteristics of families who are culturally and linguistically diverse, 2) school-imposed barriers to transition, and 3) professional insensitivity of secondary personnel.

## Characteristics of Families Who Are Culturally and Linguistically Diverse

The characteristics of people within and between particular cultural groups vary widely. Not all members of a given culture are the same with respect to their acculturation into the society, values, or beliefs of the United States. For this reason, secondary and transition personnel should not make assumptions that an individual will behave in a certain way or possess a set of values and beliefs related to their culture. Stereotyping behaviors by IEP team members can result in barriers to effective communication with youth with disabilities who are culturally and linguistically diverse and their families during the transition years.

## School-Imposed Barriers to Transition

Although IDEA 2004 strongly encourages self-advocacy and active participation of youth with disabilities and their families during the IEP transition planning process, members of groups who are culturally and linguistically diverse frequently face school-imposed barriers (see Chapter 4 for an in-depth discussion of self-advocacy). For example, parents who are culturally and linguistically diverse and have youth with disabilities may at times feel uncomfortable within the school setting because of their educational backgrounds and limited experience with American schools. IEP team members, in turn, often falsely assume that these parents are unable to grasp the material discussed in an IEP meeting.

A study by Harry, Allen, and McLaughlin (1995) revealed the following five aspects of professional educator behavior that functioned as active deterrents to African American parents' participation and advocacy for their children in special education conferences.

1. *Late notices and inflexible scheduling of conferences.* Problems included 1) parents receiving notices 2–3 days prior to a scheduled meeting despite the state's 10-day prior notice requirement, 2) administrators' reluctance to adjust meeting dates or attend meetings, and 3) scheduling of meetings at times impossible for parents to attend.

2. *Limited time for conferences.* Only 20–30 minutes were allowed for most conferences, regardless of the complexity or status of the deliberations. Parents who needed additional time were advised to continue their discussions with teachers after the meeting, despite the fact that many of the teachers were not available because they had to cover classes and no assistant was available to release them from their teaching responsibilities.

3. *Emphasis on documents rather than participation.* It was common for parents to be advised not to worry about missing a conference they could not attend because the documents would be mailed to them to sign. Many parents said they had trouble understanding the terminology in the

reports and believed that their main role was to receive information about their child's progress and to sign documents rather than to provide input to school personnel.

4. *The use of jargon.* Parents were confused by unexplained educational jargon, classification codes, test results, and information contained in technical reports. The result was that parents generally felt that the conference process was intimidating.

5. *The structure of power.* The interpersonal dynamics of the meetings placed parents at a distinct disadvantage and undermined their effort and ability to act as advocates for their children. Conferences were structured in a way that gave power and authority completely to professionals (e.g., professionals reported and parents listened); parents generally felt that the conference process was intimidating.

In short, schools can be a foreign place for families and youth with disabilities who are culturally and linguistically diverse. This can lead to a feeling of isolation when participating in a transition planning meeting. These feelings are exacerbated when IEP team members behave in ways that discourage active participation of parents who are culturally and linguistically diverse, such as abbreviating time for meetings, using a lot of educational jargon, or using authority in an intimidating manner.

Further complicating matters is the misguided perception of school professionals that parents who are culturally and linguistically diverse do not care or are apathetic to school-based approaches to transition planning. Many lack understanding of the cultural context in which parents who are culturally and linguistically diverse wish to address transition planning decisions for their child.

### Professional Insensitivity

Cultural sensitivity training begins with an understanding and respect for a family's perspective on their youth with disabilities, along with their hopes and plans for the child's future. Answers to the following questions by family members who are culturally and linguistically diverse will help provide this transition-related information.

1. What language is spoken in the home and by which members? What is the literacy level of family members?

2. What are the family's norms for personal and social development for their youth with a disability? What degree of independence is encouraged?

3. What independent living, postsecondary, and work-related goals does the family hold for the youth with a disability?

4. What are the family's views on disabilities, and how does this affect their choice of postsecondary goals and interventions?

5. What are the family child-rearing practices? Are they authoritarian and hierarchical, with children having little decision-making power, or do children possess equal and individual rights as practiced in many homes in the United States?

---

**Box 7.5.** Circle of support at The University of Hawaii

Fasy (Faz-ee) grew up in a small island country in the Pacific Ocean. He became paralyzed as a teenager when he fell from a cliff and suffered a serious spinal injury. Unable to walk, he learned to use a wheelchair. Neither the schools nor other government services provided much in special services for people like Fasy. With his determination and academic capabilities, however, he earned entry to The University of Hawaii at Manoa. A number of support services were available to him there. Due to the seriousness of his disability, Fasy required assistance to get around campus and take care of his basic needs, but extensive aide services were not available. Fortunately, in keeping with the family orientation of his Pacific Island culture, some of his family members were able to come to Hawaii specifically to support him to reach his postsecondary education goals. During much of his academic career, one or two of his brothers were always at his side, and when they were not available, other family members assisted him. With the support of his family, Fasy earned his bachelor's degree and then two master's degrees, one in history and the other in Pacific Islands studies. The challenges presented by his disability as well as cultural and language differences resulted in Fasy taking several extra years to complete his studies. His own efforts, the supports provided by his family, and the supports provided by the university, however, were successful. Now in his late 30s, Fasy is the director of one of the four campuses of his country's national university.

---

6. How much legal knowledge about parental rights and advocacy does the family possess? For example, is schooling viewed as a privilege or a right?

In summary, secondary and transition personnel must possess knowledge and sensitivity to the complex nature of cultural and linguistic diversity and the worlds from which families have come. Cultural diversity training programs are one vehicle for accomplishing this objective, provided they offer the necessary breadth and depth of understanding about various cultural groups and provide valid answers to the critical questions about a family's unique characteristics. Box 7.5 illustrates the importance of family unity in a family that is culturally and linguistically diverse.

The vignette illustrates how a cultural strength (individuals giving priority to the success of the family as a whole) can be built on to support a student with disabilities who is culturally and linguistically diverse to achieve postsecondary educational success. What is notable in this case is the ready and coordinated participation of the entire family. This collectivist orientation contrasts with the individualistic orientation of mainstream American society and should be taken into account when addressing the support needs of people with disabilities from collectivist cultural backgrounds (Leake & Cholymay, 2002).

## SUMMARY

- A family is a complex social system in which no member can be viewed in isolation.

- Awareness and sensitivity to the pressures, values, and perspectives family members bring to the school–family collaboration process and transition planning is the starting point for productive parent participation.

- Educators cannot expect a family's involvement in their children's education and development to disappear once the child enters into the phase of transition to postsecondary education; the nature of that involvement must change.

- Building self-determination in youth in transition relies on constructive parent relationships that promote self-reliance and support independent decision making.

- Changes to IDEA 2004 and the No Child Left Behind (NCLB) Act of 2001 (PL 107-110) reflect a strengthening of the long-standing federal commitment to parent involvement in the education of all children.

- Family adaptation to living with a child who has special needs can be viewed as a developmental process of growth and resilience that builds on the strengths of the family.

- The strength of teacher–family relationships is tied to the quality of preparation of teachers for such collaboration.

- Challenging parent behavior often reflects the natural anxieties and concerns that parents have for their children and the sense of deep responsibility they have for their children's transition outcomes. Professionals should work with parents from a position of understanding the depth of that responsibility.

- Secondary and transition personnel must possess knowledge of and sensitivity to the complex nature of cultural and linguistic diversity and its effects on transition planning.

This chapter examined the needs of professionals and families in the dynamic interaction with their children along the developmental path of transition to adulthood. Today, schools share the responsibility with community agencies for creating a transition service system for all students with disabilities. Students who are culturally and linguistically diverse now constitute the fastest growing segment of the educational systems in the nation. The challenge of making a successful transition through school and into post–high school roles is particularly difficult for people with disabilities of culturally and linguistically diverse heritage.

Many schools are creating school-based community resource centers to expand the participation of families in the education of their children. Together, the IDEA 2004 and NCLB set expectations for parent–professional partnerships that are unprecedented for the public school system. IDEA 2004 and NCLB emphasize the importance of the parent-professional partnership in educational services and improving educational outcomes for children and youth and the importance of strengthening the families' role in decision making and educational improvement.

## REFERENCES

Abrams, L.S., & Gibbs, J.T. (2002). Disrupting the logic of home–school relations: Parent participation and practices of inclusion and exclusion. *Urban Education, 37*(3), 384-407.

Ames, N., & Dickerson, A. (2004). Five barriers to parent involvement. *Middle Matters, 13*(1), 6–10.

Ammon, M., Chrispeels, J., Safran, D., Sandy, M., Dear, J., & Reyes, M. (2000). *Preparing educators for partnerships with families.* Sacramento: California Commission on Teaching Credentialing.

Artiles, A.J. (2003). Special education's changing identity: Paradoxes and dilemmas in views of culture and space. *Harvard Educational Review, 73*(2), 164–202.

Berg, J., Donaldson, M.L., & Johnson, S.M. (2005). *Who stays in teaching and why: A review of the literature on teacher retention.* Boston: Harvard Graduate School of Education.

Bernhard, J.K., Freire, M., Pacini-Ketchabaw, V., & Villanueva, V. (1998). A Latin-American parent's group participates in their children's schooling: Parent involvement reconsidered. *Canadian Ethnic Studies, 30*(3), 77–99.

Black, S. (2005, October). Rethinking parent conferences. *American School Board Journal.* Retrieved July 27, 2004, from http://www.asbj.com/MainMenuCategory/Archive/2005/October/RethinkingParentConferencesDoc427.aspx

Blank, M. (2001). *School–community partnerships in support of student learning.* Washington, DC: Institute for Educational Leadership, Coalition for Community Schools.

Brilliant, C., & Duke, G. (2001). Parental involvement in education: Attitudes and activities of Spanish-speakers as affected by training. *Bilingual Research Journal, 25*(3), 251–274.

Carnegie Council on Adolescent Development. (1995). *Great transitions: Preparing adolescents for a new century.* New York: Carnegie Corporation.

CBS. (2008). *60 minutes: The "Millennials" are coming.* Retrieved January 10, 2009, from http://www.cbsnews.com/stories/2007/11/08/60minutes/main3475200.shtml

Christenson, S.L., & Sheridan, S.M. (2001). *Schools and families: Creating essential connections for children's learning.* New York: Guilford Press.

Christie, K. (2005). Changing the nature of parent involvement. *Phi Delta Kappan, 86*(9), 645–646.

Clark, G.M. (2007). *Assessment for transitions planning* (2nd ed.). Austin, TX: PRO-ED.

Cline, F., & Fay, J. (2006). *Parenting with love and logic.* Bedford, OH: Pinion Press.

Cole, D. (2007). *Warning! Helicopter parents at 1,000 feet!* Retrieved December 15, 2008, from http://www.cbsnews.com/stories/2007/08/16/backtoschool/main3174106_page2.shtml

Council for Exceptional Children. (2001). *Content standards for all beginning special education teachers.* Arlington, VA: Author.

Cummins, J. (2001). Empowering minority students: A framework for intervention. *Harvard Educational Review, 71*(4), 656–676.

Dearing, E., McCartney, K., Weiss, H.B., Kreider, H., & Simpkins, S. (2004). The promotive effects of family educational involvement for low-income children's literacy. *Journal of School Psychology, 42,* 445–460.

Education Commission of the States. (2004). *Parental involvement policy.* Retrieved December 4, 2005, from http://www.publiceducation.org/pdf/nclb/parental_involvement.pdf

Elfers, A.M., Knapp, M.S., Zahir, A., & Plecki, M.L. (2005). *Preparation and support for teaching: Teachers' response to state education reform.* Working paper prepared for the Center for Strengthening the Teaching Profession.

Epstein, J.L. (2001). *School, family, and community partnerships: Preparing educators and improving schools.* Boulder, CO: Westview Press.

Family Educational Rights and Privacy Act (FERPA) of 1974, PL 93-380, 20 U.S.C. §§ 1232g *et seq.*

Fortin, J. (2008). *Hovering parents need to step back at college time.* Retrieved February 4, 2008, from http://www.cnn.com/2008/HEALTH/family/02/04/hm.helicopter.parents/index.html?iref=newssearch

Garcia, E. (2005). *NCLR Escalera Project: Taking steps to success.* Washington, DC: National Council for La Raza, Division of Workforce and Economic Development.

Haller, T., & Moorman, C. (2008). *Teaching the Attraction Principle™ to children: Practical strategies for parents and teachers to help children manifest a better world.* Merrill, MI: Personal Power Press.

Harry, B., Allen, N., & McLaughlin, M. (1995). Communication versus compliance: African American parents' involvement in special education. *Exceptional Children, 61*(4), 364–377.

Hausslein, E.B., Kaufmann, R.K., & Hurth, J. (1992, February). From case management to service coordination: Families, policymaking, and Part H. *Zero to Three,* 10–12.

Havinghurst, R. (1972). *Developmental tasks and education* (3rd. ed.). New York: Random House.

Henderson, A., & Mapp, K. (2002). *A new wave of evidence: The impact of school, family, and community connections on student achievement.* Austin, TX: Southwest Educational Development Laboratory.

Henderson, K. (2008). *Optional IDEA alternative dispute resolution.* Alexandria, VA: National Association for State Directors of Special Education.

Higher Education Opportunity Act of 2008, PL 110-315.

Individuals with Disabilities Education Improvement Act (IDEA) of 2004, PL 108-446, 20 U.S.C. §§ 1400 *et seq.*

Jacobs, J.E., & Bleeker, M.M. (2004). Girls' and boys' developing interests in math and science: Do parents matter? *New Directions for Child and Adolescent Development, 106,* 5–21.

Kochhar-Bryant, C., & Greene, G. (2008). *Pathways to successful transition for students with disabilities: A developmental process.* Upper Saddle River, NJ: Prentice Hall.

Kreider, H., Caspe, M., Kennedy, S., & Weiss, H. (2007). *Family involvement in middle and high school students' education.* Cambridge, MA: Harvard Family Research Project.

Leake, D., & Cholymay, M. (2002). Addressing the needs of culturally and linguistically diverse students with disabilities in postsecondary education. *National Center on Secondary Education and Transition: Information Brief, 3*(1).

Levine, M. (2006). *The price of privilege: How parental pressure and material advantage are creating a generation of disconnected and unhappy kids.* New York: HarperCollins.

Lightfoot, S.L. (2001). *Partnerships with families: The presence of parents can transform the culture of a school.* Retrieved August 15, 2003, from http://www.nwrel.org/cfc/frc/beyus12.html

Mapp, K. (2004). Family engagement. In F.P. Schargel & J. Smink (Eds.), *Helping students graduate: A strategic approach to dropout prevention* (pp. 99–113). Larchmont, NY: Eye on Education.

McDonough, P.M. (2007). *Parent involvement for improved college access.* Los Angeles: University of California, Graduate School of Education and Information Studies.

Mcleod, P. (2005). *Instructional strategies for English learners with disabilities.* Washington, DC: Council of Chief State School Officers.

MetLife. (2005). *MetLife survey of the American teacher: Transitions and the role of supportive relationships: A survey of teachers, principals and students.* New York: Harris Interactive.

Morningstar, M., & Wehmeyer, M. (2008). The role of families in enhancing transition outcomes for youth with learning disabilities. In J. Patton & G. Blalock (Eds.), *Transition and students with learning disabilities: Facilitating the movement from school to adult life* (2nd ed.). Austin, TX: PRO-ED.

National Center for Education Statistics. (2002). *The condition of education.* Washington, DC: U.S. Department of Education, Office of Education Research and Improvement.

National Center for Family Literacy. (2004). *Stories of impact: Improving parent involvement through family literacy in the elementary school.* Louisville, KY: Author.

National Coalition for Parent Involvement in Education. (2001). *Institute for responsive education promoting family and community involvement in education.* Fairfax, VA: Author.

National Joint Committee on Learning Disabilities. (1994). *Secondary to postsecondary education transition planning for students with learning disabilities.* Retrieved September 4, 2009, from http://www.ldonline.org/article/Secondary_to_Postsecondary_ Education_ Transition_Planning_for_Students_with_Learning_Disabilities

National Joint Committee on Learning Disabilities. (2007). *Transition to school and work: A blueprint for your child's success after high school.* Retrieved September 4, 2009, from http://www.ldonline.org/article/Transition_to_School_and_Work:_A_ blueprint_for_your_child's_success_after_high_school

National Longitudinal Transition Study-2. (2005). *Changes over time in postschool outcomes of youth with disabilities.* Retrieved January 23, 2008, from http://nlts2.org/pdfs/ str6_completereport.pdf

Newman, L. (2004). *Family involvement in the educational development of youth with disabilities. A special topic report of the National Longitudinal Transition Study-2.* Menlo Park, CA: SRI International.

No Child Left Behind Act of 2001, PL 107-110, 115 Stat. 1425, 20 U.S.C. §§ 6301 *et seq.*

Nord, C.W., & West, J. (2001). *Fathers' and mothers' involvement in their children's schools by family type and resident status.* Washington, DC: U.S. Department of Education, National Center for Education Statistics.

North Central Regional Educational Laboratory. (2001). *Urban parent involvement overview.* Retrieved June 23, 2004, from http://www.ncrel.org/sdrs

Northwest Evaluation Association. (2005, April 8). *The impact of the No Child Left Behind Act on student achievement and growth: 2005 edition.* Retrieved July 27, 2009, from http://www.nwea.org/research/getareport.asp?ReportID=46

Novick, R. (2001). *Family involvement and beyond: School-based child and family support programs.* Portland, OR: Northwest Regional Education Laboratory.

Obiakor, F.E., & Wilder, L.K. (2003). Disproportionate representation in special education. *Principal Leadership, 4*(2), 16–22.

Pacer Center. (2007). *Parent tips for transition planning.* Minneapolis, MN: Technical Assistance Alliance for Parent Centers.

Pena, D. (2000). Parent involvement: Influencing factors and implications. *Journal of Educational Research, 94*(1), 42–55.

Perkins, D.F. (1997). *Adolescence: Developmental tasks* [Fact sheet FCS 2118]. Department of Family, Youth, and Community Services, Florida Cooperative Extension Service, Institute of Food and Agricultural Sciences, University of Florida; retrieved September 4, 2009, from edis.ifas.ufl.edu/pdffiles/HE/HE82000.pdf

Pleet, A. (2000). *Partnering with parents of youth with disabilities in the transition.* Annual conference of the National Transition Alliance, Transition Research Institute, University of Illinois, Champaign.

Price, T. (2005). *Development of an instrument to measure dispositions of teachers toward culturally and linguistically diverse families.* Unpublished dissertation, George Washington University, Washington, DC.

Raimondo, B., & Henderson, A. (2001). Unlocking parent potential. *Principal Leadership, 2*(1), 26–32.

Redmond, P. (2008). *Here comes the chopper: Helicopter parents.* Retrieved December 12, 2008, from http://www.guardian.co.uk/education/2008/jan/02/students.uk

Salend, S.J., Garrick-Duhaney, L.M., & Montgomery, W. (2002). A comprehensive approach to identifying and addressing issues of disproportionate representation. *Remedial and Special Education, 23*(5), 289–300.

Shapira, I. (2008, July 6). What comes next after Generation X? *The Washington Post,* p. C01.

Study of State and Local Implementation and Impact of the Individuals With Disabilities Education Act. (2003). *Highlights from the 1999–2000 school year: Year 1 data collection.* Bethesda, MD: Abt Associates.

Technical Assistance Alliance for Parent Centers. (2005). *Developing parent leadership: A grant writing manual for community parent resource centers.* Minneapolis, MN: Author.

Tingley, S. (2006). *How to handle difficult parents: A teacher's survival guide.* Fort Collins, CO: Cottonwood Press.

Turnbull, A., Turnbull, H.R., Erwin, E., & Soodak, L. (2006). *Families, professionals, and exceptionality: Positive outcomes through partnerships and trust* (5th ed.). Upper Saddle River, NJ: Merrill/Prentice Hall.

U.S. Department of Education, Office of Special Education and Rehabilitative Services. (2003). *National symposium on learning disabilities in English language learners.* Washington, DC: Author.

U.S. Government Accountability Office. (2003). *Federal actions can assist state in improving postsecondary outcomes for youth.* Washington, DC: Author.

Wandry, D., & Pleet, A. (2002). *The role of families in secondary transition: A practitioner's facilitation guide.* Arlington, VA: Council for Exceptional Children.

Zarrett, N., & Eccles, J. (2006). The passage to adulthood: Challenges of late adolescence. *New Directions for Youth Development, 111,* 13–28.

Zehler, A.M., Fleischman, H.L., Hopstock, P.J., Pendzick, M.L., & Stephenson, T.G. (2003). *Descriptive study of services to LEP students and LEP students with disabilities.* Arlington, VA: Development Associates.

Zhang, D., Wehmeyer, M., & Chen, L.J. (2005). Parent and teacher engagement in fostering the self-determination of students with disabilities: A comparison between the U.S. and the Republic of China. *Remedial and Special Education, 26,* 55–56.

# Gathering Data to Determine Eligibility for Services and Accommodations

*Lyman L. Dukes, III*

## WHAT YOU'LL LEARN IN THIS CHAPTER:

✔ The relationship between transition assessment and being "otherwise qualified" for college or program entry

✔ How transition assessment works

✔ What tools you can use to gather transition assessment data

✔ The role of the student in the transition assessment process

✔ How to select measurable postsecondary goals and measure progress toward them

✔ How to use the Nationally Ratified Summary of Performance template with transition assessment

✔ How to complete a summary of academic and functional performance (SOP) for a student who will attend college

## MEET JAMES DELGADO

Hi. My name is James Delgado. I'm a student with a language-based learning disability who is interested in going to college. I was diagnosed with a learning disability during the fourth grade. I was really lucky that my special education resource teacher, Ms. Miller, was so nice about ensuring that my parents participated in decisions about the services I received during elementary school. They knew about the accommodations Ms. Miller arranged so that I could do well in school and demonstrate that I could fit in academically just like the other students in the regular class. Since then, my parents have always been there to guide me through the school process. I remember Ms. Miller encouraging my parents to be active participants in my education, and one of my favorite memories was multicultural awareness week when my mom and dad came in and cooked Spanish food for my fifth-grade class. More recently, they've helped me find summer work in my areas of interest—graphic design and photography. I've also met with my school transition specialist and guidance counselor who have helped me better identify what colleges and college majors might be good matches for me. I'm just about a month from finishing high school and have spent time with my high school resource teacher preparing for my last individualized education program (IEP) meeting and presenting the SOP she helped me complete. Most important, I will finish high school with a 3.1 grade-point average and am planning to go to a 4-year college away from home, live on campus, and work part time during the summers in graphic design or photography.

## CHAPTER OVERVIEW

Transition assessment plays a critical role in the post–high school outcomes of students with disabilities. Upon entry to high school, if not before, students must begin to consider their goals for adult life (i.e., postsecondary goals). The Individuals with Disabilities Education Improvement Act (IDEA) of 2004 (PL 108-446) dictates that a student's goals for education/training, employment, and, if appropriate, independent living be developed no later than age 16 (§ 300.320b). The student and family should lead in determining these goals and play a purposeful role in the entire transition process (Field & Hoffman, 2007). Transition assessment, which is mandated by law, should aid students in identifying preferences and interests, post–high school goals, instructional and transition service needs, and supports to meet identified goals. Effective and ongoing assessment ensures that as the goals of the student and family shift, the IEP and subsequent instructional activities and supports will shift in concert. The SOP, which provides the student the opportunity to summarize the transition assessment data compiled throughout high school, serves as a culminating opportunity for the student to reflect on his or her strengths and needs and the accommodations and services he or she used in high school that were effective. In addition, the SOP

---

**Box 8.1.** Critical questions when considering college attendance

• What knowledge, skills, and strategies are necessary for the student to be successful in college?

• What knowledge, skills, and strategies does the student currently possess?

• What knowledge, skills, and strategies does the student need to develop during high school?

• What reasonable and appropriate accommodations are necessary and are best aligned with what may be provided in a college setting?

• What community linkages may be helpful or necessary?

---

allows the student to consider what role the accommodations and services may play in adult academic and employment environments.

This chapter provides an overview of the transition assessment process. Methods for gathering data are addressed, and the importance of student and family participation is highlighted. Both measurable postsecondary goals and the SOP are described and examples of each are provided.

## RELATIONSHIP BETWEEN TRANSITION ASSESSMENT AND BEING "OTHERWISE QUALIFIED"

According to IDEA 2004, students with disabilities are entitled to a free appropriate public education (FAPE), to include special education and any necessary related services that must be provided in a manner that meets the unique needs of the student and facilitates his or her post–high school goals in education or training, employment, and, when appropriate, independent living (300.1[a]). Colleges are not under the same obligation, however. Instead, Section 504 of the Rehabilitation Act of 1973 (PL 93-112), the Americans with Disabilities Act (ADA) of 1990 (PL 101-336), and Americans with Disabilities Act Amendments Act (ADAAA) of 2008 (PL 110-325) prohibit discrimination based on disability and ensure *equal access* (italics added) for people with disabilities who are "otherwise qualified" (Madaus, 2005).

Students are advised to consider their postsecondary goals when entering high school. In fact, decisions made during the first years of high school can affect one's capacity to attend some postsecondary institutions. Transition assessment data aids in determining student postsecondary goals and identifying appropriate instructional experiences and transition service needs that are necessary to meet those goals. If the student and family have identified college as a postsecondary goal, then the IEP team should initiate the transition assessment process by considering the questions identified in Box 8.1. Consider, for example, that students who have not completed a college preparatory track of mathematics courses or those who have not successfully completed 2 years of high school foreign language courses may be denied admission to the college and/or college program of their choice.

Effective transition assessment begins with creating an assessment plan that is individualized in order to meet the specific needs of the student (Morningstar, 2008c). Critical skills in college environments include, but are not limited to, self-determination and self-advocacy skills; understanding rights and responsibilities; study, note-taking, and time management skills; reading, math, and writing ability; and social skills and recreational activities. Selected assessment activities should reflect the skills about which the team needs data. An individualized assessment plan for a student includes examining existing data in the student's case file and evaluating any knowledge or skill area for which the assessment team does not already have applicable data. In response to the data, relevant and productive learning experiences and transition services are identified and implemented to address areas in which the student needs improvement. In a nutshell, an individualized assessment plan that leads to preparation in knowledge and skill areas appropriate for college maximizes the chances of being "otherwise qualified" for college entry after high school graduation. The definition of transition assessment is examined next.

## TRANSITION ASSESSMENT DEFINED

*Transition assessment,* according to Sitlington, Neubert, Begun, Lombard, and LeConte, is defined as an

> Ongoing process of collecting data on the individual's strengths, needs, preferences, and interests as they relate to the demands of current and future living, learning, and working environments. Information from this process should be used to drive the IEP and transition planning process and to develop the student's SOP document detailing the student's academic and functional performance and postsecondary goals. (2007, pp. 2–3)

In summary, the first step of a typical transition assessment data gathering plan is to determine the student's interests, preferences, strengths, and needs. Once it has been established that college is a realistic option and the preferred goal of the student and family, the process should shift to building a course of study that has the greatest likelihood of resulting in college entry. Transition assessment, including both formal and informal measures, can provide the data necessary to make evidence-based decisions regarding what skills the student should learn and what accommodations and supports are appropriate given the student's goals. Transition assessment should occur on a continuous basis and be implemented in a fashion that allows the student and family to regularly (e.g., at least annually) revisit critical decisions regarding the student's goals for adulthood.

### Principles of Transition Assessment

Morningstar (2008a) identified five principles for transition assessment. They are described in the following sections.

## Use a Variety of Assessment Methods

First, a variety of assessment methods should be used in order to generate the data necessary to answer your questions. Because life demands are varied (e.g., school, home, work), it is necessary to assess skills using a variety of methods. As Clark stated, "Standardized and non-standardized, quantitative and qualitative, group and individual, educational and non-educational, professional and non-professional—each approach has some value at certain points and for certain needs" (2007, pp. 78–79). Clark went on to note that this does not mean one should use a "shotgun" approach. Methods should be selected that ensure both efficiency and effectiveness. Selected methods should be reflective of the assessment questions one is trying to answer.

## Use Multiple Sources

Next, assessment information should be verified by multiple sources. Colleges and their disability support service programs are obligated to provide "equal educational opportunity," not a FAPE. In the interest of providing students an equal opportunity rather than unfair advantage, colleges typically base accommodation decisions on examination of multiple data sources. The use of multiple sources, as opposed to one source, is intended to ensure clear and compelling support of the services provided to students with disabilities. It is critical that accommodation decisions made by secondary personnel follow suit. Accommodation decisions should be supported by multiple data sources, and these decisions should be reflected in student disability documentation records. Furthermore, students should be able to explain (i.e., demonstrate self-advocacy) how the accommodations they have received are appropriately and reasonably related to their diagnosed disability.

## Work Collaboratively

Although one person should be responsible for coordinating the transition assessment process, this does not mean one person should assume responsibility for all relevant transition tasks. Possible participants include special and general education teachers, paraprofessionals, school counselors, school psychologists, technology specialists, and college disability service representatives. Completing assessment tasks should be appropriately split among the transition assessment team. The assessment coordinator is in the position to lead the discussion about the needs of each student.

## Ensure Student Participation

Next, the student should participate to the greatest extent possible. Given that the ultimate goal of transition assessment is to improve outcomes for *students* as they enter adulthood, student participation should be considered a guiding principle of the data gathering and examination process. Students should not only be invited to meetings, which is required by IDEA 2004, but they also can and should be active participants in meetings. In addition, students can and should participate in the data gathering and analysis process, identifying transition goals, and determining whether the goals have been achieved. See Chapter 4 for more detailed information regarding student participation.

### Align IEP Goals with Postsecondary Goals

Last, determining the degree to which the transition IEP is preparing the student to achieve his or her goals for adulthood completes the process. Once students have identified postsecondary goals—in this case, college attendance—then it is necessary to ensure that annual IEP goals are those that measurably move the student toward his or her goal of college attendance. Consider, for example, that assessment results determine a student does not understand how to describe her disability, nor does she know what she might be interested in studying once in college. Suitable annual IEP goals for this student would include developing self-advocacy skills and completing interest assessments and subsequent visits to work sites relevant to identified career interest areas.

> Make a list of the knowledge and skill areas to be assessed. Identify a minimum of three to five assessment tools that will allow you to gather information in the domain areas you have listed for the student.

## What Is an "Age-Appropriate Transition Assessment?"

The National Secondary Transition Technical Assistance Center (NSTTAC) noted that the "activities, assessments, content, environments, instruction and/or materials" used should be chosen in light of the chronological age of the student (2007a, p. 1). The following principles should be considered when identifying age-appropriate transition assessments (Sitlington, Neubert, & Leconte, 1997).

1.  Assessment methods must be selected based on the types of information needed and the decisions to be made regarding transition planning and various postsecondary outcomes. For example, if a student is interested in college, then assessing the types of college options and the services they provide to students with disabilities would be helpful.

2.  Assessment methods selected must be appropriate given the learning characteristics of the student, including any cultural and linguistic differences. Consider the following factors: the cultural norms of the student and family, the possibility that past or present discrimination may affect assessment results, and the need for assistance with communication between the school and the student/family. Clark (2007) made the following suggestions to mitigate the aforementioned concerns.

If there are any concerns after the meeting with the student and family, then connect with members of the cultural community to clarify any matters that remain unclear; ask the student/family to dialogue about past or present discrimination concerns; and make translators or interpreters available to ensure effective school–family communication.

3.  Assessment methods must incorporate assistive technology or accommodations that will allow an individual to demonstrate his or her abilities and potential. Using reasonable and appropriate accommodations will allow the student and school staff to gain an accurate picture of the student's strengths and needs.

4.  Assessment methods must occur in environments that resemble actual vocational training, employment, independent living, or community environments. Although one cannot replicate college prior to attendance, certain skill sets are known to promote college completion. Given that student self-determination is considered critical for college success, evaluating the degree to which a student independently leads activities such as the IEP meeting would be appropriate. In addition, one might evaluate the degree to which a student independently develops educational goals, gathers data regarding goal attainment, and interprets and acts on the data.

5.  Assessment methods must produce outcomes that contribute to ongoing development, planning, and implementing next steps in the individual's transition process. School professionals must regularly reflect on the degree to which assessment results are being effectively used to move the student toward his or her goals for adulthood. Are the assessment outcomes reflected in the annual IEP goals? Have the student, family, and school personnel reflected on how present assessment results and current IEP goals align with possible IEP goals for any subsequent school years and the student's postsecondary goals for education, employment, and independent living?

6.  Assessment methods must be varied and include a sequence of activities that sample an individual's behavior and skills over time. That is, more than one data gathering method should be used and assessment should be ongoing. Student interests, strengths, and needs will change over time.

7.  Assessment data must be verified by more than one method and by more than one person.

8.  Assessment data must be synthesized and interpreted to individuals with disabilities, their families, and transition team members. Consider the extent to which the student and family have been prepared to participate in the data gathering/interpretation process. The process should be led, to the degree appropriate, by the student and family.

9.  Assessment data and the results of the assessment process must be documented in a format that can be used to facilitate transition planning. Options for housing results include school cumulative files, IEP files maintained by the case manager, student portfolios, or some combination of the three (Clark, 2007).

## Transition Assessment Data: The What and When

Figure 8.1 provides a helpful time line for when specific transition-relevant skills should be assessed (Clark, 2007; Virginia Department of Education, 2008). The time line indicates that assessing these skill sets can begin as early as elementary school and is an iterative process across the entire K–12 school experience. Again, because student preferences, interests, and strengths change over time, it is critical that transition assessments be consistently revisited. Readers should bear in mind that the time line is only a guide. Depending on the student, assessments may begin before the suggested time line date and may go on beyond the dates indicated (Virginia Department of Education, 2008).

## Tools for Gathering Transition Assessment Data

According to Clark (2007), data should be collected in up to eight transition-relevant domains. Sitlington and Clark stated that these areas are "basic to minimum compliance for appropriate assessment of both academic and functional performance as well as to meeting the basic transition service considerations for interests and preferences" (2007, p. 134). The eight areas are as follows.

1.  *Interests:* Gather data regarding what a person likes to do. In the case of students interested in college, this may help him or her choose an appropriate program of study.

2.  *Preferences:* These are related to choices one makes among interest areas. Typically, they are driven by one's ability to make informed personal choices. It is critical that students have the opportunity to both develop and exercise choice-making skills.

3.  *Cognitive development and academic achievement performance:* Academic achievement is a cornerstone of the postsecondary experience. Helping students determine their cognitive and academic strengths as well as those areas in which they may need support will go a long way toward setting them up for college entry and completion.

4.  *Adaptive behavior:* Although these skills may not be applicable to all students interested in college, they certainly may apply to some. For example, personal hygiene and the ability to drive or use public transportation can be issues depending on disability. If necessary, these skills should be reflected in a comprehensive assessment plan.

5.  *Interpersonal relationship skills:* It has been argued that social skill deficits are as debilitating or more so than many cognitive or academic weaknesses. Skills to be assessed in this area include understanding differences between socially appropriate and inappropriate behavior, sensitivity to diversity, and social behavior specific to college settings (e.g., professor–student interactions).

6.  *Emotional development and mental health:* Again, although not applicable to all, some students can benefit from assessing emotional and mental

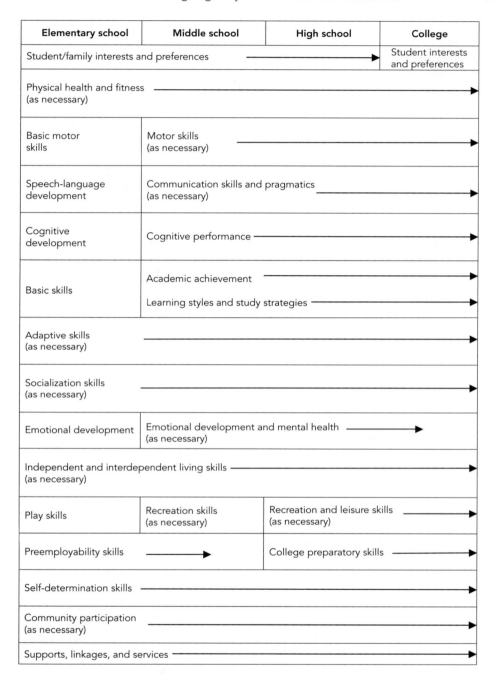

| Elementary school | Middle school | High school | College |
|---|---|---|---|
| Student/family interests and preferences →→→→→→ | | | Student interests and preferences |
| Physical health and fitness (as necessary) →→→→→→→→→→ | | | |
| Basic motor skills | Motor skills (as necessary) →→→→→→→→→→→ | | |
| Speech-language development | Communication skills and pragmatics (as necessary) →→→→→→→→→ | | |
| Cognitive development | Cognitive performance →→→→→→→→→→→→ | | |
| Basic skills | Academic achievement →→→→→→→→→→ | | |
| | Learning styles and study strategies →→→→→ | | |
| Adaptive skills (as necessary) →→→→→→→→→→→→→→→ | | | |
| Socialization skills (as necessary) →→→→→→→→→→→→→→→ | | | |
| Emotional development | Emotional development and mental health →→→ (as necessary) | | |
| Independent and interdependent living skills →→→→→→→→→→ (as necessary) | | | |
| Play skills | Recreation skills (as necessary) | Recreation and leisure skills →→→→→ (as necessary) | |
| Preemployability skills →→→→ | | College preparatory skills →→→→→→ | |
| Self-determination skills →→→→→→→→→→→→→→→ | | | |
| Community participation (as necessary) →→→→→→→→→→→→→→ | | | |
| Supports, linkages, and services →→→→→→→→→→→→→→→ | | | |

**Figure 8.1.**   Transition assessment time line for college-bound students. (From Virginia Department of Education Training and Technical Assistance Center. [2008]. *Virginia Department of Education transition assessment packet 2008*. Retrieved September 26, 2008, from www.vcu.edu/ttac/transition/doc/assessment_packet.doc; adapted by permission.)

health. Greater numbers of students with psychiatric disabilities are seeking college entry. Challenges include low self-esteem, anger management, and suicide. College demands can exacerbate these complexities. Assessing these areas and preparing emotionally for the expectations of college will be vital for some students.

7.  *Employability and vocational skills:* Determining student interest in particular career/vocational areas should allow students to make more informed decisions regarding college program interest areas. Consider matters such as the degree to which a student likes to work with others or work alone, the degree to which a student likes to work at a desk all day or move around, whether he or she likes to follow a set schedule or regularly change activities, and the degree to which he or she likes to be directed by others or be self-directed.

8.  *Community participation:* Critical skills for students who are considering college include assessing and training in self-advocacy, self-determination, knowledge of disability rights and responsibilities, and the ability to set and meet both long- and short-term goals. Students should be provided opportunities to lead disability-related meetings, discuss their disability with relevant school personnel, and set and maintain data regarding their academic goals.

> Have students set goals for the course grade(s) they would like to earn during each 9-week period. In addition, have students personally maintain a running record of their assignment scores and determine their course average at least weekly. Meet with the students weekly to discuss progress toward the 9-week goal.

In addition, Sitlington and Clark (2007) noted that assessment has historically focused on just academic and behavioral data, but the new regulations guide schools to instead assess a range of adult outcomes. Certain disability groups (e.g., emotional behavioral disorders, autism spectrum disorders [ASDs]) may be more significantly affected by their ability to emotionally or behaviorally cope with college settings than with their ability to perform academically. These challenges should not be overlooked during the assessment process. Ultimately, data collected in the previously noted domains provide the foundation for developing measurable postsecondary goals, the annual goals included in the IEP, and the summary data to be included in the SOP (Clark, 2007).

Formal assessment tools are standardized evaluation instruments whose results have been proven to be both valid and reliable (NSTTAC, 2007a). Formal methods provide the user with official scores and also allow for comparisons across students (Sitlington & Clark, 2007; Virginia Department of Education, 2008). Informal assessment methods, however, are not standardized and, therefore, do not provide the validity and reliability of

**Table 8.1.**   Formal and informal assessment tools for college-bound students

*Formal assessment tools*
Academic achievement tests
Adaptive behavior scales
Aptitude tests
Cognitive functioning assessments
Employability scales
Interest inventories
Personality scales
Quality-of-life scales
Self-determination scales
Social skills inventories
Transition knowledge and skills inventories

*Informal assessment tools*
Applied technology/vocational education prerequisites
Behavioral or functional skills inventories or checklists
Case file reviews
Curriculum-based assessments
Learning styles inventories
Medical appraisals
Observational reports from various sources (parents, teachers, employers)
Situational assessments (specific to student placement options)
Personal futures planning activities/procedures
Rating scales and checklists for general and specific planning areas
Social histories
Structured interviews from various sources (students, parents, teachers)

*Source:* Clark (2007).

formal methods (NSTTAC, 2007a). Given that colleges typically emphasize using formal measures when making accommodation decisions, the assessment team should ensure multiple formal measures are included that support the accommodations used during high school and those recommended on the SOP. This is not to say informal measures should be ignored. They can provide valuable data in support of the formal measures included in the student's documentation file. In summary, a range of data gathering tools, both formal and informal, should be used to generate data in the eight aforementioned domains. Examples of formal and informal assessment tools are noted in Table 8.1, while Box 8.2 spells out guidelines for the selection of appropriate assessment instruments.

## Steps in the Transition Assessment Data-Gathering Process

As has been emphasized, transition assessment should be approached as a process. Morningstar (2008c) suggested the following steps for implementing transition assessment.

1.  *Guiding questions:* Guiding questions can lead school personnel through the process of facilitating the determination of student and family post–high school goals and helping a student develop annual measurable

**Box 8.2.**   Selecting appropriate assessment instruments

The National Secondary Transition Technical Assistance Center (NSTTAC; 2007a) identified three guidelines for selecting appropriate assessment instruments.

1.  Familiarize yourself with the different transition assessment tools and their characteristics.

2.  Select assessment tools that help *the student* answer the following questions.

    —Who am I?

    —What do I want to do with my life now and in the future?

    —What are some of life's demands that I can meet now?

    —What are the main barriers to getting what I want from school and my community?

    —What are my options in the school and community for preparing me for what I want now and in the future?

3.  Choose assessment tools and methods that are suited to your students. Consider the following when making this decision: the nature of the student's disability, his or her postsecondary goals, and reasonable options within his or her respective community.

postsecondary goals to be included in the transition IEP. The guiding questions are as follows:

a.  Do we understand this student's preferences, interests, strengths, and needs?

b.  In what ways can we prepare this student for the future?

c.  What do I already know about this student to determine his or her postsecondary goals?

d.  What methods and sources will provide this information?

e.  To what extent can the student participate in the assessment process?

f.  How will the assessment data be collected and used in the transition planning process?

g.  Is the student making progress toward specific postsecondary goals?

2.  *Assessment plan:* An assessment plan should be customized depending on the type of information one is seeking (e.g., consider the critical questions in Box 8.1); it should be appropriate given the learning and response characteristics of the student (e.g., appropriate given the nature of the student's disability); the assessor should make reasonable and

appropriate accommodations and assistive technology available to assist the student in demonstrating ability; it should include multiple data-gathering tools and should be ongoing; and data should be gathered by more than one professional. These personnel may go well beyond those who are leading the transition process (e.g., special and general education teachers, paraprofessionals, school counselors, school psychologists, technology specialists, college disability service representatives).

3. *Assessment selection:* Multiple assessment measures should be used, including the analysis of background information (e.g., cumulative records, portfolios), standardized data (e.g., achievement test data, self-determination scales), and informal assessments (e.g., interview data, social histories; see Table 8.1 for additional suggestions). A number of free and commercially available transition assessment instruments are also available that are designed to gather data specifically regarding transition-relevant skill sets (e.g., Transition Planning Inventory [Clark & Patton, 1997]; Casey Life Skills [Casey Life Skills, n.d.]).

4. *Using data:* Remember that gathering data is only the initial step. The data must then be used to achieve some outcome. Transition assessment data should first lead to decisions about appropriate postsecondary goals for students based on preferences, interests, strengths, and needs.

5. *Integrating data and IEP:* Transition assessment data should be linked to the IEP through developing present levels of performance within the IEP, to annual IEP goals given present levels of performance and identified postsecondary goals, to appropriate instructional activities and accommodations and auxiliary aids, and, ultimately, to the completion of the SOP. Consider James again, the student introduced at the outset of the chapter. In Box 8.3, James and his case manager have spelled out his present levels of performance and the IEP goals for his 11th-grade year.

## Student Role in the Transition Assessment Process

The expression "nothing about me without me" has often been used by adults with disabilities to express the importance of promoting respect for their dignity as people and right to self-determination (Field & Hoffman, 2007). The Division on Career Development and Transition (DCDT), a division of the Council for Exceptional Children (CEC), published a position paper highlighting the need to increase opportunities for self-determination and, in turn, improve transition outcomes for students with disabilities (Field, Martin, Miller, Ward, & Wehmeyer, 1998). Moreover, self-determination has emerged as an evidence-based practice (Cobb, Lehmann, Gonchar-Newman, & Alwell, 2008). Self-determination is best approached as an organizing principle for all transition activities rather than as a discrete skill to be taught (Field & Hoffman, 2007). As Martin, Van Dycke, D'Ottavio, and Nickerson observed, however, "unfortunately, schools often do not engage students in the transition assessment and planning process, thus missing a prime opportunity to increase student involvement and self-determination skills" (2007, p. 13).

**Box 8.3.**    James Delgado's present levels of performance and individualized education program (IEP) goals for 11th grade

- *Present levels of performance:* Strength areas include overall grades during high school (3.1 grade point average) in a college preparatory course of study. Particular academic strengths include math. Transition assessment data indicate that functional skills areas such as social skills and communication are also strengths. James met the self-determination training goal and the Self-Regulated Strategy Development (SRSD; Harris & Graham, 1996) writing strategy goal identified in the previous IEP.

- *Needs:* Recent aptitude and achievement data and school performance indicate a language-based learning disability that specifically affects James' ability to read, write, and spell at a high school level. Given his desire to attend a 4-year college, James needs to develop effective study skills and test-taking strategies. In addition, he needs to develop effective reading strategies.

- *Postsecondary goals:* James' interest to attend a 4-year college away from home remains the same as in previous IEP meetings.

- *IEP goals:* Goal 1: James will master the Survey, Question, Read, Recite, Review (SQ3R; Robinson, 1970) reading strategy. Goal 2: James will master the FIRST-letter mnemonic strategy (Nagel, Schumaker, & Deshler, 1986). Goal 3: James will master the paired associates strategy.

Historically, school personnel have controlled virtually all aspects of the instructional and transition planning process. A study that examined the behavior of IEP meeting participants (Martin et al., 2006) determined that special education teachers typically controlled all aspects of the meeting and were most satisfied with meeting results. Students, however, spoke the least and were the least satisfied. Moreover, students and family members did not enjoy the meetings and did not believe their participation was meaningful. In essence, students were included only as "token IEP members" (Martin et al., 2007, p. 15). In contrast, Martin et al. (2007) noted that student participation in IEP meetings results in greater student meeting attendance; better expression of transition-relevant strengths, needs, interests, and goals; better recall of IEP goals following meetings; and improved family satisfaction with the transition IEP meeting outcomes. Moreover, student meeting participation improves self-determination skills (Martin et al., 2006).

Student-directed transition planning processes provide multiple opportunities to put the student in a leadership role, beginning with gathering, examining, and reporting assessment data to building the SOP as a senior exiting high school. It is not sufficient to ask a student what he or she would like to do after high school in the context of a speedy and intimidating IEP meeting (Field & Hoffman, 2007). Student participation in ongoing

**Box 8.4.**   The role of James and his family

James' resource teacher considers student and family participation in the transition assessment process to be critical to student success. She included James and his family in the following ways.

- James, with the guidance of his resource teacher, completed the self-directed transition planning curriculum (see http://www.education.ou.edu/zarrow/?p=37&z=7).

- James annually revisited his postsecondary goals and stated those at the beginning of each individualized education program (IEP) meeting.

- James led his IEP meetings throughout high school.

- James helped prepare letters describing his learning disability and reasonable and appropriate accommodations and delivered the letters to his general education teachers. He subsequently described to each teacher the relationship between his limitations and the accommodations he requested.

- As a component of his IEP, James mastered multiple strategies that are aligned with success in college environments (e.g., study skills strategy, reading strategy).

- James and his resource teacher worked together to examine and interpret the results of the transition assessments he completed.

- James maintained an assessment portfolio, which was reviewed by both himself and his family prior to each IEP meeting.

- James was an active participant in completing the summary of performance as a senior.

transition data-gathering processes allows for meaningful participation over time. School personnel can help the student set up and maintain an ongoing transition assessment portfolio, used throughout high school, in which all transition assessment data are housed. (See http://www.rockingham.k12.va.us/rcps_sped/SVRP/Table-of-Contents.htm for an example of a transition assessment portfolio.) Using a transition assessment portfolio can facilitate dialogue among the student and the student's family, the student's case manager, and the remaining transition IEP team. With the portfolio data in hand, they should periodically review the data, dialogue about results, and make conclusions regarding appropriate next steps in the student's high school career. Martin and colleagues (2007) at the University of Oklahoma have developed a student-directed transition planning process that culminates in a student-directed SOP (see Chapter 4 for more information on this process). The role James and his family played in the transition assessment process is described in Box 8.4.

Use the following strategies to promote self-determination in transition assessment settings: 1) provide student choice among possible IEP goals; 2) teach students to appraise performance toward an IEP goal and improve performance based on the appraisal (e.g., ask a student to explain what he or she did and how he or she can perform differently next time); 3) teach students how to set goals, evaluate performance, and make adjustments before trying again; 4) teach students to break long-term goals into smaller steps; 5) teach students when to ask for assistance; and 6) teach students to self-manage (e.g., maintain data, provide self-praise).

## MEASURABLE POSTSECONDARY GOALS

A *measurable postsecondary goal* is a statement that describes what a student would like to do following completion or exit from high school. It must take the student's preferences, interests, and strengths into account. Beginning by age 16, or earlier if deemed appropriate by the IEP team, students must have included in their current IEP measurable postsecondary goals in training or education, employment, and, when appropriate, independent living (IDEA 2004, § 300.320[b]). Measurable postsecondary goals are born from data gleaned from age-appropriate transition assessments completed either by or with the student. Transition assessment data provides insight into a student's current preferences and interests and also highlights a student's strengths and needs. Once a student's post–high school preferences and interests are determined, the transition IEP team, in collaboration with the student and family, may brainstorm how to capture the student's post–high school preferences and interests in the context of a *measurable* postsecondary goal. NSTTAC (2006) noted that a goal is measurable when it is easily determined if it has occurred or has not occurred. Examples and nonexamples of measurable postsecondary goals are given in Box 8.5.

It is important to understand the relationship of transition assessment data with both measurable postsecondary goals and the annual transition IEP. Student preferences, interests, strengths, and needs, determined through using formal and informal assessment tools (see Table 8.1), provide the data necessary to write measurable postsecondary goals. The measurable postsecondary goals result in determining the transition IEP's course of study. The resulting course of study and present level of performance data serve as the gauge for then determining the student's annual IEP goals and service needs, accommodations, and so forth. As with other aspects of the transition process (e.g., transition IEP, SOP) students should play a central role in developing measurable postsecondary goals.

### Writing Measurable Postsecondary Goals: Tips and Examples

IDEA 2004 requires that measurable postsecondary goals be written in the areas of education/training, employment, and, if appropriate, independent living (§ 300.320[b]). To the greatest extent possible, students should participate in the actual process of writing their measurable postsecondary goals. Student

**Box 8.5.**   Examples and nonexamples of measurable postsecondary goals

This is an example of a measurable postsecondary goal in the education/training domain: "Upon completing high school, John will enroll in courses at Ocean County Community College."[1] This goal meets Indicator 13 (I-13) standards for the following reasons:

- Participation in postsecondary education is the focus of this goal.

- Enrollment at a community college can be observed—either John enrolls in courses or he does not.

- The expectation, or behavior, is explicit because John either enrolls at the community college or he does not.

- Enrollment at a community college occurs after graduation, and it is stated that this goal will occur after graduation.

The following is a nonexample in the same area: "Upon graduation, John will continue to learn about life skills and reading." This goal does not meet I-13 standards for the following reasons:

- Participation in learning is the focus of this goal, but no specific place or program is specified.

- The expectation for learning, or behavior, is not explicitly stated.

This is an example of a measurable postsecondary goal in the education/training domain: "Allison will obtain a 4-year degree from a liberal arts college with major in child development."[2] This goal meets I-13 standards for the following reasons:

- Participating in postsecondary education is the focus of this goal.

- Obtaining a degree at a college can be observed—either Allison gets a degree or she does not.

- Obtaining a college degree occurs after graduation from high school.

The following is a nonexample in the same area: "The Fall after graduation from high school, Allison plans to enroll in a 4-year university in the Southeast." This goal does not meet I-13 standards for the following reasons:

- *Plans* does not indicate something that must occur after high school and can be ongoing after exit. *Will enroll* would make this a measurable postsecondary goal.

[1]Note that there would likely be less specificity in the postsecondary goals articulated by younger students than those in their last years of high school. John's goal could be made more specific by including a phrase such as "will enroll in the general associates degree program at . . . ."

[2]It is not necessary to specify the student's major for the goal to be measurable; however, increased specificity in postsecondary goal statements (when the student articulates this information) can improve the relevance of services provided during high school.

From National Secondary Transition Technical Assistance Center. (2007b). *Indicator 13 training materials.* Charlotte, NC: Author; retrieved October 7, 2008, from http://www.nsttac.org; adapted by permission.

**Table 8.2.** Web-based transition assessment resources

*Self-Determination Assessments*
AIR Self-Determination Assessment: http://education.ou.edu/zarrow
The Arc Self-Determination Scale: http://education.ou.edu/zarrow
ChoiceMaker Self-Determination Assessment: http://www.sopriswest.com

*Adaptive Behavior Assessments*
Scales of Independent Behavior-R: http://www.riverpub.com
Informal Assessments for Transition Planning: http://www.proedinc.com
Enderle-Severson Transition Rating Form: http://www.estr.net

*Individual Interest Inventories*
My Future: http://www.myfuture.com/toolbox/workinterest.html
I Oscar: http://www.ioscar.org
Career Voyages: http://www.careervoyages.gov
Career Clusters: http://www.careerclusters.com
OK Career Information Systems (need user name): http://www.okcis.intocareers.org

*Occupational Outlook Handbook*
http://www.bls.gov/oco/home.htm
http://www.bls.gov/k12/index.htm

*Job Videos*
http://www.acinet.org/acinet/videos.asp?id=27,&nodeid=27

*Career Planning Assessment Guide*
http://www.ncwd-youth.info/resources_&_publications/assessment.html

*Choose and Take Action (Assessment Video for Students with Intellectual Disabilities)*
http://www.sopriswest.com

*Transition Planning Assessment Tools*
Transition Planning Inventory (TPI): http://www.proedinc.com
Casey Life Skills: http://www.caseylifeskills.org

*Self-Directed Transition Planning*
http://education.ou.edu/zarrow/

*Nationally Ratified Summary Of Performance Template*
http://www.unr.edu/educ/ceds

*Transition Assessment Portfolio*
http://www.rockingham.k12.va.us/rcps_sped/SVRP/Table-of-Contents.htm

From Morningstar, M.E. (2008b). *Online assessments and resources.* Retrieved October 7, 2008, from http://www.transitioncoalition.org; adapted by permission.

ownership of the goals is critical to achieving his or her aspirations. O'Leary and Maitrejean (2008) suggested that students as young as 11 or 12 years old begin practicing writing post–high school goals. They also noted that students who cannot articulate post–high school goals begin by participating in the process of career testing and exploration. The following web site is a great resource for beginning career exploration: http://www.careerclusters.org. Additional career exploration options are provided in Table 8.2.

O'Leary and Maitrejean (2008) outlined a few simple steps for developing measurable postsecondary goals. Students can be easily taught to use the process.

1. Begin writing the goal with the phrase "After high school . . ." or "After graduation . . ."

2.  Next, use *results-oriented* terms such as *enrolled in, work,* and *live independently.* The terms used should be both observable and measurable. That is, can it be seen and can it be quantified?

3.  Last, use descriptors such as *full time* and *part time.*

Thus, a possible goal would look like this: "After graduation, Jamie will enroll full time in the University of South Florida St. Petersburg Nursing Program." Bear in mind that only education/training and employment goals are required. Independent living goals are included if the transition IEP team deems one appropriate given the nature of the student's needs and his or her postsecondary vision.

In summary, postsecondary goals are linked to the course of study, present levels of performance, annual goals, and the coordinated set of activities included in the transition IEP. Annual IEP goals must provide the student the opportunity to develop the skills necessary to meet the measurable postsecondary goals he or she has articulated. Consider, for example, a student interested in attending college who has been diagnosed with an ASD. Often, such students are challenged by social interactions and, in particular, communication. If a student with an ASD has identified college as a postsecondary goal, then his or her annual IEP goals should reflect the skills he or she will need to develop to be successful in that environment. In this case, training in developing social skills and knowing personal interests would be appropriate goals. The following year, the IEP goal might be extended to connect personal interests with social opportunities so that the student has the chance to practice those skills in authentic settings in a personal area of interest (Shea & Mesibov, 2005). Multiyear planning across annual IEPs better allows students to be appropriately prepared for college academic and social environments. Both examples and nonexamples of measurable postsecondary goals are provided in Box 8.5.

## SUMMARY OF PERFORMANCE

The SOP was mandated under IDEA 2004 and must include recommendations regarding how to assist the student in meeting his or her postsecondary goals (§ 300.305[e][3]). The intent of the SOP is to provide a student with one document that summarizes all relevant formal and informal transition assessment data. Given that legislation no longer requires an exit assessment for students with disabilities (§ 300.305[e][2]), the SOP takes on particular importance as it relates to post–high school academic experiences. An SOP should make clear and compelling connections among a student's formal testing data, informal assessment data, classroom performance information, and the reasonable and appropriate accommodations and services used during high school (Dukes, Shaw, & Madaus, 2007). The SOP, if effectively utilized, can provide a rich array of information that supports a student's request for accommodations and auxiliary aids in postsecondary environments.

The SOP has a number of important uses. One, it serves as a capstone for the entire transition assessment process. It is the gathering place for all the data collected during the high school years. Bear in mind, also, that the guiding philosophy should be to put the student, to the greatest degree possible, in a leadership role during the assessment process. Ultimately, it is the student who will be responsible for explaining the SOP contents to the college disability service professional(s). Therefore, a second important aspect of the SOP is to provide the student the opportunity to demonstrate that he or she can clearly and effectively explain the following:

- His or her postsecondary goals

- The nature of his or her disability

- The nature of the assessment data that has been selected for inclusion

- The connection between the assessment data and the accommodations and auxiliary aids recommended for use in college settings

- A historical perspective regarding his or her strengths and needs, supports that have been effective during high school, and how his or her disability has affected his or her school experience over time

> Maintain a summary of performance portfolio beginning in the freshman year of high school. Engage the student in an annual dialogue about what to include in the portfolio, and ask the student to explain why those documents are being included.

## Nationally Ratified Summary of Performance Template

The IDEA 2004 mandate requiring an SOP for all students graduating or aging out of the K–12 schools did little to specify what should be included in an SOP. In an effort to ensure the SOP would meet the postsecondary documentation requirements under Section 504 and ADA 1990, experts who represented organizations involved in transition around the country worked together to develop an SOP model. Following 2 years of work, an SOP template was completed and ratified by seven national and international professional disability organizations (National Transition Assessment Summit, 2005). The summit members and ratifying organizations have encouraged both state education agencies and local education agencies (LEAs) to adopt the template or adapt it to meet their specific needs. Dukes et al. stated that "the guiding philosophy of the template is that the SOP is an opportunity to condense an array of information into a clear, understandable, and usable document that facilitates student self-determination in adult life" (2007, p. 144). Dukes et al. described the five parts of the nationally ratified SOP as follows.

### Part 1: Background Information

This section is designed to include demographic information regarding the student. It also indicates that the student's disability be identified and on what date the student was diagnosed. A request is made that the most recent evaluation data be attached to the completed SOP. This is particularly important for students going on to college as the institution's disability services contact person will use the attached evaluation data to assist in determining any reasonable and appropriate accommodations and auxiliary aids for which the student might be eligible. As mentioned previously, for the purposes of identifying college supports, the attached documentation should include multiple measures that corroborate the supports used in high school and those recommended for the college environment.

## Part 2: Student's Postsecondary Goals

The post–high school goals of the student, to a great degree, dictate what information will be highlighted in upcoming sections of the SOP. If a student is attending college, for example, then data regarding the student's academic and cognitive skills should be highlighted. Data regarding functional skills, in most cases, will be less critical. As discussed, IDEA 2004 requires that measurable postsecondary goals be identified for each student 16 and older, or earlier if deemed appropriate by the transition IEP team. Students and their families should take the lead role in determining postsecondary goals. By law, these goals should address education or training, employment, and, if appropriate, independent living. The goals included in Part 2 of the SOP are a reflection of the measurable postsecondary goals the student and family articulated during the transition assessment process.

## Part 3: Summary of Performance

This section is designed to include information in academic, cognitive, and functional skill areas. It is critical that personnel completing the SOP use it as an opportunity to highlight a student's strengths, needs, preferences, and interests by using multiple data sources. If the SOP merely repeats the test scores that are included on the attached disability documentation, then a valuable opportunity to explain the student's strengths and needs in light of the documentation scores has been lost. School personnel should also use this as an additional opportunity to dialogue with the student and family about how the evaluation data reflects the student's strengths and needs.

It is also worth noting that data included in Part 3 of the SOP should reflect the goals identified in Part 2. For example, if the student and family have indicated college as a goal, then the academic and cognitive content areas become particularly important. In fact, Madaus and Banerjee (2008) found that postsecondary disability service providers place significant importance in the formal measures of ability and achievement when determining eligibility for services for students with learning disabilities. In light of the seeming need for formal standardized evaluation data, it would behoove the transition IEP team to consider the need for recent formal standardized measures for students who plan to attend college following high school (Madaus & Shaw, 2007). With that said, ideally, a wide array of data sources, both formal and informal, should be used in Part 3 to highlight the student's strengths and needs.

## Part 4: Recommendations to Assist the Student in Meeting Postsecondary Goals

This section should highlight suggestions for accommodations, adaptive devices, assistive services, compensatory strategies, or collateral support services for the purposes of enhancing access to postsecondary education or employment. School personnel completing the SOP must be especially careful with this section. Employers and postsecondary institutions are not under the same legal obligation as secondary schools. Therefore, students and families should be explicitly told that the accommodations and other supports listed here are *recommendations only*. If school personnel are not judicious in making recommendations, then students and families may have the expectation of certain supports that are not reasonable in the college and employment milieu. In addition, students and families should be told that accommodations and supports not identified in the SOP may be necessary in the future because postsecondary environments provide supports that are situation specific. Therefore, the student may encounter a circumstance in which an accommodation is needed that was not necessary in the secondary setting.

### Part 5: Student Input

The intent of this section is to add the student voice to the SOP document. Self-determination skills are considered to be a critical component of quality transition service provision (Field, 2003). Therefore, although this section is noted as optional, it is highly recommended. Student participation is the key to helping students understand their disability and the reasoning behind the supports used to accommodate their limitations that are a function of the disability. Postsecondary personnel will be particularly interested in the student's perspective given that he or she will typically be of adult age and will be the postsecondary service provider's point of contact during college.

In summary, the SOP is the document in which the student and his or her case manager should spell out the student's disability and functional limitations and how those limitations substantiate the reasonable and appropriate accommodations and services the student has used during high school. Academic, cognitive, and functional skill data should be provided, and these data should, ideally, reflect the use of multiple assessment tools. In addition, the assessment data noted in the SOP should support the accommodations and services that are recommended for postsecondary settings such as college and employment. In summary, the SOP serves as the opportunity to connect assessment data with the accommodations and services that have been used by the student. A completed SOP that James Delgado created with the assistance of his case manager has been included as an appendix at the end of the chapter. A blank copy of the nationally ratified SOP is available at http://www.unr.edu/educ/ceds/sop.template.pdf.

## SUMMARY

Transition assessment serves as the starting point for determining a student's aspirations for adulthood. Aspirations for adulthood are articulated as a student's measurable postsecondary goals and are also highlighted in Part 2 of the student's SOP, the document with which the student leaves the high school setting. The student's annual IEP goals and instructional activities must be aligned with the student's postsecondary goals. Transition assessment must be ongoing and must include multiple assessment methods and multiple assessors. Student and family participation in the assessment process is critical to achieving adult life aspirations. Therefore, they should be included in all aspects of the transition assessment process. In college environments, students with disabilities will be required to meet the same academic obligations as any other student. Their college success, to a great degree, will depend on the opportunities they have in high school to be self-determined students. The transition assessment process should be treated as an important opportunity to gather key information and garner active student participation.

## REFERENCES

Americans with Disabilities Act (ADA) of 1990, PL 101-336, 42 U.S.C. §§ 12101 *et seq.*

Americans with Disabilities Act Amendments Act (ADAAA) of 2008, PL 110-325.

Brinckerhoff, L.C., McGuire, J.M., & Shaw, S.F. (Eds.). (2002). *Postsecondary education and transition for students with learning disabilities* (2nd ed.). Austin, TX: PRO-ED.

Casey Life Skills. (n.d.). *Casey Life Skills.* Retrieved December 12, 2008, from http://www.caseylifeskills.org

Clark, G.M. (2007). *Assessment for transitions planning* (2nd ed.). Austin, TX: PRO-ED.

Clark, G.M., & Patton, J.R. (1997). *Transition Planning Inventory.* Austin, TX: PRO-ED.

Cobb, B., Lehmann, J., Gonchar-Newman, R., & Alwell, M. (2008). *Self-determination for students with disabilities: A narrative meta-synthesis.* Retrieved August 25, 2008, from www.nsttac.org

Dukes III, L.L., Shaw, S.F., & Madaus, J.W. (2007). How to complete a summary of performance for students exiting to postsecondary education. *Assessment for Effective Intervention, 32,* 143–159.

Field, S. (2003). *Self-determination: Assuming control of your plans for postsecondary education.* Washington, DC: George Washington University, Heath Resource Center.

Field, S., & Hoffman, A. (2007). Self-determination in secondary transition assessment. *Assessment for Effective Intervention, 32,* 181–190.

Field, S., Martin, J., Miller, R., Ward, M., & Wehmeyer, M. (1998). Self-determination for persons with disabilities: A position statement of the division on career development and transition. *Career Development for Exceptional Individuals, 2,* 113–128.

Florida Department of Education. (n.d.). *Florida Comprehensive Assessment Test (FCAT).* Tallahassee: Author.

Hammill, D., & Larsen, S. (1996). *Test of Written Language, Third Edition (TOWL-3).* Austin, TX: PRO-ED.

Harris, K.R., & Graham, S. (1996). *Making the writing process work: Strategies for composition and self-regulation.* Cambridge, MA: Brookline Books.

Individuals with Disabilities Education Improvement Act (IDEA) of 2004, PL 108-446, 20 U.S.C. §§ 1400 *et seq.*

Kochhar-Bryant, C.A. (2007). *What every teacher should know about transition and IDEA 2004.* Boston: Pearson Education.

Madaus, J.W. (2005, Jan./Feb.). Navigating the college transition maze: A guide for students with learning disabilities. *Teaching Exceptional Children, 37*(3), 32–37.

Madaus, J.W., & Banerjee, M. (2008). *An examination of service provider perceptions of learning disability documentation components.* Unpublished data, Storrs, CT.

Madaus, J.W., & Shaw, S.F. (2007). Transition assessment: Introduction to the special issue. *Assessment for Effective Intervention, 32,* 130–132.

Maitrejean, L., & O'Leary, E. (2006). *Measurable postsecondary goals.* Retrieved August 25, 2008, from transitioncoalition.org/transition/file.php?path=files/docs/mpsg_umbrella1213220286.pdf

Martin, J.E., Marshall, L.H., Maxson, L., Jerman, P., Hughes, W., Miller, T., & McGill, T. (1997–2000). *ChoiceMaker.* Frederick, CO: Sopris West.

Martin, J.E., Van Dycke, J., Christensen, W.R., Greene, B.A., Gardner, J.E., & Lovett, D.L. (2006). Increasing student participation in IEP meetings: Establishing the self-directed IEP as an evidence-based practice. *Exceptional Children, 72,* 299–316.

Martin, J.E., Van Dycke, J., D'Ottavio, M., & Nickerson, K. (2007). The student-directed summary of performance: Increasing student and family involvement in the transition planning process. *Career Development for Exceptional Individuals, 30*(1), 13–26.

Morningstar, M.E. (2008a). *Implementing the age appropriate transition assessment requirements of IDEA 2004.* Presentation to the Henrico County Public Schools, Henrico County, VA.

Morningstar, M.E. (2008b). *Online assessments and resources.* Retrieved October 7, 2008, from http://www.transitioncoalition.org

Morningstar, M.E. (2008c). *Transition assessment: The big picture.* Presentation at the Kansas University Transition Summer Institute, Lawrence.

Nagel, D.R., Schumaker, J.B., & Deshler, D.D. (1986). *The FIRST-letter mnemonic strategy.* Lawrence, KS: Edge Enterprises.

National Secondary Transition Technical Assistance Center. (2006). *NSTTAC indicator 13 checklist form A.* Retrieved September 12, 2008, from http://www.nsttac.org/pdf/checklista.pdf

National Secondary Transition Technical Assistance Center. (2007a). *Age-appropriate transition assessment guide.* Charlotte, NC: Author.

National Secondary Transition Technical Assistance Center. (2007b). *Indicator 13 training materials.* Charlotte, NC: Author.

National Transition Documentation Summit. (2005). *Nationally ratified summary of performance template.* Retrieved September 10, 2008, from http://www.unr.edu/educ/ceds/sop.template.pdf

Noonan, P., Morningstar, M., & Clark, G. (2003). *Transition assessment: The big picture.* Retrieved October 6, 2008, from http://www.transitioncoalition.org

O'Leary, E., & Maitrejean, L. (2008, February). *Effective transition planning.* Presentation at the Wisconsin Transition Conference, Wisconsin Dells.

Rehabilitation Act of 1973, PL 93-112, 29 U.S.C. §§ 701 *et seq.*

Robinson, F.P. (1970). *Effective study* (4th ed.). New York: Harper & Row.

Shea, V., & Mesibov, G.B. (2005). Adolescents and adults with autism. In F.R. Volkmar, R. Paul, A. Klin, & D. Cohen (Eds.), *Handbook of autism and pervasive developmental disorders: Diagnosis, development, neurobiology, and behavior* (4th ed., Vol. 1, pp. 288–311). New York: Wiley.

Sitlington, P.L., & Clark, G.M. (2007). The transition assessment process and IDEIA 2004. *Assessment for Effective Intervention, 32,* 133–142.

Sitlington, P.L., Neubert, D.A., Begun, W.H., Lombard, R.C., & LeConte, P.J. (2007). *Assess for success: A practitioner's handbook on transition assessment* (2nd ed.). Thousand Oaks, CA: Corwin Press.

Sitlington, P.L., Neubert, D.A., & Leconte, P.J. (1997). Transition assessment: The position of the division on career development and transition. *Career Development for Exceptional Individuals, 20,* 69–79.

Transition Coalition. (2008). *Transition assessment web sites.* Retrieved October 7, 2008, from http://transitioncoalition.org/transition/section.php?pageId=73

U.S. Department of Education. (2007). *Students with disabilities preparing for postsecondary education: Know your rights and responsibilities.* Washington, DC: U.S. Government Printing Office.

Virginia Department of Education Training and Technical Assistance Center. (2008). *Virginia Department of Education transition assessment packet 2008.* Retrieved September 26, 2008, from http://www.vcu.edu/ttac/transition/doc/assessment_packet.doc

Wechsler, D. (1991). *Wechsler Intelligence Scale for Children, Third Edition* (WISC-III). San Antonio, TX: Harcourt Assessment.

Wehmeyer, M. (2002). *Self-determination and the education of students with disabilities.* Reston, VA: Clearinghouse on Disabilities and Gifted Education.

Woodcock, R.W., McGrew, K.S., & Mather, N. (2001). *Woodcock-Johnson III Tests of Achievement.* Itasca, IL: Riverside Publishing.

# APPENDIX

## James Delgado's
## Summary of Performance

..................................................................

Part 1: Background Information

**Student name:** James Delgado

**Date of birth:** 7/6/91

**Year of graduation/exit:** 2009

**Address:** 123 Main Street

Any Town, FL                                    33312

(Street)                    (Town, state)                    (Zip code)

**Telephone number:** 555-123-4567

**Primary language:** English

**Current school:** Any Town High School

**City:** Any Town

**Student's primary disability (diagnosis):** Learning disability (language based)

**Student's secondary disability (diagnosis), if applicable:** N/A

**When was the student's disability (or disabilities) formally diagnosed?** Fourth grade/October 2000

**If English is not the student's primary language, what services were provided for this student as an English language learner?** N/A

**Date of most recent IEP or most recent 504 plan:** 5/1/2008          **Date this summary was completed:** 4/19/2009

**This form was completed by:** Jane Resource          **Title:** Resource teacher/case manager

**School:** Any Town High School          **E-mail:** jresource@anytownhigh.edu          **Telephone number:** 555-123-4567

**Please check and include the most recent copies of assessment reports that you are attaching that diagnose and clearly identify the student's disability or functional limitations and/or that will assist in postsecondary planning.**

- ☒ Psychological/cognitive
- ☐ Neuropsychological
- ☐ Medical/physical
- ☒ Achievement/academics
- ☐ Adaptive behavior
- ☒ Social/interpersonal skills
- ☒ Community-based assessment
- ☒ Self-determination
- ☒ Informal assessment: Interest inventory
- ☒ Informal assessment: Reading style preference checklist
- ☒ Other: Parent/student interviews

- ☐ Response to intervention (RTI)
- ☐ Language proficiency assessments
- ☒ Reading assessments
- ☐ Communication
- ☐ Behavioral analysis
- ☒ Classroom observations (or in other settings)
- ☒ Career/vocational or transition assessment
- ☐ Assistive technology

**Part 2: Student's Postsecondary Goal(s)**

1. Attend 4-year college away from home

2. Live in residence hall at college/university

3. Work part time in photography/graphic design in summers during postsecondary studies

If employment is the primary goal, the top three job interests: _____

**Part 3: Summary of Performance (complete all that are relevant to the student)**

| ACADEMIC CONTENT AREA | Present level of performance (grade level, standard scores, strengths, needs) | | Essential accommodations, assistive technology, or modifications utilized in high school, and why they were needed |
|---|---|---|---|
| | | Standard Score (SS) | Percentile | |
| **Reading** (basic reading/decoding; reading comprehension; reading speed) | Woodcock Johnson III- Tests of Achievement (WJ III ACH) | | | Accommodations: Extended time (time and a half) on examinations in courses that require extensive processing of written language (e.g., language arts, other writing intensive courses) |
| | Word Attack | 88 | 20 | |
| | Letter–Word Identification | 87 | 19 | |
| | Passage Comprehension | 84 | 15 | |
| | Reading Fluency | 82 | 12 | |

(continued)

| | | |
|---|---|---|
| | Scores on the WJ III and performance on school assignments/examinations demonstrate problems with decoding. Reading comprehension is troublesome because phonological difficulties require a lot of attention, leaving only a small amount of attention available for comprehension of the reading.<br><br>Statewide assessment: Florida Comprehensive Assessment Test (FCAT) reading score: 354 out of 500 (with extended time)<br><br>Reading style preference checklist: Learns best through listening to audio textbooks and following along in the text, discussing reading, and having extra time to complete reading assignments<br><br>IEP data: Reading goal: Met goal in 2006–2007 academic year by using SQ3R reading strategy | Modifications: None<br>Assistive technology: Audio books (disk or text to speech)<br>Compensatory strategies: Repeating to self any directions that are written, asking for directions to be orally provided, using the Survey, Question, Read, Recite, Review (SQ3R) reading strategy (examining pictures, tables, and figures provided in textbooks) |
| **Math** (calculation skills, algebraic problem solving, quantitative reasoning) | WJ III ACH     SS     Percentile<br>Calculation     94     33<br>Applied Problems     104     61<br>Math Fluency     100     50<br><br>WJ III scores and school performance do not indicate any major issues with mathematical ability. A closer look at WJ III test items and schoolwork (e.g., course grades) suggest geometry and algebra are more challenging for James. Based on school performance, quantitative reasoning skills are typically above average—James is able to use math in his photography and graphic design work.<br><br>Statewide assessment: FCAT math score: 374 out of 500 (extended time not provided)<br>Course grades: B average in algebra II in 2007–2008 academic year | Accommodations: None<br>Modifications: None<br>Assistive technology: Calculator (utilized by all students in class)<br>Compensatory strategies: None |

| Language (written expression, spelling) | | | |
| --- | --- | --- | --- |

| WJ III ACH | SS | Percentile | Accommodations: |
| --- | --- | --- | --- |
| Spelling | 80 | 9 | Extended time (time and a half) for examinations that require extensive reading/writing |
| Writing fluency | 84 | 15 | Modifications: None |
| Writing samples | 82 | 12 | Assistive technology: Computer (laptop) for word processing purposes (e.g., on a written class examination), Inspiration software for organizing writing ideas, spell check, word prediction software for out-of-class writing assignments |
| Editing | 84 | 15 | Compensatory strategies: Outline any lengthy writing tasks |

James is challenged by writing and spelling tasks. His WJ III scores provide evidence of his written language difficulties as does his performance on school tasks (e.g., essays, curriculum-based writing samples) that require writing and spelling.

Test of Written Language, Third Edition (TOWL-3)

Performance on the TOWL-3 showed many misspellings, poor penmanship, and inconsistent use of upper- and lowercase letters.

Statewide assessment: FCAT writing score: 3 out of possible 6 (with time and a half)

IEP data: Writing goal: Met goal in 2006–2007 academic year by using an expressive writing strategy—Self-Regulated Strategy Development (SRSD)

Class assignments (teacher created): FCAT practice writing prompts—student averaged 3.7 out of 6

Homework: 94% average on homework in language arts during 2007–2008 academic year (parents report checking most homework)

---

**Learning skills** (class participation, notetaking, keyboarding, organization, homework management, time management, study, test taking)

General education teacher planning notes: James is typically an active class participant unless a lot of reading or writing is required (e.g., language arts, science, history).

Exceptional Student Education (ESE) teacher anecdotal data/ESE teacher classroom observation data: He is able to use a computer to take notes (with word prediction software), but prefers recording lectures and getting notes from classmates. James sometimes uses a software application for organizing his ideas for a writing assignment. He is challenged by reading and writing for examinations.

Parent interview (completed parent questionnaire)/student interview: James has used a typing text to learn how to type (29 words per minute with 3 or less errors). His parents often assist him with organizational tasks (e.g., preparing an outline for a writing assignment) and managing his daily schedule.

Accommodations: Extended time for examinations (processing speed), notetaker or recording of teacher lectures (handwriting and spelling difficulties require excessive attention and reduce focus on lecture)

Modifications: None

Assistive technology: PDA, word prediction software, essay writing software

(continued)

| COGNITIVE AREAS | Present level of performance (grade level, standard scores, strengths, needs) | Essential accommodations, modifications, and/or assistive technology utilized in high school and why they were needed |
|---|---|---|
|  | IEP data: Student met annual goals in the 2007–2008 academic year by using the Kansas study and test-taking strategies (e.g., the FIRST-letter mnemonic strategy, the paired associates strategy) <br><br> Grade report: He typically earns a B average in his classes, with time and a half for essay tests. | (Note: These are suggestions intended solely for the student) Compensatory strategies: Break large tasks into smaller steps, plan daily activities each morning |
| **General ability and problem solving** (reasoning/ processing) | Wechsler Intelligence Scale for Children, Third Edition (WISC-III) <br> Verbal IQ: 114　　Performance IQ: 86　　Full Scale IQ: 101 <br><br> Coding and symbol search scores are an indication of impaired processing speed. <br><br> WISC-III cognitive scores (Visual Matching, Decision Speed, Planning, Pair Cancellation) indicate difficulties with processing speed. <br><br> College entrance examination　　　Score <br> Verbal　　　　420 <br> Math　　　　　580 <br> Writing　　　3 (developing mastery) <br> Taken with 50% extended time in 11th grade | Accommodations: See reading, written language, and learning skills sections <br> Modifications: None <br> Assistive technology: See written language section <br> Compensatory strategies: None |
| **Attention and executive functioning** (energy level, sustained attention, memory functions, processing speed, impulse control, activity level) | Classroom observation/formal testing observation: James does not appear to have trouble with sustaining attention or maintaining attention on activities of interest. Based on observational data, he is capable of maintaining appropriate attention levels throughout a 50-minute high school class period. He does struggle with reading and spelling but is able to concentrate on tasks when instructed to do so. It should be noted that these are subjective statements based on informal observation and are not supported by objective data because none are available. | Accommodations: See reading, written language, and learning skills sections <br> Modifications: None <br> Assistive technology: See written language section <br> Compensatory strategies: |

| | Present level of performance (strengths and needs) | Essential accommodations, modifications, and/or assistive technology utilized in high school and why they were needed |
|---|---|---|
| | WISC-III cognitive: See comments in general ability and problem-solving section regarding processing speed | Taking larger tasks and breaking them into smaller steps, taking/writing class notes using a lot of white space |
| **Communication** (speech-language, assisted communication) | N/A: Student functions within typical limits | Accommodations/modifications/ assistive technology: None |
| **FUNCTIONAL AREAS** | **Present level of performance** (strengths and needs) | **Essential accommodations, modifications, and/or assistive technology utilized in high school and why they were needed** |
| **Social skills and behavior** (interactions with teachers/peers, level of initiation in asking for assistance, responsiveness to services and accommodations) | Teacher observation: James demonstrates age-appropriate skills with regard to his interactions in school settings. He is sometimes frustrated with his performance in classes that require a lot of reading (e.g., science, history) and will sometimes not complete tasks in these courses.  IEP data/Transition Planning Inventory assessment: He is willing to ask for assistance and understands his need for necessary accommodations and modifications.  Social skills inventory: He is actively involved in the photography and yearbook clubs. | Accommodations/ modifications/assistive technology: None |
| **Independent living skills** | Parent conference/Transition Planning Inventory assessment: He is performing at age-appropriate levels in self-care, leisure skills, personal safety, and transportation. James may need to learn age-appropriate banking and budgeting skills, however. | Accommodations/ modifications/assistive technology: None |
| **Environmental access/mobility** (assistive technology, mobility, transportation) | Parent conference/Transition Planning Inventory assessment: James has average to above average skills in this functional area. | Accommodations/ modifications/assistive technology: None |

(continued)

| Category | Assessment data | Accommodations/strategies |
|---|---|---|
| | | Compensatory strategies: James has 20/60 vision and must wear glasses or contact lenses while using a motor vehicle (including drivers education in high school), based on doctor requirements |
| **Self-determination/ self-advocacy skills** (ability to identify and articulate postsecondary goals, learning strengths, and needs; independence and ability to ask for assistance with learning) | Parent interview/IEP data: ChoiceMaker Self-Determination assessment: Student has successfully mastered the goals/objectives within its three sections—choosing goals, expressing goals, and taking action. Please see attached curriculum matrix for specific skills mastered. Examples of James's self-determination and self-advocacy skills include scripting and leading his IEP meetings, assisting in weekly data collection and evaluation related to his IEP goals, and requesting support for learning from his teachers and parents as needed. In addition, James has identified his postsecondary goals of living in a dorm at a university away from home. James should continue to practice developing self-determination and self-advocacy skills given their significant importance in a college setting. | Accommodations/ modifications/assistive technology: None

Compensatory strategies: He has had extensive high school training in self-determination and self-advocacy |
| **Career-vocational/transition/ employment** (career interests, career exploration, job training, employment experiences and supports) | Transition Planning Inventory assessment/Interest Inventory data: James has expressed interest in both photography and graphic design. He has taken community-based courses to learn computer applications typically used in photography/graphic design settings.

IEP data: During the past year, he has shadowed people in both professions and has worked in the field of photography.

Community-based assessment: Teacher and employer evaluations are attached, which demonstrate potential in the profession. | Accommodations/ modifications/assistive technology: None

Compensatory strategies: James has reported using a computer to complete written work. He should consider using assistive technology that reads the information to him for lengthy reading. |
| **Additional important considerations** | James wears glasses to correct his vision, which is 20/60 without glasses. | He wears glasses or contacts to correct his eyesight. |

**Part 4: Recommendations to Assist the Student in Meeting Postsecondary Goals**

What are the essential accommodations, modifications, assistive technology, or general areas of need that the student will require to enhance access in the following post-high school environments (only complete those relevant to the student's postsecondary goals)?

| | |
|---|---|
| **Higher education or career-technical education** | Accommodations/assistive technology: James should explore using a notetaker or tape recording lecture courses. Time and a half should be provided for examinations in courses that require extensive reading and/or writing. James should also continue to gain access to his academic texts on CD. <br><br> Areas of need/compensatory strategies recommended: Based on his current needs, James should bring a laptop to college to use in his classes. He should use some sort of calendar that is regularly accessible (e.g., PDA, computer program if he regularly carries his laptop). This program should also have a feature that notifies him through e-mail when important appointments or due dates are upcoming. When possible, he should complete tests using a word processor rather than writing by hand. James would also benefit from meeting with his instructors to talk about assignments both before and after completing them. He should use a learning lab or learning specialist to address ongoing concerns such as goal setting, organization, and time management. If course lectures are recorded (e.g., podcast), then James should consider downloading these to use for later review. |
| **Employment** | Accommodations/modifications/assistive technology: None <br><br> Areas of need/compensatory strategies recommended: James is interested in graphic design and photography and has experience with both. During summer part-time work, James should use a computer to complete any written work. In addition, he should use a PDA and other back-up methods for reminding himself of what dates and times he works. |
| **Independent living** | Accommodations/modifications/assistive technology: None <br><br> Areas of need/compensatory strategies recommended: James will be living in a residence hall, and informal assessment reports suggest that he would benefit from training regarding finances and meeting appointments and deadlines. He should use a computer program for budgeting and banking, a calendar (e.g., PDA) for appointments and assignments, and break longer assignments into smaller parts within the calendar. James should post a morning routine (e.g., check calendar, confirm daily schedule on PDA, pack necessary daily school/work items) in his room so that he does not overlook important daily tasks. |
| **Community participation** | Accommodations/modifications/assistive technology: None <br><br> Areas of need/compensatory strategies recommended: None |

*(continued)*

**Part 5: Student Input (highly recommended)**

Summary of performance: Student perspective

A. How does your disability affect your schoolwork and school activities (such as grades, relationships, assignments, projects, communication, time on tests, mobility, extracurricular activities)?

I have great parents and a great case manager at school. They have helped me make the most of my abilities. I have a hard time with staying organized and getting my work done on time, but my mom and dad especially help me with due dates. I use the extra time accommodation to take tests at school, and I use my computer a lot. I have a lot of friends and enjoy my photography club and photography work. I use my mom's car to go out and have been on a few dates. I can't wait to study design and photography at a college. I think my grades should be good enough to get in.

B. In the past, what supports have been tried by teachers or by you to help you succeed in school (aids, adaptive equipment, physical accommodations, other services)?

Teachers have tried a lot of ways to help me with my schoolwork. Only a few of the supports have been good at helping me with my grades. During ninth grade I started bringing a laptop to my classes. I use it to take notes and do my in-class assignments. I connect it to a printer in class to turn in assignments. I also have been using extra time to take tests since I was in middle school. Sometimes I take tests in a room alone, but I do not do it very often. I have also been using books on disk for a long time. This has helped me a lot. I have trouble keeping up with the reading homework if I don't use the books on disk. Sometimes I have tape recorded my teacher talking in class, and sometimes I have gotten the class notes from a friend in the class. I also use a PDA to keep a schedule, and I use my digital watch to ring when it is time for class. Oh, and sometimes I have taken tests that are read to me, not in the resource room where I work on reading and writing, but in science and history.

C. Which of these accommodations and supports has worked best for you?

Well, I kind of ignore my digital watch. I know I should pay more attention to it. I also forget about my PDA a lot. I know I will have to use it when I live on my own. I'm lucky my mom and dad help me with my homework. I really use the books on disk, and the extra time for tests is really important. Having tests read to me helps some, but if I have extra time I don't really need it read. Using my computer in class helps a lot and having someone help me with taking notes is a big help too. I enjoy carrying my computer to classes.

D. Which of these accommodations and supports have not worked?

I guess I don't really need to take tests in another room. Also, reading tests to me isn't something I think I really need. I don't think I really need to tape my teacher, but if I can't get help with notetaking, then I would want to tape the teacher. A few times when I was younger my teacher would shorten my test or say I could change some assignments, but my mom and dad told the teacher she didn't need to do that for me.

E. What strengths and needs should professionals know about you as you enter the postsecondary education or work environment?

I know what my disability is and I can explain to my teachers why I need accommodations. I bring each of them a note every year and tell them that the note explains the accommodations I need, and I also tell them about my disability. I learned about this by working with my resource teacher with advocacy lessons. I did really well the time I worked as a photography assistant. The work was awesome and I was excited to do something that I loved. The photographer even wrote a note to my parents about what a great job I did. I work hard at school. I take whatever time I need to understand my assignments. I use strategies for writing and I use my laptop to try to finish work on time because I don't write very quickly. I am motivated to go to college and I think I know how hard it will be. I do well with photography and design and math work. With accommodations, I do okay with classes that have a lot of reading and writing, mostly Bs and some Cs. I had a really hard time trying to learn Spanish, which is a language my dad knows. I have a lot of friends. I already know how to do a lot of things on my own so I should be able to live in a dorm.

I have reviewed and agree with the content of this summary of performance.

Student signature: _____ James Delgado _____ Date: ___ 5/2/09 ___

# 9

# The College Search

Nick Elksnin and Linda K. Elksnin

## WHAT YOU'LL LEARN IN THIS CHAPTER:

✔ The subjective/emotional aspects of finding the right college

✔ How a systematic college search is a two-step process

✔ What personal variables are involved in the initial student–college match

✔ What variables are involved in the subsequent student–disability services match

✔ How to assist students in compiling a short list of colleges

✔ What some different college search resources are and how to find out about others

## CLAYTON

Clayton is a 16-year-old in the first semester of his junior year at Wexhall High School. He began receiving accommodations in his classes after he was diagnosed with attention-deficit/hyperactivity disorder (ADHD) in the fourth grade. These accommodations included sitting in front of the classroom, receiving extended time on tests and examinations, and scheduling core academic classes in the morning. In addition, Clayton was taught how to monitor his attention to task and to organize and prioritize homework assignments. Clayton's parents also hired a coach when he started high school to help him keep on track with his college preparatory classes and his many extracurricular activities. Clayton has a 3.2 GPA. He likes and does well in English and history. He is not crazy about math, but earned Bs in algebra and geometry. Friends and family frequently ask him where he wants to go to college. Clayton's parents have told him that he needs to start thinking about colleges, but he wants them to stop pressuring him so he can enjoy his junior year. The fact of the matter is that the notion of going to college is a scary prospect. He does not know what he wants to study or where he wants to go. He figures he will end up at State U where most of his buddies say they are headed. His girlfriend Monica will go to a small, exclusive, private college where her mom and dad met. Clayton has thought about how great it would be for Monica and him to go to the same school, but he does not think his grades and SAT scores will be high enough.

## WHY IS SEARCHING FOR A COLLEGE SO DIFFICULT?

Many high school students are like Clayton; they do not have any idea about selecting a college. For many students, the prospect of living in a foreign environment for 2 or 4 years is a scary thought.

The process of selecting the right college is often a study in contradictions. Although students, parents, and some high school personnel like to think that the college search is based on linear objective data such as tuition costs, size of institution, and academic requirements, the reality is that the search for a college often is highly emotional and intensely personal. A student's final choice is often subjective rather than objective. It is not uncommon to hear students exclaim that they just "fell in love with the campus." The emotionally charged aspects of searching for and selecting a college should come as no surprise to high school personnel who understand adolescent development.

### Think Back for a Moment

The purpose of this chapter is to inject objectivity into the college search process. At the same time, we recognize that emotions will come into play as well and ask high school personnel to think back to when they selected a college. How did you search for colleges? How did you finally select your alma mater? Do any of your reasons for your ultimate choice of colleges look like those in Box 9.1?

**Box 9.1.** Ten questionable reasons for selecting a college

1. The baseball/basketball/football team is great.
2. I heard that the classes are easy.
3. All of the girls/boys/professors are hot.
4. My mom/dad/aunt/uncle/brother/sister went there.
5. It is cheap and the only place my parents will pay for.
6. My girlfriend/boyfriend/friends is/are going there.
7. I heard that you party all the time and can miss class.
8. Everybody says it is a good school.
9. Due to the location, I can surf/ski/hang out any time.
10. I want to find myself.

**Box 9.2.** Ten better reasons for selecting a college

1. My proposed major area of study is offered.
2. The school has a good reputation in my area of study.
3. I can live at home and commute as classes are offered at flexible times and there is public transportation.
4. The campus is away from home, but not too far away.
5. The small classes allow for opportunities to interact with instructors.
6. The quality of the library (e.g., computer labs, student center) is top notch.
7. Costs are reasonable and student aid is available.
8. It will be easy to transfer to another institution.
9. I can get a good job with my degree and major.
10. I have no idea of my major, but I can easily explore different areas to help me choose one.

As adults, we would rather forget we used criteria such as these during our own college selection process, although we might admit to knowing someone who did. And, in fairness, some of us actually used a more measured, rational, and systematic decision-making process that involves qualities such as those noted in Box 9.2.

---

**Box 9.3.**   Succeeding in college

Success in college is a challenge for students with and without disabilities. More than half of high school students want to go to college, but less than half complete a 4-year degree (Berkner, He, Mason, & Wheeless, 2007). The National Longitudinal Transition Study-2 reported that half of students with disabilities also planned to go to college, but only about 39% of these students actually matriculated (Wagner, Newman, Cameto, & Levine, 2006).

---

It is easy to lose credibility with students if we fall into the adult trap of "do what I say, not what I did." Even if our own college selection process was rational and logical, it is best not to paint our experience in laudable or exemplary terms. Instead, we need to remember how emotional and difficult the college search process can be and empathize with the students we are attempting to guide. At the same time, we need to acknowledge that our current roles as teachers, counselors, psychologists, or administrators attest to our ability to identify a college from which we graduated. We are credible examples of a successful college search because we completed college.

The goal of this chapter is to provide a framework for guiding students with disabilities through the college search process. Searching for a college that is the right fit is a difficult proposition for all students (see Box 9.3). Students with disabilities have the additional challenge of recognizing personal, social, and learning characteristics that are related to their particular disability and then determining if a college can provide relevant services and supports. In short, students with disabilities must possess knowledge of self (e.g., likes and dislikes, academic and nonacademic interests, employment goals), knowledge about characteristics of their disability (e.g., difficulty processing information, problems with organization, misreading social cues), and knowledge about a particular college (e.g., admissions, student support services, majors offered) in order to conduct an effective college search. (See Box 9.4.)

## When Should the College Search Begin?

It is easy to say that college searching cannot happen too soon, potential legacy applicants notwithstanding. Before answering the "when to begin" question, however, students must honestly answer this question, "Do I have what it takes go to college?" Brinckerhoff, McGuire, and Shaw recommended that *"a realistic assessment of potential* [emphasis added] for college or vocational school" (2002, p. 39) take place at the end of 10th grade as part of the formal individualized education program (IEP)/individualized transition plan (ITP) process. This assessment should be based on a candid review of student academic performance, including courses taken, grades earned, and PSAT/SAT or ACT test scores. (See Chapter 2 for ways in which high school

---

**Box 9.4.** The college search and students with disabilities

*How is the college search different for students with disabilities?*
Students with disabilities "experience two parallel but interconnected processes in the transition from high school to college. The first is a college-choice process similar to their nondisabled peers. The second process is a 'transition' process defined under special education law" (Harbour, 2008, p. 13).

*Why is the college search more difficult for students with disabilities?*
The most important concept to grasp is that the student with a disability needs all the same competencies as any other college students plus whatever special skills or strategies are needed to cope with the disability (WNY Collegiate Consortium and Disability Advocates, 2006).

---

professionals can help students make a realistic decision about going to college.) The search for a college should begin no later than the 11th grade if going to college is deemed a viable goal.

## SYSTEMATIC COLLEGE SEARCH

Systematic College Search (SCS) is a two-step match process designed to make examining the more than 4,000 public, private, 2-year, and 4-year institutions of higher education in the United States more manageable (Barr, Hartman, & Spillane, 1995). The first step involves having the student identify 6–10 colleges of interest. This step requires that students understand and articulate their personal preferences.

The goal of the second step is to shorten the list of prospective institutions by aligning student learning needs with student disability services programs and supports offered by colleges identified during the first step. The one to three colleges identified during the second step become likely candidates for application. In most cases, high school personnel such as school counselors, special education teachers, transition coordinators, and parents will guide students with disabilities through the college search process. There are a number of private for-fee professional consultants, however, who assist students with a wide range of college issues (e.g., building résumés, completing applications, selecting majors and courses, visiting campuses, prioritizing acceptances), including searching for colleges. Consultants who are members of professional associations must meet certain training and experience standards. See Box 9.5 for related resources.

### Step 1: Identifying College
### Characteristics that Align with Personal Preferences

West and Taymans reminded us that "students must determine the characteristics of colleges that will make them happy and support their

**Box 9.5.** College consultants organizations

*Higher Education Consultants Association*
http://www.hecaonline.org

*Independent Educational Consultants Association*
http://www.educationalconsulting.org

*National Association for College Admission Counseling*
http://www.nacacnet.org

success" (2001, p. 4). Although totally subjective, envisioning happiness at a college is a critical personal variable. Personal preferences can change, but a college search has to start with stated personal preferences.

It is difficult for many students to articulate, much less predict, the features, elements, and characteristics of a college that would make them happy. Much of this difficulty is limited by personal experiences. For example, answering the question, "Would you be happier attending a large or a small college?" may be influenced by a student's experience attending a small versus a large high school or living in a metropolitan area as opposed to a rural area. Conventional wisdom suggests a large college or university would prove to be overwhelming and impersonal for a student who attended a high school of fewer than 400 students. A student who attended a small high school may actually crave the diversity of people and experiences available at a larger college, however. Similarly, a student who grew up in a large city may crave the sense of community and individual attention offered by a smaller institution. Thus, high school personnel must help students think beyond what makes them happy and consider what they like and what they *think* they may like about the college experience. After students are able to articulate knowledge of their likes and dislikes, their academic and nonacademic interests, and their career goals, they can consider the following college characteristics.

### Size

The size of a college or university has both personal and academic implications. A smaller college may allow for a more personal intimate feel on campus. Classes may be smaller, with professors rather than teaching assistants providing the bulk of instruction. Small classes may encourage faculty members to provide personal attention to students. Advisors may be assigned fewer advisees at a smaller institution, allowing them to offer greater personal service. Some large universities create academic intimacy by organizing students into specialized learning communities, however (e.g., honors college).

A smaller college may have a limited number of majors. Larger schools may have a greater number of large, impersonal, lecture-style classes, but offer a wide variety of majors and minors. Departments within institutions may enroll large or small numbers of majors. The size of institutions, departments, and classes presents potential positives and negatives depending on the current and/or predicted preferences of an individual student.

## Location

The location of a college affects a number of variables as well. Going "away to college" is usually viewed by students as "being on your own and out of the house." Leaving the area where one attended high school offers students the opportunity to meet new people and experience dormitory or apartment living. Attending school closer to home, however, allows a student to benefit from existing social and disability support systems while commuting to the new learning environment.

Geography comes into play when selecting a college as well. A student who lives on the East Coast may have become enchanted with the Southwest and is now interested in attending school in that area of the country. Students who experienced 18 years of cold winters may prefer to attend a college in the Sunbelt. Career interests also influence choice of geographic location. A student interested in oceanography may be better served investigating colleges located on the coast. Conversely, students interested in urban studies may wish to consider city campuses.

## Extracurricular Opportunities

Students are advised to consider their level of participation when evaluating extracurricular activities colleges offer. Levels of participation range from active participant (e.g., playing football, playing in the band) to enthusiastic observer (e.g., cheering for the team, being a member of the audience during live performances). Opportunities for personal enrichment or activities that enhance long-term goals are equally valuable. It is important for students to consider how some extracurricular activities provide immediate personal enrichment and how others are compatible with long-term goals. Attending football games played by a top-ranked team may fulfill an immediate personal goal, whereas writing for the school newspaper may be an important résumé builder for a future journalist. Students may need to determine which activity is of greater importance when searching for colleges. For example, a student may need to select a smaller college that has a lower-ranked football team but with increased odds of becoming editor of the school paper. A solid baseball player may have a greater chance of playing ball at a smaller institution. A student with athletic coaching aspirations may elect to attend a university with an array of coaching internships. An effective college search involves determining availability of campus clubs, organizations, team sports, intramural athletics, affinity groups, and community-based opportunities at colleges and universities. Knowing which opportunities exist enables students to determine if a particular college is compatible with expressed interests and goals.

## Physicality

It is difficult to evaluate the physical aspects of a particular college without visiting the campus. There are, however, ways to ferret out information during the first step of the college search. For example, size of the student body affects how a college or university is physically organized. A large number of students requires a large campus, whether it is located in a rural (i.e., built out) or an

**Box 9.6.**   Undecided

Close to 40% of incoming college freshmen are "undecided" when it comes to a major, and approximately 75% of college students change their majors at least once during their college career (Nadler, 2006). Clearly, high school students are presented with a daunting task when asked to name a major while searching for colleges.

urban (i.e., built up) environment. A larger campus means that there is more distance between dormitories (or apartments) and classrooms, libraries, student services, and cafeterias. Topography comes into play as well. Some colleges were literally built on a hill, later expanding down and beyond the hill. The size and topography of a campus affects the amount of time required to get to class, as well as building accessibility and need for transportation.

### Courses of Study

Selecting a college major helps students determine what college coursework will be required to fulfill long-held career goals and obtain future employment (Andrews, 1998). High school personnel, however, must stress to students that a choice of major or focused course of study is not an irrefutable or irrevocable decision. Choosing a major is difficult, if not impossible, for students who have limited knowledge of subject matter or career paths. Deciding on a major prior to taking introductory college-level coursework is at best a guesstimate or moving target. High school students need to be reassured that most incoming college freshmen have not decided on a major. (See Box 9.6.)

Nevertheless, it is important to become knowledgeable about the majors a college offers and the course requirements for major and minor areas of study. Students often have ill-conceived notions of a college major course of study. For example, the decision to major in education is made easy for a student who desired to be a high school math teacher for many years. The student may not realize, however, that many colleges require 2 years of foreign language coursework to earn an education degree. This requirement has major implications for the student with language-based learning disabilities. Availability of a particular major is an important decision point in the systematic college search process, however. Students who seriously consider majoring in psychology often believe courses exclusively focus on introspection, personal interaction, and psychological issues. They may not realize, however, that fulfilling a psychology major also entails successfully completing several upper-level courses in statistics and research.

When going through the first step of the systematic college search, students need to make sure that their initial choice of major is available while

---

**Box 9.7.**   Finding out more about college majors

*Book of Majors 2009* (College Board, 2008a)
This guide provides detailed descriptions of 190 of the most popular college majors, along with academic preparation required for each, career opportunities, employment prospects, and so forth. A directory that lists majors offered at individual colleges also is included.

*College Majors Handbook with Real Career Paths and Payoffs, Second Edition* (Fogg, Harrington, & Harrington, 2004)
Majors and career paths are organized within seven categories: behavioral and medical sciences, business and administration, education, engineering, humanities and social sciences, natural sciences, and technology. Each chapter describes a major, required coursework, and employment outcomes.

*The Everything College Major Test Book: 10 Tests to Help You Choose the Major That Is Right for You* (Nadler, 2006)
The 10 tests are designed to help students determine their interests, aptitudes, and abilities, which in turn will help identify potential college majors.

*Guide to College Majors* (Princeton Review, 2007a)
The guide provides information about more than 350 of the most popular college majors.

---

recognizing that the college course of study selected while in high school may change during the college experience. Box 9.7 includes resources students can use to investigate college majors or courses of study.

### Reality Check

There are two additional factors students must consider in addition to determining how well specific colleges match personal likes and dislikes with respect to size, location, extracurricular opportunities, physicality, and courses of study. Likes, wishes, and dreams, although important, have to be tempered with two bottom-line reality issues—affordability and selectivity. If the student or student's family cannot afford the cost of attending a college, then it must be eliminated from the list. It is important for the students to objectively examine their academic records, including GPA, class rank, test scores (e.g., SAT, ACT), and record of extracurricular activities to determine if they meet a college's entrance criteria. Examining the most recent freshman class's average SAT/ACT scores, class rank, and GPA also will help students determine if their records match those of successful applicants. The case study of Clayton illustrates how these factors affect the college search.

## CLAYTON

At the request of his parents, Clayton's guidance counselor asked him to come up with a list of personal preferences about college. He provided the following responses:

*Size:* I'd like to attend a large university. My class has more than 700 kids in it, and my high school has almost 3,000 students. I don't see myself going to a school that's the same size or smaller than my high school. The only way I'd go smaller would be to go to my girlfriend's school.

*Location:* Sometimes it's scary thinking about leaving home to go to school. State U is only 2 hours away so it wouldn't be hard to come home on weekends, and a lot of friends from high school will be going there. But I've lived in this state all my life and I'd like to go to a school where I can do outdoor stuff such as hiking, kayaking, and rock climbing. A school in or near the mountains—in the West or Southwest—would be perfect.

*Extracurricular opportunities:* I'm on the track team, but I'm not sure I want to be on a college team. I really like tennis, but I'm not good enough for a team, but I'd like to play for fun. I like watching just about any sport. My brother graduated from a big university 4 years ago and was in a fraternity. I think I'd like to join a fraternity, too. There was always something to do at my brother's school—football games, basketball games, concerts, and parties. I cover men's varsity sports for my high school paper and would like to write for a college paper.

*Physicality:* A big campus is okay with me—more students, more to do, more places to go.

*Courses of study:* I looked through the College Majors Handbook you gave me. I'm a pretty good writer and get good grades in English. I like all kinds of sports—watching and playing them. I'm thinking journalism might be a good major for me or maybe physical education.

*Affordability and eligibility:* My parents said they would pick up tuition for a public college or university. They said it's okay to go out of state. Private schools would mean I'd have to get loans or scholarships. I'm doing okay, not great, academically. I got 1100 on the PSAT. My GPA is about a 3.2, and I could pull it up if I took AP history and English classes. Right now I'm ranked in the top 20% of my class.

After Clayton decided on his preferences, he searched for colleges that might be a good match for him. His final list included State U, three mid-size universities, and four large-size universities. Of the seven out-of-state universities, all were public. Four were in Western states, one was in the Southeast, and two were in Midwestern states bordering his home state. All of the schools had his preferred majors. He put Monica's school on the list, but removed it after thinking that he probably couldn't get in and his parents wouldn't pay for it even if he did. Clayton was now ready to consider which schools offered the types of disability services he might need as a college student.

Completing the first step of the systematic college search should result in a list of 6–10 colleges that possess characteristics (e.g., size, location, extracurricular opportunities, physicality, courses of study) that are a good match. Colleges that were unaffordable or too academically competitive were eliminated. Completing the student profile (see Figure 9.1) will help students articulate their personal preferences, which will help drive the systematic college search. The next step is to winnow the list of 6–10 institutions by considering how well student disabilities services meet the needs of the student.

## Step 2: Matching Student Needs with Student Disability Support Services Programs

### Student Disability Support Service Delivery

Disability support services can be described as basic or comprehensive (Brinckerhoff, 2006, 2007). Colleges and universities that offer basic services ensure that requirements of the Americans with Disabilities Act (ADA) of 1990 (PL 101-336) and the Rehabilitation Act of 1973 (PL 93-112) are met and that reasonable accommodations are made at no cost to students. Madaus (2005) characterized basic programs as generic, less intense, and available to all students with disabilities. Accommodations may include course substitutions, reduced course loads, recorded texts, and extended test time. It is also important to determine services that, although available to all students, may be of particular benefit to students with disabilities. These supplementary services may include writing labs, math labs, technology labs, and group tutoring. Colleges may also offer classes designed to improve time management, organizational, and study skills. Brinckerhoff (2007) reported that schools offering basic services often employ a single full- or part-time staff member who may not have experience and training in disabilities-related issues. By offering basic services, colleges and universities meet their legal obligations under Section 504 of the Rehabilitation Act of 1973 and ADA, but they may not meet the complex needs of some students with disabilities. Schools offering this level of service tend to be smaller, although this is not always the case.

Madaus (2005) characterized comprehensive services as intense and highly individualized. Colleges that provide comprehensive services typically offer a much wider array of services, including one-to-one supports such as tutoring, specialized instruction, self-advocacy training, and in-house psychoeducational assessment. Intensive services such as coaching may be provided on a fee basis. Some comprehensive programs limit enrollment and require that students meet additional eligibility requirements. Often, comprehensive programs have a director trained in disability-related issues who oversees a staff of full- and part-time professionals.

### Student Disability Support Service Standards

College disability support services have undergone rapid growth and evolution. The type and range of services available are as diverse as the number of available colleges and universities. The Association on Higher Education And Disability (AHEAD) published disability support services *Program Standards and Performance Indicators* that "present a consensus among experts in the field

Name _____ Grade _____ School _____ Enrollment _____ *(Circle)* Rural Suburban Urban

*(Circle)*

GPA _____ SAT_____ ACT _____ Class Rank_____ General College Prep AP Honors

Subjects I enjoy _____

I get good grades in these subjects _____

I participate in _____

Outside of school I like to _____

Things I like or want to know more about _____

Areas I might want to major in _____

My goal after graduating from college is to _____

*(Circle)*

The size of the college I want to attend: Small Medium Large Why? _____

*(Circle)*

I want to: Live at home Go to a school not too far from home Go to school far from home

*(Circle)*

I want to live: At home In a college dormitory In an apartment

Outside of class I would like to _____

My ideal college would allow me to _____

Rate the next items, ranking as follows: 1 = Not Important, 2 = Somewhat Important, 3 = Very Important

A college with small classes                1   2   3

A college with winning sports teams          1   2   3

A college that is easy to physically navigate  1   2   3

A college with lots of activities            1   2   3

A college that is more quiet and laid back   1   2   3

A college that reflects my personal values   1   2   3

A college that is focused on academics       1   2   3

I learn best _____

Accommodations in my high school classes that work well are _____

_____

**Figure 9.1.** Student profile.

**Box 9.8.** Specialized colleges

Two colleges expressly designed for students with disabilities currently are available.

Landmark College in Putney, Vermont, serves students with dyslexia, ADHD, and specific learning disabilities. During the first year of the associate's degree program, students learn strategies and acquire skills to enable them to be successful college students. The goal of the program is to enable students to transfer to a 4-year college program. See http://www.landmarkcollege.org.

Beacon College in Leesburg, Florida, offers associate and baccalaureate degrees (e.g., liberal studies, human services, computer information services) for students with learning disabilities. See http://www.beaconcollege.edu.

regarding minimum essential services" (2006, p. 1). Shaw and Dukes suggested that a program "that demonstrates it fulfills these indicators can justifiably claim that it is state-of-the-art" (2006, p. 15). It is helpful for high school personnel to determine if, and how, a particular college's disability support services program meets each of the AHEAD standards.

### Specialized Colleges

The more than 4,000 traditional 2- and 4-year colleges in the United States offer student disability services that vary widely in terms of intensity, comprehensiveness, and quality. When considering these institutions, students with disabilities must take care that their needs will be met once arriving on campus. Another option is specialized colleges, whose sole focus is to support students who learn differently. See Box 9.8 for more information.

## Learning Characteristics of the Student

When conducting a systematic college search, students with disabilities are placed in the demanding situation of 1) understanding and articulating how they learn and 2) projecting accommodations they will need in an unfamiliar (i.e., college) environment. Making sure the match between the student with disabilities, the institution he or she will attend, and the student disabilities services offered by that institution is critical to ensuring success in college (McGuire & Shaw, 1987; Vogel & Micou, 2001).

### Self-Knowledge

Helping students with disabilities understand how their disability affects them academically and socially is a big part of transition planning. Self-awareness of the following characteristics will help students determine accommodations they may need in order to be successful in college.

- Type and severity of disability
- Processing abilities

- Level of attention
- Level of motivation
- Self-advocacy skills
- Organizational skills
- Time-management skills
- Compensatory skills
- Coping/stress management skills
- Study skills
- Test-taking skills
- Social skills
- Academic skills

## Current Accommodations

Having students consider how the accommodations and modifications they are receiving in high school relate to their disability characteristics is useful before they predict which accommodations will be needed in college. Accommodations and modifications offered at high school and college levels are described in detail in Chapter 3. The level of support and types of accommodations needed in college directly relate to level of achievement reached and types of skills acquired in high school. A demonstrated ability to complete demanding college preparatory courses, study effectively and efficiently, work independently, and use technology appropriately provide a solid base for students to build on in college. Assisting students in matching their learning characteristics with needed accommodations, as illustrated by the case study of Clayton, is essential for college success.

### CLAYTON

Clayton sat down with the transition specialist at his high school and made a list of disability characteristics that affected learning, along with the accommodations that worked for him.

| Characteristic | Current accommodation |
|---|---|
| Difficulty paying attention in large classrooms | Preferential seating in lecture classes |
| Difficulty paying attention in class in the afternoon | Scheduling core academic classes before lunch |
| Difficulty completing essay examinations within time limit | Extended time on essay examinations |
| Difficulty keeping track of assignments, appointments, and meetings | Academic coach assistance |

*(continued)*

(continued)

Clayton then made a list of accommodations he thought he might need as a college student: front row seating in lecture halls, additional time on essay examinations, and a coach to help him organize and prioritize. He was worried about taking calculus and thought he might want to gain access to tutoring and/or math lab services. He then obtained information about the types of services offered by each of the eight schools he identified. All eight schools offered the basic types of services Clayton needed. Only two schools offered coaching services for a fee. Of these schools, one had a lower student-to-faculty ratio, and Clayton thought he would do better in smaller classes. He put the two schools on his final list, however, along with State U. His current academic coach recommended a non-university–affiliated coach who lived near State U.

Having students complete a profile for each college (see Figure 9.2) will make it easier to compare colleges with respect to characteristics and student disabilities services.

## SYSTEMATIC COLLEGE SEARCH RESOURCES

### Published Guides

Published guides have long been a resource for comparing different colleges across a multitude of variables. They are a good place to begin a systematic college search. Guides usually list colleges alphabetically or by state, but there are many organizational systems. Often, supplementary checklists and questionnaires are included. Published guides are found in libraries and high school guidance departments, or they can be individually purchased. Hardcopy guides are a one-stop way to shop, similar to catalog shopping (see Box 9.9). A drawback is that most guides are designed for the general student population, and information about student disabilities services is limited or lacking.

Guides designed for students with disabilities provide more in-depth information about student disability services and disability-related issues. The guides in Box 9.10 offer a good starting point for a systematic college search. They do not cover every aspect of student disability services available at every institution, but tend to focus on colleges that provide comprehensive student disability services.

### Searching for Colleges on the Internet

Students can obtain extensive information about colleges on the Internet (see Box 9.11 for examples of college search web sites). If students do not have Internet access at home, then it is readily available at school and in public libraries. They may be asked for their e-mail addresses and demographic

College _____ Location _____ Miles from home _____

(Circle)
Type:  2-year  4-year  Public  Private  Co-ed  Single-gender  Religious  Cost _____

(Circle)
Size:  Small (less than 2,000)  Medium (2,000–15,000)  Large (15,000+)

(Circle)　　　　　　　　　　　　　　　(Circle)
Setting:  Rural  Suburban  Urban  Housing options:  Dorm  Apartment

Extracurricular options _____

Majors of interest _____

Average freshman  GPA ____  SAT/ACT ____ /_____  Class Rank ____ Acceptance Rate ____
(Circle)　　　　　　　　　　　　　　　　　　　　　(Circle)
Do I meet published minimum requirements?  Yes  No  Am I competitive (or close)?  Yes  No

Student support services (e.g., counseling center, writing lab, math lab) _____

_____

Student disabilities services _____

_____

_____

_____

Which of the disability services are useful to me in high school? _____

_____

_____

_____

(Circle)
I will be able to arrange an on-campus tour that will include a tour of student disability services: Yes  No

Date/time _____ Contact _____ Telephone _____

E-mail _____ Campus location _____

(Circle)
I need to visit:　　Food service options　　Library　　Student center　　Academic departments

Other: _____

_____

**Figure 9.2.**　College profile.

**Box 9.9.** General college guides

*College Handbook 2009* (College Board, 2008b; 2,100 pages)
Presents information about every accredited 2- and 4-year college in the United States, including entrance requirements, freshman class profiles, class sizes, financial aid, housing, majors, and sports programs.

*Four-Year Colleges 2009* (Oram, 2008a; 2,832 pages)
Presents information about every 4-year college in the United States, including setting, enrollment, tuition and fees, degree programs, student–faculty ratios, and campus life.

*Two-Year Colleges 2009* (Oram, 2008b; 720 pages)
Presents information about every 2-year college in the United States, including entrance requirements, enrollment statistics, degree programs, and campus life.

**Box 9.10.** College guides designed for students with disabilities

*K & W Guide to Colleges for Students with Learning Disabilities, Ninth Edition* (Princeton Review, 2007b; 848 pages)
Information about more than 300 colleges is included in this guide, including types of disability services offered, admissions requirements for programs, course waivers, and substitution policies.

*Peterson's Colleges for Students with Learning Disabilities or ADD, Eighth Edition* (Seghers, 2007; 560 pages)
This guide includes information about programs designed for students with learning disabilities or attention-deficit disorder at more than 1,100 2- and 4-year colleges.

information before they are permitted to access a site. Some sites offer college search tools that match schools with student preferences related to type of school, location, majors/degrees offered, honors programs, study abroad programs, and student disabilities services. Some search tools will compare a student's record with college entrance requirements and freshman class profiles to predict admission to a particular school. Of course, this type of comparison can only be made if a student is willing to disclose personal data such as GPA, SAT and/or ACT scores, class rank, and courses taken. Online search sites have the advantage of being continually updated. (See Box 9.11.)

Students also have the option of investigating schools by going directly to the college web site. Alternatively, some state higher education commissions provide extensive online information regarding college

---

**Box 9.11.** College search web sites

http://www.princetonreview.com/com.aspx?uidbadge=%07
http://collegesearch.collegeboard.com/search/index.jsp
http://www.educationplanner.org
http://www.nces.ed.gov/collegenavigator/ [no registration required]
http://cnsearch.collegenet.com/cgi-bin/CN/index/ [go to custom search]

---

offerings in a specific state (e.g., http://www.collegefortexans.com, http://www.schev.edu/students/collegeListAlpha.asp).

The College Board (2008b) recommended that students go beyond the home page of a college web site and surf the site as an "enrolled student." (See http://www.collegeboard.com/student/csearch/majors_careers/45103.html for tips on surfing college web sites.) Keep in mind that the amount of information available online is overwhelming. It is also difficult to evaluate quality and accuracy of information as marketing is the primary goal of many sites.

## Campus Visitation

On-site campus visits have been long considered the "gold standard" for gathering information and as a final step in placing colleges on the "short list." In addition to gaining an impression and developing a feel for the campus, being on campus allows a student to ask questions of students, faculty, and staff. It is essential that students and parents plan before visiting a campus. Knowing what to look for, the right questions to ask, and the right people to ask go a long way to making a visit productive. Peterson's (2008) provides lists of specific suggestions for making a campus visit worthwhile. See Figure 9.3 for a list of questions to ask during a campus tour.

A campus visit also allows students with disabilities to gather information about student disabilities services that may be unavailable in guides, catalogs, and on web sites. Interacting with students, faculty, and staff enables the student with a disability to determine if claims about services are accurate. Matching student needs and student services is a critical component of the second step in a systematic college search. In the end, this match may only be accomplished through on-site interviews. Students can assess student disability services programs by asking questions such as those presented in Figure 9.4. Students can tailor questions to their disability to get a better idea of the types and quality of services offered by a college of particular interest.

## Virtual Campus Tours

Although not the same as an actual visit, virtual tours provide an opportunity to visualize physical aspects of a college campus, which may not be obvious

Here are things you should not miss while visiting a college. Take a look at this list before planning campus trips to make sure that you allow enough time on each campus to get a sense of what the school—and the life of its students—is really like.

- Take a campus tour.

- Have an interview with an admissions officer.

- Get business cards and names of people you meet for future contacts.

- Pick up financial aid forms.

- Participate in a group information session at the admissions office.

- Sit in on a class of a subject that interests you.

- Talk to a professor in your chosen major or in a subject that interests you.

- Talk to coaches of sports in which you might participate.

- Talk to a student or counselor in the career center.

- Spend the night in a dorm.

- Read the student newspaper.

- Try to find other student publications—department newsletters, alternative newspapers, literary reviews.

- Scan bulletin boards to see what day-to-day student life is like.

- Eat in the cafeteria.

- Ask students why they chose the college.

- Wander around the campus by yourself.

- Read for a little while in the library and see what it's like.

- Search for your favorite book in the library.

- Ask students what they hate about the college.

- Ask students what they love about the college.

- Browse in the college bookstore.

- Walk or drive around the community surrounding the campus.

- Ask students what they do on weekends.

- Listen to the college's radio station.

- Try to see a dorm that you didn't see on the tour.

- Imagine yourself attending this college for four years.

**Figure 9.3.** Campus visit checklist. (Source: "Campus visit checklist: Making the most of your trip" Copyright © 2009, the College Board. www.collegeboard.com. Reproduced with permission.)

from pictures in guides, catalogs, or brochures. Tours may involve clicking areas of the campus map to see academic buildings, dormitories, laboratories, and so forth. Some colleges offer video tours of their campuses, and a few colleges have webcams installed around campus so students can see what is going on in real time. Taking virtual tours can help students 1) decide if they want to make a campus visit, 2) prepare for an upcoming campus visit, and 3) substitute the virtual tour for an on-site tour if time and money are an issue. See Box 9.12 for more information on virtual tours.

1.  Is there a separate admissions process for students with learning disabilities?

2.  What documentation is required? Are accommodation determinations based on the high school IEP recommendations?

3.  Is there a separate learning disabilities program?

4.  Are there selective criteria for admission to the learning disabilities program?

5.  Is there a separate fee for enhanced learning disabilities services?

6.  How many students with learning disabilities do you serve?

7.  What is your graduation rate for all freshmen? For students with learning disabilities?

8.  What is your graduation rate for all students? For students with learning disabilities?

9.  Does your institution offer remedial and/or developmental courses for credit towards graduation?

10. Does your institution offer substitutions for foreign language or math courses? If so, what documentation is required? What is the process?

11. Do you ever offer waivers? Under what circumstances?

12. Do you have staff members trained in the area of learning disabilities?

13. What is the counselor/student ratio?

14. How long does a student wait to get in to see a counselor? A day? A week?

15. How do you handle emergencies? Are there walk-in hours?

16. How are testing accommodations handled? If I qualify to take my exams with extended time how much time can I have? Where do I take the test? What if my exam is in the evening and your office is closed? If I need a distraction-free space will I always get it?

17. What services do you offer?

   ___ Tape recorders ___ Alternative forms of testing ___ Notetaker

   ___ Option to tape lectures ___ Extended time on exam ___Reading machines

   ___ Typing services ___ Computer availability ___ Taped textbooks

   ___ Distraction-free space ___ Calculator during exams ___ Support groups

   ___ Priority registration ___ Study groups ___ Other (describe) _____

18. Do you offer tutoring? If so, is it offered by:

   ___ Learning disabilities specialist ___ Faculty member ___ Graduate assistant

   ___ Peer tutor ___ Paraprofessional

19. Are tutors trained to work with students with learning disabilities?

20. Is there a fee for tutoring?

21. Do you offer career planning? Can graduates use career services?

22. Does the academic adviser work in tandem with the learning disabilities specialist?

23. Do you offer study skills and/or learning strategies courses? Are they offered for credit?

24. What is the climate on your campus for students with learning disabilities?

25. Do you expect the services that you are telling me about today to all be there in the future?

26. Are there regular workshops for faculty members about working with students with learning disabilities?

27. How many complaints do you get from students about faculty or staff members in a year? How are they handled?

28. Does your campus have an ADA/504 compliance officer?

29. Have any lawsuits or OCR complaints been filed against your campus?

30. Is there strong support from the faculty members and administration for this program?

**Figure 9.4.** Questions to ask about college student disability services programs. (From Brinckerhoff, L.C., McGuire, J.M., & Shaw, S.F. [2002]. Appendix 2.8. Questions to ask during the college search. In *Postsecondary education and transition for college students with learning disabilities* [2nd ed.]. Austin, TX: PRO-ED. [Reprinted from *Questions to Ask During the College Search,* by L.S. Block, 1998, Columbus, OH: Block Educational Consulting. Retrieved December 28, 2000, from http://www.ldreport.com/ld_questions.htm] Copyright 2000 by Block Educational Consulting. Reprinted with permission.)

---

**Box 9.12.**   Virtual tours

Go to these web sites to tour colleges and universities of interest.
http://www.campustours.com
http://www.collegeboard.com/student/csearch/college-visits/index.html

---

## SYSTEMATIC COLLEGE SEARCH: CONSIDERATIONS FOR STUDENTS WITH SPECIFIC DISABILITIES

### Learning Disabilities

The key for success for students with learning disabilities is to "know how to learn." If they were taught to be strategic learners in high school, then they improved their time management, organization, memory, note-taking, and test-taking skills. They learned specific strategies for improving reading comprehension and rate of reading speed, as well as ways to make content more accessible and meaningful. By the time students with learning disabilities leave high school, they should have a good idea of the types of accommodations needed in college. If students determine that only basic support services are required, then they may wish to consider colleges without comprehensive student disability services. These students may only require generic student services such as labs and group tutoring and not need any type of disability service. If students anticipate a need for more intensive supports because of the rigorous academic demands of a college or major, however, then they may wish to err on the side of caution and limit their search for schools that offer a wide array of disability services.

The difficulty for students with learning disabilities is predicting what learning supports they *may* need in an unknown college environment. Often, students will not know the types of services needed until they are well into the first semester of their freshman year. A safe bet is for the student to select a school that offers more than minimum services, understanding that the full range of services may never be needed. Students with learning disabilities also need to carefully consider their major, selecting majors that match academic strengths and knowing which academic weaknesses can be accommodated or not. For example, a student with a learning disability in the area of mathematics may want to avoid majors in chemistry, mathematics education, or engineering.

### Attention-Deficit/Hyperactivity Disorder

The ability to self-manage is the primary challenge for students with ADHD. Students learn to manage through cognitive behavioral strategies, such as self-monitoring of attention, and with the help of medication. Challenges include staying on task, organizing their time, and focusing on peers and adults. Students who manage their medication and who monitor inattentiveness and impulsivity are less likely to need college disability services. Many students with ADHD know what needs to be done; however, they just cannot get it done (Taymans, West, & Sullivan, 2000). In this instance, students may benefit from coaches who help them organize work, meet deadlines, and have ongoing academic dialogue with peers and teachers. If students can independently function and successfully manage their medication, then college options are expanded. College search considerations can focus more on personal preference issues, then move to the disability services match. When management and functionality are more problematic, students with ADHD need to consider colleges that provide more intensive disability support services, including on- and off-campus coaching services. Considering colleges that offer summer transition programs for incoming freshmen allow for a "trial run" and more opportunity to evaluate the disability services match.

## Asperger Syndrome and Autism Spectrum Disorders

Students functioning in the milder range of autism spectrum disorders (ASDs), such as Asperger syndrome, will need to consider issues relating to the social aspects of college life. Campus life issues include social isolation, inappropriate classroom interaction, and problems with daily living skills such as eating and doing laundry. Many students with Asperger syndrome need mentoring and ongoing social skills instruction and feedback. Goals for college students with Asperger syndrome include expanding social circles, linking personal interests with social opportunities, improving time management, promoting independent living, and reducing stress (Shea & Mesibov, 2005). Students may benefit from having their own room to reduce the stress of managing idiosyncratic behavior. Because of the intensity of services required, students with Asperger syndrome need to search for colleges that offer comprehensive disability services, including assignment of coaches and personal assistants.

## Emotional Disabilities and Behavior Disorders

When high school students with emotional disabilities and behavior disorders enter college, they are generally regarded as having psychiatric disabilities as documented by medical personnel. Supports in the student's community such as parents, counselors, and therapists are left behind when the student leaves for college. Searching for colleges that offer comprehensive student disability services will be critical to make sure needed supports are available. Based on previous history, students need to predict if they may need to take a reduced course load or take a semester off during an acute psychiatric episode. Students may not function fully independently when it comes to managing their illness. In this case, having a case manager, coach, or peer mentor may be a viable option.

Finding out about services provided to all students by college counseling centers, such as group counseling and support groups, will help students with psychiatric disabilities determine if their ongoing needs can be met. If students take medication on a regular basis, then they need to know if student health personnel (e.g., psychiatrists, other physicians) prescribe and monitor medications. Students with psychiatric disabilities may wish to avoid disability disclosure if "generic" supports provided to all students meet their needs (see Chapter 10 for a discussion of self-disclosure).

## Traumatic Brain Injury

Students with traumatic brain injury (TBI) have diverse and complex medical, academic, and social needs. The nature of these needs is influenced by recency and severity of the injury. The degree of independence required for a specific college environment has significant implications for the student with TBI. Students who recently completed a rehabilitation and/or cognitive retraining program may be better served by living at home and attending one or two classes at a nearby community college. Course load can be increased gradually, ultimately enabling the student to transfer to a 4-year college. Students with less severe injuries may thrive in a 4-year college where they live on campus. Selecting 4-year schools in the student's community or away from home requires an honest assessment of the student's needs and the degree to which they can be met by student disability services. The physical aspects of a potential campus can make the student's daily life manageable or impossible. Large, complex campus environments may be impossible to navigate. Accessibility to academic buildings, housing, and transportation is a significant issue. A result of TBI is that the students cannot differentiate their preinjury from their postinjury selves. Therefore, students with TBI will need the assistance of parents, counselors, neurologists, and neuropsychologists to help them determine which college environments are realistic.

Problems following a TBI are broad and varied, such as inattention, impulsivity, disinhibition, memory loss, problem-solving deficits, expressive and receptive language difficulties, and social imperception. Addressing these problems requires services such as skills training, tutoring, coaching, and group and individual counseling. Often, these services are only available in comprehensive student disability services programs.

## SUMMARY

What are important considerations when students with disabilities search for the right college?

- College selection for many students is an emotional, subjective decision. Students with disabilities often are attracted to colleges and universities for nonacademic reasons. Whether an institution is a good match for the student with disabilities and offers needed disability services may not be given serious consideration without prompting or coaching by high school personnel.

- The systematic college search includes two steps. The first step identifies 6–10 colleges that promote personal satisfaction/happiness, as well as meet criteria related to size, location, extracurricular opportunities, physicality, and courses of study. In addition, this level of search considers affordability and selectivity.

- During the second step of the systematic search, the student matches learning characteristics with the types of services and supports provided by the 6–10 institutions identified during the first step. High school

personnel can assist in this effort by identifying college disability support
services that reflect AHEAD (2006) standards. This level of search will
refine the list to about one to three prospective schools. There are
specialized colleges for students with learning disabilities requiring a high
level of support.

- Published guides, online searches, campus visits, and virtual tours are
  resources to assist students and high school personnel with the college
  search. Finally, paid professional consultants are available to assist
  students with disabilities in the college search process.

- High school personnel should consider specific college search requirements
  for students with disabilities such as learning disabilities, ADHD, ASDs,
  emotional disabilities/behavior disorders, and TBI.

## REFERENCES

Americans with Disabilities Act (ADA) of 1990, PL 101-336, 42 U.S.C. §§ 12101 *et seq.*

Andrews, L.L. (1998). *How to choose a college major.* Chicago: NTC/Contemporary Publishing Company.

Association on Higher Education and Disability (AHEAD). (2006). *AHEAD program standards and performance indicators.* Retrieved August 22, 2008, from http:///www.ahead.org/uploads/docs/resources/final-program-standards-with-performance-indicators.doc

Barr, V.M., Hartman, R.C., & Spillane, S.A. (1995). *Getting ready for college: Advising high school students with disabilities.* Washington, DC: HEATH Resource Center.

Berkner, I., He, S., Mason, M., & Wheeless, S. (2007). *Persistence and attainment of 2003–04 beginning postsecondary students: After three years* (NCES 2007-169). Retrieved October 8, 2008, from http://nces.ed.gov/pubsearch

Brinckerhoff, L.C. (2006). *College for students with LD and/or AD/HD.* Retrieved August 20, 2008, from http://www.greatschools.net/cgi-bin/showarticle/3111

Brinckerhoff, L.C. (2007). Postsecondary learning: New challenges and opportunities. In A. Roffman (Ed.), *Guiding teens with learning disabilities* (pp. 167–221). New York: Princeton Review.

Brinckerhoff, L.C., McGuire, J.M., & Shaw, S.F. (2002). Appendix 2.8. Questions to ask during the college search. In *Postsecondary education and transition for college students with learning disabilities* (2nd ed.). Austin, TX: PRO-ED. (Reprinted from *Questions to ask during the college search,* by L.S. Block, 1998, Columbus, OH: Block Educational Consulting. Retrieved December 28, 2000, from http://www.ldreport.com/ld_questions.htm)

Brinckerhoff, L.C., McGuire, J.M., & Shaw, S.F. (2002). *Postsecondary education and transition for students with learning disabilities* (2nd ed.). Austin, TX: PRO-ED.

College Board. (2008a). *Book of majors 2009.* New York: Author.

College Board. (2008b). *College handbook 2009* (46th ed.). New York: Author.

Collegeboard.com. (2008). *Ten tips for searching college websites.* Retrieved August 24, 2008, from http://www.collegeboard.com/student/csearch/majors_careers/45103.html

Collegeboard.com. (2009). *Campus visit checklist: Make the most of your trip.* Retrieved August 30, 2008, from http://www.collegeboard.com/student/csearch/college-visits/101.html

Fogg, N.P., Harrington, P.E., & Harrington, T.F. (2004). *College majors handbook with real career paths and payoffs* (2nd ed.). Indianapolis: JIST Works.

Harbour, W.S. (2008). *Disabled students' access to information about postsecondary disability services during their college search process.* Unpublished thesis, Harvard Graduate School of Education, Cambridge, MA.

Madaus, J.W. (2005). Navigating the college transition maze: A guide for students with learning disabilities. *Teaching Exceptional Children, 37,* 32–37.

McGuire, J.M., & Shaw, S.F. (1987). A decision-making process for the college-bound student: Matching learner, institution, and support program. *Learning Disability Quarterly, 10,* 106–111.

Nadler, B.J. (2006). *The everything college major test book: 10 tests to help you choose the major that is right for you.* Avon, MA: Adams Media.

Oram, F. (Ed.). (2008a). *Four-year colleges 2009.* Lawrenceville, NJ: Peterson's.

Oram, F. (Ed.). (2008b). *Two-year colleges 2009.* Lawrenceville, NJ: Peterson's.

Peterson's. (2008). *Questions to ask on a campus tour.* Retrieved August 30, 2008, from http://petersons.com/education_planner/selecting_article.asp?sponsor=2859&articl eName=Questions_to_Ask_on_a_Campus _Tour

Princeton Review. (2007a). *Guide to college majors.* New York: Author.

Princeton Review. (2007b). *K & W guide to colleges for students with learning disabilities* (9th ed.). New York: Author.

Rehabilitation Act of 1973, PL 93-112, 29 U.S.C. §§ 701 *et seq.*

Seghers, L. (Ed.). (2007). *Peterson's colleges for students with learning disabilities or ADD* (8th ed.). Lawrenceville, NJ: Peterson's.

Shaw, S.F., & Dukes, L.L. (2006). Postsecondary disability program standards and performance indicators: Minimum essentials for the office for students with disabilities. *Journal of Postsecondary Education and Disability, 19,* 14–24.

Shea, V., & Mesibov, G.B. (2005). Adolescents and adults with autism. In F.R. Volkmar, R. Paul, A. Klin, & D. Cohen (Eds.), *Handbook of autism and pervasive developmental disorders: Vol. 1: Diagnosis, development, neurobiology, and behavior* (4th ed., pp. 288–311). New York: Wiley.

Taymans, J.M., West, L.L., & Sullivan, M. (2000). *Unlocking potential: College and other choices for people with LD and AD/HD.* Bethesda, MD: Woodbine House.

Vogel, S.A., & Micou, L.L. (2001). *Postsecondary decision-making for students with learning disabilities* (2nd ed.). DeKalb: Northern Illinois University.

Wagner, M., Newman, L., Cameto, R., & Levine, P. (2006). *The academic achievement and functional performance of youth with disabilities: A report from the National Longitudinal Transition Study-2.* Menlo Park, CA: SRI International.

West, L.L., & Taymans, J.M. (2001). *Selecting a college for students with learning disabilities or attention deficit disorder (ADHD).* Arlington, VA: ERIC Clearinghouse on Disabilities and Gifted Education (ERIC Document Reproduction Service No. ED461957).

WNY Collegiate Consortium and Disability Advocates. (2006). *Effective college planning.* Retrieved July 20, 2008, from http://www.ccdanet.org/ecp/collegesuccess

# Helping Students with Disabilities Navigate the College Admissions Process

*Manju Banerjee and Loring C. Brinckerhoff*

## WHAT YOU'LL LEARN IN THIS CHAPTER:

✔ Key elements of the college admission process for students with disabilities

✔ What a transition plan is as defined by the Individuals with Disabilities Education Improvement Act (IDEA) of 2004 (PL 108-446)

✔ How to plan a time line to prepare for transition to college

✔ What types of documentation are necessary to satisfy colleges' requirements for accommodations and support services

✔ What the differences are between open admission, early

decision, and early action processes

✔ What processes are necessary to receive testing accommodations for the ACT or SAT

✔ What questions a student should be prepared to ask during the campus interview with postsecondary disability support personnel

✔ Pros and cons of self-disclosure of a disability in the application process

✔ Needs of students with disabilities for admission into college

## CHAPTER OVERVIEW

For decades, college aspirations were an improbable dream for most students with disabilities, but not anymore. Increasing numbers of students with disabilities are graduating with high school diplomas and seeking admission into postsecondary institutions. Between 1996–1997 and 2005–2006, the percentage of students with disabilities who graduated with a regular high school diploma increased from 43% to 57% (Knapp, Kelly-Reid, & Ginder, 2008). Postsecondary education is clearly a viable option for students with disabilities. Yet, navigating the college admission process can be daunting. Today, getting into college has a different connotation from just a few years ago. Changes in disability legislation, differences in transition planning protocol across states, the growing array of postsecondary options, differing college admissions criteria, and increasing thresholds of basic skills and competencies required in college make the admission process different from approaches of only a few years ago. This chapter addresses college admissions information and procedures in general, as well as pertinent transition information for students with disabilities seeking to go on to college. Specific topics discussed are the transition plan, time line for college preparation, differences in admission protocol among varying postsecondary institutions, high-stakes admissions testing, searching for information on college web sites, postsecondary disability services, and recommendations for putting together an effective transition plan for admission into college.

## KEY CONSIDERATIONS IN THE COLLEGE ADMISSION PROCESS

Many students with disabilities view themselves as lacking the ability to go to college. The reality is that students with disabilities often do not have the requisite course preparation, active engagement in their own transition process, and advocacy skills necessary for admission into and graduation from college. Transition from high school to college starts with understanding the rights, responsibilities, and opportunities offered under the high school transition plan and implementing a realistic time line for college preparation.

### The Transition Plan

Making a smooth transition from secondary to postsecondary education is challenging for any student, but for students with disabilities, the process can be particularly daunting. Post–high school goals for students with disabilities, however, are similar to those of students without disabilities. In 2004, 47% of students with disabilities reported that their transition goal was to go to college, whereas another 40% indicated some form of postsecondary education or vocational training as their transition goal (National Longitudinal Transition Study-2 [NLTS-2], 2004). The process of getting into college starts with transition planning in high school, which includes appropriate measurable postsecondary goals based on age-appropriate transition assessment, a description of transition services including a plan of study, and a time line for initiating and completing transition activities. The transition plan is part of a student's individualized education program (IEP), which specifically addresses services and activities geared toward meeting the student's post–high school goals. Transition services are a coordinated set of activities managed by the school (and sometimes by other community agencies) to promote successful transition to postsecondary education, employment, and independent living. IDEA 2004 stipulates that transition services must be 1) results oriented; 2) focused on improving the academic and functional achievement of the student with a disability; and 3) based on the student's strengths, preferences, and interests. Transition services for college include counseling the student on an appropriate plan of study to pursue in high school with an emphasis on college prep and/or advanced placement courses and skills instruction consistent with this goal. Although there are several players in transition planning, students' preferences and interests are an integral part of the planning process. Students are encouraged to develop decision-making and self-determination skills and actively participate in the transition services offered by the school. An in-depth discussion of the importance of self-determination skills is provided in Chapter 4.

IDEA 2004 dramatically expanded the requirements for transition planning from a mere statement of needed transition services to the development of appropriate measurable postsecondary goals based on age-appropriate transition assessment. In determining such goals, the IEP team—including the student—must identify instructional and educational experiences that will help the student prepare for a successful transition. It is the responsibility of the IEP team to define every transition activity that should occur, identify individuals who have primary responsibility for such activity, and specify the dates when each activity must begin and end.

Assessing strengths, preferences, and interests as they relate to current and future educational, personal, social, and vocational goals is an important part of transition services. As Sitlington, Neubert, and Leconte noted, "Assessment data serve as the common thread in the transition process and form the basis for defining goals and services to be included in the Individualized Education Program (IEP)" (1997, p. 70–71). Transition assessment data are used to develop IEP goals and objectives for the transition plan; make instructional and programming decisions; determine present levels of academic and functional performance; and identify the strengths, interests, and preferences of the student (National Secondary Transition Technical Assistance Center, 2008). Transition assessment also provides information on students' strengths outside of academic and career ambitions (Kortering, Sitlington, & Braziel, 2004).

According to IDEA 2004, a transition plan must be included in the first IEP that is in effect after a student turns 16 years of age. IEP teams, however, can choose to begin transition planning at an earlier age if the team deems it appropriate. Nationally, by the age of 14 years, 75% of students with disabilities have a transition plan, whereas 96% have a transition plan by the time they are 17 or 18 years of age (NLTS-2, 2004). It is generally believed that starting the transition plan earlier rather than later gives students an increased opportunity to develop the skills and competencies necessary for college.

## Plan of Study

Courses taken in high school can have a significant bearing on whether students make it to college, particularly a college of choice. The least restrictive environment for students with disabilities planning to attend college is typically the general education curriculum. Conventional wisdom used to be to steer students away from courses that may exacerbate their academic challenges. For example, students with difficulty in quantitative reasoning were often advised to avoid algebra courses in high school. Such advice, however, is no longer tenable. College admissions officers are particularly interested in challenging courses that have been attempted by students in secondary grades. This is especially the case for postsecondary institutions that have prescribed mathematics and foreign language requirements. A student's history of attempting a foreign language and grades received during the attempts can become valuable information in petitioning for an academic adjustment or course substitution in a foreign language once in college. Wagner, Newman, Cameto, Levine, and Marder (2003) noted that about one in five students with a disability took a foreign language course in high school, underscoring the importance of such college preparatory courses. The authors added that enrollment in vocational courses has declined in favor of more academically rigorous college preparatory courses. Students with learning disabilities, speech-language and other health impairments, and emotional, hearing, visual, and orthopedic impairments are more likely than students with intellectual disabilities, those at the severe end of the autism spectrum, and those with multiple disabilities to take academically oriented college preparatory courses in high school.

Advanced college preparatory courses can pose a dilemma for many students with disabilities. The opportunity to demonstrate preparedness for the academic rigors of college has to be weighed against a reduced grade point average (GPA) that often results from taking challenging courses. The take home message, however, is irrefutable—students with disabilities need to take courses in the general curriculum, specifically courses that are oriented toward and often become prerequisites for postsecondary education.

## TIME LINE FOR TRANSITION

Students' active engagement and participation in the transition process is essential for effective transition planning (Brinckerhoff, McGuire, & Shaw, 2002). The goal of transition is preparation for college, not simply to get into a particular institution. The following section addresses a recommended time line for college preparation starting in pre–high school to senior year.

### Pre–High School Preparation

For students with college aspirations, the process starts before they reach high school. As a first step, students and key transition personnel working with the student must ensure that the student's course enrollment is diverse and challenging. Students should consider taking a well-balanced portfolio of classes that include courses in English, mathematics, science, history, geography, foreign language, fine arts, and computer and technology literacy. Transition planning in eighth grade should identify course offerings in high

---

**Box 10.1.** Study skills for college

Study skills necessary for college include techniques and strategies for

- Reading large volumes of text in print as well as in digital format
- Reading and comprehending information that is not explicitly discussed in class by course faculty
- Taking notes in large lecture halls as well as in small-group discussions
- Participating in face-to-face class engagement and virtual learning communities
- Participating in online and technology-blended courses
- Searching for information within open learning environments such as the Internet
- Researching, organizing, and writing term papers
- Taking tests in multiple settings and in varying formats
- Memorizing technical terms, formulas, and definitions
- Participating in clinical and experiential settings

---

school, their level of difficulty (e.g., advanced placement, honors, college preparatory, basic), and the sequence in which these courses are offered. Many high schools partner with local community and other nearby colleges to offer courses to their high school students. Ideally, pre–high school is the time to explore course options between the high school and local postsecondary institutions that students may be eligible to attend. The objective is to investigate courses that will best prepare the student for his or her college of choice. Students' IEP transition plan should reflect these courses in the plan of study.

In addition to identifying an appropriate plan of study, students must actively address remediation of lingering basic skills deficits in reading, mathematics, writing, and oral language. Although many colleges offer remedial courses, it is not guaranteed across all postsecondary institutions. Basic skills requirements can become gatekeeper courses for students with disabilities once they enter college if not properly addressed in their transition plan. Students may have to spend additional time in college to address remedial coursework before they graduate. Furthermore, some private and parochial high schools do not view remedial coursework as part of their mission. Some states also allow students to take community college placement tests such as the Accuplacer in high school.

Pre–high school is also the time to start identifying and becoming familiar with a repertoire of study skills and learning strategies that the student can adapt and expand as academic rigors increase in college (see Box 10.1). The range of study skills for this generation of college-bound students includes technology-based strategies and experience with hardware such as laptops, smartphones, personal digital assistants, and iPods. Students who are comfortable and knowledgeable about open learning environments such as the Internet have a distinct advantage over their peers once they are in college (Parker & Banerjee, 2007).

## Freshman Year

By freshman year in high school, the transition planning process is typically well underway. Students are encouraged to be active participants in their own transition planning (Madaus, 2005). Active participation starts with students gaining an understanding of the specifics of their own disability and functional limitations due to the disability. *Functional limitations* refer to the way a disability affects processing and performance under given circumstances and in particular settings. For example, students with dyslexia typically have functional limitations in visual processing that affect decoding and reading comprehension. Freshman year is not too early for students to practice explaining their strengths and challenges to others as part of a self-advocacy goal in the transition plan.

Steps toward independence include working with the transition team and a college guidance counselor to register for planned courses during all 4 years of high school, ensuring that course credits needed for the desired high school diploma are in place, and preparing for and passing all end of course examinations. For students who receive a course substitution and/or waiver in high school, there must be documentation of a clear and justifiable rationale for this action. If a course waiver or substitution is indeed warranted, then it must be anchored in the disability and supported by the disability documentation. It should not be based on student, parent, or teacher preferences.

Students are well advised to begin a transition portfolio of relevant disability documentation, letters of support, verification of test accommodations used on statewide assessments, copies of past IEPs, and copies of other appropriate materials and artifacts. Keeping a personal copy of school records is helpful. Documents from multiple sources help to build a strong case for requested accommodations once in college and also provide a rich resource for completing the summary of performance (SOP; see Chapter 8).

Freshman year is also the time to move from a remedial approach toward a compensatory approach in learning and instructional planning. In other words, in addition to basic skills tutoring and remediation, students should start identifying reasonable accommodations and compensatory strategies that support their learning. *Accommodations* are adaptations and modifications to presentation, expression, and engagement by the student in different settings and under varying time conditions. Typical accommodations include receiving extended time for tests; using a reader or scribe, calculator, spell checker, or word processor; and using a distraction-free environment for testing. In high school, the instructional plan is geared toward academic success and keeping pace with peers. The IEP identifies the students' present level of academic and functional performance, which serves as the basis for determining annual measurable goals and short-term objectives. At least one annual goal must address postsecondary or other vocational transition activities. Test accommodations in primary and secondary settings are guided by state policies and regulations (Lazarus, Thurlow, Lail, Eisenbraun, & Kato, 2006). At the postsecondary level, accommodations are determined based on verifying disability status under the American with Disabilities Act (ADA) of 1990 (PL 101-336), student intake, program technical standards, and requirements identified by the course instructor. During their freshman year, students should start familiarizing themselves with learning strategies and accommodations they are likely to use in college, including auxiliary aids and services (see Chapter 3 for more detailed information regarding this topic).

## Sophomore Year

Sophomore year is the time to reinforce many of the college preparation initiatives started in ninth grade. During this time, students should continue active participation in IEP planning, take courses that prepare them for college, keep working to remediate basic skills, and continue to add to their transition portfolio.

An important goal for students and parents during sophomore year is to make sure that the student's disability documentation records are current. If the disability documentation is dated, then parents can request a documentation update. Under IDEA 2004, schools are no longer required to conduct a triennial evaluation of the student's disability status, but must consider the request for an evaluation update from parents and/or the student, if appropriate. Requesting reevaluation for the explicit purpose of getting into college or providing eligibility for disability services in postsecondary environments can no longer be the only rationale for retesting students. Most postsecondary institutions have guidelines for disability documentation, and students and parents are well advised to review these guidelines starting in sophomore year in preparation for college. More information on preparing disability documentation for college is provided in a later section of this chapter.

Students should consider preparing for and taking the Preliminary Scholastic Aptitude Test (PSAT) in their sophomore year. The PSAT is a standardized test administered by the College Board in October. It is considered a preparation test for the SAT and follows a similar format to the SAT, which is a part of the admissions requirement for many competitive postsecondary institutions. In addition to gauging the level of preparedness for the SAT examinations, scores on the PSAT determine qualification for the National Merit Scholarship. High-stakes entrance examinations are a reality for most students contemplating college. Most competitive institutions still require students to submit either SAT or ACT scores. Two-year, county, and community colleges do not have SAT/ACT requirements, but require students to take an entrance examination or placement test such as the Accuplacer or Compass. Preparation for taking these examinations should start in the 10th grade. Taking these tests at this time gives students the opportunity to retake the tests later to improve their score, if desired. As of March 2009, students can choose which score on the SAT they would like to report to colleges, thus limiting admissions personnel from viewing scores received on less successful attempts and the number of attempts made.

For students with disabilities, this is *the* time to identify and apply for high-stakes test accommodations. Test accommodations on college admission or college placement tests are not necessarily the same as test accommodations on statewide assessments such as the Connecticut Academic Performance Test (CAPT) or the Massachusetts Comprehensive Assessment System (MCAS). The latter accommodations are determined by state policy on assessment and the student's IEP, whereas accommodations for college examinations are determined based on testing agency disability documentation guidelines and documentation review protocol. Students and parents are often surprised when a request for certain accommodations on the SAT or ACT is denied despite the student having received similar accommodations for high school examinations. The accommodation history of the student is only one of several factors that testing agencies consider.

By this time, students should start to hone in on specific study skills such as conducting a literature search on a topic, using library facilities, implementing strategies for reading with auxiliary aids and assistive technologies, reading from traditional and nontraditional sources, and assembling information from multiple venues to address a query or write a paper. Developing awareness of and fluency with assistive technologies that can be used in college is particularly important. It is not too early to dialogue with guidance counselors about college, attend college fairs, and talk to college representatives who visit high schools.

## Junior Year

Junior year is the time to consolidate college preparation plans, continue the initiatives started in freshman and sophomore year, and identify a short list of potential colleges. Students should focus on matching their interests and abilities to the academic program and campus life at the colleges on their short list. Most students identify one or two colleges that are probably a "reach" for them (i.e., colleges that may be difficult for them to get in); a few that are "target" colleges (i.e., where they are most likely to get admission based on their academic and extracurricular profile); and some colleges that are "safety" colleges (i.e., where they are fairly confident of getting admitted). Spreading out the list of identified colleges in this way helps to avoid later disappointment.

Considering the type of disability support services offered by postsecondary institutions is key when identifying the college short list. Students should plan on-campus visits during the junior year, which should include a visit to the disability services office. Students, and not simply their parents, should be prepared to talk to postsecondary disability service personnel about support services that are available and criteria for gaining access to services (see Box 10.2). Disability support office personnel typically do not accept disability documentation before a student is admitted to the institution, but students and parents can benefit from having a conversation with disability services staff about the level of support needed by the student and support options offered by the college or university support program.

Information about admissions, math and foreign language prerequisites, and technology requirements, as well as details regarding residential campus

---

**Box 10.2.** Queries about disability support services

Students should inquire about the following when searching for information on postsecondary disability support services.

- Application to the disability services office, which may be different from application to the college

- Fee-for-service student support options

- Range of support services offered, including access accommodations and one-to-one strategy instruction

- Diagnostic and screening services offered by the office or college affiliates

- Disability documentation guidelines and process used in making accommodation decisions

- Protocol for receiving accommodations

- Availability of assistive technologies for demonstration, on-site use, and/or short-term loan

- Availability of financial aid for beyond-access support services

---

life and disability services are usually available on college web sites. Some college web sites have a dialogue box in which prospective students can pose questions and receive answers from college personnel. High school juniors should practice posing queries to admissions and disability services personnel on the college web site in preparation for the campus visit. The college catalog, whether hard copy or online, is another important source of information on programs offered and the requirements for different majors. Students are well advised to carefully review the college undergraduate catalog when identifying a short list of colleges. Although it is not usually required that students identify a major program of study in their college application, students should start thinking about possible career goal(s) and majors that support such goal(s). Identifying career goals can help guide the college application process.

Junior year is also the time to consider retaking any high-stakes entrance examinations (e.g., SAT, ACT). Students should plan to take high-stakes tests so that they have adequate time to retake these tests, if necessary, and still be in compliance with college application deadlines. If eligible, students are well advised to take these tests with accommodations. Taking high-stakes tests with accommodations helps to establish a track record of eligibility for accommodations and, in some cases, may facilitate the availability of these accommodations once admitted to college. It is important to reiterate, however, that accommodations used in K–12 settings do not automatically transfer to entrance examinations or college. Students should keep a list of accommodations and auxiliary aids used in school in their transition portfolio to help build a case for accommodation requests in college. It would

**Box 10.3.**   Transition portfolio

A transition portfolio should include copies of a student's latest psychoeducational and other educational evaluations; copies of the student's latest individualized education program, summary of performance, medical records, high school transcripts, ACT or SAT scores, and letters attesting to use of accommodations on these tests; a list of accommodations and auxiliary aids used in school; academic support services needed in college; letters of recommendation; and information about work and extracurricular activities related to the choice of major. Some colleges and universities do provide academic adjustments, such as math or foreign language substitutions. Students may be able to avail themselves of this option but are required to present evidence supporting such a request. Students should include letters from appropriate teachers attesting to any waiver, reason for the waiver, and/or testimony regarding struggles in math or foreign language. Letters from tutors can also be helpful.

also be helpful to request that the list of accommodations be included in the SOP until graduation from high school.

Many competitive postsecondary institutions require one or more personal essays. Junior year is also the time to start working on the college application essay. Usually high school English teachers and guidance counselors can help students prepare for the college essay. Some students with disabilities use private transition consultants to help them prepare for college entry. Use of such services is not paid for by the schools and the choice to use these services is an individual decision.

The college application packet has several components, including the application form, college essay, high-stakes test scores, high school transcripts, and letters of recommendation. Junior year is a good time to begin requesting letters of recommendation from teachers and other individuals such as the soccer coach, band coordinator, and the athletic director. Counselors, drama directors, and employers may also be asked to write letters of recommendation. The importance of learning effective self-advocacy skills prior to college cannot be overemphasized. Whether asking for letters of recommendation, posing questions to admissions personnel on the college web site, or being actively engaged in the transition planning process, students can and should use every opportunity to become their "own experts."

## Senior Year

Students should meet with the high school guidance counselor early in their senior year to start reviewing their transition portfolio for materials that they will need for the college application (see Box 10.3). Under IDEA 2004, schools must provide students with disabilities an SOP upon graduation from high school with a regular diploma or due to exceeding the age of eligibility. The SOP is "a summary of the child's academic achievement and functional performance, which shall include recommendations on how to assist the child in meeting the child's postsecondary goals" (§Sec. 300.305[e][3]). Students should talk to their guidance counselor about receiving the SOP and include it in the transition portfolio. Although the SOP is helpful information regarding the student's disability, most colleges still require a current psychoeducational evaluation or a medical report from a qualified physician to determine eligibility and protection under the ADA.

During the senior year, students should continue to develop self-advocacy skills, study skills, and compensatory strategies for college. Some colleges require an admissions interview. Students should practice for the college interview by role playing with their transition coordinator or guidance counselor. The campus visit takes on particular significance during this time, and students should prepare for the campus tour by making a list of questions they would like to ask about academics, disability services, placement examinations, admissions procedures, financial aid, housing, social activities, and athletics.

Most colleges require applications to be filed by December of the senior year. Students should give themselves ample time to meet application deadlines and make sure they know how to complete college application forms online. The personal essay or statement is one element of the college application that is particularly relevant to students with disabilities. Most applications invite students to respond to three essay themes: 1) tell us about yourself, 2) why you want to attend this institution, and 3) a creative open-ended question that invites the student to express his or her opinion about a national issue or a person who had a significant influence on his or her life. If the institution has a reputation for being receptive to students with disabilities, then students may choose to be open and candidly discuss their disability in their college essay (see Figure 10.1 for a sample essay written by a prospective student with learning disabilities and attention-deficit/hyperactivity disorder [ADHD]). In other instances, it may be prudent not to disclose the disability until after admission.

## Preparing the Disability Documentation

The disability documentation is one of the most important pieces of written evidence that students with disabilities will need to initiate the process of accommodations and support services following college admission. The disability documentation verifies the student's eligibility for protection under the ADA and provides detailed and specific information to college personnel for making accommodation decisions. Traditionally, psychoeducational and neuropsychological evaluations have comprised the disability documentation for students with learning disabilities and/or ADHD. For other disabilities, the documentation may be a comprehensive letter or medical record from a physician or a psycholinguistic evaluation by a speech-language pathologist.

Most postsecondary institutions have guidelines for disability documentation posted on their college web sites. The Association on Higher Education And Disability (AHEAD) has identified seven essential elements of

I began my schooling in a private elementary school near my home in Boston. I remember that it was a nightmare for me during class time. I had a fear of being asked to read aloud because my ability level was much lower than that of my classmates. Anxiety would take hold of me whenever a reading task was assigned by my teachers. Back in second grade, I was separated from the rest of the class into a group of three kids in the corner of the room. We were learning to read basic words from flash cards when everyone else was reading E.B. White's *Charlotte's Web*. Academic periods were humiliating, so I eagerly anticipated being able to join the rest of my classmates in phys ed and music.

Finally, in fifth grade I was formally diagnosed as having dyslexia. I discovered that my difficulty with reading and spelling had nothing to do with intelligence. There was now an answer for my lack of progress and a solution for the problem. My parents were initially upset, but I was glad to be back in a public school with the other kids in my old neighborhood. There I received help with my homework at the Academic Skills Center. I was placed in an instructional support class, or a resource room, where I met with a learning specialist four times a week. Not only did the learning specialist help me do my homework, but he forced me to stay organized and develop time management skills. For the first time in my life, I felt like I could live up to the academic expectations of others!

People thought going to the resource room would be a negative experience for me because I have dyslexia. It was actually quite the opposite. My education has been a more positive experience for me because I didn't dwell on my disability. It decided that this was not going to hold me back from what I wanted to accomplish with my life. Having dyslexia has actually enhanced some of my personal skills such as being a very confident verbal communicator. At a young age, I had to learn to communicate clearly and concisely when speaking because I knew that I labored over putting my thoughts on paper. Now that I am in my senior year of high school, I am using a laptop computer for all of my writing assignments and notetaking in class lectures. I feel like I am now a stronger writer.

Compensating for dyslexia means that I need extra time to complete tasks. Many of my friends don't understand that. I have even lost friends due to the difficulties of balancing studies with social activities. I realize now that I can excel in a competitive university environment with the use of technologies and the help of a learning support center. Having dyslexia has been difficult, but I've come to believe in myself and my ability to succeed.

Thank you for considering me for the class of 2013!

Sincerely yours,

J.J.

**Figure 10.1.**    Sample application essay that discloses disability.

quality disability documentation (see http://www.ahead.org/resources/best-practices-resources/elements). Institutions can adopt their own guidelines for disability documentation; therefore, high school students should review institutional documentation guidelines carefully in preparing their own disability documentation for college (see Box 10.4).

Students must be aware of certain considerations when getting their disability documentation ready for college. One consideration is the recency of the evaluation. The recency or shelf-life requirement for disability documentation can vary from institution to institution. Most institutions have a 3- or 5-year recency requirement for learning disabilities documentation, a 3-year recency requirement for ADHD, and 6 months for psychiatric disabilities and traumatic brain injuries. Some institutions give consideration to

---

**Box 10.4.**  Disability documentation guidelines

Most postsecondary documentation guidelines require the following:

- Identification and diagnosis of a disability under the ADA by a qualified professional

- Objective and self-reported evidence that forms the basis for the diagnosis and attests to functional limitations due to the disability and its effect on academic performance under varying conditions

- Academic, developmental, and/or past medical history that may have a bearing on the student's current functioning

- Recommendations for accommodations and support services, including a rationale based in the evaluation findings for each accommodation

---

documentation that may be dated if it is based on adult measures of assessment.

Although documentation guidelines are important in getting the documentation ready for college, it should be remembered that documentation guidelines describe general protocol and practices used by the institution in determining ADA protections. Documentation guidelines are *not* legal mandates. Most institutions look for the initial documentation to be comprehensive and include test scores from an assessment battery, in addition to historical evidence and clinical judgment. In preparing the disability documentation for college, students should pay particular attention to the documentation guidelines of the institutions they have targeted and ask questions of disability personnel if in doubt. Often, all that is needed is a *documentation update* rather than a complete reevaluation. A documentation update is typically conducted when the initial documentation is dated and/or there is need to affirm eligibility and verify the current and continuing effect of the student's functional limitations (Banerjee & Brinckerhoff, 2006).

## Differences in Admission Requirements

Today there are increasing numbers of postsecondary options available to students with disabilities who are considering higher education. Admissions requirements for these institutions of higher education lie along a continuum from less to more selective. Least selective post–high school programs focus on whether the student meets minimum requirements, usually a high school diploma or a GED, and accept students on a first-come, first-serve basis. For students with disabilities who are not yet ready for a competitive college experience, nondegree programs may be appealing. These campus-based programs focus on life skills training for students with below-average intellectual functioning. Most students who opt for such programs would find the admissions requirements for a degree program to be too challenging. They may, however, be interested in and benefit from experiencing "college life" while continuing to learn and prepare for independence in adulthood. Students enrolled in these programs often learn practical, community-based vocational training that complements daily living (e.g., engaging in personal hygiene, cooking, shopping, cleaning, managing money) and social skills training. The residential life component of such programs is integral to the college experience. Students typically live in apartments with supervision and work locally as they develop daily living skills. Some programs that adhere to this model may also have collaborative relationships with the local community college. Two such examples are the Horizons School in Birmingham, Alabama, (http://www.horizonsschool.org) and the Threshold program at Lesley University (http://www.lesley.edu/threshold/threshold_home.htm). The admission protocols in these settings often depend heavily on disability documentation and the IEPs that describe the student's current functional limitations and abilities as well as their motivation to succeed in school (Brinckerhoff, 2007). Personal interviews are often required. Letters of recommendation that attest to the student's aptitude, interpersonal skills, and readiness for college, rather than standardized test scores (e.g., ACT, SAT), are given more weight in the review process. Depending on the setting, a high school diploma with a 2.0 GPA in academic subjects or a GED is required for admission.

## Community and Two-Year Colleges

Many students with disabilities who elect to go on to postsecondary education start by spending a year or two at a local community college. This is a particularly attractive option for students who may have a low high school GPA, are missing pieces of the college preparatory curriculum, or have weak scores on the ACT or SAT that make more competitive institutions out of reach. An advantage of community colleges is that they do not require standardized entrance examinations such as the ACT or SAT. One of the best attractions of community colleges is that they allow students to "try out" the college experience close to home, near family and friends.

Like community colleges, 2-year junior colleges are economical and offer a high-quality education. Given that the program of study for an associate's degree is usually 2 years in length, students have quicker access to employment and more flexibility to plan a schedule that may better meet their transition needs. Students may take a few courses of interest, a series of vocational courses to train for a particular vocation, or pursue an associate's degree with the intention of transferring to a 4-year institution. The admissions protocol for students to apply to a community or 2-year college is straightforward—minimal grades and a professed interest in college education. If the student has graduated from high school or has a GED, then they will be accepted. Most offer "open admission," but prospective students need to be aware that more community colleges are now requiring academic prerequisites for certain departments. Technical majors or nursing programs, for example, usually require preparation in math or science. For most community and 2-year institutions, the admissions requirements are not demanding, but students have to demonstrate proficiency on basic skills placement tests upon admission. In many instances, students cannot take credit-bearing courses until they have placed out of basic skills remedial courses.

## Technical Training Options

Students with disabilities who prefer hands-on learning may be interested in pursuing careers in areas that deemphasize reading and writing skills and capitalize on experiential training. "Tech-prep" programs are becoming increasingly popular choices for those students who would like to study in a setting that can offer them a partnership between secondary vocational technical schools and community colleges. Other students may have more success in college settings that feature a co-op curriculum that focuses on coursework and direct work experience rather than an institution with a more traditional liberal arts curriculum (Brinckerhoff, 2007).

## Four-Year Colleges

More selective and competitive institutions are at the other end of the admissions spectrum. According to the College Board (http://www. collegeboard.com), the application-to-admissions ratio at the most competitive colleges is 10–15 to 1. These colleges and universities accept only 1 in 10–15 applicants. About half of the postsecondary schools in the United States are 4-year colleges that can generally be classified as liberal arts colleges or universities. These schools typically grant a bachelor's degree and can be public or private. Liberal arts colleges often appeal to students who are looking for a smaller college environment and a broader liberal arts curriculum that promotes lifelong learning. Four-year colleges offer students a broad range of academic disciplines and typically have more competitive admission requirements than 2-year settings. There is little agreement as to the importance of one or more of these factors over another, but generally speaking, academic performance, college preparatory courses, and school experience is given significant weight. Because competition for admission is fierce, students may be denied admission because of a relative weakness in any one of these factors.

Large universities offer the broadest range of educational, athletic, and social experiences. Public universities are known for providing a high-quality education at a reduced cost to in-state residents. It is important to note that each college within a large public university may have its own standards for admission. For example, it is not unusual for the College of Engineering to require a higher GPA and SAT score than the School of Education at the same institution. Honors colleges within a university usually have admissions standards that are much more competitive than the general admissions requirements. An honors college within a university is essentially a "school within a school" that has its own stringent admissions policies, hand-picked faculty members, and attractive scholarship packages. The big advantage of these programs is that they offer all the benefits of a large university while still allowing students to enjoy a challenging curriculum in the intimate setting of a smaller school. Although public universities often provide a high-quality education at a reduced cost to in-state residents, out-of-state students can expect to pay a premium not unlike the costs associated with private 4-year settings.

Many large universities and land-grant colleges have regional campus colleges. Regional campus colleges extend access to the educational opportunities offered by the main campus/institution to a particular locality and offer flexibility in schedule and tuition costs that may be especially attractive for some students. Admissions requirements at regional campuses are similar but less demanding than those at the main campus. For example, regional campuses may have a lower SAT score threshold requirement. Many students with disabilities start their transition to postsecondary education at a regional campus and then transfer to the main campus when they acquire the necessary course and grade portfolio for admission to the more selective option.

## Online Degree Programs

As technology advances and distance learning becomes more commonplace, online associate's and bachelor's degree programs are gaining in popularity. Online learning is particularly appealing for students who already have strong computer skills and need a flexible class schedule to fit around home or work responsibilities. For students with disabilities, online courses can be a mixed blessing. For students with excellent keyboarding skills and poor social skills, online courses can be an advantage because they do not have to leave the comfort of home. For students with weak keyboarding skills or difficulty tracking a discussion thread, it may be a challenge to be a full participant in such courses.

## Early Decision, Early Action, and Rolling Admissions

Awareness of the application protocol regarding early decision, early action, and rolling admissions is important to consider when applying to 4-year competitive institutions. More and more, prospective students are opting to apply *early decision* or *early action*. If a rising senior knows exactly what he or she wants in a college and feels passionate about a particular school, then he or she may want to consider applying early decision because, in general, colleges admit a higher proportion of students as early applicants than from the regular applicant pool. An early decision application is one obvious way that an applicant can let a college know that this institution is clearly his or her first choice. Early decision is usually binding, which means that if admitted, the prospective student must withdraw any other applications and attend that institution. The guidance counselor must also attest with a "letter of commitment" that the student will attend the institution, if admitted. If a high school senior applies early, in most cases by November 1st of the senior year, then typically he or she will receive a response within 6–8 weeks. If the student is not accepted outright, then he or she may receive a "deferred" admission letter that advises the student that his or her application will again be considered in the spring with all other applicants. In many cases, this may pay off, but the admissions office wants to review more applicants before committing to this particular student. The admissions landscape is shifting with regard to early decision as some highly selective universities are dropping that option.

In contrast, *early action* is not binding but it does require that the prospective student make an admission decision earlier in the process. It is still possible to bank an initial acceptance and apply to additional colleges during the regular admissions cycle and wait until early May to make a decision.

*Rolling admissions* means that applicants are evaluated as they arrive and decisions are mailed usually within 4–6 weeks. Students need to know that under this plan the incoming class is filled on a first-come first-serve basis. It should be noted that rolling admission plans usually have financial aid and/housing priority deadlines, so it behooves students to apply early. Regardless of the setting, students with disabilities need to start early when planning for the transition from high school to college.

### The Common Application

The Common Application is available online and accepted by more than 340 member colleges and universities (http://www.commonapp.org). Most applicants choose to submit the form electronically. According to the Common Application web site, in 2007, more than 1.4 million applications were sent to member colleges electronically. This included school reports, transcripts, midyear reports, letters of recommendation, and teacher evaluation forms. Colleges subscribing to the Common Application pledge to give it equal weight to a standard application. One advantage of the Common Application is that it has three very general personal statement choices that the student prepares. In this way, time can be saved, and students can focus on developing two or three essays that can be submitted for all their applications. The Common Application is appealing for students with disabilities because they can consolidate their energies into one application instead of having to complete separate application forms, as well as a variety of essays, for each institution. This can be a major advantage for students with learning disabilities in particular.

Students may also apply online via PrincetonReview.com. A similar time-saving approach is to connect with the CollegeLink program, a fee-based service that allows applicants to complete a single application on their personal computer that can be forwarded to more than 500 institutional subscribers. CollegeNet.org provides a similar service, and for a small fee, prospective students can print out applications and apply electronically using the application form for more than 1,500 colleges.

## Application to Disability Services

The vast majority of colleges and universities in the United States and Canada have a disability support services office on campus that is staffed by qualified professionals who can assist students with skills such as self-advocacy and arranging reasonable and appropriate accommodations. These staff members typically provide prospective students and their parents with a broad range of information about how accessible and accommodating the campus is to students with disabilities (Duffy & Gugerty, 2005). Additional campus resources and publications regarding housing arrangements, personal counseling, and specialized support services (readers, notetakers, tutors, and interpreters) are typically available both online and on paper from the disability support services office.

Some institutions have an optional box on their admissions application form for prospective students to check if they would like additional information regarding the support services available to students with disabilities. Under the law, an institution may not ask prospective students to self-identify on the application if they have a disability, but they can legally ask if the applicant would like disability-related information. In such instances, prospective students who have requested information will typically receive a personalized letter from the director of the disability support services office thanking them for their interest along with a packet of disability-related resource materials. Some disability support services offices have a separate application for admission if they have a specialized support program for students with disabilities. These enhanced support programs are often found in large public or private universities and often involve regular personalized instruction with a learning specialist, access to a specially equipped computer lab, and personal counseling. This additional application form is usually sent separate from the standard application form and is completed only if the student wants to receive specialized or enhanced services at an additional fee. These application forms request that the student submits an additional processing fee, recent disability documentation, high school transcripts, and a personal essay. Specialized programs often have an enrollment cap and wait lists are not uncommon, so it is important to apply early if enhanced services are desired.

## Standardized Testing in the Admission Process

Tenth-grade students can take the PSAT in order to prepare for the SAT. The purpose of the PSAT is to provide the student with practice for the subsequent SAT testing and to give the student an early indication as to how they may fare on the SAT. The scores range from 20 to 80 and are designed to correspond to the SAT scale of 200–800. The ACT has a similar practice examination called the PLAN. Like the PSAT, its primary purpose is to provide families and schools with a way to evaluate a student's progress in the curriculum so that changes can be made, if necessary. The PLAN is targeted for students in their sophomore year. Students with IEPs or 504 plans should be encouraged to take these tests with accommodations. The results of the PSAT and PLAN can help determine areas of strength or weakness and guide future course selection in high school. The College Board and the ACT have extensive supports that include "retired" test questions that are available free of charge on their respective web sites to assist students in preparing for these tests. The ACT Online Prep is another test preparation program designed by the ACT that offers additional test practice questions, a practice essay with real-time scoring, a diagnostic test, and a personalized study path. The College Board also has the SAT Test Practice Center with a variety of sample questions and test-taking suggestions. If a student does not perform well on these tests, then he or she may want to consider enrolling in a commercially available test prep course with Princeton Review or Kaplan. In the last few years, the online test prep market has gained in popularity. These online services typically cost $400–$800 and results may be mixed according to WebWatch, a reporting service from the nonprofit publisher for *Consumer Reports*. Some free services (e.g., Number2.com) may be just as good for ACT or SAT prep compared with these more costly services.

During the fall of the sophomore year of high school, or more typically in the junior year, about 4 million students take either the ACT or the SAT. The SAT is composed of three sections: 1) critical reading, which has sentence completion and passage-based reading comprehension questions; 2) mathematics, which is based on math that college-bound students typically learn in their first 3 years of high school; and 3) writing, which has both a multiple-choice section and an essay section. The standard administration of the essay section must be written with a number 2 pencil and is 25 minutes in length. Approximately 30% of the score for the writing section is based on this essay. The entire test is 3 hours and 45 minutes for the standard administration. All multiple-choice questions are scored the same way—one point for each correct answer and one quarter point subtracted for a wrong answer. No points are subtracted for answers that are left blank.

The College Board subject tests are 1-hour subject-specific examinations whose subjects include English, foreign language, history, and natural sciences. Many colleges use the subject tests for admission, course placement, and to advise students about course selection. Some colleges specify the subject tests they require for admission or placement; others allow applicants to choose which tests to take. It is important to review college catalogues to find out whether the schools require these scores for admission. Students are well advised to take subject tests toward the end of their junior year or beginning of the senior year while the content is still fresh in their mind.

The ACT offers students one of two options. They may register for only the ACT or the ACT Plus Writing. Some colleges require the ACT writing test and others do not. The ACT contains multiple-choice test items in four areas: English, mathematics, reading, and science. Each of these tests contains questions that offer either four or five answer choices. The English test is a 75-question, 45-minute test that measures a student's understanding of standard written English (punctuation, grammar and usage, and sentence structure) and of rhetorical skills (strategy, organization, and style). Spelling and vocabulary are not tested. The mathematics test is a 60-question, 60-minute test designed to assess the mathematical skills that students have typically acquired in courses up to the beginning of 12th grade. The test presents multiple-choice questions that require the student to use reasoning skills to solve practical problems in mathematics. Using calculators is permitted on the mathematics test. The ACT reading test and the ACT science test are each 40-question, 35-minute tests. The reading test measures reading comprehension, and the science test measures a variety of reasoning and problem-solving skills in the natural sciences. The optional ACT writing test is a 30-minute essay test that measures writing skills similar to entry-level college composition courses. Students are asked to write a response to a prompt question in which they have to assume a particular viewpoint or perspective.

## Requesting Accommodations on the SAT or ACT

If a student's documentation supports a disability-related impairment that directly affects test performance, then he or she should apply for testing accommodations on these high-stakes college admissions tests. Testing accommodations may include a reader, a writer, a recorded version, large-type, large-block answer sheets, extended time, use of a private room, or multiple testing days. The College Board requires any accommodation request in excess of 100% additional time (double time) or any request for multiple-day testing be accompanied by a copy of the student's IEP or 504 plan. The school psychologist or the private diagnostician who wrote the report should be sure that the disability documentation is complete according to the documentation guidelines posted on the testing agency's web site. The College Board has adopted a set of documentation guidelines prepared by Educational Testing Service that provide guidance to parents, consumers, and educational testing professionals about the type of documentation necessary to verify accommodation requests for students with learning disabilities, ADHD, visual impairments, physical disabilities, or psychiatric disabilities. The College Board also has a process whereby the student's high school can supplement older testing with teacher observations on the student's use of accommodations in the classroom.

The scores on the ACT and the SAT are no longer flagged as "nonstandard test administration" when they are sent to the institution. As a result, the admission director will not know which students took the tests with accommodations. As of January 2009, the College Board will follow the ACT by allowing students to select only their best scores to be sent to a given institution for consideration.

## Sorting Out College Options

Most students need instruction and guidance on ways to use college resource guides or directories, including available computer-guided software, to assist them in the college search process. Internet sites such as Collegenet.com, Collegeview.com, and Collegelink.com allow prospective students to search for colleges based on type, geographic region, intercollegiate sports, major, tuition fees, available financial aid, and other factors. Students can then use the "hot links" from these sites to the home pages of the school for more information, to compare and contrast school offerings, or to apply online. As students scan web pages looking for their preferred institutions of higher education, they should make a list of the schools that are the most interesting in terms of location, level of competitiveness, and curriculum offerings. Students should pay careful attention to the stated admissions criteria, which often vary widely from one institution to another. Based on this cursory search on the Internet, catalogs can be either downloaded or requested by mail for a more detailed analysis. If this process becomes too emotionally charged for the family, then parents may want to consider hiring a college consultant who can assist with the college search process.

## Finding the Right Level of Disability Support

Students should be advised to choose the school first and then the disability support services. Typically, this is not done, and parents initially shop for the disability support service program that they have heard about and do not consider whether the institution is really the best fit for their son or daughter given the course offerings, curriculum, and faculty–student ratio. After students have identified 10–15 institutions that are at the appropriate level of competitiveness (e.g., selective, more selective, most selective) based on the

**Box 10.5.**   College guides for learning disabilities
support services

Students can find information on college learning disabilities support
services in the following guides:

- *The K &W Guide to Colleges for Students with Learning Disabilities,
  Ninth Edition* (The Princeton Review, 2007)

- *Peterson's Colleges for Students with Learning Disabilities or ADD,
  Eighth Edition* (Seghers, 2007)

popular college guides, then students should think carefully about the level of
disability support services they may need after high school. By cross-matching
the institution with the level of support services necessary, students can
generate a list of five or six schools to investigate fully. Further consultation with
some college guides specific to learning disabilities can be helpful as well (see
Box 10.5). Once the list is narrowed down, students and parents should plan a
campus visit that might include taking a campus walking tour, sitting in on a
class, or visiting a residence hall, athletic facility, computer lab, or library.

Given that college admissions personnel cannot ask directly if a student
has a disability, students need to think carefully about whether they want to
disclose this information in the application process. If a student has overcome
significant odds and achieved academically, then disclosing the disability in
a personal statement that highlights his or her record of accomplishment
could be a real benefit. The goal of disclosure is to highlight academic
strengths not weaknesses. It might be worth explaining to an admissions
officer if a student with a learning disability has a high school transcript with
mediocre grades for his or her freshman and sophomore years and then his or
her grades improved significantly once he or she was identified as having a
disability and qualified for accommodations. Similarly, if the student lacks a
variety of extracurricular activities due to outside tutoring or work demands,
then this could be shared by the student in the interview. Regardless of the
decision, it is important that prospective students know that postsecondary
institutions are not required to waive or lower admissions criteria because a
student has a disability.

After gathering preliminary information about a particular college or
course of study, students should narrow their choices down by making a
follow-up telephone call to the director or coordinator of disability services
and arrange for a personal interview. Typically, it is the parent that makes
these arrangements, but this is one more instance in which students should
be given the opportunity to make their own arrangements. Given that college
is a significant financial investment, students and parents should take the
time to meet the disability support staff directly. Students with disabilities
who perform better verbally than on paper should consider scheduling an
interview with the admissions office and with the disability support service
office. Often, these interviews with the disability support service office are

nonbinding and have little if any direct effect on the admissions outcome but such fact finding can be extremely helpful. These informational sessions with disability support service staff may be done individually or in small groups with prospective students and their parents. It should be noted that most disability support service directors/coordinators prefer to meet individually with the student without parent prompting in order to get an accurate reading of the student's level of motivation, social skills, and self-knowledge. If the institution a student is considering has a highly rated disability support services office, then there should be no harm in disclosing the disability in the interview. If, however, the school does not have strong services for students with disabilities, then it might be better not to discuss the disability at this early stage of the application process. The following questions may be worth considering by students when they meet disability support service staff.

- How many students with disabilities are registered with the disability support service office?

- Is there a program for students with a specific disability (e.g., learning disabilities, Asperger syndrome) on campus?

- What kinds of accommodations are offered for students with special needs?

- Are there support groups for students with disabilities?

- Do students with disabilities have automatic early registration privileges that allow them to select the courses and professors they want?

- What is the attitude of the school toward accommodating a student who is unable to pass math and/or foreign language requirements?

- Are there provisions for course waivers or substitutions in foreign languages?

- Are counselors available on an ongoing basis for disability counseling and support?

- Is there a computer specialist that is available to assist students with disabilities with their assistive technology needs?

- Is input from the disability support service office allowed as part of the admissions and selection process?

- Is it possible to meet other students with disabilities who use the support services or to exchange e-mail addresses so that additional questions can be asked peer to peer?

After visiting the campus, it is advisable for the student to write a thank-you note to the interviewer. This brief handwritten note (not an e-mail) should come from the student and not the parent if it is to make a positive impression on the admissions officer.

## Financial Aid and Scholarships

Given the high cost of attending college, parents often need to be reminded to file financial aid application forms early. These forms, known as the Free Application for Federal Student Aid (FAFSA), can be found online at http://www.fafsa.edu.gov. According to the National Center on Education Statistics report for 2003–2004, approximately 63% of all undergraduates received some form of financial aid. Federal and state government education institutions and private agencies are committed to making higher education accessible to students, regardless of need. Students with disabilities may have some additional expenses that need to be factored into the financial aid request. For example, some colleges may charge an additional fee for specialized academic skills support, or students may need to buy assistive equipment for their computer or purchase e-files for their iPod. All these expenses should be anticipated so that the financial aid package will be adequate for the upcoming year.

Scholarships and grants are the best form of financial aid because they do not have to be paid back. Scholarships are typically offered to students with unique abilities that the school is seeking to promote, such as exceptional talent in music, art, or athletics. Scholarships are typically conditional to the student taking a standard course load and maintaining a satisfactory GPA over 4 years.

Federal grants for undergraduate study include Pell Grants, Federal Supplemental Educational Opportunity Grants (FSEOG), Academic Competitive Grants (ACG), and National SMART Grants. Pell Grants are the most common type of federal aid offered to undergraduate students and form the basis on which supplemental aid or other financial support may be added. Pell Grant recipients also receive priority for FSEOG awards that are provided to students with exceptional financial need and for National SMART Grants for math and science students. The ACG was introduced in 2007 and is for students who have attended secondary school programs that have been identified by the government as achieving a high standard of academic rigor.

Federal work-study programs are another way for students to address the tuition burden. Work-study is an actual part-time job that typically pays the current federal minimum wage and sometimes higher depending on the work performed. The amount of work-study support students receive depends on their level of financial need and the funding level provided by the school.

When scholarships, grants, and work-study are not sufficient to cover tuition costs, students may take out loans. Loan payments typically commence about 6 months after graduation. There are three federal loan programs available to students depending on their financial need. One example is the Federal Perkins Loan, which is a low-interest loan for students with significant financial needs. The Stafford Loan is another popular program that features a fixed interest rate and a yearly cap on the maximum amount a student may borrow. Finally, private loan companies may be another option worth considering. For example, MyRichUncle is a national student loan company offering federal and private loans to undergraduates, graduates, and professional students.

## Putting All of the Pieces Together

When it comes time to apply for college, students must decide on elements of their profile that present them as successful future college students. Regardless of the type of disability, students need to be reminded that the high school transcript is the number one credential needed for establishing their potential for college success. Letters of recommendation from teachers are secondary to the transcript. Letters of recommendation from family members, friends, clergy, or elementary school teachers carry little weight in the application process. A letter from a general education teacher in one of the student's college preparatory classes who reports that this student is ready for the rigors of college despite a disability is likely to capture the attention of the admissions committee. If the student has chosen to self-identify in the application process, then a letter from the resource room teacher might also be appropriate if it substantiates the student's level of motivation and achievement potential to do college-level work. Letters from special education teachers can shed valuable light on the student's prospects for future success if they realistically highlight the student's abilities and potential.

Students should be advised to fill out applications neatly in ink or directly on the computer. For the essay, they should write about a topic that is exciting to them, rather than something that "sounds intellectual" or is too routine. A student's disability or an unexpected health complication early in life can be a good topic if it is handled in a creative and self-affirming manner. A student who provides a brief historical overview of his or her disability and then focuses on just one or two events that changed his or her life may come across better on paper than, for example, a student with dyslexia who attempts to tell his or her life story in two pages (Brinckerhoff, 2007). Applicants should also be advised not to send more information than is recommended and to avoid exaggerating their achievements—a thick file does not necessarily impress admission staff. Admissions officers have tremendous integrity and such ploys are frowned on. Finally, students should ask their guidance counselors to review all application forms 2–3 weeks prior to the application deadline.

Letters of acceptance generally begin to arrive in mid-March. Many colleges, however, routinely hold the final acceptance notice until they have an additional quarter of high school grades. Students should not be alarmed as this process is often standard at more competitive institutions. If a student has not heard within 4–6 weeks of the date that admissions decisions typically are made, however, then the student, not the parent, should call. It is possible that documentation may still be missing or transcript grades were inadvertently not sent. If a student receives several letters of acceptance, then he or she is in the pleasant position of having to rank-order the college choices. If the student is unsure about which college to accept, then a follow-up telephone call or a second visit may be appropriate. After carefully deciding which college to attend, based on the previous considerations, the student should write a brief acceptance letter and mail in the deposits with the housing request early.

## Basic Services or a Comprehensive Support Program?

Under the ADA, each college and university must provide some minimal level of support to students with disabilities at no cost to ensure that reasonable accommodations are available (e.g., textbooks in an audio format, notetakers, additional time on examinations, provision for course substitutions, reduced course load). The most loosely defined or basic services are those in which there is a disability contact person on campus who typically wears many hats. Such a person may have some limited training in disability matters but, in fact, may be an attorney, counselor, or nurse. These generic support services are available to ensure equal educational opportunity for any student with a disability but little more. This individual typically consults with other offices on campus, such as the writing lab or tutorial program, to support students who are at risk. More campuses are now hiring at least one individual to serve

**Box 10.6.** The Strategic Alternative Learning Techniques (SALT) Center

The SALT Center at The University of Arizona (http://www.salt.arizona.edu) houses a full-time staff of 22 professionals who serve as ADHD coaches, counselors, graduate assistants, peer mentors, learning disability specialists, technology specialists, and peer tutors. The SALT program offers a 1-day mandatory orientation program for new students before registration. Subject area tutoring is provided by graduate assistants, professional tutors, and trained peer tutors. Additional support in career planning, learning strategies, self-advocacy, stress management, practical computer skills, test-taking, time management, and writing skills are provided collaboratively with on-campus and off-campus services. An extensive web site includes written policies and procedures regarding course substitutions, learning disabilities accommodations, and documentation requirements. For students seeking support beyond the mandated services, an additional fee applies depending on the level of service desired.

as the designated point person for all disability matters. Remediation and support is provided one-to-one in small groups for study skills and time management. Programs for college survival skills, medication management, and written composition skills are provided through on-campus or off-campus services. Faculty are notified by the coordinator of the students with disabilities office regarding all accommodation needs. For admission to the program, students are required to submit a psychoeducational report. The application deadline to the support program is rolling/continuous.

Comprehensive disability support service programs that go beyond the legally mandated services are characterized by having more than one person who directs the support services. Typically, the director or coordinator has expertise in one or more areas of disability and oversees a staff of several full-time professionals and part-time learning specialists. In addition to the basic accommodations noted previously, these campus offices typically have extensive written policies and procedures, faculty and staff awareness training, a wide range of tutorial supports, academic advisement, and frequent monitoring of student progress. In some instances, because of the specialized nature of the services provided, these programs offer a limited number of slots for students with disabilities and charge an additional fee. Separate applications are standard, as well as an additional service fee.

A summer transition program is often included in this comprehensive service delivery model. Some of newest innovations in these settings include ADHD peer coaching, tech prep tutorials for students, and technology loaner libraries for students. Sometimes this model includes in-house diagnostic testing as part of the program. Content tutoring may also be available in addition to learning strategy instruction. The Strategic Alternative Learning Techniques (SALT) Center at The University of Arizona (see Box 10.6.) is an example of a comprehensive learning disabilities support program, and

---

**Box 10.7.**   Landmark College

Landmark College (http://www.landmark.edu) is a 2-year liberal arts college serving students with learning disabilities and/or ADHD. Enrollment is approximately 475 students, with nearly 95% of the students residing from out of state. Class sizes are small and instruction is personalized. Many of the college faculty are adults with learning disabilities who assist students in developing self-understanding, self-advocacy, and lifelong learning skills. It is also one of the most costly private learning disabilities postsecondary institutions in the country. Landmark offers several summer programs, including a 3-week summer program specifically for high school students, a 2-week transitions program for recent high school graduates, and a 5-week summer session for visiting college students.

---

Landmark College in Putney, Vermont (see Box 10.7) is an example of a specialized learning disabilities postsecondary college.

## SUMMARY

The intent of this chapter was to highlight the fact that getting into college is a *process*. Preparing for making the transition to college is more than simply gaining admission into a postsecondary institution. Students with disabilities can be better prepared to make informed choices regarding the array of postsecondary options available to them by understanding their rights and responsibilities, as well as the effect that their disability may have on learning. Getting into college involves engaged and strategic planning and preparation by students. With support from high school teachers, guidance counselors, special educators, and parents, students can become masters of their own transition planning and be well equipped to choose the postsecondary setting that best matches their academic preparation, ability profile, and career interests.

## REFERENCES

Americans with Disabilities Act (ADA) of 1990, PL 101-336, 42 U.S.C. §§ 12101 *et seq.*

Banerjee, M., & Brinckerhoff, L.C. (2006, June). *Updating LD/ADHD documentation: Securing accommodations for high stakes tests and college coursework.* Paper presented at the Association on Higher Education and Disability, San Diego.

Brinckerhoff, L.C. (2007). Postsecondary learning: New challenges and opportunities. In A. Roffman (Ed.), *Guiding teens with learning disabilities: Navigating the transition from high school to adulthood* (pp. 167–221). New York: The Princeton Review.

Brinckerhoff, L.C., McGuire, J. M., & Shaw, S.F. (2002). A comprehensive approach to transition planning. In L.C. Brinckerhoff, J.M. McGuire, & S.F. Shaw (Eds.), *Postsecondary education and transition for students with learning disabilities.* (pp. 25–69). Austin, TX: PRO-ED.

Duffy, J.T., & Gugerty, J. (2005). The role of disability support services. In E.E. Getzel & P. Wehman (Eds.), *Going to college: Expanding opportunities for people with disabilities.* (pp. 89–115). Baltimore: Paul H. Brookes Publishing Co.

Getzel, E.E. (2005). Preparing for college. In E.E. Getzel & P. Wehman (Eds.), *Going to college: Expanding opportunities for people with disabilities* (pp. 69–83). Baltimore: Paul H. Brookes Publishing Co.

Individuals with Disabilities Education Improvement Act (IDEA) of 2004, PL 108-446, 20 U.S.C. §§ 1400 *et seq.*

Knapp, L.G., Kelly-Reid, J.E., & Ginder, S.A. (2008). *Postsecondary institutions in the United States: Fall 2007, degrees and other awards conferred: 2006-07, and 12-month enrollment: 2006-07.* Washington, DC: National Center for Education Statistics.

Kortering, L., Sitlington, P., & Braziel, P. (2004). The use of vocational assessment and planning as a strategic intervention to help keep youths with emotional or behavioral disorders in school. In D. Cheney (Ed.), *Transition of students with emotional or behavior disorders: Current approaches for positive outcomes.* Arlington, VA: Council for Children with Behavior Disorders and Division on Career Development and Transition.

Lazarus, S.S., Thurlow, M.L., Lail, K.E., Eisenbraun, K.D., & Kato, K. (2006). *2005 state policies on assessment participation and accommodations for students with disabilities* (Synthesis Report 64). Retrieved November 10, 2008, from http://cehd.umn.edu/NCEO/OnlinePubs/Synthesis64/

Madaus, J.W. (2005). Navigating the college transition maze: A guide to students with learning disabilities. *Teaching Exceptional Children, 37*(3), 32–37.

National Center for Education Statistics. (2005). *2003-04 National Postsecondary Student Aid Study (NPSAS:04) undergraduate financial aid estimates for 2003-04 by type of institution.* Retrieved July 1, 2009, from http://nces.ed.gov/Pubsearch/pubsinfo.asp?pubid=2005163

National Longitudinal Transition Study-2. (2004). *A special report of findings from the National Longitudinal Transition Study-2.* Retrieved October 20, 2008, from http://www.nlts2.org/reports/2004_11/nlts2_report_2004_11_complete.pdf

National Secondary Transition Technical Assistance Center. (2008). *Activity report: February 2008.* Retrieved July 1, 2009, from http://www.nsttac.org/pdf/february_report2008.pdf

Parker, D.R., & Banerjee, M. (2007). Leveling the digital playing field: Assessing the learning technology needs of college-bound students with LD and/or ADHD. *Assessment for Effective Intervention, 33*(1), 5–14.

The Princeton Review. (2007). *The K & W guide to colleges for students with learning disabilities* (9th ed.). New York: Random House.

Seghers, L. (Ed.). (2007). *Peterson's colleges for students with learning disabilities or ADD* (8th ed.). Lawrenceville, NJ: Peterson's.

Sitlington, P.L., Neubert, D.A., & Leconte, P.J. (1997). Transition assessment: The position of the Division on Career Development and Transition. *Career Development for Exceptional Individuals, 20,* 69–79.

Wagner, M., Newman, L., Cameto, R., Levine, P., & Marder, C. (2003). *Going to school: Instructional contexts, programs, and participation of secondary school students with disabilities.* Menlo Park, CA: SRI International.

# 11

# Planning for the Transition to College

*Stan F. Shaw*

## WHAT YOU'LL LEARN IN THIS CHAPTER:

✔ What key elements must be considered in the transition planning process

✔ How to implement a comprehensive transition planning process that begins when the student enters high school

✔ How to write an individualized education program (IEP) that includes all the necessary

elements to foster college access and readiness

✔ What secondary personnel can do to promote a school infrastructure that fosters effective transition to college

✔ What specific approaches and strategies can enhance the transition of students with specific disabilities

**EMILY**

Emily is a student with attention-deficit/hyperactivity disorder (ADHD) and a learning disability who has difficulty with organization, time management, information processing, and written expression. She was a student with a disability under the Individuals with Disabilities Education Improvement Act (IDEA) of 2004 (PL 108-446) during most of her middle and high school years. Her transition goal was to attend a 4-year college. She completed a challenging college prep curriculum in high school with a *B* average. She was admitted to two of the competitive 4-year colleges to which she had applied. When she arrived on campus she provided the Office for Students with Disabilities with her summary of performance (SOP) and formal evaluation data that documented her disability and justified her need for accommodations such as extra time on tests. She just completed her freshman year at a college more than 100 miles from home. She has a 2.76 grade point average (GPA) in psychology and is successfully managing the independence of college life.

How did Emily get to this point? More important, what did high school personnel do in collaboration with Emily and her parents to cultivate a successful transition from secondary education to college? This chapter presents options for the transition planning process that school personnel can implement to promote the postsecondary success demonstrated by Emily. First, key concepts that have been presented in previous chapters can be reviewed in Box 11.1.

## IMPLEMENTING THE TRANSITION PLANNING PROCESS

IDEA 2004 calls for an annual IEP to include "appropriate measurable postsecondary goals based upon age-appropriate transition assessments related to training, education, employment, and, where appropriate, independent living skills" (§ 300.320[b]). Too often, regulatory mandates are perceived as just additional paperwork that school personnel have to complete. These requirements, however, come from an evidence-based need for school personnel to address the poor outcomes for students with disabilities. Although it is acknowledged that postsecondary education has demonstrated its utility for providing productive outcomes for students with disabilities, it will not occur without addressing IDEA 2004 mandates with due diligence (see Box 11.2).

### Transition Services

IDEA 2004 defined *transition services* as

A results-oriented process that is focused on improving the academic and functional achievement of the child with a disability to facilitate the child's movement from school to postschool activities, including postsecondary

---

**Box 11.1.**    Big ideas, thus far

1.   Students with disabilities can be successful in college.

2.   College can have a positive effect on a student's quality of life.

3.   There are significant differences in terms of expectations and legal requirements when moving from high school to college.

4.   Because students in college have to self-advocate and request services, it is necessary to help the student develop and practice self-determination skills to the greatest extent possible.

5.   It is critical for the student to be provided reasonable accommodations that have the likelihood of being available in postsecondary settings. It is important that the student participate in selecting and evaluating those accommodations.

6.   Implementing a schoolwide model including response to intervention and/or positive behavioral supports can promote the development of the student's academic and social skills within the general education curriculum, which will enhance his or her ability to successfully make the transition to college.

7.   Preparing students to meet the general technology competency expectations of colleges (e.g., spreadsheets, graphics, multimedia, Internet), as well as technology-based learning strategies (e.g., functioning in a web-based class, online research, netiquette for virtual learning communities) will foster success in college.

8.   Helping students use an array of assistive technology will enable them to become independent learners.

9.   Encourage parents to relinquish their advocacy role to their children based on both the change from the Individuals with Disabilities Education Improvement Act (IDEA) of 2004 (PL 108-446) to Section 504 of the Rehabilitation Act of 1973 (PL 93-112) in postsecondary education and the need for student self-determination.

10.  The SOP can be used as a vehicle for schools to gather informal and formal assessment data that students can use to document their disability and justify the need for postsecondary accommodations.

---

education, vocational education, integrated employment (including supported employment), continuing and adult education, adult services, independent living, or community participation. [It] is based on the individual child's needs, taking into account the child's strengths, preferences and interests. (§ 300.43)

How can the IEP be developed to include "appropriate measurable postsecondary goals" (§ 300.320[b])? What are the most appropriate services

**Box 11.2.**   What the Individuals with Disabilities Education Improvement Act (IDEA) of 2004 (PL 108-446) says about the transition planning process

The transition services section of IDEA 2004 requires that:
Beginning no later than the first IEP [individualized education program] to be in effect when the child turns 16, or younger if determined appropriate by the IEP team, and updated annually, thereafter, the IEP must include
(1) Appropriate measurable postsecondary goals based upon age-appropriate transition assessments related to training, education, employment, and, where appropriate, independent living skills; and
(2) The transition services (including courses of study) needed to assist the child in reaching those goals. (§ 300.320[b])

that can be provided to assist the student to meet these goals, and how do you assess the efficacy of those services? The requirement that students be invited to attend the IEP meeting, combined with the focus on student strengths and preferences, further reinforces the critical importance of student self-determination, which is now unquestionably fostered by IDEA 2004. This is particularly heartening in terms of postschool outcomes because studies have demonstrated that effective self-determination skills improve employment (Wehmeyer & Schwartz, 1997) and postsecondary education (Field, Sarver, & Shaw, 2003) outcomes. What can IEP teams do to nurture active student participation? These questions and issues related to enhancing the school structure to foster transition are addressed in this chapter.

## When to Begin

Increasing the age at which transition planning must be included in the IEP is an important modification created by IDEA 2004. Under the Individuals with Disabilities Education Act Amendments (IDEA) of 1997 (PL 105-17), an annually updated statement of "transition needs" was required beginning at age 14. For college-bound students, this statement might have focused on "the child's course of study." At age 16, a "statement of needed transition services" was required. IDEA 2004 eliminated the age 14 mandate but specifically noted that planning may begin at a younger age if "determined appropriate by the IEP team" (§ 300.320[b]). It is productive that many states have promulgated regulations that maintain age 14 as the time to begin transition planning. All school personnel are encouraged to begin the transition planning process early enough so that students can consider college as a goal and start their freshman year in high school taking the necessary college preparation curriculum. Transition planning begins with the IEP team working with the student to specify postsecondary goals and select an appropriate course of study.

## Student Involvement in the IEP Process and Selection of Accommodations

Chapter 4 presented the rationale for and importance of fostering student self-determination prior to leaving high school. The IEP process is the most natural venue for that effort. Because laws applicable to postsecondary education settings (i.e., Section 504 of the Rehabilitation Act of 1973 [PL 93-112], the Americans with Disabilities Act Amendments Act [ADAAA] of 2008 [PL 110-325]) require the student to self-identify, provide disability documentation, and request reasonable accommodations, it is critical that students begin that process in high school through active participation in IEP team activities.

Although some high school freshmen who have not been self-advocates may initially have a difficult time, it is important for a designated member of the IEP team to foster that involvement. A premeeting with the student to discuss postsecondary goals or using worksheets (see Chapter 4) that present the students voice to the IEP team can be one bridge to self-advocacy. IEP team discussions that seek student input, ask the student about needed accommodations for specific courses, and ask for student feedback on use and utility of accommodations will help develop student self-determination. Consider additional ideas for involving the student in the IEP process presented in Chapter 4.

## Role of School Personnel in Implementing the Transition Planning Process

The IEP team has consistently been presented as the group of professionals with statutory responsibility for transition planning. There are, however, many secondary personnel with responsibilities for the transition process. Although professional roles are fluid depending on the availability, interests, and expertise of staff, specific staff roles might traditionally include the following.

### School Principal or District Administrator

The school principal (or assistant principal) or district administrator (e.g., special education director or supervisor) plays a key role in setting the tone for the school regarding the importance of the transition planning process and the expectation that it can promote critical student outcomes, rather than just serving as a paperwork burden. This role includes making sure school forms and processes are state of the art (e.g., practical and effective procedures for student involvement in IEP, constructive SOP forms and directions), personnel are prepared to carry out their responsibilities, roles are clear and appropriate, and the effectiveness of the process is evaluated.

### Transition Coordinator

Many high schools have transition coordinators who lead the transition effort in the school from developing, managing, and monitoring the school's transition process to collaborating with outside agencies including vocational rehabilitation and postsecondary institutions. They may teach specific transition courses (e.g., strategic instruction, short-term training) or develop special programs (e.g., summer transition programs, internships, joint programs with community colleges).

## Special Educators

The role of special educators is in a state of flux as a result of the placement of most students with disabilities in the general education curriculum and particularly because of the increasing implementation of response to intervention (RTI) and positive behavior supports (PBS). They now typically support students within the general education classroom. Chapter 5 describes an effective role in the schoolwide support model with a particular focus on intensive instruction to foster strategic learning. Special educators also play a key role in the IEP process by helping other team members and students to determine goals and accommodations and evaluate progress. In schools where administrative support is less than optimal, special educators can work with other school personnel to collaborate with parents to demonstrate the productive outcomes that result from effective transition planning. In addition, the state transition coordinator, who can provide training or describe model programs in other districts, can be an effective ally in this effort.

## General Educators

Classroom teachers have increasing responsibility for serving students with disabilities included in their classes. They need to collaborate with members of the IEP team to provide access to the general education curriculum by granting specified accommodations, conducting ongoing assessment of student performance, and communicating with special education and related services personnel. Secondary teachers have always had students planning to attend college, so their insights and expertise can be very helpful in the transition process.

## Counselors

Although school counselors have the traditional role of working with students to foster transition to postsecondary education, they need to take their skills in college placement and adapt them to the unique needs of students with disabilities. The American School Counselor Association (2004) position statement on the roles of school counselors working with students with special needs included providing support for postsecondary transition, assisting with establishing and implementing accommodations, and serving on the school's multidisciplinary team. To that end, counselors can include students with disabilities in many generic college search activities and provide special supports related to the college selection, access, and disability documentation needs of students with disabilities. The *Guidance and Career Counselors' Toolkit: Advising High School Students with Disabilities on Postsecondary Options* (HEATH Resource Center, 2006) is an excellent resource to support counselors in these efforts.

## School Psychologists and Other Related Services Personnel

School psychologists and other related services personnel (e.g., physical therapists, social workers, speech-language pathologists) have roles related to the provision of interventions (e.g., counseling, therapy) and assessment. They are often core members of the IEP team. Their educational assessment/diagnostic skills make them ideal professionals for collecting and sharing data useful for assessing transition and completing the SOP.

## DEVELOPING A TRANSITION IEP FOR COLLEGE

The IEP is a critically important document—it is the school's contract with the student. The IEP describes the services necessary to foster transition outcomes and the accommodations and supports needed to succeed in the general education curriculum and to participate in districtwide assessments.

### Key Elements in the Transition IEP for College

A student's transition IEP must now list appropriate, measurable postsecondary goals based on age-appropriate transition assessments, as well as the transition services needed to help the student reach those goals. Under IDEA 2004, the transition goals to be included in a student's IEP must relate to training, education, employment, and, when appropriate, independent living skills. This book addresses the goal of transition to education, specifically, admission to a 2- or 4-year college. The transition IEP must include the following elements.

#### Student Preferences

Student preferences are included to ensure that students are actively involved in the transition planning process. This is important because the likelihood of success increases if we are working at something we prefer. IDEA 2004 requires that the IEP team take into account the student's strengths, preferences, and interests. Therefore, it is necessary to assess the student's preferences so that postsecondary goals are appropriately chosen. To do that, the IEP team should assess the student's potential, desires, skills, and aptitude by gathering information on strengths, preferences, and personal goals identified through surveys and interviews (see Chapter 8 for transition assessment options). Ideally, this transition assessment process will lead to the student being able to personally share goals and dreams and define expectations as an active member of the IEP team.

#### Anticipated Postsecondary Outcomes

Because transition is a results-oriented process, it must include measurable postsecondary goals based on age-appropriate transition assessments. One of the biggest problems with transition plans has been that goals have not been specific enough to be measured and therefore do not provide the accountability required by IDEA 2004. The problem has been exacerbated by the fact that objectives are no longer required by federal statute, although many state regulations still do require objectives for each IEP goal. Effective practice suggests a broad goal such as, "Sarah will acquire the skills to enroll in a 2- or 4-year college," followed by specific objectives that would lead her to achieve that outcome and provide a basis to plan services and monitor progress. To help IEP teams with appropriate objectives for that outcome, see

**Table 11.1.** Secondary personnel should implement the following activities as part of a 4-year transition planning process

---

### Grade 9: Preparing for high school success

Develop a transition plan that helps students identify postsecondary goals with particular focus on the importance and availability of gaining access to postsecondary education.

Discuss culture, family, language, and the community context in developing postsecondary outcomes with the student.

Consult with students to plan the most academically challenging college preparatory program of courses in the general education classroom.

Encourage students to actively participate in IEP meetings, and suggest activities that meet their postsecondary goals.

Identify effective accommodations in areas of weakness, such as math, writing, or foreign language classes.

Review the diagnostic data with students to help them develop an understanding of the nature of their own disability and their need for accommodations.

Plan supports that foster independent learning and success including study skills, time management, test-taking strategies, social skills, and interpersonal communication skills.

Create an SOP folder for each student to collect ongoing data from formal and informal assessments related to goals, functional performance, and utility of accommodations.

### Grade 10: Transition planning begins

Teach students about the different rights and the responsibilities of high schools and colleges under IDEA 2004, Section 504, and the ADA.

Encourage students to self-advocate with parents, teachers, and peers.

Connect students with mentors and role models from culturally diverse backgrounds.

Counsel students (and parents) to carefully consider implications of academic choices, particularly in regard to avoiding the temptation of "retreating" to lower-track classes and being wary of course waivers.

Help the student prepare to become a coleader of the transition planning team at the IEP meeting.

Encourage students to "try out" accommodations and auxiliary aids in high school classes that are likely to be available in college (e.g., taped textbooks, notetakers, laptop computers, extra time on examinations).

Role-play with the student how, when, and where to discuss and request needed accommodations.

Include use of assistive technology aids (e.g., talking calculators, 4-track tape recorders, optical scanners, hand-held spell-checkers, voice-activated software, electronic day planners) and learning technologies (e.g., Internet, online instruction, course management systems like Blackboard or Vista) that might be necessary in college.

Meet with the student to develop a plan and time line for taking the PSAT/SAT and/or ACT and consider necessary accommodations, if warranted.

Review grades and test scores at the end of the year to assess options for college or other postsecondary education.

Encourage students to consider working a part-time summer job or volunteer position to foster self-determination and fiscal resources for college.

### Grade 11: Transition planning in the junior year

Consider requesting a complete psychoeducational evaluation to be conducted by the beginning of 12th grade as an IEP goal.

Help the student explore advantages and disadvantages of community colleges, vocational technical schools, 4-year colleges, and other postsecondary education options.

Plan a meeting with local department of rehabilitation services counselor to determine eligibility for services and/or other agency representatives to consider eligibility and assistance in the areas of vocational assessment, job placement, and/or postsecondary education/training.

Finalize arrangements for the SAT or ACT with necessary accommodations.

Work with the student on his or her college search.

Consider a private learning disabilities preparatory school or a "13th year" program if postsecondary education does not seem to be a viable option.

Encourage students to consider enrolling in a summer orientation program specifically for students with disabilities.

Encourage the student to apply for a summer job, volunteer position, or career-related work experience.

**Grade 12: Transition planning in the senior year**

Review and consider retaking the SAT or ACT to improve scores.

Discuss financial considerations with students and search the Internet for financial supports.

Collaborate with the department of rehabilitation services to consider eligibility for job guidance, enrolling in internships, or job shadowing experiences that permit hands-on skill building.

Complete the SOP with the student, making sure to attach copies of formal evaluations to support acceptance of college disability documentation requirements.

Encourage the student to consider taking a college course for credit over the summer or in conjunction with a summer orientation program.

---

*Note.* Adapted from *Postsecondary Education and Transition for Students with Learning Disabilities, 2nd Ed.* (pp. 38–42), by L.C. Brinckerhoff, J.M. McGuire, and S.F. Shaw, 2002, Austin, TX: PRO-ED. Copyright 2002 by PRO-ED, Inc. Adapted with permission.

examples of objectives in the appendix at the end of the chapter (Connecticut State Department of Education, 2007). These objectives provide clear direction regarding activities and transition services that Sarah would need to achieve her postsecondary education goal. Whether Sarah achieves her goal, the IEP team could demonstrate accountability for the appropriate transition program they planned.

### Transition Services

The IEP also must describe transition services to assist the student in reaching transition goals and related objectives. Avoke and Simon-Burroughs (2007), however, cautioned that students from culturally and linguistically diverse backgrounds are at high risk for negative postschool outcomes and may not have a positive response to traditional transition planning activities. IEP team members, therefore, are encouraged to adapt transition activities to the individual context in order to develop a more accurate understanding of how to enhance student outcomes. For example, although self-determination has been encouraged as a key tenet of this book, it must be tempered with the understanding that in some families and cultures there may be conflict with that value (Sitlington, Clark, & Kolstoe, 2000). See Chapter 4 for additional information on culturally responsive transition planning.

The following section emphasizes transition services, including a course of study, special education, related services, and technology as needed. Table 11.1 provides a general time line of transition activities through the high school grades. It is not meant to be an exhaustive list or to limit a school to that particular sequence but rather to exemplify the range of activities that may be implemented over time to fulfill postsecondary education outcomes.

### Course of Study

As a result of the competitive global economy and the increased need for higher-level skills for productive employment, high schools have increased academic requirements for graduation, and about half the states have implemented or are planning to implement exit examinations. More specifically, since 2006, 28 states have increased their graduation requirements for students with disabilities (Burdette, 2008). The Education

Commission of the States (2008) reported that many high schools across the country require 4 years of English, at least 3 years of math, as well as coursework in science, social studies, and foreign language. For students who hope to enroll in 4-year colleges, it is best to plan a high school curriculum that, *at a minimum,* includes 4 years of English, 3 years of math (including algebra and geometry), 2 years of laboratory sciences, 2 years of social studies (including American history), and 2 years of foreign language.

Standards-based education—the concept that common expectations applied to all students can be a catalyst for improved educational outcomes—has become a driving force in determining what should be taught and measuring what students should be expected to know (Kochhar-Bryant & Bassett, 2002). Given that almost half the states now require high school exit examinations, those standards have become ubiquitous in secondary schools. Transition services, however, require the school to provide interventions to accommodate individual student needs across a broad range of domains, including personal adjustment, independence, and social development. This makes IEP teams the focal point for overcoming the discontinuity between transition services and standards and related exit examinations. Kochhar-Bryant and Bassett recommended "opportunity standards" as a construct to bridge the gap between group standards and individual needs guaranteed by IDEA 2004. The opportunities needed by students with disabilities in their planned program may include individualized instruction, a responsive curriculum, adequate time for learning, positive behavioral interventions, valid assessment, and access to technology. The recommendations in Chapter 3 regarding the provision of accommodations, the activities presented in Chapter 4 to build independence, and the provision of technology described in Chapter 6 will all be useful options for the IEP team to consider to fulfill these opportunity standards.

### Special Education

Special educators can provide services to help students succeed in academic courses. They can provide academic or behavioral supports within the schoolwide model as presented in Chapter 5. Transition outcomes can be enhanced when special educators teach courses or modules that promote strategic learning (e.g., time management, organization, test preparation, study skills).

### Related Services

Counselors, social workers, and school psychologists are related services personnel with particularly important roles to play in providing transition services. Counselors have the training and experience to assist with many of the college search activities specified in Chapter 9. Social workers, counselors, and school psychologists have skills to support the social development and behavioral adjustment of students with disabilities (e.g., autism spectrum disorders [ASDs], serious emotional disturbance) so they can cope with the challenges inherent in the postsecondary education environment.

### Technology

Although this section is labeled "technology," IDEA 2004 requires IEP teams to consider assistive technology. As noted in Chapter 6, there is a broad range of transition technology that needs to be considered for incorporation into the IEP. In addition to traditional assistive technology devices (e.g., personal data managers, audio recorders, talking calculators, screen readers), it is critical to prepare students to meet the many technology competency expectations of colleges (e.g., graphics, multimedia, use of the Internet), as well as technology-based learning competencies (e.g., functioning in a web-based class, online research, netiquette for virtual learning communities; Shaw, Madaus, & Banerjee, 2009). Students with cognitive disabilities in college who have to deal with functional limitations caused by their disability will have great difficulty trying to also master new technology required in college classes. IEP teams that do a thorough assessment of technology needs and provide the necessary services to help students use both assistive and learning technologies will greatly enhance transition outcomes (Brinckerhoff & Banerjee, 2006).

## Uses of the Transition IEP

It is important to have high school accommodations approximate those that would be allowed in postsecondary education under Section 504 and the ADA (Brinckerhoff, McGuire, & Shaw, 2002). Providing supports for a student to gain admission to postsecondary education that will not be allowed in college potentially sets the student up for failure in the college setting. Course waivers, typically in math or foreign language, may make the student ineligible for admission to many 4-year colleges or require the student to take remedial courses at a community college. In some cases, the student would be required to take a number of college courses in this major area of weakness because of high school waivers. It is better for the IEP team to work with the student to identify course accommodations that allow the student to complete these courses in high school.

When considering accommodations, however, it is helpful to wean the student from accommodations that would not be allowed in college. Colleges will not provide accommodations that are believed to be inappropriate or unreasonable. An accommodation will not be provided if the disability documentation does not clearly justify the need for that accommodation. Course modifications (e.g., student only does half as much work as other students, grade is based on a different scale or content, student is not penalized for spelling mistakes in a writing class) will often not be permitted. Most colleges do not provide "untimed" tests but rather extended time based on the specific assessment data (e.g., student processing time requires time and a half only on math examinations). The IEP team is encouraged to help the student learn to succeed using supports and accommodations that will be allowed at the next level of education.

Madaus and Shaw (2006) suggested that the SOP should be part of the IEP process and under the purview of the IEP team. It has been recommended that SOP data collection should, ideally, begin in the freshman year and information continue to be added to the SOP file throughout the course of the student's high school years. Although IDEA 2004 calls for the SOP to be completed before high school graduation, the student and IEP team should collaboratively determine the most efficacious timing. For some students it may be helpful to have it completed early to use the data to support a request for accommodations on college entrance examinations. The National Disability Documentation Summit (Shaw, 2005) noted that involving the

---

**Box 11.3.**   Why is universal design needed?

Providing classroom accommodations has been the primary means to ensure equal access to instruction for students with disabilities. Although accommodations are often a necessary and appropriate means to provide access, they can foster a number of problematic dynamics, particularly for the growing number of students with cognitive disabilities that are not apparent to teachers and classmates. Field, Sarver, and Shaw (2003) noted that providing accommodations requires teachers to make time-consuming and difficult modifications for individual students. Most important, it forces students to disclose their disability in each class where accommodations are necessary, to specify their disabilities and limitations, and to request "special" treatment (i.e., reasonable accommodations). Although access to accommodations is guaranteed by the law, "it is often a frustrating, embarrassing, unpleasant, stigmatizing, and unending process for students with disabilities" (Field et al., p. 346).

---

student in developing the SOP is an important element in self-determination and that, in the end, the student "owns" the SOP to use in postsecondary environments (Dukes, Shaw, & Madaus, 2007).

An effectively written SOP can be the key element in documenting the student's disability and justifying the need for specific accommodations. The National Summit model SOP (see Chapter 8) includes previous formal evaluations, specification of functional limitations, and a history of accommodations that have been used successfully over time. Such evidence can be effective in supporting requests for reasonable accommodations in the college setting.

## INTEGRATING TRANSITION
## INTO THE SCHOOL'S INFRASTRUCTURE

Although the transition planning process and the transition IEP are key elements in fostering access to college, there are also a number of school elements, if available, that can provide productive supports for students seeking college admission. Some, such as universal design, are schoolwide, whereas others, such as counseling or career programs, are specific programs that may be included in the student's transition IEP as needed.

### Universal Design

Universal design is an approach to instruction that seeks to overcome the challenges associated with providing individual accommodations course by course (see Box 11.3). The general concept of universal design includes a specific set of principles to systematically incorporate accessible features into

**Table 11.2.**  Framework for considering alternative paradigms

|  | Special education | Universal design |
|---|---|---|
| Disability | An abnormality or impairment that exists within the individual | A component of human diversity and variation |
| Eligibility | Identify, test, and label individual students to document the presence of a disability and determine access to services | Consider the learning needs of a broad range of students to inform instructional and curricular design |
| Inclusion | Include students with disabilities whenever appropriate in the general curriculum | Design instruction and be inclusive of a wide range of learners |
| Instruction | Individually determined special education services available only to eligible students | Universally designed instruction available to all students |
| Accommodations and modifications | Available only for those students with documented disabilities | Available to all students via alternative methods for accessing instruction and curriculum |
| Assessment | Assure that students with disabilities are included in high-stakes assessment | Assure that standards are developed to be accessible to the widest range of students |
| Resource allocation | Special education services are viewed as depleting general education resources | Elements of universal design add value for a broader range of students |

From Shaw, S.F., McGuire, J.M., & Scott, S.S. (2004). *A framework for considering alternative paradigms* (pp. 1, 2). Storrs: University of Connecticut, Center on Postsecondary Education and Disability; reprinted with permission.

a design instead of retrofitting changes or accommodations (see Table 11.2). As it is applied in the field of architecture, universal design results in creating environments and products that can be used by a wide range of diverse individuals (McGuire, Scott, & Shaw, 2006). Legislation has promoted applying universal design in architecture (e.g., providing curb cuts, ramps, automatic doors, accessible bathrooms) so that all people, including those with physical disabilities, can gain access to stores, schools, and other facilities. Federal legislation has described universal design in education as universal design for learning. It is defined as:

> a scientifically valid framework for guiding educational practice that (A) provides flexibility in the ways information is presented, in the ways students respond or demonstrate knowledge and skills, and in the ways students are engaged; and
> (B) reduces barriers in instruction, provides appropriate accommodations, supports and challenges, and maintains high achievement expectations for all students including students with disabilities. (Higher Education Opportunity Act of 2008 [PL 110-315])

Therefore, just as a student in a wheelchair needs *no* disability services in a physically accessible environment, a student with a learning disability may not need disability services in an *instructionally accessible environment*. Scott, McGuire, and Shaw (2003) developed an inclusive paradigm for teaching by adapting the framework of universal design and its principles to reflect the instructional practices that have been acknowledged as effective with students with disabilities.

Universal design anticipates the needs of diverse learners and incorporates effective strategies into curriculum and instruction to make learning more accessible (Scott et al., 2003). Such an environment will foster student self-determination because options are available that allow the student to select personally productive approaches to learning (Field et al., 2003). Efforts to improve instructional accessibility should be given as high a priority as providing physical access was in previous decades.

Universal design is, therefore, becoming part of the public dialogue about inclusive educational practices. IDEA 2004 references to universal design include the definition from the Assistive Technology Act Amendments of 2004 (PL 108-364) (Section 602 [35]); requirements to support using technology based on universal design principles to maximize accessibility to the general education curriculum (Section 611 [e][2)][C)][v)]); and using universal design principles in developing and administering districtwide and alternative assessments (Section 612 [a][16][E]).

Secondary schools that begin to implement universal design features would reduce the need for accommodations and enhance transition to postsecondary education for all students. This can be implemented by providing 1) curriculum that provides multiple means of representation, 2) curriculum that provides multiple means of expression, and 3) curriculum that provides multiple means of engagement (Center for Applied Special Technology [CAST], 2006). Examples of universal design include providing course material online for all students or examinations that do not have time limitations or are completed electronically so students can choose to use needed assistive technology. The National Center on Accessing the General Curriculum is providing a vision of how new curricula, teaching practices, and policies can be woven together to create practical approaches for improved access to the general curriculum for students with disabilities (Center for Applied Special Technology, 2004). CAST also developed practical guides that provide teachers with ideas about ways to integrate universally designed learning tools and strategies into the curriculum (see http://www.cast.org).

## Counseling Programs

A formal counseling program could provide productive supports for student transition. Promising elements of such a program include teaching learning strategies, exploring career options, learning educational rights under Section 504 and the ADAAA, and developing awareness of postsecondary options. Opportunities for high school students to visit a local college or having college students with disabilities visit the high school can be very productive. Involving outside agency personnel such as vocational rehabilitation counselors provides additional support and extends the effort beyond high school. A unique component of such an effort is a follow-along process in the first year of postsecondary education that involves helping the student become accustomed to campus, visit disability services, and join academic support groups (Aune, 1991).

Mentoring is a specific kind of counseling program in which the relationship between the mentor and the student can be a key factor in successful transition. Mentoring is a supportive relationship between a student and someone more senior in age or experience who offers support, guidance, and assistance as the younger partner plans a new area of experience such as transition to college. Many disability services offices have encouraged their students to mentor high school students through formal or informal programs. Students with disabilities are likely to listen to someone who has successfully made the transition to college while coping with the same challenges they face. Such a program can be initiated by contacting the college disability services office in your region. The *Guidance and Career Counselors' Toolkit: Advising High School Students with Disabilities on Postsecondary Options* (HEATH Resource Center, 2006) is a resource for initiating such a program. The Edge Foundation (http://www.edgefoundation.org), which is developing and evaluating college mentoring programs, can be a helpful resource. A different kind of counseling that has a broader focus on careers and employment may also be effective for transition to postsecondary education.

## Career Programs

Although the emphasis of this book is on transition to degree programs at 2- and 4-year colleges, there is data to suggest that programs that focus more on careers and short-term postsecondary training can foster productive postsecondary education outcomes. For example, the Bridges Project (Lamb, Brown, Hodges, & Foy, 2004) offered a course for students with disabilities that focused on exploring careers and developing self-determination skills. Participants were required to observe and interview someone from their chosen career, gather information on that career, and plan a workshop for college faculty on classroom accommodations for students with disabilities. Although such a short-term effort may be productive, Iowa's High School High Tech (HSHT) program provided a more longitudinal support system.

In HSHT, students were involved in site visits, job shadowing, internships, and college preparation (e.g., choosing an appropriate college, developing study skills, seeking reasonable accommodations). In addition, they received extensive hands-on training in technology and related high-tech careers and were supported through follow-along in college to ensure access to college supports (Nietupski et al., 2004).

A more comprehensive collaboration is evident in the Occupational Skills Training (OST) program. The OST is a collaboration between high schools, colleges, the Office of Vocational Rehabilitation, and the employment community (Flannery, Yovanoff, Benz, & Kato, 2008). Guiding principles of this kind of program include "a) a focus on specific occupations, b) a curriculum that can be completed within one year or less, and c) hands-on instruction and/or worksite-based training" (Flannery et al., p. 27). This type of short-term postsecondary training provides a college experience (i.e., these programs are often offered at community colleges) that does not require the academic background and time commitment of degree programs but can provide for productive employment outcomes. This could be an effective dual enrollment program for high school students who transition to the world of work. The OST provides the student with an individual training plan, support in the classroom and on the worksite, direct occupational skills training by the employer, and a case manager. The employment outcomes for OST graduates include significantly higher wages and hours worked than for those who did not graduate (Flannery et al., 2008). Additional information on community-based programs for young adults can be found at http://www.transitioncoalition.org. It seems that collaborative efforts between secondary and postsecondary institutions would be most productive, given the importance of programs that follow the student from high school into college. Next, how additional collaborations can be developed and implemented will be discussed.

## Joint Programs Between High Schools and Colleges

There are many examples of collaboration among high schools, colleges, state agencies, and professional organizations that are worth emulating. Some states have successfully built bridges in the areas of college disability documentation, legal requirements, and communication in which the discontinuity between secondary and postsecondary education has often been problematic. With regard to college disability documentation, task forces organized by the state transition coordinator that involve the state affiliate of the Association on Higher Education And Disability (AHEAD) have brought together all relevant stakeholders to develop statewide documentation guidelines that were agreed on by secondary schools and colleges in the state (Reilly & Wilkerson, 2008). This makes navigating the transition maze considerably easier for students planning to attend college in their home state.

Other states have addressed the much debated SOP, which was a new requirement specified in IDEA 2004. Stakeholders from Iowa worked under the leadership of the state transition coordinator to develop a unique solution that involved two SOP forms. One form is for students who are making the transition to employment and the other is for meeting the more stringent documentation needs for transition to college (Wassenaur & Guy, 2008).

Many states have an ongoing effort to provide annual workshops for consumers and/or professionals on transition topics. There may be separate training efforts for consumers (e.g., students, parents) and professionals. Given that these workshops often attract 300–700 attendees, some states will run them in different regions of the state or in catchment areas for different colleges. The hallmark of these workshops is a balanced presentation that will often include general information on effective transition with an overall theme of self-determination, differences between secondary and postsecondary expectations, and, often, a panel composed of students with disabilities who have made a successful transition to college. Breakout sessions typically address the needs of professionals (e.g., what knowledge and skills do students need for a successful transition to college, staff development in formulating effective transition plans for college, approaches to transition assessment, writing an SOP for college), students (e.g., What do I need to do to prepare for college? What are the realities of college life?), and parents (helping your child become a self-advocate, change in parental role as your child shifts from high school to college).

These statewide collaborations have also resulted in developing various state transition brochures and information sheets. Connecticut's Interagency Transition Task Force has developed an extensive *Transition Training Manual and Resource Directory* (2004) that includes sections on laws, transition curricula, interagency collaboration, transition to postsecondary education, self-advocacy, financial independence, and resources. It is available at http://www.state.ct.us/sde/deps/special/index.htm.

# ADDRESSING THE NEEDS OF STUDENTS WITH SPECIFIC DISABILITIES

It is necessary to begin by acknowledging that no two students are alike and that the disability does not define the individual. Nevertheless, there are often issues related to each disability that are pervasive that require consideration. Although the interventions are presented under a specific disability, they may have utility in addressing similar behaviors in students with other disabilities.

## Learning Disabilities

Students with learning disabilities make up about half the population of students with disabilities. Their characteristics are very diverse. They exhibit difficulties such as problems with calculation, the inability to comprehend written words, very slow processing, and limited short-term memory. Because most of these characteristics relate directly to academic success, students with learning disabilities are often challenged in the area of learning. Yet, by definition, they also have academic abilities in areas not directly related to the learning disability and often exhibit the intelligence to succeed in college.

The first barrier that must be addressed is the incorrect perception that these students are stupid or lazy. It is vital that the IEP team maintain a balance between addressing both student strengths and weaknesses. Students with learning disabilities have academic skills that need to be identified, encouraged, and utilized. Assessment is an important related issue. It is imperative that effective formal and informal assessment data be collected to pinpoint functional limitations and needed interventions and accommodations because of the atypical profile these students present and the fact that their disabilities are "hidden" (see Chapter 8). Implementing strategic instruction (e.g., time management, organizational skills, memory skills, language and communication skills, notetaking, outlining) is the key to successful transition for students with learning disabilities (see Chapter 5). Research indicates that students with learning disabilities who can apply instruction regarding how to learn become independent learners who can achieve success even in the most competitive college environment. This fact raises one final issue that must be addressed in the transition process. If students with learning disabilities have achieved academically, then they may no longer be identified under IDEA 2004 given that they do not meet criteria for special education services. Under these circumstances, it may be productive for the transition process to include students with learning disabilities (and other disabilities such as ADHD) who are no longer served under IDEA 2004, but have 504 plans instead.

## Attention-Deficit/Hyperactivity Disorder

Students with ADHD also face challenges when they enter college, including staying on task, organizing time, focusing, and interacting with peers and adults. In addition, they no longer have the structure provided by high school and the support system of home, and this is compounded by increased demands for self-directed study, persistence, and organization. Supports such as special education services, behavioral interventions, and individual counseling will often not be available in college. It is important for students classified as ADHD to be prepared for these significant changes if they are to succeed in postsecondary education. Supports that will promote college achievement include activities such as providing students with information, listening as the student verbalizes plans, helping the student identify options, encouraging student choice, and asking questions that help students reflect on and learn from the self-determination process. The ADHD coaching process has the potential to be an effective model for encouraging the aforementioned behaviors, and it is increasingly available in college settings. Although coaching is not yet an evidence-based practice, there is preliminary data to suggest its utility (Parker, 2004). Coaching involves an ongoing relationship in which the agenda comes from the student and the focus is on helping the student create practical strategies for daily living. The coach helps the student attend to the task and provides encouragement throughout the process. A professional or peer coach can support the student to set goals, focus, prioritize, persist in staying on schedule, and complete tasks (Edge Foundation, 2008). A coach uses questions as the primary communication tool because the fundamental tenet of coaching is a belief that students know the answers to their own questions (Parker, 2004). A nonjudgmental sounding board and confidence builder can be an effective intervention for transition to college. Resources for ADHD coaching are available at http://www.adhdcoaches.org; http://www.coachfederation.org; http://www.adhdcoachinstitute.org; and http://www.edgefoundation.org.

## GARY: A STUDENT WITH ATTENTION-DEFICIT/HYPERACTIVITY DISORDER

School has been a struggle throughout Gary's life. Disorganization is a hallmark of his life and it includes an inability to plan, study, attend to tasks, or complete assignments. He also has deficits in written expression and math. His strengths are above-average intellectual ability, verbal skills, and the ability to relate to peers and adults. Transition planning for Gary involved careful analysis of those strengths and weaknesses to identify appropriate long-term goals. The IEP team, in collaboration with Gary and his parents, decided that a 4-year college with few required general education courses (particularly in math) and with significant disability supports was a reasonable goal. Transition services included special education support in the area of study skills and organization throughout his high school years. The most critical support was a peer coach who would ask Gary if he could specify his homework, determine his time line for completing long-term assignments, and check his daily planner to identify daily/weekly school responsibilities. The school counselor worked with Gary to identify vocational interests and apply for part-time or summer jobs so Gary could explore areas of interest and vocational goals.

## Asperger Syndrome and Autism Spectrum Disorders

Students with ASDs, particularly those with Asperger syndrome, are increasingly seeing college as a realistic option. These students often present unique characteristics including issues with self-concept and self-awareness and restrictive and repetitive patterns of behavior, interests, and activities. They may have deficits in social skills, particularly social perception; difficulty interacting with peers; and sensory processing challenges and sensitivities. Specific problems typically include motivation, perspective taking, organizing written work, rigidity, and impulse control. These characteristics can also be strengths when working in a class or area of study that relates to student interests. The challenge for secondary personnel is to identify the supports and accommodations that each student finds helpful in adjusting to what often seems like a confusing and hostile environment. A helpful approach is to attempt to achieve a balance between accommodations that facilitate management of everyday challenges while providing training and supports that assist the student in developing self-advocacy and life skills. Providing a coach can be productive to help the student work through daily problems, learn coping strategies, and have an emergency outlet when social situations become overwhelming. There are a growing number of colleges that will also provide a coach for students who can document need and utility of that support (Edge Foundation, 2008; Thierfeld-Brown, Wolf & Bork, 2008).

## Emotional Disabilities and Behavior Disorders

The initial challenge for students with emotional or behavior disorders who are beginning college is a matter of classification. In postsecondary environments, such students are referred to as "students with psychiatric disabilities" and are typically required to have medically based disability documentation. Challenges at college include a less structured environment; being away from the traditional support system of home, community, and parents; and the need to self-advocate. These multiple challenges require a comprehensive transition effort. One such approach is *supported education,* which provides an array of services that include a case manager or peer mentor to provide one-to-one support, skill training related to time management, studying, and interpersonal skills. Stress management and assistance, which may require both school and community multidisciplinary resources (e.g., school counselor, vocational rehabilitation, private psychiatrist), may also be needed supports. In addition, many students may need to take a reduced course load or even a semester off when disability-related challenges are particularly acute.

## Traumatic Brain Injury

Students with traumatic brain injury (TBI) often face challenges not typical of other students discussed thus far. In addition to the deficits caused directly by the injury, they are aware of how they functioned prior to the "trauma," which makes it challenging for them to understand and accept their limitations. This causes difficulty accepting goals that are more reflective of current functional levels. In addition, there are often physical/medical problems (e.g., migraine headaches, mobility issues, speech problems) that complicate transition planning.

A multidisciplinary effort involving educators; speech-language, physical, and occupational therapists; neuropsychologists; vocational rehabilitation counselors; and possibly cognitive therapists and neuro-optometrists is often necessary. These students require a coordinated and sustained *team* effort with a case manager to monitor progress and call meetings to address problems. There may be need for intensive cognitive training to deal with memory problems, counseling to address family interactions and frustration resulting from the disability, coaching to foster self-advocacy skills, and an assistive technology evaluation to identify low-tech or high-tech accommodations that will compensate for weaknesses.

The multiple challenges faced by these students requires careful planning of postsecondary education opportunities. Even for a student who had excellent preinjury school grades, when considering college options, current skills and knowledge must be paramount so that the student is still "otherwise qualified" and in a position to succeed if a competitive college is selected. Helping the student and family identify support personnel (e.g., therapists, counselors, neuropsychologists) in the college setting is critical if the student is not going to be living at home. A community college that would allow the student to live at home for the first year or two of college might also be an appropriate consideration even for a student who aspires to a 4-year degree.

## SALLY: A STUDENT WITH TRAUMATIC BRAIN INJURY

The car Sally was driving was hit by a drunk driver when she was a freshman in high school. Before the injury she was a straight A student with plans to attend a competitive college like her two older brothers. Postinjury she has dealt with significant cognitive impairments including short-term memory problems and limited ability to concentrate and learn new material. She and her family are extremely frustrated by the fact that she cannot perform academically anywhere near her preinjury level and are realizing that her preinjury goals (i.e., admission to a competitive 4-year college) may not be met. As a current high school junior, Sally's transition team needs to address her dreams in a realistic framework. Transition services should include intensive cognitive intervention and identifying effective accommodations and appropriate long-term goals.

## PLANNING FOR THE MONTHS BEFORE BEGINNING COLLEGE

Although being admitted to college is an achievement to be savored, it must not be the end of the transition process if the intent is to provide an effective foundation for success. Secondary personnel need to address the following issues in collaboration with the student to make the transition to college as seamless as possible.

Review the SOP in light of the selected college's disability documentation requirements to ensure that the data support the necessary services and accommodations.

Self-disclosure is a complex issue in the adult environment. It requires the student to know if, when, and how to disclose a disability. For example, professors do not have the right to details of the disability once college disability services has approved documentation. Students should also consider whether roommates or classmates need to know about the disability and, if so, what information should be shared.

Consider what the student needs to acclimate to the postsecondary environment. Considerations should include visits to the college to become familiar with the campus layout and location of critical offices and buildings. Legal rights under Section 504 and the ADAAA and how they are different from IDEA 2004 need to be reviewed.

The student may need help with decisions regarding courses to take in the first year and, particularly, about course load. Summer courses or a summer transition program (either provided by the selected college or by another postsecondary institution) should be considered in order to reduce freshman year course load.

Given the social pressures and emotional stressors associated with the transition to postsecondary education, it is important to help the student find a support system at the college, identify local counseling or mental health professionals (college based or private), and plan for the increased necessity for self-advocacy.

## SUMMARY

- Transition should begin at the beginning of high school or shortly thereafter so that a 4-year course of study can be developed to meet college admission requirements, effective accommodations can be identified, and services can be provided over time to ameliorate academic and behavioral deficits.

- All school personnel, including the building administrator, special and general educators, and related services personnel, should be part of the transition team supporting this critical effort to help students gain access to postsecondary education.

- Key elements of the transition planning process include identifying student preferences, determining postsecondary education goals, and providing transition services.

- Transition services may include a course of study that balances school standards with individual transition needs that can be conceptualized as "opportunity standards," including individualized instruction, a responsive curriculum, adequate time for learning, access to technology, positive behavioral interventions, and valid assessments.

- When selecting accommodations, it is necessary to avoid course modification that will not be allowed in postsecondary education and could limit college access.

- The IEP team should recommend transition supports and accommodations that will also be allowed in postsecondary education.

- Implementing universal design in high schools would enhance the ability of students with disabilities and all students to learn without modifications and accommodations, limiting the need for school personnel to provide individualized instruction.

- Developing structured elements that foster transition such as counseling/mentoring, career programs, or collaborative efforts with institutions of higher education or state agencies can provide productive and easily accessible options for transition planning.

## REFERENCES

American School Counselor Association. (2004). *Position statement: Special-needs students.* Alexandria, VA: Author.

Americans with Disabilities Act Amendments Act (ADAAA) of 2008, PL 110-325.

Assistive Technology Act Amendments of 2004, PL 108-364, 29 U.S.C. §§ 3001 *et seq.*

Aune, E. (1991). A transition model for postsecondary bound students with learning disabilities. *Learning Disabilities Research and Practice, 6,* 177–187.

Avoke, S.K., & Simon-Burroughs, M. (2007). Providing transition services for students with disabilities from culturally and linguistically diverse backgrounds. *Journal of Special Education Leadership, 20,* 66–72.

Brinckerhoff, L., & Banerjee, M. (2006). *Tech preparation: New challenges and opportunities for college-bound teens with LD and/or ADHD.* Retrieved September 4, 2008, from http://www.schwablearning.org/pdfs/expert_loring.pdf?date=8-21-06&status=new

Brinckerhoff, L.C., McGuire, J.M., & Shaw, S.F. (2002). *Postsecondary education and transition for students with learning disabilities* (2nd ed.). Austin, TX: PRO-ED.

Burdette, P. (2008, March). *Graduation requirements for students with disabilities: Policy recommendations.* Alexandria, VA: National Association of State Directors of Special Education.

Center for Applied Special Technology. (2004). *National Center on Accessing the General Curriculum.* Retrieved June 30, 2008, from http://www.cast.org/ncac

Center for Applied Special Technology. (2006). *Teaching every student.* Retrieved July 21, 2008, from http://www.cast.org/teachingeverystudent/toolkits/tk_introduction.cfm?tk_id=21

Connecticut Interagency Task Force. (2004). *Transition training manual and resource directory.* Retrieved July 30, 2008, from http://www.sde.ct.gov/sde

Connecticut State Department of Education. (2007). *Topic brief: Writing transition goals and objectives.* Retrieved July 30, 2008, from http://www.sde.ct.gov/sde/lib/sde/PDF/DEPS/Special/Transition_GO.pdf

Dukes, L.L., Shaw, S.F., & Madaus, J.W. (2007). How to complete a summary of performance for students exiting to postsecondary education. *Assessment for Effective Intervention, 32,* 143–159.

Edge Foundation. (2008). *Coaching.* Retrieved August 4, 2008, from http://www.edgefoundation.org

Education Commission of the States. (2008). *High school graduation requirements: Quick facts.* Retrieved August 3, 2008, from http://www.ecs.org/html/IssueSection.asp?Issueid=145&ssID=0&s=Quick+Facts

Field, S., Sarver, M., & Shaw, S. (2003). Self-determination: A key to success in postsecondary education for students with learning disabilities. *Remedial and Special Education, 24,* 339–349.

Flannery, K.B., Yovanoff, P., Benz, M.R., & Kato, M.M. (2008). Improving employment outcomes of individuals with disabilities through short-term postsecondary training. *Career Development for Exceptional Individuals, 31,* 26–36.

HEATH Resource Center. (2006). *Guidance and career counselors' toolkit: Advising high school students with disabilities on postsecondary options.* Retrieved July 10, 2008, from http://www.heath.gwu.edu

Higher Education Opportunity Act of 2008, PL 110-315, 20 U.S.C. §§ 1001 *et seq.*

Individuals with Disabilities Education Act Amendments (IDEA) of 1997, PL 105-17, 20 U.S.C. §§ 1400 *et seq.*

Individuals with Disabilities Education Improvement Act (IDEA) of 2004, PL 108-446, 20 U.S.C. §§ 1400 *et seq.*

Kochhar-Bryant, C.A., & Bassett, D.S. (2002). *Aligning transition and standards-based education: Issues and strategies.* Arlington, VA: Council for Exceptional Children.

Lamb, P., Brown, M., Hodges, B., & Foy, D. (2004). *Building bridges toward science careers for youth with disabilities.* Retrieved July 16, 2008, from http://www.ncset.org/publications/viewdesc.asp?id=1494

Madaus, J.W., & Shaw, S.F. (2006). The impact of the IDEA 2004 on transition to college for students with learning disabilities. *Learning Disabilities Research and Practice, 21,* 273–281.

McGuire, J.M., Scott. S.S., & Shaw, S.F. (2006). Universal design and its applications in educational environments. *Remedial and Special Education, 27,* 166–175.

Nietupski, J., McQuillen, T., Duncan-Berg, D., Weyant, J., Daugherty, V., Bildstein, S., O'Connor, A., Warth, J., & Hamre-Nietupski, S.M. (2004). Iowa's high school high tech goes to college program: Preparing students with mild disabilities for careers in technology. *Journal of Developmental and Physical Disabilities, 16,* 179–192.

Parker, D.R. (2004). *Voices of self-determined college students with ADHD: Undergraduates' perceptions of factors that influence their academic success.* Unpublished doctoral dissertation, University of Connecticut, Storrs.

Rehabilitation Act of 1973, PL 93-112, 29 U.S.C. §§ 701 *et seq.*

Reilly, V., & Wilkerson, D. (2008, August). *Dealing with the documentation dilemma: A statewide approach.* Association on Higher Education and Disability Annual Conference, Reno, Nevada.

Scott, S.S., McGuire, J.M., & Shaw, S.F. (2003). Universal design for instruction: A new paradigm for adult instruction in postsecondary education. *Remedial and Special Education, 24,* 369–379.

Shaw, S.F. (2005). IDEA will change the face of postsecondary disability documentation. *Disability Compliance for Higher Education, 11*(1), 7.

Shaw, S.F., Madaus, J.W., & Banerjee, M. (2009). 20 ways to enhance access to postsecondary education for students with disabilities. *Intervention in School and Clinic, 44,* 185–190.

Shaw, S.F., McGuire, J.M., & Scott, S.S. (2004). *A framework for considering alternative paradigms.* Storrs: University of Connecticut, Center on Postsecondary Education and Disability.

Sitlington, P.L., Clark, G.M., & Kolstoe, O.P. (2000). *Transition education and services for adolescents with disabilities.* Boston: Allyn & Bacon.

Thierfeld-Brown, J., Wolf, L., & Bork, R. (2008, August). *In and out: Transitions for students with autism spectrum disorders.* Association on Higher Education and Disability Annual Conference, Reno, Nevada.

Wassenaur, C., & Guy, B. (2008, August). *The Iowa transition initiative: Support for Accommodations Requests (SAR) implementation.* Association on Higher Education and Disability Annual Conference, Reno, Nevada.

Wehmeyer, M.L., & Schwartz, M. (1997). Self-determination and positive adult outcomes: A follow-up study of youth with mental retardation or learning disabilities. *Exceptional Children, 63*(2), 245–255.

# APPENDIX

## Objectives to Use for Postsecondary Education Goals

### Postsecondary Education

Goal: *Student will acquire the skills to successfully transition to a 2- or 4-year college/university.*

Student will enroll in academic classes that will prepare him or her for the educational challenges of postsecondary education.

Student will meet with guidance counselor/special education teacher to discuss academic requirements of pursuing a college degree.

Student will demonstrate skill in developing a positive school profile that will be used in the college application process.

Student will participate in at least one extracurricular activity in order to develop relevant nonacademic skills.

Student will describe his or her disability in terms of learning strengths and weaknesses.

Student will attend postsecondary options fairs, events, and group sessions provided by the school.

Student will participate in the traditional standardized tests necessary for acceptance to postsecondary institutions (PSAT, SAT, and ACT).

Student will complete the paperwork necessary to take the ACT/SAT with accommodations.

Student will schedule a visit with the disability services coordinator for at least two colleges/universities to determine the levels of service available.

Student will describe the accommodations/modifications available in the postsecondary settings visited.

Student will explain the difference between protection under IDEA 2004, Section 504 of the Rehabilitation Act of 1973, and the ADA.

Student will ensure that all current evaluation data required by postsecondary institutions has been gathered.

Student will participate in direct skills training in becoming a positive self-advocate:

• Learn whom to ask and when to ask for assistance.

From Connecticut State Department of Education. (2007). *Topic brief: Writing transition goals and objectives* (pp. 3–6). Retrieved October 28, 2008, from http://www.sde.ct.gov/sde/lib/sde/PDF/DEPS/Special/Transition_GO.pdf; adapted by permission.

- Practice describing what is needed in order to become a successful student.

- Develop and practice negotiation skills to help get what is wanted/needed.

- Develop strategies for seeking assistance.

- Discuss disability needs in the context of seeking accommodations.

Student will practice needed postsecondary education strategies:

- Time management

- Test preparation

- Study partner/study group

- Note-taking techniques

- Stress reduction techniques

- Text anxiety reduction activities

Student will develop the skills to organize work with efficiency.

Student will develop strategies to enhance study skills.

Student will determine what documentation data is required by the selected postsecondary institution in order to receive needed accommodations.

Student will research resources within and outside the college to find support.

Student will seek eligibility for vocational rehabilitation services.

Student will identify private tutoring, if necessary.

Student will submit a résumé and postsecondary list of options to a counselor.

Student will write a personal essay to use in college applications.

Student will investigate availability of financial aid and complete paperwork.

## Self-Advocacy

Goal: *Student will demonstrate self-advocacy skills in order to communicate learning style and academic and behavioral needs.*

Student will complete a learning style inventory and be able to describe learning style.

Student will communicate to others the strengths and weaknesses of learning style.

Student will review the modifications/adaptations page of his or her IEP.

Student will communicate with teachers to seek help, clarify instructions or requirements of academic tasks, and make them aware of accommodations.

Student will learn skills to facilitate his or her IEP.

Student will identify effect of behavior on self and others and how it affects learning.

Student will assess accuracy of assignments and tests by reviewing for errors and making necessary revisions.

Student will accept the consequences of being unprepared for class by discussing the consequences and developing a strategy to avoid problems in the future.

Student will demonstrate the skill of obtaining information from teachers regarding tests, quizzes, projects, and so forth.

Student will develop and carry out a plan for making up work missed due to absence.

Student will accept responsibility for utilizing resource period services to meet classroom objectives.

Student will discuss specific topic behaviors (positive and negative) and their effect on academic classes and/or social performance of self.

Student will seek guidance/direction when facing new or difficult situations.

Student will appropriately confront topics/issues that are uncomfortable with support.

Student will plan and implement alternative solutions for school problems as they occur with adult guidance.

Student will deal with academic and social situations positively and appropriately and discuss feelings regarding these situations.

Student will accept praise and/or criticism from peers or adults and utilize this to change social and behavioral outcomes.

## Organization and Study Skills

Goal: *Student will demonstrate organization and study skills in order to participate successfully in academic classes.*

Student will self-monitor homework by maintaining an assignment notepad that lists all assignments and dates due.

Student will monitor long-term assignments by breaking down assignments, setting up blocks of time for completing each part, and recording and monitoring progress.

Student will show preparation for class by reporting to class on time with necessary materials for class.

Student will complete assigned tasks by following oral and written directions.

Student will complete assigned tasks by beginning within a reasonable amount of time and finishing within a specified time frame.

Student will work toward effective task completion by remaining on task, ignoring distractions, and working independently for a specified period of time.

# Index

Page references to tables, figures, and boxes are indicated by *t*, *f*, and *b* respectively.

study skills for college, 233–234,
233*b*, 236
time line for, 234–238
*see also* Cognitive strategy
instruction; Schoolwide positive
behavior support (SWPBS);
Transition assessment; Transition
planning
PSAT, *see* Preliminary Scholastic
Aptitude Test
Psychiatric disorders, *see*
Emotional/behavioral disabilities,
students with

Reasonable accommodations, 27–28
*see also* Accommodations and
modifications
Reduced course loads, 56
Regional campus colleges, 244
Rehabilitation Act of 1973 (PL 93-112),
Section 504
college disability services, 213
compared to other legal mandates, 11,
14, 26, 39–40
creating a plan, 16–17
example plan, 17, 18*f*–19*f*
overview, 11, 26
Subparts D and E, 12–14, 14*t*, 26–27,
42–43, 51
Related services personnel
in individualized education program
(IEP) meetings, 70
provision of transition services, 266
role in implementation of schoolwide
response to intervention (RTI)
model, 92
role in transition planning, 262–263
Remedial work, 1, 118–120, 233
Response to intervention (RTI)
determining eligibility for services, 9
schoolwide model for support, 88
Rolling admissions, 245

SAT, 235–236, 246–248
Scholarships, 251
School counselors, 262, 271–272
Schoolwide positive behavior support
(SWPBS)
examples, 89*t*
need for, 100–101
overview, 101–105, 102*f*, 110
research on, 105–106
Secondary level
accommodations and modifications,
39, 41–42, 234–235, 267
assistive technology use, 121–123
career programs, 271–272

contrasted with postsecondary
settings, 23–24, 25–26
counseling programs, 270–271
curriculum considerations, 20–21,
265–266
diploma options, 20
dropout risk, 100
exit examinations, 265, 266
freshman year transition planning,
234–235
graduation rates, 230
joint programs with colleges, 233,
272–273
junior year, 236–238
personnel roles in transition planning,
145*t*, 261–263
school–parent collaboration, 148–153,
150*t*
Section 504, Subpart D, 12–13, 14*t*,
26, 42
self-assessment of schools, 91
senior year, 238–239
sophomore year, 235–236
support services, 25–26
universal design, 268–270, 268*b*, 269*t*
*see also* Preparation for college;
Transition planning
Section 504, *see* Rehabilitation Act of
1973, Section 504
Self-advocacy, *see* Self-
determination/self-advocacy
Self-Determination Assessment Battery,
69
Self-determination/self-advocacy
assessment, 68–69, 173
case examples, 75–76
for college accommodations, 58*b*
definition, 66
goal attainment skills, 72–75
importance of, 11, 23–24, 66–68
need for, 1
objectives, 282–283
questions for students, 74*t*, 76–77
student leadership opportunities and,
70–72, 71*t*, 107
Take Action instructional program,
73–76, 74*t*
transition assessment and, 179–182,
181*b*
Self-determined learning theory, 67
Self-Directed IEP, 71–72, 71*t*
Self-disclosure by students
during application process, 49, 249
to employers, 59
percentage of students, 46, 57, 59
preparing students for, 277
resources, 60*b*
as student responsibility, 45–46, 54
timing of, 49–50